ROMAN SEXUALITIES

Photograph of *Lagynos*, Roman, late first–second century A.D.
The Art Museum, Princeton University. Bequest of Professor Albert
Mathias Friend, Jr. *Photo Credit:* Bruce M. White.

ROMAN SEXUALITIES

Edited by
Judith P. Hallett and
Marilyn B. Skinner

PRINCETON UNIVERSITY PRESS

PRINCETON, NEW JERSEY

LIBRARY OF CONGRESS CATALOGING-IN-PUBLICATION DATA
ROMAN SEXUALITIES / EDITED BY JUDITH P. HALLETT
AND MARILYN B. SKINNER.
P. CM.
INCLUDES BIBLIOGRAPHICAL REFERENCES AND INDEX.
ISBN 0-691-01179-6 (CL : ALK. PAPER) ISBN 0-691-01178-8 (PBK. : ALK. PAPER)
1. SEX CUSTOMS—ROME—HISTORY. 2. SEX IN LITERATURE.
3. ROME IN LITERATURE. 4. CLASSICAL LITERATURE.
5. FEMINIST CRITICISM. 6. ROME—HISTORY.
7. ROME—SOCIAL LIFE AND CUSTOMS.
I. HALLETT, JUDITH P., 1944– . II. SKINNER, MARILYN B.
HQ13.R65 1998   306.7'0945'63—DC21   97–12684 CIP

THIS BOOK HAS BEEN COMPOSED IN JANSON

PRINCETON UNIVERSITY PRESS BOOKS ARE
PRINTED ON ACID-FREE PAPER AND MEET THE GUIDELINES
FOR PERMANENCE AND DURABILITY OF THE COMMITTEE
ON PRODUCTION GUIDELINES FOR BOOK LONGEVITY
OF THE COUNCIL ON LIBRARY RESOURCES

HTTP://PUP.PRINCETON.EDU

PRINTED IN THE UNITED STATES OF AMERICA

1 3 5 7 9 10 8 6 4 2
1 3 5 7 9 10 8 6 4 2
(PBK)

CONTENTS

ACKNOWLEDGMENTS

Zmyrna mei Cinnae nonam post denique messem
quam coepta est nonamque edita post hiemem.

Nine harvests and nine winters since conception,
my Cinna's *Zmyrna*, brought at last to birth.
(*Catullus 95.1–2*)

IF PREPARATION of this book did not actually require the full amount of time Cinna put into his masterpiece, it assuredly seemed that long to both of us. We therefore wish to recognize the special contributions of everyone who assisted us.

First, we owe a massive debt of gratitude to our original third co-editor, Amy Richlin, who resigned for personal reasons. In approaching prospective contributors, soliciting manuscripts, and generously offering advice on draft after draft of the introduction, she contributed greatly to the success of the project, and she was with us all the way in spirit.

Working with the staff of Princeton University Press has been a truly pleasurable experience. Former History and Classics editor Lauren Osborne responded enthusiastically to the initial proposal, and her successor, Brigitta van Rheinberg, provided expert guidance at every stage of the editorial process. Editorial assistant Alessandra Phillips kept us informed of all new developments. The judicious observations and criticisms of two anonymous referees greatly improved individual chapters. James Tatum, who read the entire manuscript twice, helped us to focus on our ultimate objectives as we revised and condensed.

Seeing the manuscript into print was made considerably easier by the care and diligence of the personnel who worked with us: production editor Karen M. Verde, copyeditor Sherry Wert, and our fellow classicist Jeffrey S. Carnes, who indexed the volume. Promotion copywriter Linda S. Truilo welcomed our suggestions for presenting the book to prospective buyers.

The jacket illustration and frontispiece show an unusual *lagynos* or flask, from the late first to second century C.E., probably from Knidos, now in the study collection of the Princeton University Art Museum. Color photographs were funded in part by subvention awards from the Provost's Author Support Fund of the University of Arizona and from the Graduate Research Board of the University of Maryland at College Park. For overseeing the photography, arranging reproduction fees, and sharing information on provenance and parallels for the vase type, we are very much indebted to Karen E. Richter, Assistant Registrar of Photo Services at the museum. We are also extremely grateful to Shelley Haley and David Soren for helpful comments about the iconography of this vessel and its likely origins.

Separately, Judith Hallett wishes to express her personal thanks to all her families, domestic, departmental, and professional. Marilyn Skinner, in turn, warmly appreciates the steadfast support of her husband, the patience of her colleagues, and the affection of her household and barn companions. Above all, she recognizes the vital assistance of the undergraduate students in her "Women in Antiquity" course, who, year after year, continue to supply her with delightful insights into ancient sex/gender systems.

ROMAN SEXUALITIES

INTRODUCTION

QUOD MULTO FIT ALITER IN GRAECIA ...

Marilyn B. Skinner

A S ITS TITLE, *Roman Sexualities*, indicates, this set of twelve essays by recognized and emerging authorities on ancient Rome is more focused, in both scope and objectives, than were earlier treatments of a comprehensive "Greco-Roman" sexual ideology. By applying feminist tools of analysis to an illustrative group of Latin texts, the studies contained here uncover local elaborations of a common Mediterranean sex/gender system. Generic links between those elements of an indigenous Roman "sexuality"—which, following Halperin, Winkler, and Zeitlin (1990b: 3), I would define as "the cultural interpretation of the human body's erogenous zones and sexual capacities"—encourage my own editorial attempt to integrate particular conclusions advanced in these essays into a coherent whole. This broad, though incomplete, synthesis admittedly comprises personal and perhaps idiosyncratic readings of Roman sexual discourses. Neither my co-editor nor any of my fellow contributors would agree with every claim I make. In creating such a schematic profile, however, my first aim is to demonstrate that Roman constructions of sex should constitute a discrete research area within the general field of ancient sexuality. As enumerated here, the unusual features of that sex/gender system may interest not only colleagues in Latin literature and Roman social history but also a larger academic audience, particularly specialists in modern Mediterranean anthropology, women's studies, and the overall history of sexuality.

In its basic characteristics, the Roman sex/gender system was hardly unusual. Its conceptual blueprint of sexual relations, like that of classical Athens, corresponded to social patterns of dominance and submission, reproducing power differentials between partners in configuring gender roles and assigning them by criteria not always coterminous with biological sex. Intercourse was construed solely as bodily penetration of an inferior, a scenario that automatically reduced the penetrated individual—woman, boy, or even adult male—to a "feminized" state. Insertive and receptive modes of pleasure were consequently polarized, each considered appropriate to only one sex, with desire for cross-sex gratifications stigmatized as "diseased" (*morbosus*) and with mutual interchange of gender roles often vilified as the nadir of corruption in freaks like the emperor Caligula (Suet. *Calig.* 36.1). While this map of sexuality was undoubtedly pan-Mediterranean, we are concerned here with certain modifications found in materials that circulated in Rome and its provinces from about 70 B.C.E. to slightly after 200 C.E., a period conventionally designated by historians as the epoch of the late Republic and early to middle Empire.

During that span of time, the city-state of Rome was transformed through long decades of civil war from a republic governed by an oligarchic senate into a quasi-hereditary principate. The institution of imperial rule, as Peter White observes, "reoriented political and social life in Rome and complicated the vocations of the upper class" (1993: 110). Changed conditions of political existence are mirrored in the literary record of the educated elite, who grew more and more preoccupied with preserving personal autonomy and honor in an atmosphere of constraint. Meanwhile, as the megalopolis itself asserted control over the whole Mediterranean basin, then over western Europe, the Balkans, and the Middle East, its population became increasingly multiethnic, polyglot, and culturally fragmented, containing greater numbers of immigrants and foreign-born ex-slaves. Hostility toward other ethnic groups, particularly Greeks and eastern Mediterranean peoples, correspondingly escalates in Latin literature, along with class prejudice against enterprising and newly rich freedmen.

Though social stratification was pronounced at Rome, leading citizens of Italian and provincial communities and, occasionally, persons of lesser distinction enjoyed remarkable opportunities for advancement thanks to a fortunate combination of wealth and personal connections. To a degree unparalleled in classical or even Hellenistic Greece, patronage was "central to the Roman cultural experience" (Wallace-Hadrill 1989b: 65). Horizontal networks of support informed all areas of life, at all levels of society, mediating hierarchy through finely gradated degrees of *amicitia*, "friendship," an institution premised upon a voluntary exchange of favors between the *patronus* and his dependent or *cliens*. Patronage relations played an organic part in Republican-era contests for magistracies and social dominance among the leading families; after the establishment of the Principate, patron-client ties became even more crucial to maintaining an appearance of aristocratic dignity and consequence. For less-exalted parties, conversely, the gracious euphemism *amicitia* did not always succeed in glossing over awkward disparities in status. In the wake of civil wars and loss of political clout by the hereditary nobility, we find literary texts displaying heightened obsession with inequalities in rank and power, accompanied by the extreme defensiveness manifest in the constant scapegoating of targeted subgroups. As a fundamental tenet, the present collection presupposes that these historical and social contingencies were projected onto the dominance-submission grid of Roman sexuality, creating documents in which ostensibly crude sexual narratives serve as an ordered semantic system for articulating social anxieties.

The notions of sexuality my colleagues and I explore are those refracted in literary texts and allied discourses such as law and medicine, which are pressed into service as convenient, though by no means transparent, witnesses to cultural mindsets. Although this body of evidence preserves mainly the outlook of a well-educated cadre and does not comprehend either regional differences or the radical shift in religious and cultural values during the later Empire, it has the advantage of being substantially accessible in translation to nonspecialist readers. Erecting a platform for general discussion is an essential step in staking out a newly defined area of scholarly inquiry. Thus I submit this sketch of Roman sexual ideology as a preliminary outline extracted from readily available documents and subject to refinements and corrections based on a much wider range of evidence. Artifacts such as the clay *lagynos* chosen to illustrate this volume, for example, may offer alternative perspectives on sexuality through images presumably viewed in domestic or menial settings (see discussion of the vessel in Johns 1982: 125–27), while inscriptions and graffiti can furnish insight into the attitudes of nonelite and peripheral populations.

We may speak of "sexualities" because the picture is a collage. As Jonathan Walters demonstrates in his chapter, "Invading the Roman Body," preservation of corporeal integrity was for men of high rank the defining mark of both sexual normalcy and social position. This nexus of virility, inviolability, and prominence set corresponding standards for their dependents: a daughter's conspicuous chastity and fecundity, for example, conferred luster on a family comparable to that earned by a son's military or civic success (Prop. 4.11.29–36, 71–72). However, Roman discourses on sex are more engrossed with departures from established norms, chiefly because they employ putative anomalies in gender role and moral irregularities as symbolic frameworks for identifying and denigrating alterity in class, ethnicity, lifestyle, and political agenda. It is consequently possible to tease out ideological tenets from the polemic deployment of negative stereotypes. Different forms of sexual trespass can be associated with particular societal concerns. For example, according to one controversial theory canvassed in several of these essays, accusations of effeminacy may have been intended to tap audience prejudice against nonconformist lifestyles, including those of alternative sexual subcultures. Because women of the senatorial class were implicated in the power networks of male kin, lurid tales of their adulteries could encapsulate corollary messages of political and social destabilization. The caricature of the *tribad*, or mannish female equipped with dildo, must have reassured males of their natural physiological advantages. Finally, we find lyric and elegiac poets deliberately confessing to the *nequitia*, "wantonness," that operates as an erotically charged synonym for other aberrant stances, including that of the woman writer. Essays in this collection examine both conventionally gendered objects of Roman sexual discourse and their deviant counterparts and also seek to recover hints of contrasting female perspectives on the human body, on sexuality, and on textuality.

In doing so, *Roman Sexualities* attempts to complicate a scholarly dispute whose breadth and fervor may be ascribed to the fact that the subject has only lately been sanctioned as appropriate for academic discussion. On the European continent, to be sure, investigations of ancient sexual mores, with particular attention to pederasty in fifth- and fourth-century B.C.E. Athens, have a long, albeit somewhat checkered, intellectual pedigree (Halperin, Winkler, and Zeitlin 1990b: 7–13). Among Anglo-American classicists, on the other hand, frank exchange of ideas on such matters has become customary only during the last two decades. Henderson's lexical survey of obscenity in Attic comedy (1975) and Dover's exploration of Greek homoerotic conventions in literature and vase painting (1978) are now recognized as legitimating studies. Current excitement over ancient erotics, however, dates primarily from the appearance in English translation of the second and third parts of Michel Foucault's *Histoire de la sexualité*. In the first volume of the *History*, published in France as *La Volenté de savoir* in 1976, the French philosopher had advanced the proposition that categories of sexual identity are everywhere culturally mediated and, to use the generally received term, "constructed" (1980: 105–6). Subsequently applying his genealogical method to antiquity, Foucault in *L'Usage des plaisirs* (*The Use of Pleasure: The History of Sexuality*, vol. 2, 1985) and *Le Souci de soi* (*The Care of the Self: The History of Sexuality*, vol. 3, 1986) identified classical Greece and the later Greco-Roman empire, respectively, as chronological moments at which male sexual subjectivity took on ethical configurations markedly unlike those deemed "normal" in present-day societies—moments that eventually became turning points in the Western cultural production of the desiring subject. Though argument about its merits arose at once and still continues, that account of ancient sexuality has already become "deeply influential and profoundly provocative—with great cause" (Goldhill 1995: xi). Within little more than a decade, experts on Greek and Roman culture have produced a number of thoughtful engagements with elements of Foucault's thesis.

In Hellenic studies, the mass of literature has now reached such ample proportions that a brief overview must necessarily be selective. The edited collection *Before Sexuality: The Construction of Erotic Experience in the Ancient Greek World* (Halperin, Winkler, and Zeitlin 1990a) sparked off widespread interest in classical and later Greek erotic discourses with its stimulating theoretical introduction to the cultural production of meanings and the social construction of sexual identities. From that foundational publication, the course of several research trajectories may be traced. One trajectory extends Foucault's cognitive paradigm by using it as point of departure for more specialized inquiries into ancient cultural poetics (Halperin 1990a; Winkler 1990). Another tries to correct errors or omissions in his handling of source materials and scholarship (D. Cohen 1991a: 171–73). Yet another combines constructionist premises with such other postmodern stances as that of feminist critical theory (M. A. Katz 1989; Zeitlin 1990; duBois 1995: 127–62). Concurrently, the temporal and geographical range of analysis has been extended far beyond archaic and classical Greece. Texts of the Second Sophistic era, in the second century c.e., are closely scrutinized in conjunction with *Le Souci de soi* (Gleason 1995), especially the Greek novel, where an alternative code of erotic conventions may perhaps be found (Konstan 1994; Goldhill 1995). Thus classical scholarship produced in more or less direct response to Foucault occupies a prominent place in the ongoing investigation of ancient Greek erotic beliefs and practices.

According to Amy Richlin, however, that preoccupation with Greek cultural phenomena on the part of Foucault and his followers overlooks specificities in Roman practice already uncovered by earlier feminist researchers (Richlin 1991: 168–71; 1992b: xiv–xvii; see further Skinner 1996). Foucauldian-oriented work on the constitutive elements of Roman sexual ideology has been relatively limited, confined to imperial Rome of the first two centuries c.e. and centered upon the question of whether conjugal relations took on new meanings during that period. In the third volume of *The History of Sexuality*, Foucault posited an "inflection" in Roman moral thinking about sexuality that ultimately led to the devaluation of romantic attachments to boys in favor of a symmetrical, mutually binding marital relationship (Foucault 1986: 147–85, 189–232). In rebuttal, Cohen and Saller have pointed to a "centuries-long, repetitious debate" about the value of marriage that produced "varied layers of discourse" on the topic but assumed an inevitable subordination of wife to husband consonant with the pronouncements of Xenophon and Aristotle (1994: 44–55). While Cohen and Saller's account, buttressed by Treggiari's magisterial survey of Greek and Roman marital ideals (1991: 183–319), offers a strong corrective to Foucault, it tends, even more than Foucault himself, to subsume Roman eroticism of the classical era under the rubric of a homogeneous "Greco-Roman" sexuality. Yet researchers in related areas of Roman studies such as cultural history and Latin literary criticism have long observed sex and gender protocols distinct enough from those of classical or Hellenistic Greece to warrant treating Roman sexuality as an independent system—at least in my view. Those permutations include separate constructions of the notion of "Woman" and of women's familial role, a more rigorous ethical climate surrounding pederasty, and a conspicuous tendency to sexualize both hostility and shame. Let us briefly explore each in turn.

"Conceptions of sexuality in ancient Rome," Catharine Edwards reminds us, "are inseparable from conceptions of gender" (1993: 75). In Roman public discourse—as, unequivocally, in that of Greece—the notion of Woman can be a marker of radical alterity. Though ordinarily synonymous with what is excluded from male self-fashioning, however, Roman concepts of Woman also serve to affirm, by extension, the very qualities culturally assigned to men. Dissimilar Greek and Roman ideas of women's domestic and familial obligations and, conversely, of women's ability to operate in the public sphere correspond to differences in each society's abstract construct of "Woman." As retold by the archaic Greek poet Hesiod (*Th.* 570–616; *Op.* 47–105), myth makes Pandora the ancestress of a race (*genos*) of female beings separate from mankind, fashioned by Zeus primarily as a constraint on human endeavor, though also required for propagation of the species (Zeitlin 1995: 69–70). Over the next three centuries, according to the well-known argument of Page duBois, Greek thought proceeded to conceptualize Woman as a mere vehicle of reproduction, rather than an associate in reproductive labor. In consequence, she was rendered passive, receptive, closely bound up with interiority, and eventually alienable (duBois 1988: 165–66).

Social conventions bear out that reading of Greek gender symbolism. The basic unit of the Greek city-state was the *oikos*, the individual household headed by a master or *kyrios*. Marriage was the agreed-upon transfer of authority over a woman from one *kyrios* to another. In Athens, male guardianship of women extended to all external transactions involving the household, not excepting the legal and financial management of a wife's dowry; women's tasks were confined to "that within" (*ta endon erga kai epimelēmata*, Xen. *Oec.* 7.22). Indeed, the wife was connected with the interiority and privacy of the *oikos* to such a degree that, as a matter of etiquette, a respectable woman's name would not be mentioned in public (Schaps 1977). Her domestic duties included weaving textiles, administering household stores, and supervising servants, but were most often summed up in terms of a single mission, the bearing and nurturing of a male heir. Thus documents from classical Athens suggest a practice of "regarding the married woman as an invisible link between two families of men" and transmit a "fantasy of descent from male to male" (Pomeroy 1995: 119). Insofar as she stands for what is shielded from public gaze, particularly the intimate secrets of domestic life, Woman is regarded as a vessel of propagation maintained in protective custody (M. A. Katz 1989: 171–73).

Though the legal position of Athenian women was doubtless an extreme case, and women's roles throughout the Hellenic world were considerably modified during the next few centuries, marked differences between cultural expectations for Roman matrons and for their counterparts in contemporary Greek communities did not escape ancient observers. Whereas Greek custom discouraged women's presence in public space, elite Roman families of the late Republic exploited it as yet another occasion for competitive advertisement: ostentatious displays of wealth by noblewomen testified to past military achievements of male kin. The second-century B.C.E. historian Polybius accordingly treats his Greek audience to a catalogue of the splendid regalia paraded by Aemelia, widow of the famous general Scipio Africanus, when she attended matronal cult ceremonies (Polyb. 31.26). Subsequently the biographer Cornelius Nepos remarks upon the Roman wife's great social visibility, both as hostess in her own home and as a guest at dinner parties, adding, "In Greece it's very different" (*quod multo fit aliter in Graecia, Prooemium* 6–7). Again, the parental responsibilities of the *materfamilias* were often contrasted with those of Greek women. In the upper-class Roman household, wet-nursing and infant care were chores assigned to slaves (Bradley 1991: 13–75), while the biological mother was instead idealized as a vigilant overseer of the older child's intellectual and moral development, an obligation shared on an equal basis with her husband (Dixon 1988: 104–40). Her disinclination to breast-feed thus became a moralizing topos among philosophers (Musonius 3; Gell. 12.1). Moreover, her putative indifference to the welfare of young children, as opposed to the Greek mother's care and devotion, earned a rebuke from the physician Soranus of Ephesus, who blamed the high incidence of rickets in Rome on failure to supervise a toddler's movements (*Gynecology* 2.44).

In Roman society a father's stringent economic and legal control over his household (*familia*) and his direct descendants, involving juridical life-and-death power even over adult children, paradoxically allowed his married daughters to occupy a somewhat equivocal position in their own domestic units. By the time of the late Republic, the majority of Roman wives did not pass beneath a husband's authority (*manus*) upon marriage, but instead remained full members of their natal family, subject to paternal rule (*patria potestas*) while their father lived and, with certain restrictions, ultimately eligible to become his legatees or heirs (Gardner 1986:

163–203). Even during a father's lifetime, the political weight assigned to daughters of the aristocracy as critical intermediaries in marriage alliances required them to further the goals of their natal family among relatives by marriage (Hallett 1984). Meanwhile, the husband in a marriage without *manus* had no legal jurisdiction over his wife and no voice in the management of her property. While she would need a tutor's authorization for major transactions, a propertied woman with no living direct male ascendants could therefore operate with a good deal of freedom in the commercial realm (Gardner 1986: 14–22; Garnsey and Saller 1987: 130–36).

Conceptions of the maternal relationship encouraged upper-class Roman women to take an active interest in the administration of their own finances (Dixon 1988: 41–70, 168–209). Since the public success of offspring reflected well upon parental training, women were disposed to invest emotionally and economically in their sons' political careers and assist their upward progress through vigorous participation in patronage networks. Power to make valid wills, disposing of property as they saw fit, gave such women an incentive to increase their wealth and an ongoing influence over the children who would be their expected beneficiaries. Some Roman husbands, Dixon observes, had confidence enough in their wives' flair for business to designate them as the trustees of a minor child's patrimony. In most Greek states, a son would instead have received holding power over the complete estate, including the maternal dowry, with the accompanying obligation to support his mother from its income (1988: 50–51).

Such material considerations suggest that in the elite Roman sex/gender system, the conceptualization of Woman was inherently bipartite—a cognitive phenomenon without exact equivalent in the Greek scheme of gender polarity (Hallett 1989b). Although they frequently attribute Otherness to females as a group, Latin authors do single out certain women for displaying praiseworthy attributes said to be typical of men and rare in members of their own sex. The desirable quality, such as courage, has allegedly been transmitted through the paternal line of descent or learned by example from male agnates: its emergence in a female testifies to the strength of the trait carried by the bloodline. As Hallett remarks, the penchant for likening a woman's temperament and character to that of her father and brothers coincides with the economic, political, and social functions women continued to perform as representatives of their natal family after marriage (ibid.: 67).

In examining the Roman "sexual script for women's social roles," Eva Stehle makes a corollary observation: "Because female sexuality is not constructed as hostile *per se* to the dominant structure, women performing their sexual roles can be adopted as a metaphor for expressing Roman political ideals" (1989: 145). A woman's satisfactory performance of her marital and reproductive duties might symbolize proper moral conduct in the public sector, just as neglect of such duties was symptomatic of a collapse of civic order (Hor. *Carm.* 3.6.17–20; see Joshel, this volume). Hence images of imperial women were included on public monuments at times of dynastic crisis in order to convey ideological messages about the central relationship of family life and reproduction to the welfare of the community (Kampen 1991: 243). That notion of women as "Same" as well as "Other" presupposes a female body partly assimilated to the male constitution, one whose sex-specific functions, such as lactation or even pregnancy, did not constitute its entire raison d'être. In combination with other evidence considered in the following chapters, it also implies that gender boundaries were more fluid for Romans than for Greeks, and thus more prone to destabilization.

Although homoerotic passivity in adult males was condemned by Greeks and Romans alike, the two cultures took different ethical positions on pederasty. Despite its being a source of deep social unease, courtship of freeborn youths was nevertheless institutionalized in democratic Athens and philosophically extolled as an educational process (Foucault 1985: 187–225; D. Cohen 1991a: 171–202). In Rome, conversely, the rape or seduction of a young male citizen was *stuprum*, an offense subject to criminal punishment (Fantham 1991; Richlin 1993b: 561–66; see now C. A. Williams 1995: 531–35), possibly under the *lex Sca(n)tinia* (Cantarella 1992: 106–14). While relations with boys were permissible as a sexual practice, they were viewed chiefly as a means of sexual gratification and, in law, were all but restricted to slave concubines. This difference in moral outlook is most often ascribed to a Roman "cult of virility," a conquest mentality that precluded a prospective soldier or statesman acceding to the demands of another (Veyne 1985: 31; Cantarella 1992: 218). It has also been attributed to reflex apprehension about the strenuous demands of Roman masculinity, rendered as the fear of falling into a polluted category (Richlin 1993b: 536–37). *Patria potestas* was doubtless a negative determinant, since the influence of a lover on a youth would have posed a serious threat to the *paterfamilias*'s absolute authority.

Finally, competitive pressures pervade the intimate connections between desire, animosity, and degradation in the collective Roman psychology. As distinguished from that of classical Greece, Roman society was simultaneously more repressive in some domains of erotic activity and more exhibitionist in others (Hallett 1988: 1265–66). Lilja opines that "Roman sexuality seems to have been characterized by a strong note of violence and aggressiveness, when compared with the sexuality of the Greeks" (1983: 135). Sexual consciousness at Rome was undeniably permeated with a love of explicitly violent spectacle. The incompatible and volatile extremes of "beauty and violation, power and powerlessness, control and abandon" encountered in the late Republic and early Empire were concentrated, according to Carlin Barton, in the figure of the gladiator, a cultural icon infused with the spectators' own vain longing for honor and their unbearable sense of sensual satiety and despair (1993: 79–81).

In the political and social arena, among rivals struggling for preeminence, the language of combat was notoriously obscene: Latin oratory, iambic poetry, and satire are all reservoirs of crude sexual insult. While philologists were attempting lexical and sociolinguistic clarifications of that sexual vocabulary (e.g., Adams 1982), feminist scholars pioneered the application of critical and analytical tools to its semiotic content. Researchers soon concluded that a wide spectrum of abstract power relations and grades of social stratification were reified in sexual terms, with claims to superiority put forth, for example, as graphic threats of rape. Richlin's comprehensive treatment of such invective motifs, *The Garden of Priapus: Sexuality and Aggression in Roman Humor* (1983), was a landmark study that immediately familiarized students of Roman social history with the agonistic thrust of Latin obscenity. Lately, Edwards has shown that moralizing discourses openly attacking vice served positive ends as well, asserting a greater capacity for self-control on the part of the senatorial class and hence a better right to rule, flaunting moral rectitude as "symbolic capital," and checking individual self-aggrandizement that posed a threat to the interests of peers (1993: 24–28).

Research has simultaneously uncovered a correlative thematics of erotic abjection, in which the social odium attached to the lover was concretely portrayed as impotence or emasculation (Skinner 1986, 1991). Consequently, entire genres were positioned on an axis of hypermasculinity versus "softness": just as satire inscribes a poetics of priapic braggadocio, so elegy, in its incessant flirtation with the passive subject position, fluctuates among three intersecting gender modalities, the masculine, the effeminate, and the feminine (Henderson 1989; Wyke 1994). The cross-sex allure of pantomime and its prurient ballets of female suffering danced by a male artist may be a related phenomenon. Such transvestite theatrical fantasies can be assimilated to tales of rape in Ovid's *Metamorphoses* that feature a concomitant dissolution of bodily boundaries; contemporary theories of pornography explain the voluptuous appeal of female victimization scenarios by identifying them as vehicles for supplying Roman audiences with a vicarious taste of masochistic pleasure (Richlin 1992e: 173–78). Extending this trajectory into the domain of architecture, Fredrick has noted that in atrium houses, which were theaters of prestige for the nobility, rooms where public business was conducted show a decorative preference for frescoes of mythological heroines that solicit a voyeuristic or fetishizing response from the viewer, whereas private areas set aside for leisure frequently exhibit disturbingly sensuous images of male vulnerability (1995: 282). In its present modified form, which acknowledges a constant vacillation in the male imaginary between fantasies of subjugating the Other and being subjugated oneself, that early feminist endeavor to show a deep-rooted association between sexuality and aggression in Roman thought continues to prove fruitful.

As the preceding review of topics indicates, the explosive vitality of research in the area of ancient sexuality, though given considerable impetus by Foucault's publications, is also driven by the convergence of numerous earlier lines of inquiry, some more than fifteen years old and firmly established by now in both England and America. Through its sustained inquiry into gender configurations, one approach, that of feminist criticism, has played a leading part in developing a general paradigm of ancient sexual ideology. Otherwise disparate in methodology, the essays in *Roman Sexualities* are all heavily indebted to feminist theory. Every contributor subscribes to the assumption that gender analysis is a primary tool of cultural and literary criticism. All share the perception that Roman public discourses on sexuality are privileged means of conceptualizing and articulating social concerns metonymically. In classical Latin literature and Roman law and medicine, the authors find gender asymmetry mapped onto power differentials between ages, classes, ethnic groups, and professions, blurring distinctions in kind. Employing incisive techniques of feminist analysis, these essays unpack the ideological messages encoded in textual representations of conformity to or deviation from the ideational norm underpinning the Roman sex/gender system.

Although each of the following essays can be read independently as an addition to the literature of its own subject field, and each essayist must be regarded as arriving at conclusions apart from his or her fellows, the model of the Roman sex/gender system that emerges from this enterprise may be considered, in part, a collective invention, consolidating an array of perceptions. Of necessity, it is an elastic model, capable of accommodating different readings of complicated evidence. Those readings, however, unite in stressing the metonymic properties of sexual discourse in Roman society—the (re)affirmation of privilege in scenarios of phallic hostility and the implicit acknowledgment of cultural strain when power differentials are clouded through an imagined transfer of gender markers. As a key part of the investigative process, they provide a taxonomy of zero-degree or "normative" maleness, its deviations, and its intersections with other status denominators. What I have termed in my own chapter "a reciprocal synecdochic bond between sex and power" is therefore examined from a variety of aspects and correlated with topical concerns over social boundaries highly valorized in Roman culture and yet unusually porous.

In the following survey, I have tried to impart a sense of the distinctive contribution made by each essayist. Then, by bringing theoretical insights together, pointing out areas of agreement and disagreement, and extending certain inferences, I attempt to draw overall conclusions that indicate directions to be pursued in later investigations.

Unmarked Sexuality: The *vir*

Roman Sexualities logically begins with a radical synopsis of the rules of Roman manhood. In "Invading the Roman Body: Manliness and Impenetrability in Roman Thought," Jonathan Walters investigates the cultural model of the *vir*, or adult male citizen. This chapter throws fresh light on what it meant to be a man in ancient Rome by illustrating how Roman notions of manhood were part of a wider hierarchy of social statuses. In conjunction with his sexual role as penetrator and his civic role as *pater-familias*, the freeborn male citizen, as Walters reminds us, enjoyed immunity from physical violation in accordance with social station. Being able to defend the parameters of the body from invasive assault was both the touchstone of masculinity and the prerogative of a gentleman. Applications of the term *vir* are limited: it is not bestowed upon youths, members of the working classes, disreputable persons, or slaves. Consequently, a term that at first glance only indicates the biological sex of an individual turns out to recognize, in addition, his entitlement to the privileges that accompany the male gender role, and does so by appealing to status criteria that may appear irrelevant to the modern observer.

Language that correlates passive male sexual behavior with female experience mystifies gender, Walters contends, by using the modifier "womanish" to mark off what is not proper for men. The ambiguous place in society of the adolescent freeborn male (*praetextatus*) and his protected position under the law confirm that the male body, as a social configuration, possessed sacrosanct boundaries. Conversely, vulnerability to beating was an earmark of quasi-servile status, and thus the structural equivalent of sexual availability. However, the body of the Roman citizen-soldier is an anomalous case. As a free man the soldier was sexually inviolable but subject to physical punishment by a superior officer as a condition of military discipline. While the soldier's wounds test the limits of the distinction between penetrable and impenetrable bodies, his scars, if honorably earned, become permanent credentials of his status as "true man." Thus Walters combines gender, sexuality, social standing, and conceptions of the body into a formulation that illumines the contributions of his eleven colleagues, for an entire spectrum of alternative sexualities takes its departure from that dense ideological connection between an adult male citizen's physical integrity, his rank, and his presumed virility.

Wayward Sexualities

Comprehension of the unarticulated expectations governing normative sexuality and sexual conduct can often be achieved by examining lifestyles and activities defined as transgressive. Progressing from the set of assumptions about masculinity explored by Walters, Holt Parker's "Teratogenic Grid" furnishes us with a novel schematic analysis of Roman sexual deviance. Parker's tidy configuration is reductionist in principle, designed to strip the taxonomy of sexual acts found in iambic, epigrammatic, and satiric texts down to its essentials—and to uncover the humor in that phallomorphic system. For the other side of the picture, this essay should be read in conjunction with my own contribution, which exposes the fragile infrastructure of Roman manhood.

Parker takes issue with Foucault's contention that sexual acts were not categorized in antiquity as "licit" or "illicit." Roman ideology, he maintains, creates acceptable or perverse "sexual personas" by isolating specific practices and reifying the performers as exclusive practitioners of the habit in question. The normal male, *vir*, energetically penetrates his object through one of three orifices: the vagina, the anus, or the mouth. By definition, the female recipient, the *femina* or *puella*, is penetrable through each orifice. The symmetrical economy of the system also constructs monstrous antitypes of "passive" man and "active" woman, namely the *cinaedus* or *fellator* and the *tribas*. Anal and oral receptivity, the two modalities of passive male behavior, are themselves designated as discrete preferences. Imposition of the contemporary terms "homosexual" and "heterosexual" on Roman sexual relations is fraught with difficulty, Parker concludes, as there is really almost no overlap between ancient and modern schematizations of sexual behavior.

By factoring in the determinant of penetrability, Parker's chapter enlarges Walters's argument that Roman sexual ideology superimposes caste markers upon putatively value-free denominations for biological human males. Walters observes that *vir* is an appellation reserved for adult citizens of relatively high status; Santoro L'hoir (1992) has shown that a lower-class male is labeled *homo*, for which the female equivalent is *mulier*. The archetypal sexually receptive female is, however, the *puella*, designated as such not (or not only) because of her youth and charm, but because her status is coterminous with that of the *puer* or slave (cf. Golden

1985 on *pais*, "child" and "slave"). As a slave equivalent, she lacks carnal bounds: all fissure, all flesh, she is open to any rival *vir* and hence promiscuous by nature. Only the elegiac poet/lover experiences her as *dura*, "hard," because he alone is unable to enter her. Since the trope of "love as war" represents the narrator as abusing her verbally and physically, elegiac violence, as Fredrick proceeds to show, emerges as still another strategy for casting the erotic object as receptive.

In "Unspeakable Professions: Public Performance and Prostitution in Ancient Rome," Catharine Edwards presents a theoretical explanation for the marginalization of one coterie, the actors, gladiators, and prostitutes branded as *infames*, "of ill repute." Persons so classified were stigmatized by the law as examples of the dishonorable; yet some members of the senatorial elite and even the imperial family are said to have wanted to join their ranks. Edwards's essay suggestively explores the logic of this seeming paradox. Individuals in occupations tainted with *infamia* were prevented from enjoying the full rights of citizenship, she argues, because their work was intimately associated with low forms of sexual behavior. Involvement in the provision of vulgar pleasures subjected them to public gaze and required them to put their bodies, like those of slaves, at the service of others. Hence Edwards's study reinforces Walters's correlation between bodily integrity and legal and social standing. The uneasy relationship between the most conspicuously degraded members of the citizenry—persons notorious for their sexual availability—and those who were supposed to be Rome's most honorable citizens further elucidates the vital connection between Roman constructions of public honor and sexual pleasure. The deliberate pursuit of *infamia* as a source of depraved gratification, alleged of Valeria Messalina by Tacitus, takes this line of thought to the logical conclusion unpacked here by Joshel.

Gender Slippage in Literary Constructions of the Masculine

The next four chapters grapple with the instability of Roman masculinity as an achieved sexual/social condition. *Vir* was a slippery grade, admitting of qualification, its accuracy as predicate always open to question. Anthony Corbeill's "Dining Deviants in Roman Political Invective" studies allegations of effeminacy in connection with the invective topos of dining. His demonstration that forms of self-indulgence are related through a network of associations adds coherence to the total picture of Roman sexuality by revealing why, in establishing a man as guilty of one crime, the speaker can necessarily implicate him in all. As a venue of private entertainment, Corbeill explains, the banquet provides a convenient site for allegations of secret depravity. Invective on the theme of gluttony is accompanied by accusations of financial profligacy, erotic passivity, and dancing: if credited, these instances of ineffective self-management label an aspiring politician unfit for public office. Roman orators regularly cite appearance as evidence of dissipation, though obesity, surprisingly, was not used as a criterion: dress, adornment, and physical movement constitute instead the defining attributes of the sexually submissive male.

Like Parker, Corbeill maintains that the Roman stereotype of the *cinaedus*, whose sexuality was contrary in its very essence to that reckoned proper for men, belies Foucault's contention that homoerotic behaviors did not play a part in defining the individual as a sexual type. However, the respective views of Parker and Corbell on the materiality of this figure conveniently illustrate the range of current scholarly speculation about the relation of text to historical fact. Richlin (1993b) suggests that the *cinaedus*, though colored by fictitious details, may point to the existence of circles of men who violated prescriptions for virile behavior. Edwards, in turn, contends that the *cinaedus* is a construct and that accusations of *mollitia*, "softness," slander the target by exploiting a cultural confusion between elegance and weakness (1993: 67–68). For Corbeill, the persuasive power of rhetorical descriptions of sexually passive men strongly implies the existence of individuals corresponding in recognizable ways to the stereotype. Finally, Parker argues that the question needs more precise formulation: while the appellation *cinaedus* denotes a category of thought to which Roman speakers, as a historically verifiable practice, commonly assigned contemporaries, we cannot determine whether it was also used as a badge of self-identification by persons with traits resembling those ascribed to *cinaedi*.

Temporary adoption of a "feminized" persona by the first-person speaker of lyric and elegiac verse is, however, a recognized phenomenon in late Republican and Augustan poetry. Beginning with the tumultuous decades of civil war and proceeding into the Augustan period, when constraints on individual autonomy became palpable (Foucault 1986: 81–95), psychic virility developed an acute sensitivity to the slightest diminution of social standing. Through erotic commonplaces, especially that of *servitium amoris*, or "enslavement to love," poets explored the dynamics of intercourse between social superiors and inferiors (Lyne 1979). My own chapter and those of Oliensis and Fredrick shed cumulative light on those concerns.

In "*Ego mulier*: The Construction of Male Sexuality in Catullus," I draw together a number of previous lines of inquiry in an effort to explain the Catullan speaker's self-identification with wronged heroines and the widespread popularity of poetic narratives that allowed male readers to take the woman's part. This follow-up investigation advances my earlier hypothesis that structural affinities between the dominance and submission pattern of sexual relations and the agonistic bent of political relations allowed Catullus to represent political reversals as physical assaults on his manhood (Skinner 1979, 1989, 1991). Yet parallel applications of a literary motif of masculinity voluntarily renounced—through castration, as in the case of the mythic Attis of poem 63, or through obeisance to a tyrannical *puella domina* such as Lesbia—suggest that the poet is also responding to a compelling desire on the part of audiences for occasional escape from the psychological stresses of the adult male gender role. Consumption of poignant erotic verse like the suite of Catullan epigrams lamenting Lesbia's infidelity, for example, may have afforded disappointed aspirants to office temporary relief from the rigid isomorphism of sex and power by permitting them to voice a repressed sense of outrage vicariously, through imaginative empathy with a wronged protagonist. It is no accident, I think, that narratives of tragic passion and elegiac laments of betrayed love became commonplaces of Latin literature during Catullus's lifetime and remained popular for two generations afterward. By tempering the strain of self-presentation, romances of gender transposition kept the fabric of Roman masculinity intact during the political turbulence of the late Republic and early Augustan age.

In addition, I observe that the pledge of companionship (*foedus amicitiae*) of Catullus and Lesbia is tantamount to a bond of *clientela*, with Lesbia playing the role of aristocratic patron and Catullus occupying the subordinate place of lesser *amicus*. Whatever the truth of a surmised liaison between the Veronese poet and one of the female members of the prominent Claudian clan, the *amicitiae* of Augustan poets and their highly placed male friends offer actual examples of unequal alliances that, according to Ellen Oliensis in "The Erotics of *amicitia*," are associated textually with gender asymmetry. While the roles of *amator* and *cliens* are structurally similar—one courts the goodwill of a mistress, the other of a patron—they differ in the degree to which each can exert control over the relationship. The literary beloved is at the poet's rhetorical disposition. Mention of a patron's name, however, evokes an extraliterary public world in which the speaker is at a disadvantage in comparison to his great *amicus*. Since, as Oliensis states, "any asymmetrical relation between two Roman men is conceivably also a sexual relation," the client's inferiority affiliates him with occupants of the feminine position in the erotic act. Augustan poetry dealing with the theme of patronage acknowledges the threat to psychosexual virility implicit in the client's dependence upon a patron. However, it also turns his structural femininity to advantage by designating poetic exchange as a channel of potential reciprocity. Oliensis's study increases the reader's sensitivity to the covert operations of sexuality in Roman discourse by showing that erotic nuances are present in every account of hierarchical transactions between men.

On the other hand, David Fredrick's essay, "Reading Broken Skin," intervenes in current discussion about technologies of gender in elegy by questioning feminist studies that lock the first-person speaker into a permanently feminized or effeminate posture. Fredrick adapts film theory's psychological model of viewer oscillation between scopophilia and voyeurism to explain the lover's alternate impulses to fetishize his *puella* and to punish her sadistically. As literary strategies, these two ways of figuring the beloved correspond to the generic antithesis of elegy and epic: Callimachean aestheticism mandates sublimation of the fragmented but artistically elegant female body, while violence recuperates epic mass and bloodshed. The generic code of elegy consequently attempts to hold the opposition of penetrator and penetrated suspended within the subject position of the lover himself. Using an approach drawn from media studies to refine present notions of elegiac gender inversion, this chapter initiates a potentially rewarding dialectic over generic stylizations of male eroticism.

Male Constructions of "Woman"

"Woman," in ancient thought, is an inherently self-contradictory concept. I pointed out earlier that the feminine, as the pole of Otherness in a dualistic system, was equated by Hesiod with the demands of physical existence, including the sexed body that cannot be transcended. Yet "body" itself is a protean formulation, for it can also incorporate that dimension of human existence that escapes rational systemic control. Femininity is therefore an unstable signifier, and Roman discourses, ambivalent as they are about sexual difference, will turn out to be riddled with uneasy doubts even when they purvey ostensible scientific truth concerning Woman.

Amy Richlin reveals the equivocal nature of women's bodies as constructed by popular belief in "Pliny's Brassiere," her investigation of folk traditions preserved in Pliny the Elder's *Natural History* and other sources. Roman medicine "colonizes" the female body as a wellspring of power. Its unique effluvia (menstrual blood, milk) may help or harm; as natural products those fluids are especially effective upon objects of culture. Women's own cooperation is necessary in particular cases, and they themselves are said to employ aphrodisiacs, abortifacients, cures for barrenness, and charms for averting the evil eye. Richlin here applies a double hermeneutic to Roman medical texts, focusing first on a decidedly

Roman Pliny, the male observer who uses a brassiere to relieve his headache, then on the woman from whom he borrowed it. By introducing this overlooked material into standard accounts of ancient sexuality, Richlin hopes to do for Roman women what Foucault did not: to imagine them as subjects exercising a quite elaborate care of the self, in popular rather than elite culture, sometimes conforming to social norms, as in strategies for promoting conception, and sometimes flouting them, as in devices for inducing abortion.

As Richlin observes, the Roman cultural system was distinguished by "perilously permeable" class, ethnic, and gender boundaries. Dichotomies of same/other and active/passive are built into each of those three categories, leading to their inevitable conflation: thus an impoverished, freed, or slave individual of non-Italian, and especially Greek or eastern Mediterranean, background will inevitably be feminized as well. Yet the caricatures of ambitious, nouveau riche freedmen in Petronius's *Satyricon* and Juvenal's third satire indicate that greater opportunities for mobility generated nightmares of hybrid-status persons able to gain advantage over Roman citizens by operating outside the bounds of ethnic and class identity. Those satiric plots reverse the usual antithesis by marginalizing the native-born speaker and endowing the obnoxious foreign upstart with phallic potency (Juv. 3.109–12).

Social tensions brought about corresponding mutations in female, as well as male, gender roles. Latin authors, particularly during the imperial period, undercut residual notions of female passivity by portraying women of the ruling class as possessing illegitimate political power and therefore being sexually out of control. In historical and satiric texts, the pleasure-seeking instincts of Woman drive her to encroach upon male prerogatives: given the chance, she appropriates for herself the coveted role of sexual agent. The rampant lust of females close to the throne is a hallmark of imperial corruption, epitomizing heinous breaches of executive, as well as moral and social, propriety.

In "Female Desire and the Discourse of Empire," Sandra Joshel reads Tacitus's construction of Valeria Messalina as "a fiction for the terms through which the Romans experienced their own present and its history." Messalina's ravenous but ultimately unsated appetites, along with her elided speech, are rhetorical tactics for differentiating the alleged political excesses of the Julio-Claudian regime from the climate of imperial operations experienced by Tacitus's contemporaries. Viewed from a senatorial standpoint, the empress's fierce concupiscence is a sign of the extravagant growth of imperial power itself. In using an avatar of desiring Woman to displace male agency, the narrative fabricates improbabilities that make historiographic reconstructions of the political background extremely tenuous. Joshel's chapter accordingly invites historians to turn away from vain searches for the "facts" of Messalina's career to a more informative consideration of her symbolic meanings.

In its most extreme form, deviation from the female gender role produces the figure of the *tribas* or woman-penetrating woman. An essential contradiction in terms, active female same-sex desire could only be represented in the Roman imaginary as pseudophallic. Masculine psychological identity in a woman was accordingly believed (or at least said) to be accompanied by genital deformity. In her pioneering investigation of this stereotype, "Female Homoeroticism and the Denial of Roman Reality in Latin Literature" (1989), Judith Hallett demonstrated that each of its features encapsulates the putative "unnaturalness" of women-only sexual encounters. Reprinted here, her essay, which plausibly explains the eccentricities of the type in terms of Roman cultural poetics, underpins further discussions of the topic by Gordon and Parker in this volume.

Latin literature habitually dissociated the *tribas* from the contemporary Roman present; her sexual practices, Hallett argues, were Hellenized and retrojected into the past. This puissant (and occasionally breached) literary tradition endowed her with monstrous organs allegedly capable of performing the duties of a penis. Attribution of male apparatus, in defiance of biological fact, epitomized her rejection of conventional heterosexuality and its expectations for feminine receptivity. The Roman tendency to deny potentially threatening aspects of cultural and physical reality produces a muddling of prescriptive and descriptive in discourses on female sexuality, necessitating caution in assessing the material content of all such representations. Hallett's analysis of the *tribas* as a falsified, yet textually empowered, construct may have implications for the analogous fashioning of the *cinaedus*.

But in Roman thought these pretensions to masculinity on the part of the woman-penetrating woman cannot help but prove vain. Just as Messalina's heterosexual appetites were portrayed as insatiable, driven as they were by a deeper impulse to self-degradation, so the priapism assigned by our sources to the *tribas* is fraudulent, amounting to no more than a sorry endeavor to transcend inescapable female inferiority. Parker and Hallett, in their respective treatments of Martial 7.67, agree that the poet depicts the *cunnilinctrix* Philaenis as a "failed man" whose lack of genuine equipment dooms her to the performance of self-betraying pathic acts. Ovid's depiction of the erotic persona of Sappho, Pamela Gordon then responds in "The Lover's Voice in *Heroides* 15," fits precisely the same literary pattern. Ovid's version of Sappho's amatory career makes her convert in her mature years to loving a younger man, repudiating her "shameful" desire for women. The implication that female homoeroticism is a perverse mode of conduct radically at odds with nature is a reflex of Roman moral attitudes, to be sharply distinguished from erotic sentiments found in the surviving fragments of the historical Sappho. In her pursuit of the beautiful Phaon, moreover, Ovid's heroine enacts the part of a Greek male *erastēs*. Even while seeking a heterosexual love object, she shows her unfeminine bent. Her lewd objectification of Phaon's appearance and her callous dismissal of past partners are qualities reminiscent of the faithless male lover, not the sad abandoned woman. Unlike her fellow heroines, she speaks of her sexual experiences in graphic terms, even recounting the equivalent of a "wet dream." The pastiche of male eroticism she enacts is, employing Luce Irigaray's adroit pun, not homosexuality but "hom/m/osexualité." In this collection, then, Hallett, Parker, and Gordon engage in a three-way conversation that brings intriguing cultural data to bear on one of Ovid's most frequently discussed texts.

The Sappho of the *Heroides* is not only a case of "corrected" female desire but also an artistic has-been. "Ovid portrays her no longer in full possession of her literary powers," Joan DeJean observes, "but at a time when her genius and towering poetic stature have diminished" (1989: 67). Citing passages in which the speaker herself attributes her creative block to abandonment (*Her.* 15.13–14, 195–98), Gordon points out that Sappho has "lost her Muse along with her lover." As a *tribas* in the company of her girlfriends on Lesbos, that cradle of plaintive song and seething vice, she had been quite capable of exercising her lyric gift. In the heterosexual domain, however, she can only self-identify as a *puella*—indeed, with an arch gesture toward Catullus (100), a forsaken *Lesbis puella*. The observation that Ovid's Sappho is now a *silenced* poet is highly suggestive, for it raises the question of whether, at least in Rome, Woman herself can speak.

Roman configurations of Woman in elegy implicate the textual in the erotic by conflating the *puella* with the Muse as source of artistic inspiration (Prop. 2.1.1–16) or, alternatively, with the poetic product itself (Wyke 1987; Cameron 1995: 303–38; for further discussion, see Fredrick's essay). Either way, she is only "a fictionalized object put to the service of the poet so that she may perform a thousand different roles" (Gold 1993a: 88). When glimpsed composing to the lyre (e.g., at Prop. 2.1.9–10, 2.3.19–22), the *puella* has been adorned with meretricious trappings, like a Barbie doll in police uniform. As a relational projection of male identity, she cannot be an autonomous poetic agent any more than she can be a sexual penetrator. Lascivious verse, according to a model of reception well attested in Roman culture, assigns its reader the pathic position, first titillating, then satisfying him in priapic fashion (cf. Catull. 16; Mart. 1.35.5, 3.69.2; see now Fitzgerald 1995: 49–51). Female inability to write, at least on erotic themes, follows directly from female incapacity to play the man's part authentically. Into Sappho's warped sexual longings, consequently, Ovid has inscribed a frustrated desire for authorship, for the stylus no more hers by right than the penis.

Female Construction of the Desiring Subject

Written during the Augustan period, six brief erotic elegies by the poet Sulpicia, niece of M. Valerius Messalla Corvinus, offer the only firsthand literary evidence, outside of fragments, for the existence of a female slant on Roman sexual ideology. Recent criticism has observed that Sulpicia deploys standard elegiac themes in unorthodox ways (Hinds 1987: 43–44; Roessel 1990: 247). In her chapter, "*Tandem venit amor*: A Roman Woman Speaks of Love," Alison Keith argues that the male poet/lover, though professing to flout traditional moral expectations, is actually complicit with prevailing morality when he assumes that regulating women's sexuality through sanctions against infidelity will serve social ends. In the *Aeneid*, the canonical balance sheet of Augustan values, Dido's tragedy drives home the baneful political consequences of female sexual transgression, just as personal lyric, epigram, and elegy show its destructive effects upon a man's private life. Sulpicia's epigrams, however, challenge both sets of competing discourses through direct allusions to the story of Dido. By employing Vergilian diction, themes, and imagery, the woman poet invites her reader to imagine a positive outcome for Dido's affair. At the same time, she breaks the timeworn connection between political visibility and deviant sexuality by displacing her involvement with her lover Cerinthus to the textual sphere, which allows her to voice female passion in a franker, less constrained way. By demonstrating how she adapts not just one but two of the master discourses of Augustan culture, Keith advances the growing perception of Sulpicia as an original and unique voice in Latin literature.

I would like to take this line of interpretation one step further. In the repository of Roman male fantasy, as we have seen, the *puella* able to compose verse on her own initiative is an anomaly. Thus Sulpicia confronts a formidable artistic problem. Like the Ovidian Sappho, she can locate herself within the elegiac tradition only by becoming her beloved's compliant *puella*; but to be a poet/lover she must occupy the active position. To attain creative agency, then, she appropriates previously existing sexual metaphors for the poetic text as intellectual property and as producer of meanings. Writing is elsewhere said to be bound by ties of chastity to its author, who strives to keep it unsullied (Hor. *Epist.* 1.20.3–5), or, in other circumstances, to be pledged to the single critic permitted to know its secrets (Courtney 1993: 306 = Suet. *Rhet.* 18.2). Sulpicia's programmatic poem ([Tib.] 3.13 = 4.7) inverts those tropes, making literary communication the outcome of lavish sexual accessibility. As Fredrick and Keith independently observe, the speaker equates candid self-expression with self-exposure when she proclaims her intent to "bare" her love (*nudasse*) rather than "cover" it (*texisse*). Her corresponding refusal to preserve her verse under seal for one chosen reader revokes the model of exclusivity governing not only the elegiac relations of lover and mistress but also the audience's reception of poetic meanings, inviting a free play of signification. That openness culminates in a recognized union of deserving equals: in the end, she envisions herself "spoken of as having been with an honorable man honorably" (*cum digno digna fuisse ferar*, [Tib.] 3.13.10).

In the same manner as the explicit *tabellae*, or pictures of couples having intercourse, that hung in aristocratic Roman bedrooms and offered a distancing perspective on the conjugal activity of their married occupants (Myerowitz 1992: 149), Sulpicia's poetry allows its implied male reader to reflect upon his given stance as dominant partner in the erotic encounter. Her own simultaneous enactment of the poet/lover and *puella* roles, meanwhile, inserts an additional chip into the mosaic of Roman sexualities. Like the scanty traces of an unorthodox type of male self-fashioning conceivably embedded in the *cinaedus* figure, or the possibility, advanced by Gordon, that the caricature of the *tribas* may target real displays of female homoerotic resistance, Sulpicia's poetry hints that actual Roman gender performances were perhaps more complicated, and actual sexualities more supple, than the mass of prescriptive and polemic documents would indicate.

Questions for Further Exploration

Even if the above paradigm is accepted in all particulars—and that is hardly likely to happen—many issues raised in passing would still remain unresolved. In the first place, the scheme I offer here scarcely touches on the complex intersections of sexual subject positions with class or ethnic status. In Roman sexual ideology, as in the Latin language, positing the binary opposition of "man" to "woman" is altogether too simplistic. The privileged designation *vir* is calibrated by degrees of separation from what is female, effete, enslaved, and foreign. One nexus of terms is organized around the capacity to resist penetration, that is, the enjoyment of relative freedom from external constraints: here the *cinaedus* or *pathicus* and the *puella* set the negative parameters of ideal manhood. Male receptivity and female penetration, reified as a dichotomy of *cinaedus* and *tribas*, then delimit extremes of gender boundary destabilization occurring in the absence of a virile male center. Another cluster, brilliantly analyzed by Santoro L'hoir (1992: 9–46), situates the *vir* and his consort the *femina* on a higher economic and social plane, contrasted in this instance with the lower-class *homo* and *mulier*. I personally would like to know much more about how all these identifiers function in a general sociolinguistic system.

Clearly, further research on the rhetoric of sexuality is in order, with special attention to finding evidence of how marginal populations—women, slaves, noncitizens—designate themselves in respect to the conjunction of class and gender.

Again, as this synthesis has attempted to make clear, the sexual behaviors found in our sources are still in need of thorough clarification as *texts*. Roman discourses on sex and gender had largely to do with the currents of political, social, and economic power and their erratic, seemingly arbitrary, workings. Disturbing changes in the social milieu were represented as deviations from sexual norms; violations of "natural" gender relations bear witness to the confusion caused by economic realignment and patterns of class mobility. Laments of distressed mythic heroines and ineffectual lovers seem to project anxieties triggered by a radical shift in the structure of government, while transvestite drama offered an imaginative escape from such anxieties perhaps supplanted, in the later imperial period, by a compulsion to deeper philosophical or religious commitment. In Rome, sexual metaphor may have been a means of codifying for relatively easy apprehension sociological data that in a late capitalist society would more likely be disseminated in statistical or quantitative form. That ancient data is still available, provided we read the indicators properly.

Such suggestions for further inquiry are of course not meant to be all-inclusive. Many other rewarding research projects will surely be sparked off by the essays contained in this volume. The intellectual pleasures of Roman sexualities are manifold and inexhaustible.

PART ONE

UNMARKED SEXUALITY

ONE

INVADING THE ROMAN BODY: MANLINESS

AND IMPENETRABILITY IN

ROMAN THOUGHT

Jonathan Walters

THIS ESSAY investigates one aspect of the patterning of concepts of manhood as revealed, or implied, in the language of the Latin-writing elite of the Roman world. The texts from which examples are taken range in time mainly from the period between the first century B.C.E. and the early third century C.E. Most of these works are prose—juridical texts, historical narrative, rhetorical and educational texts. They are all written by male members of the ruling elite of the Roman world. Their primary intended audience was that of other such men, with whom the authors were linked by a common culture that itself rested on wealth and semihereditary social status, and that was formed by a traditional linguistic and rhetorical education. Many of the authors lived in Rome itself, at least for part of their lives, but the "Rome" that these texts embody is a matter more of class and culture than of geography. The authors were men talking, or rather writing, in public to other men—with all the biases and limitations that *that* implies. This essay does not examine how others might think or talk, or write if they could, nor even how any individual member of this male elite might think in the privacy of his own mind, nor the way in which deviant individuals or social subcultures might think and talk; it addresses only the dominant, hegemonic ideology of Roman society, expressed or implied in its central forms of public discourse.

I should like to take this opportunity of thanking Dr. Catharine Edwards for her kindness in showing me a copy of her then-unpublished essay "Unspeakable Professions: Public Performance and Prostitution in Ancient Rome," which now appears in this volume. The influence of Dr. Edwards's work on my own will be obvious to those who read our two essays. I should also like gratefully to acknowledge the advice and help given to me in connection with this essay by Professors Judith P. Hallett, Amy Richlin, Marilyn B. Skinner, and (last, but by no means least) Dr. Maria Wyke. All translations are my own.

In this essay I argue that the Roman sexual protocol that defined men as impenetrable penetrators can most usefully be seen in the context of a wider conceptual pattern that characterized those of high social status as being able to defend the boundaries of their body from invasive assaults of all kinds. (An exception to this general pattern is the case of the Roman soldier, discussed later in this essay.) This patterning makes clear the extent to which "gender" is in Roman culture intertwined with other categories of social status: some males, because of their low place in the social hierarchy, were not full men and therefore lacked this "manly" characteristic of corporeal inviolability. A Roman social protocol that employed a rhetoric of gender (itself dependent on a metaphorical use of biological sex) thus appears to be part of a wider cultural pattern whereby social status was characterized on the basis of perceived bodily integrity and freedom, or the lack of it, from invasion from the outside. The Romans did demarcate a specific area of sexuality: the writings of authors such as Lucretius[1] show that the Romans recognized a discrete area of behavior that corresponded closely with our term "sexual activity." The way in which the Romans discussed this area, the various activities that fell within it, and the actors involved were, however, conceptually linked with the patterning that they perceived in other areas of social activity, and with their views of social relationships in general.

In Latin, when a male was sexually penetrated by another, a standard way[2] of describing this was to use the expression *muliebria pati*; that is, he was defined as "having a woman's experience." Clearly, what happens to the sexually passive man is conceived of as being the same as what happens to a woman. This usage is a particular example of a wider Latin linguistic usage, in which *pati* and its cognates are used in descriptions of male homosexual activity to refer to the role played by the one who is penetrated.

The basic meaning of *pati* and its linguistic relatives is "to be the object of some event," "to have something happen to one." As a linguistic expression of the habitual pessimism of humankind, on the assumption that, for the most part, what happens to one is unpleasant, it often carries the meaning "to suffer." In the context of sexual activity, as we have seen, it denotes the "passive" partner, the receptor or the penetrated. This usage is congruent with the characterization, widespread in the public discourses of the Greco-Roman world, that sex is a one-way street, something one person does to another. The active partner was conceptualized as possessing a phallus, and the activity as necessarily involving phallic penetration. So strong was this predisposition to see a phallus as essential for sexual activity that cases of female homosexual activity are usually described in ways that assume that one of the two women has a phallus, whether as an actual part of her body (an exceptionally large clitoris) or an artificial one.[3] This usage also places emphasis on the pleasure experienced by the "active," penetrating partner in the sexual act, and the sense that the other participant is primarily there for the use of the penetrating man. Sexual activity is routinely conceptualized in Roman public discourse as penetrative, sexual pleasure (particularly in the male homosexual context) as accruing to the penetrator, and the penetrator-penetrated relationship as "naturally" involving a more powerful individual wielding power over a less powerful one.

Strictly speaking, of course, insofar as *muliebria pati* refers to vaginal intercourse,[4] it is inaccurate: no male can be penetrated in this way. The anal penetration of a male is assimilated linguistically to the vaginal penetration of a female. Curiously, we see a contrary linguistic phenomenon in the case of heterosexual anal penetration: the situation of the penetrated female is sometimes denoted by a reference to her taking the part of a *puer* (normally translated as "boy," e.g., Mart. 9.67.3). It is a curiosity of this usage that, while an expression for anal intercourse in the case of a male, *muliebria pati*, refers to a woman, the expression in the case of a woman refers to a boy. In both cases, the passive partner in the sexual act is described as something other than a "man," whether a woman or a boy. This is in accordance with Roman (and classical Greek) sexual protocols, which view the sexually "active" role as the only appropriate one for a adult male citizen, the homosexually "passive" role being appropriate for *pueri*, a term that covers both male children and male slaves of any age. In Roman society, the only culturally condoned male homosexual relationship was that between a sexually active adult citizen man and a sexually passive male, usually younger, who was a slave, an ex-slave, or a noncitizen.[5]

The use of *muliebria* to define what it is that the sexually receptive male experiences makes it clear that this is something that is supposed, in Roman thought, not to be characteristic of men. The status of *vir* and sexual *patientia*, to be a man and to be penetrated by another man's penis, are conceptualized as mutually incompatible. Seneca uses this "commonsensical" opposition when he writes of a male slave castrated to preserve his youthful beauty, "He will never be a man, so that he may be able to endure penetration by a man for a long time" (*Ep.* 122.7). The term that we usually translate by "man" (in the strict sense of "a male human being") is of restricted usage in Latin:[6] not all males are accorded that designation. First, it is restricted to adult males: males who have not attained the state of adulthood are not called *viri*; instead they are described as *pueri, adulescentes,* or other terms that define them as not yet fully grown. Male slaves, too (and ex-slaves), even if adult, are not normally called *viri*: the preferred designation for them is *homines* (which is also used in elite literature for low-class and disreputable men), or *pueri*.

Vir, therefore, does not simply denote an adult male; it refers specifically to those adult males who are freeborn Roman citizens in good standing, those at the top of the Roman social hierarchy. A term that at first appears to refer to biological sex in fact is a description of gender-as-social-status, and the gender term itself is intimately interwoven with other factors of social status (birth and citizenship status, and respectability in general) that to us might not seem relevant to gender. When, therefore, we see "men" characterized in Roman discourse as sexually impenetrable penetrators, we find that this characterization, seemingly a simple matter of what is gender-appropriate in the field of sexuality, is in reality more complex, anchored in a wider pattern of social status within which "gender" itself is embedded. Not all males are men, and therefore impenetrable: some males—the young and the unfree, for example—do not have the status of full men and are therefore characterized as potentially penetrable by other males. The boundary between the penetrable and the impenetrable is as much a matter of social status in general as it is of "gender."

A neat-seeming dichotomy between men and women, founded on biological sex, is a recurrent metaphor used in the discourse of social gender. Its use, however, serves to mystify gender, by implicitly or explicitly supporting the local gender-system of a particular culture by an appeal to "nature" (in this case, physiology).

The two genders that we normally address in modern Western thought are not mirror images of each other, nor do they each "objectively" occupy the space that the other does not, like black-and-white images that can be seen either as two black silhouettes facing each other on a white background, or as a white candlestick on a black background. The "truth" that the two genders are mutual opposites is a mystification, part of our gender system. They are two separate constructs, each with its "Other." The "woman" constructed by men, particularly perhaps when that construction is embedded in a discourse addressed primarily to other men, is a male figment, used to say something about men, not about women.[7] (In the same way, women's discourse about men, especially when directed to other women, is in practice primarily a way of talking about women themselves, not about the experienced "reality" of men's existence.)[8] The two genders operate in conceptual worlds that are, to some extent at least, separate, each using the other metaphorically as a way of mapping the perceived boundaries of its own category. In the case we are considering, a particular activity, sexual penetration, is used to mark a gender boundary.

This focus on sexual penetration is used elsewhere to define transgression and thus the proper boundaries of gender-role and sexual behavior. Seneca, for example, calls up the image of sexual activity as a matter of one-way penetration in a manipulation of notions of gender-appropriate behavior to contrast what "nature" intended for women with a nightmare vision of them as sexually penetrating and thus dominating men.[9] This schema characterizes "man" as sexual penetrator, and the penetrated as "unman," using "woman" to exemplify the unman and assimilating a homosexual act to a heterosexual one.

This may not seem as surprising as it should. One reason for this surprising lack of surprise is the effect on the modern reader of cultural assumptions that are common to both our society and that of the Romans. Both in the modern West and in ancient Rome, homosexual activity between men is commonly described in public discourse in a framework that assimilates it to heterosexual activity, reading one partner as "male" and the other as "female," and collapsing this conceptual framework into another based on the notion of an "active/passive" polarity.[10] Sexual activity, of course, can be conceived of in other ways, regardless of the gender of the participants—for example, as a cooperative activity jointly undertaken by the two participants. In terms of male homosexual activity in particular, it is, of course, equally possible to seek sexual satisfaction by being penetrated, or by nonpenetrative sexual activity.[11] I would ask the reader to bear in mind the arbitrary, locally conditioned nature of such conceptions of sexual activity in order to observe which conception is in fact being brought into play in the expressions under consideration. Readers who share the assumptions underlying the phrase *muliebria pati* should be aware of the extent to which they have already become implicated in the presumptions of that discourse, and consider to what extent their sociocultural assumptions about sexual activity have led them to collude with it.[12]

If we look at the case of the *praetextatus*, the freeborn male youth who is not yet an adult man, we see that he occupies an ambivalent position, and is an object of special concern, precisely because the Roman protocols of sexuality place him in a marginal state in the pattern of "gender" and wider social status. He is a young male who is not a full-fledged man, and is therefore "naturally" an object of sexual desire to adult males; and in the Roman public discourse of sexual desire, the only conceivable way that a "normal" man could consummate that desire is by penetrating the youth. He is, however, a man-to-be: his status is a temporary one that must, if society is to reproduce itself satisfactorily, lead to the attainment of full Roman citizen manhood, to being a *vir*. For him to be sexually penetrated, to undergo "what a woman undergoes," would disrupt that "normal" progression, tainting him with unmanliness.[13] He is neither like a fully adult man, who was conceived of as not desirable to other adult men, nor like other young males of lower social status, such as slaves, ex-slaves, and other outsiders, who were conceived of as desirable, and as legitimate objects of desire on the part of Roman citizen men, whose bodies did not have to be protected from sexual penetration that would "unman" them. In this, the *praetextatus* was like the respectable Roman matron, or the freeborn unmarried girl—naturally desirable, but not to be penetrated.

The situation of respectable females is more nuanced than that of males: it is not that they are completely impenetrable, but rather that they are only to be penetrated by their legitimate husbands. It is noteworthy in this regard that this ambiguous position of the respectable woman appears to be marked by a considerable reluctance to refer to the sexual act within marriage in Roman public discourse: this can be explained by a certain tension between such women's high social status and the "naturally" demeaning nature of the act of being penetrated. It is perhaps relevant to point out that *mulier*, from which the adjective *muliebria* comes, is used particularly of low-status and disreputable women;[14] the adjective may well refer not only to low-status women, but also to those characteristics of "being a woman" that are considered demeaning. We see this differentiation according to social status rather than gender from the legal regulation of sexual activity, and in particular from an examination of the classes of people who were protected by law from sexual assault and sexual propositioning.

It is often stated that Roman law prohibited homosexual acts between males, or between an adult man and a nonadult youth. The *lex Sca(n)tinia* is frequently mentioned in this context. Berger (1953), for instance, in his entry on *stuprum cum masculo (puero)*, writes:

> Pederasty. Originally it was punished by death, later with a fine of money. In the late empire the death penalty was inflicted again.—See LEX SCATINIA.

Under *Lex Scatinia (Scantinia)*, his entry reads:

> Against stuprum cum masculo (= pederasty, 149 B.C.). The penalty was a fine of ten thousand sesterces.

The evidence on which Berger bases his claim that the *lex Sca(n)tinia* provided for a penalty of 10,000 sesterces fine is probably Quintilian 4.2.69, which reads, "He has had illicit sexual relations with a freeborn male . . . the perpetrator shall pay the fine fixed for this offense, which is 10,000 sesterces."

As we see, there is no reference to the *lex Sca(n)tinia* here,[15] and the presumption that the sum named is the penalty for *stuprum* (illicit sexual activity) in general rather than specifically with a male, under some other legislation (most likely the *lex Iulia de vi*),[16] is strengthened by a passage in a [Quintilian] *Declamatio minor* that gives the same penalty for *stuprum* with a freeborn woman.[17] Not only is Berger on shaky ground in his assertion of the penalty attached to the *lex Sca(n)tinia*, but his summary of the provisions of Roman law in this area is seriously inaccurate, in that he fails to translate accurately what the source text actually says. The Quintilian passage refers specifically to an *ingenuus*, that is, a freeborn male, not to males in general.

That Roman law penalized attempts by males to seduce some male youths is also clear from a detailed passage by the jurist Paulus:

> He who has seduced or otherwise dishonored a freeborn youth, whether he has abducted him himself or suborned his attendant, or who has propositioned a woman or a girl, or has done anything to corrupt the morals of another, or has provided the house or money necessary for such an act, if the act is carried out shall be subject to "capital" punishment. If it is only attempted he is exiled to an island. The attendant who has been an accessory is punished with the full rigor of the law. (*Sent.* 5.4.14)

Here the social status of the youth concerned is clearly defined: he is described in the original Latin as *praetextatus*, that is, a freeborn male Roman citizen not yet of full adult status. His social status is further indicated by the assumption that he would have slaves attending him, as would evidently be the case with the females also mentioned as being an equivalent case. Obviously we are dealing here with the attempted seduction of a male youth of considerable social status (and, presumably, some wealth). This view of the matter, that the important distinction is the social status of being freeborn, rather than simply biological sex, is confirmed by the evidence of Plutarch, who gives as a reason for the wearing by free youths of the *bulla* (a form of amulet worn around the neck) that it is a sign marking them out as not to be approached by adult men for sexual purposes (*Quaest. Rom.* 101, 288a). What Berger has taken as simply referring to gender is clearly informed by class-status assumptions: not all youths were protected by the law, only those of respectable social background.

That distinctions of social status were of vital importance in relation to the sexual activity of males with females is as clear as in the case of male homosexual activity. The pseudo-Quintilian text cited above (note 17) clearly refers only to freeborn women: others, of whatever social status, are evidently outside the ambit of the law. Papinian, too, patently excludes slaves from the ambit of the Julian legislation on sexual offenses, treating unauthorized sexual activity with a slave as an infringement of the slave owner's rights to his or her property (*Dig.* 48.5.6 pr.), and this is confirmed by Ulpian (*Dig.* 47.10.25). Elsewhere, the underlying reasoning is made explicit: such sexual activity on the part of a free person with the slave of another is conceptualized as invasive not of the body of the slave (whose bodily integrity was not in itself of concern to the law), but potentially of the household of the owner (*Dig.* 1.18.21).

It is not simply slaves who stood legally outside the ambit of the Julian legislation on sexual offenses: Ulpian writes of some free women as being "those with whom extramarital sex does not count as *stuprum*" (*Dig.* 25.7.1). The example of such women given in the context is those who have been found guilty of adultery: clearly such women are low in the hierarchy of social status. Some women, even if free, are of such low status that they can be propositioned, and sex with them is, for the respectable man whose point of view the law usually assumes, not a matter of legal concern. Ulpian's reference to a possible point of mitigation in the case of sexual harassment is revealing: "If a man were to have propositioned unmarried girls, his offense is lessened if they were dressed like slaves, and very much lessened in the case of women dressed like prostitutes rather than respectable women" (*Dig.* 47.10.15.15). That is, if a man has propositioned a respectable woman "by mistake," as it were, taking her, because of her dress, for a nonrespectable, low-status woman, he is less culpable: she has, in effect, laid herself open to the assault on her respectability by appearing in public in a way that misleads others as to her social status. Clearly, the law on sexual offenses was designed to protect the respectable and their families: those of insufficient social status were not the concern of the law. Some people, even free citizens, were evidently of such low status that they (or their families) were not held to have, at least in the area of sexual activity, an "honor" to be impugned.

This connection in Roman society between social status and availability for sexual penetration long antedates the Augustan period. At the turn of the third and second centuries B.C.E., Plautus provides a list of those off-limits for a man looking for sex: "No one is forbidden to go on the public highway so long as you keep out of fenced-off farmland. So long as you keep your hands off married women, widows, unmarried girls, youths, and free boys, go for whomever you want" (*Curc.* 35–38). Significantly, all the categories of people mentioned as being potentially desirable are something other than *viri*, full men: for a man to want to penetrate another man is positioned as inconceivable. The metaphor of ownership that Plautus uses is also significant: those who belong to a family with sufficient social status and power to protect its members from invasive sexual penetration are clearly differentiated from others who are in a sense "in the public domain," open to sexual use on the part of "the man in the street."

What we see is that the right to protect one's body from the sexual assault of another, or from the sexual propositioning that was considered its verbal equivalent, is a right that is only allowed to certain categories of people, those who are respectable citizens of good birth and social standing. In the case of adult males, this sexual impenetrability is not afforded to everyone, only to those who have the status of full men, *viri* in Roman terms. This impregnability is not simply a matter of the actual penetration of the body: the contouring of the social boundary involved is the same when it is a matter of sexual propositions and pestering for sexual purposes more generally. Viewed from this perspective, such propositions can be seen as invasive in the same way as sexual penetration: the impenetrable boundaries of the social body are being drawn around those of the physical body.

Except in the context of sexual activity usually characterized as sadomasochistic, the connection between sexual activity and beating does not, perhaps, immediately occur to us.[18] Yet if we bear in mind the Roman protocol that conceptualized sexual activity as being about the penetration of the less powerful partner by the more powerful one, the act of beating and being beaten comes into focus as being very similar. As Saller (1991: 151) points out:

> More was at stake [in the case of beating] than physical pain: to the Romans the anguish was in significant measure social and psychological, the insult to *dignitas* . . . [since] the Romans attached symbolic importance to whippings [and] the whip was used to make distinctions in the public sphere between free and subject.

It was, at least in the late Republic and early Principate, one of the formal marks of Roman citizen status that one could not be beaten (Livy 10.9.4; Cic. *Pro C. Rabirio perduellionis reo* 12). For the Romans, as they chose to remember and record their own history as part of their corporate self-definition, the struggle for freedom from the tyranny of the powerful, from the time of Tarquin to the conclusion of the Struggle of the Orders, was marked at focal points by a concentration on the issue of the bodily inviolability of the Roman citizen, of whatever status, and in particular on the question of whether a citizen could be beaten. Livy records stories from the legendary past where this issue became a focus of contestation.[19] The question of corporal punishment was an area of conflict around the status of the *nexus* (debt-bondsman), an ambiguous status with elements of both citizenship and slavery.[20]

Beating was a punishment with an intimate connection with the hierarchy of social statuses, with the distinctions between free and slave, citizen and noncitizen, and being beaten was a humiliating mark of low status.[21] It was a mark of slavery that one could be beaten: the *Digest* makes clear the connection between slave status and corporal punishment.[22] Quintilian, too, while implying that beating was commonly inflicted on that other low-status group, children, makes the connection between beating and degradation to slavelike status clear,[23] and Plautus treats a scarred back as characteristic of a slave (*Amph.* 446). Even when, by the middle of the second century C.E., the major social division for purposes of criminal law had shifted from a distinction between free and slave to one between *honestiores* (the "more respectable" classes, those of munici-pal-councillor status and above) and *humiliores* (the lower orders), the li-ability to be beaten, or the exemption from it, still served as a—perhaps the—major marker of the distinction between high and low.[24] More gen-erally, *honestiores* were exempt from examination by torture, while the *hu-miliores* were not; the former, if found guilty, were punished not by an at-tack on their bodies but by a fine or exile, while the latter were subject to corporal punishment (*Dig.* 48.19.9.11 [Ulp.]). In this they were assim-ilated to the status of slaves.[25] Beating thus takes its place as one of a number of assaults on the body that, by their invasive quality, are intrin-sically demeaning. To be of high status meant to be able to protect one's body from assault even as a punishment; the mark of those of low status was that their body was available for invasive punishment.

Beating as an exemplification of what in Athens would have been called "hubristic" behavior[26] is accompanied in the exemplary stories of Rome's past by sexual violation, as we see in stories such as those of Lucretia and Verginia. Valerius Maximus (6.1.9) gives his readers a story that brings out into the open the connection between quasi-servile status and both beating and sexual availability for the master: that of T. Veturius, forced as a youth to give himself up as debt-bondsman to his creditor, who beats him like a slave because he refuses a sexual passivity that would dishonor him. The story ends well, of course: the victim goes to the consul, and the senate orders the wicked creditor imprisoned, to preserve inviolate the sexual purity of Romans, however humble they may be.

The jurist Gaius gives us a clear example of the equivalence in Roman thought between beating and sexual assault and their joint connection with social status when he writes: "Someone is demeaned not only when they are struck with a fist or a stick, even beaten, but also . . . if someone pesters a respectable woman or a freeborn youth" (even if he does not verbally proposition them).[27] To add further weight to the symbolic iden-tification for Romans of beating and sexual penetration, Aulus Gellius (9.12.7) records Cato the Elder as placing male prostitutes outside the category of those with bodily inviolability, alone of free men, even among the disreputable. They, like slaves, can be beaten, marking them off from the status of other citizens. Those who allow themselves to be penetrated sexually place themselves in the position of having the boundaries of their bodies invaded in other ways, too.

The status of being a respectable, freeborn Roman citizen was thus marked, at least in theory, on the corporeal level by bodily inviolability. Roman citizens, however low their social status, were not to be beaten, raped, or otherwise assaulted. Sexual penetration and beating, those two forms of corporeal assault, are in Roman terms structurally equivalent.[28]

The punishment of adulterers gives us further evidence of the equivalence for Romans of beating and sexual penetration, and their relationship with "manhood" and respectable social status. Normally, as we have seen, the body of a Roman citizen male was inviolable. An adulterer, however, lost that inviolability, and became subject to physical attack on his body if caught by the aggrieved husband. Plautus stages a scene in which an adulterer is beaten and threatened with castration (*Miles gloriosus* 1395–1426). Horace notes as potential punishments of a man caught having sex with a married woman being beaten to death, being raped by the husband's slaves, and being castrated, as well as losing money and reputation.[29] As the *Digest* puts it, *contumelia*, social degradation or dishonor, can take the place of killing as a punishment for the adulterer.[30] Beating, rape, and castration all fall into this category: they all symbolically degrade the adulterer, who has asserted his manhood sexually at the expense of another man. What these punishments bring about is the lowering of the adulterer from the status of full man to something less, emasculating him sexually (in the case of rape or castration), and reducing him to the status of a slave or a child (in the case of beating). In all these cases he is unmanned, diminished from *vir* to something less.

In order to get at what underlay this equivalence, we should examine what in the story of Veturius mentioned above is the factor that brings the two forms of bodily penetration together, the fact of slavery. It is a truism that Greco-Roman civilization was a "slave society," but when we glibly repeat that statement, we do not, perhaps, always remember its profound psychological, and therefore cultural, implications for members of that society. Unlike, for example, the slave society of the American South before the Civil War, in Roman society slavery was not supported by and supportive of a social distinction marked by visible differences of race. Slaves could become citizens—though, it is true, only second-class ones; conversely, a citizen had to face the possibility, however remote, of one day being enslaved. The slave, therefore, was both radically other than and, potentially, dangerously close to the free citizen.

What characterized the status of slaves was that they were not autonomous: they were under the control of their owner, under orders, most specifically that their bodies belonged to their owner, to do with as he or she wished. Slaves could be beaten, tortured, killed, and the fact that a slave, male or female, was at the disposal of his or her master for sexual use was so commonplace as to be scarcely noted in Roman sources. It was this lack of autonomy on the corporeal level, this availability of the body for invasive assaults, which characterized the status of slavery. Conversely, this equation of slavery with having, or being, a body at the disposal of another for penetration meant that having one's body penetrated was seen as slavelike. To allow oneself to be beaten, or sexually penetrated, was to put oneself in the position of the slave, that archetypal passive body.

But in this neat schema, where beating equals sexual penetration, and where to undergo either is to lose the status of a man, the Roman soldier stands out like the proverbial sore thumb. Central to the concept of Roman manhood was the image of the Roman soldier, the citizen in arms. Yet, paradoxically, the soldier can be beaten by his superiors. (He can only be beaten with a vine staff, but he can be beaten nevertheless.) Indeed, the mark of rank of a centurion was the vine staff with which he could beat citizen-soldiers. The provisions of the *leges Porciae*, which protected Roman citizens from beating, may have been extended in theory to soldiers,[31] but Tacitus's anecdote (*Ann.* 1.23.4) about the centurion known as "Fetch me another!" for breaking one vine staff after another on the back of the soldiers he was beating shows that, even under the Principate, the private soldier was seen as being subject to beating. Why soldiers, alone of Roman citizens, should be subject to such physical violence remains obscure. Clearly the difficulties of maintaining discipline under field conditions must, at least to some extent, account for this, but no satisfactory explanation for this anomaly has yet been adduced.

Viewed from this perspective, the Roman soldier, symbol of all that is manly in Roman society, is dangerously like the slave, that ever-present, unmanly inferior and outsider. One crucial difference that remains is that the body of the Roman soldier is sexually inviolable. To demonstrate this, we have the exemplary tale of Marius honoring the private soldier who killed an officer who wanted to violate him sexually.[32] To allow an officer to use a Roman soldier's body for his own sexual pleasure would be to break down the last barrier that still distinguished the manly from the unmanly, the high from the low, to bring disorder into the heart of the ordered social hierarchy of Rome.

The Roman soldier provides us with another exception to the rule that unmanly degradation results from the penetration of the body—a soldier's wounds are honorable, not dishonoring. Once again, as with beating, the situation of the soldier is dangerously close to the edge in terms of social status: the exception that highlights the rule. A man can without losing his superior status be penetrated by a sword or a vine, but not by a penis or a birch. As we see from Livy's highly colored recounting of the story cited in note 32, the scars from a soldier's wounds are conceptually placed as the polar opposite of scars from a servile beating.[33] They are his mark of manhood, the signifier, permanently inscribed on his body, of his social status as a full man.

Much of the pattern underlying the conceptualization that I have outlined can be better understood if it is seen as being based on the notion of the invasion of the boundaries of the body, and in particular on the idea of the inviolability of personal space including and surrounding the body as marker of superior status. The various ways in which the body of an inferior is acted upon in the aggressive demonstration of a power imbalance, or in the attempt to create such an imbalance, can be placed along a line of lesser or greater invasiveness. Verbal propositions and pestering, touching, beating, sexual penetration—all are seen as degrading invasions of the personal space of the victim of these assaults. The inability to defend one's body is a slavelike mark of powerlessness. It is within this wider pattern, which sees the body as potentially subject to invasion from a more powerful external force, and social superiority as, symbolically at any rate, consisting in the ability to protect one's body and even invade the body of others, that the Romans' obsession with seeing sexual activity in terms of an active/passive polarity, and their linking of this polarity with a conception of manhood, should be placed. The contours of social status demarcated by the distinction between the sexually penetrable and the impenetrable are, broadly speaking, the same as those we see when we examine the distinction between the beatable and the unbeatable. The pattern that emerges is that of a social pyramid. At the apex are the small class of *viri*, true men, adult Roman citizens in good standing, the impenetrable penetrators. Just below them are sets of people—freeborn male youths and respectable women—who are potentially penetrable because they are not, or not yet, men, but who are defined (because of their family connections with respectable Roman men) as inviolable, and therefore under the protection of the law. Below them, on the lowest slopes of the pyramid, are those, whether male or female, who are beatable and sexually penetrable. A sexual protocol that proclaims itself to be about gender-appropriate behavior turns out to be part of a wider pattern of social status, where the violability or inviolability of the body is a privileged marker of such status.

This is a pattern similar to that discernible in the world of classical Athens. Elite Roman discourse, however, has particular ways of articulating concern about the boundaries of manhood. Two areas of anxiety are manifest: the freeborn youth and the soldier. The freeborn Roman youth is characterized as potentially desirable to adult men, but as not to be sexually penetrated. His classical Greek counterpart is characterized by a finessing of the issue of his sexual penetrability, symbolized by a reluctance to enunciate the practice in polite pederastic literature (see, e.g., Theognis) or to represent the sexual penetration of Athenian youths on Attic vase-paintings. The Roman prohibition is overtly articulated, perhaps betraying a greater, or at least a different, anxiety about the process of making men. Although the citizen-soldier occupies a place in Roman culture similar to the place of the citizen-hoplite in that of classical Athens, the exemplary story of Marius and the soldier, to which there is no close equivalent in Athenian literature, suggests greater anxiety among Roman men about the soldier's status of being *under orders*, subject to corporeal punishment, and how this might compromise his manhood.

Notes

1. Lucr. 4.1030ff. See also Adams 1982: 188–89.
2. E.g., Sall. *Cat.* 13.3; Tac. *Ann.* 11.36; [Quint.] *Declamatio maior* 3.11; *Dig.* 3.1.1.6 (Ulpian).
3. See Hallett 1989a: 221ff. on the perceived need for a phallus in Roman representations of lesbian sexual activity.
4. There are references in Latin literature to the anal penetration of women (e.g., *Priapea* 3; Sen. *Controv.* 1.2.22), but these are much rarer than references to vaginal penetration.
5. See, for example, Gonfroy 1978 and Verstraete 1980.
6. As Santoro L'hoir 1992 has shown.
7. See, for instance, Wyke 1987, and Kennedy 1993, especially 28ff.
8. See, for an example of this, Roessel 1990 on Sulpicia's "Cerinthus."
9. *Ep.* 95.21: "These women are as bad as men in their sexual appetites, and, though nature made them sexually passive, they think up a new form of perversity and even . . . penetrate men." See the discussion of this passage in Hallett 1989a: 214ff.
10. This point has been noted by many scholars, including Hallett (1977).
11. As Hallett (1989a) argues, Roman use of the term *tribades* (from the Greek verb meaning "to rub") for lesbians involves both a recognition and a denial of nonpenetrative sexual pleasure. The modern notion of the "vaginal orgasm" should, however, remind us that, conceptually, rubbing and penetration are not necessarily mutually exclusive.
12. Lest we be seduced into thinking that Roman conceptions of sexuality were "naturally" similar to those of the modern West, we should remember the attack by Calvus on Pompey (Calvus fr. 18M), which equates a man who scratches his head with one finger with one who obviously wants to be penetrated by another man. How many of us make the same assumption?
13. A standard ploy of Roman political rhetoric was to accuse one's opponent of having allowed himself to be sexually penetrated by other males when he was a youth. See, for instance, Hallett 1977 on the role of accusations of effeminacy in the propaganda war between Octavian and Antony.
14. As Santoro L'hoir 1992 shows.
15. For a discussion of the ancient sources that refer to the *lex Sca(n)tinia*, see Lilja 1983: 112–21.
16. Cf. *Dig.* 48.3.4 (Marcian).

17. [Quint.] *Declamatio minor* 370. The historical reality of the laws cited in the rubrics of *controversiae* is, however, questionable.

18. On beating and other forms of violence as part of Roman sexual activity, see the essay by Fredrick in this volume.

19. E.g., Livy 2.55.5: "'I appeal to the citizenry,' he said, 'since the tribunes choose to beat a Roman citizen in full view of them.'"

20. E.g., Livy 2.23.7 (of an old soldier now in debt-bondage): "Then he showed [to his fellow citizens] his back disfigured by the marks of his having been recently beaten."

21. Cf. *Dig.* 48.19.10.2: "And the very act of being beaten is more severe than a fine."

22. E.g., *Dig.* 2.9.5 (Ulp.): "The case of a slave differs from that of a free man: in the first case punishment takes the form of beating, in the second of a financial penalty"; *Dig.* 49.14.12 (Callistratus): "Those who are condemned to the mines lose their status of freedom, since they are also subject to the slaves' punishment of beating."

23. "I do not believe that pupils should be beaten. First, because it is degrading and fit only for slaves, and undoubtedly, as is obvious in the case of adults, insulting" (Quint. 1.3.13–14).

24. E.g., *Dig.* 48.19.28.2: "Not everyone is normally beaten, only those who, though free, are of low status; more honorable people are not beaten." Cf. *Dig.* 48.19.28.5 and *Dig.* 50.2.12.

25. "Slaves are subject to the same punishment as *humiliores*" (Macer: *Dig.* 48.19.10 pr.).

26. See D. Cohen 1991b on hubris and sexual assault in Athenian law.

27. Gaius *Inst.* 3.220; Zalueta 1.227; cf. *Dig.* 47.10.15.22 (Ulp.).

28. See Adams 1982: 145–49, for the use of expressions of striking or beating as a metaphor for sexual penetration.

29. *Sat.* 1.2.41ff: "One is flogged to death . . . another is screwed by the slaves, another has his balls and randy cock cut off"; cf. *Sat.* 1.2.132–33: "You had better run away . . . unless you want to lose your money, your arse, or your reputation."

30. *Dig.* 8.5.23 (22).3: "A man who has the right to kill an adulterer has all the more right to inflict humiliation on him."

31. "[The *leges Porciae*] extended the right of appeal to Roman citizens both in capital cases and in cases involving the penalty of scourging, not only in Rome but in Italy and the provinces, and ultimately under service conditions in the field" (McDonald 1944: 19).

32. The incident is summarized by Val. Max. 6.1.12 and the Plutarchian *Regum Imperatorum Apophthegmata* (*Mor.* 202b–c) and recounted in greater detail in Plutarch's *Life of Marius*; it evidently became a commonplace example of a case of justifiable homicide, being referred to in this context by Cicero (*Mil.* 9 and, almost certainly, *Inv. Rhet.* 2.124) and Quintilian (*Inst.* 3.11.14), as well as being the subject of the [Quint.] *Declamatio maior* 3.

33. Livy 2.23.4: "He showed them on his own chest the scars that proved his valiant conduct in numerous battles."

PART TWO

WAYWARD SEXUALITIES

TWO

THE TERATOGENIC GRID

Holt N. Parker

> This goal is, briefly, to grasp the native's point of view, his
> relation to life, to realise *his* vision of *his* world.
> (Bronislaw Malinowski, *Argonauts of the Western Pacific*)

IN CONTEMPORARY Western society, we base our division of sexual categories on the axis of same versus other. Our primary division rests on the genders of the people involved. Thus we have two large-scale emic[1] categories of individuals: heterosexuals, who have sex with persons of the opposite gender, and homosexuals, who have sex with persons of the same gender.

This categorization is a rather parochial affair and a comparatively recent development even in the culture of the West.[2] It is abundantly clear from the anthropological record that this feature simply is not used in numerous other cultures. In such other cultures, sexual categories are based on divisions of age, social status, ritual category, or power relations and often cut across or simply ignore the biological classes of male and female.[3] Not only are lines drawn in different places, but more than two *genders* are recognized by various cultures.[4] Our hetero- versus homo-categories make no sense in a culture where one has more than two choices.

The ancient world, both Greek and Roman, did not base its classification on gender, but on a completely different axis, that of active versus passive.[5] This has one immediate and important consequence, which we must face at the beginning. Simply put, there was no such emic, cultural abstraction as "homosexuality" in the ancient world. The fact that a man had sex with other men did not determine his sexual category. Equally, it must be emphasized, there was no such concept as "heterosexuality." The application of these terms to the ancient world is anachronistic and can lead to serious misunderstanding. By the fifth time one has made the qualification, "The passive homosexual was not rejected for his homosexuality but for his passivity,"[6] it ought to become clear that we are talking not about "homosexuality," but about passivity.

It is very difficult for us to ignore our own prejudices and realize that what may be literally a matter of life and death in our culture would have been a matter of indifference or bewilderment to the Romans (see below).[7] But anthropological data shows that active versus passive as a basis for determining sexual categories is paralleled in a wide variety of societies.[8] Outside our own system of cultural types, "homosexual" applies meaningfully only to acts, not to people; it is an adjective, not a noun.[9] Even then we must add the warning that the adjective may serve to gather together acts of significance only to our culture.[10] We all recognize that different societies have totally different lines from ours that divide sacred and secular, edible and inedible, kin and non-kin. We are willing to believe that the Romans inhabited a different physical world, a different spiritual world, a different psychological world. We must be willing to accept that they inhabited a different sexual world as well.[11]

The Grid

Roman sexuality was a structuralist's dream. The Romans divided sexual categories for people and acts on the axis of "active" and "passive." Active has, in their scheme, a single precise meaning. The one normative action is the penetration of a bodily orifice by a penis. There are other acts that the Romans thought of as sexual (kissing, fondling, biting, hitting), but they do not determine sexual personas.[12] The Roman sexual schema is rigidly phallocentric, and this is a fact rooted in nature (cf. Mart. 11.22.9–10; Hallett 1983: 108). Thus "active" is *by definition* "male" and "passive" is *by definition* "female." Accordingly, Roman society creates exactly four sexual categories for people. There is the normal/active male (*vir*) and the normal/passive female (*femina/puella*). Each then has its antitype: the passive/abnormal man (*cinaedus*) and the active/abnormal woman (*virago/tribas/moecha*).

The sexual acts that determine a sexual persona are also divided into active and passive. This distinction of voice forms the principal axis of the grid. I have drawn it as a vertical, since it is literally the case that what is active is deemed superior (male); what is passive is deemed inferior (female).

Crossing this vertical axis is a horizontal axis of three holes (vagina, anus, mouth). The model for this axis is the female body, and the grid is encoded in the very language itself. Latin has a single verb for each sexual determinative act: *futuere*, "to insert one's penis in someone's vagina"; *pedicare*, "to insert one's penis in someone's anus"; and *irrumare*, "to insert one's penis in someone's mouth." The entire vocabulary is purely anatomical and quite precise about what is going where, as outlined in

The Grid

	Orifice		
	Vagina	Anus	Mouth
Active			
Activity	*futuere*	*pedicare*	*irrumare*
Person (VIR)	{ *fututor*	*pedicator/pedico*	*irrumator*
Passive			
Activity	*futui*	*pedicari*	*irrumari/fellari*
Person			
Male (PATHICUS)	{ *cunnilinctor*	*cinaedus/pathicus*	*fellator*
Female (FEMINA)	{ *femina/puella*	*pathica*	*fellatrix*

the accompanying table. The grid allows exactly six slots. There is the *vir*, the normal/active/male, who has open to him three possible sexual activities: to fuck someone in the vagina, the anus, or the mouth. He can be a *fututor* (vaginal inserter), a *pedicator/pedico* (anal inserter), or an *irrumator* (oral inserter). Accordingly, a *pedicator* is *not* a "homosexual"; he's a "bugger": someone who likes fucking people—of either gender—up the ass. An *irrumator* is *not* a "homosexual"; he's something we don't have a word for: a man who prefers fucking—both women and men—in the mouth. Nor is a *fututor* our "heterosexual." A *vir* while practicing *fututio* (vaginal insertion) must, of course, use women, but the Romans assumed that he would enjoy other orifices at other times in other genders.

The opposite of the *vir* is the *femina*. However, the Roman writers reserve a special term for a woman in her sexual role, and this is *puella*, which denotes not merely youth or beauty, but the specific status of "sexual object."[13] As the opposite of *vir*, the *puella* or *femina* (i.e., the normal/passive female) has open to her exactly three possible sexual passivities: to be fucked in the vagina, the anus, or the mouth. She can be a *fututa* (vaginal insertee), a *pathica/pedicata* (anal insertee), or a *fellatrix/irrumata* (oral insertee). The fact that there is no separate noun corresponding to *fututa* is in itself significant: the word for a woman who is fucked vaginally is simply *femina/puella*. A woman is defined as "one who is fucked in the vagina."

Anomalous Acts

By the very act of classification, any cultural system not only defines "normal" and "abnormal," but also creates anomalies that are perceived as monstrous because they cross the boundaries of defined categories (Douglas [1966] 1984; Murray 1983). Let us then look first at the horizontal division: the distinction between active and passive. The active is necessarily and essentially male: penetrating with one's penis. To be passive, therefore, is to play the part of a woman. This is amply attested by the phrase *pati muliebria*, "to suffer/be passive in the woman's role," and the overtones of the word *patior*, "to suffer, to allow, to be passive." Seneca said it best (*Ep.* 95.21): women are *pati natae*, "born to suffer," that is, made to be fucked (cf. Val. Max. 9.1.8). But the phrase is also frequently used of abnormal men, that is, men who allow themselves to be sexually passive.[14]

A woman cannot be properly active at all, since she has no penis. A woman cannot (in the Roman scheme of things) fuck a man.[15] Yet the very act of taking male/active sex as normative and the identification of the "active" with the "good" creates an anomaly at the very heart of the system, since it forces the identification of even the "normal" woman with the passive, the pathic, the bad (Richlin 1992a: 174). Female sexual *activity*, then, is by definition abnormal, almost an oxymoron. The sexually active woman is a monster.

Further, the vertical axis of the three holes creates its own anomalies. First, while the anus and vagina are thought of primarily as passive (mere receptacles for action), the mouth is problematic, a difficulty of conceptualization again shown in the language itself. Passive oral sex (*irrumari*) has the active counterpart of sucking (*fellare*, Adams 1982: 130–34). Thus, for the Romans, oral intercourse crosses classificatory boundaries. Disturbingly, it is both active and passive. Oral sex, however greatly desired, is already constructed as an anomalous activity.

Since the basis of the horizontal axis is the female body, a more significant gap is left when the system is inscribed on the male body. The grid is not symmetrical: only women have vaginas. Whereas a man can practice *pedicatio* or *irrumatio* on men and women alike, he can commit *fututio* only with women. What, then, happens when a man is passive?

Martial and the Logic Problem

We can see the poet Martial exploiting his culture's communal grid with the relentlessness of a logic problem. So 2.47 makes explicit the three possible active roles for a man:

> I warn you, flee the tricky nets of the infamous adulteress,
>> Gallus, o you who are smoother than a Cytherian conch shell.
> Do you trust in your buttocks? The husband is not a butt-fucker (*paedico*).
>> There are two things he does: mouth-fucks (*irrumat*) or cunt-fucks (*futuit*).

The significantly named Gallus hopes to avoid death or castration at the hands of a jealous husband by submitting to one of the standard punishments for adultery: anal rape.[16] The husband, however, is not interested in anal sex (again, the word *pedico* does not specify the sex of the victim). Gallus lacks a vagina. One orifice is left. It logically follows that Gallus is going to be raped in the mouth (a worse punishment; cf. Mart. 3.83, and see below). Similarly, 3.73:

> You sleep with well-endowed boys
> and what stands on them does not stand on you.
> What, I ask you, do you want me to suspect?
> I wanted to believe that you were a soft man (*mollem*),
> but rumor denies that you are a *cinaedus*.

Gallus is *mollis* "soft," that is, passive: this eliminates the top three cells of the grid. He sleeps with boys: this eliminates the first column; he isn't a *cinaedus*: this eliminates the second column; all that remains is to conclude that he is a *fellator*: Q.E.D.

The gap in the system is shown by the deductive puzzler of 2.28:

> Laugh aloud at the one who called you, Sextillus,
> a *cinaedus* and stick out your middle finger.
> But you are not a butt-fucker (*pedico*), nor are you, Sextillus,
> a cunt-fucker (*fututor*).
> Nor does the hot cheek of Vetustina please you.
> I confess you are none of these things. So what are you?
> I don't know, but you know there are two things remaining.

The grid allots only six slots. Sextillus is not a *cinaedus* (anus/passive), nor a *pedico* (anus/active), nor a *fututor* (vagina/active), nor an *irrumator* (mouth/active). There are only two things left: he must be a *fellator* (mouth/passive) or . . . or what? A man may be used anally (*cinaedus*), and orally (*fellator*), but how can a man be used vaginally? The answer is clear from numerous other sources: he must be a *cunnilinctor* (Richlin 1992a: 132). Thus the logic of the system demands that cunnilingus is viewed somehow as being the passive/negative side of vaginal intercourse. To be passive with respect to the mouth is to be a *fellator*, to be passive with respect to the anus is to be a *cinaedus*, to be passive with respect to the vagina is to be a *cunnilinctor*. For a man to commit cunnilingus is to be fucked by a woman.

The Ontological Status of Cunnilingus

This is, for us, a highly counterintuitive statement; but it is clear from the Roman sources that cunnilingus is viewed as a man being used by a woman and corresponds to a man being used vaginally.[17] The passive man is "fucked" by a woman. Cunnilingus, as about the only sexual act in the

Roman schema where a man can be passive (i.e., nonpenetrating) with a woman, becomes the testing ground for whether *cinaedus* matches up with our concept of "homosexual." It is clear that it does not. In cunnilingus we have men engaged in sexual activities with women, which violates our very definition of "homosexual," but still being passive. In the Roman sexual system, the dividing line is active versus passive (penetrated versus penetrating), not same versus other. Thus, for a man to give oral sex is for him to be passive with respect to his mouth, and the disgrace is the same whether he is servicing a man or a woman (Veyne 1985: 31). Cunnilingus, like fellatio, is an oral violation, and the two are frequently lumped together, as in the logic of Martial 2.28 above (cf. also 3.81; 12.59.10). So Martial asks the rhetorical question (3.88):

> The brothers are twins but they tongue different groins.
> Tell me, are they more unlike or alike?

Men who perform fellatio are expected to perform cunnilingus as well. Just as the active male is indifferent to the gender of the person he violates, so the (orally) passive male is indifferent to the gender of the person who violates him. So in Ausonius *Epigrams* 78, where raging oral lust in a married *fellator* drives him to the perverted extremity of cunnilingus with his own wife.

Thus, cunnilingus is a monstrosity in the system. It is active, a type of failed intercourse (Mart. 3.81, 3.84, 11.25, 11.61), but also passive; note Martial's outrage in 11.61, where he attacks a man so passive that his mouth becomes a cunt for a cunt. Cunnilingus is passive, and so in the Roman system an essentially feminine activity. This can be seen clearly in Martial 7.67 (1–3, 13–17), where Philaenis misunderstands the categories of the grid (Richlin 1992a: 134; Hallett 1989a: 215–16):

> Philaenis the tribad (*tribas*) butt-fucks (*pedicat*) boys
> and fiercer than a husband's erection
> hacks eleven girls every day. . . .
>
> . . . .
>
> After these things [various manly exercises], when she's horny,
> she doesn't suck (*fellat*)—she thinks this unmanly (*parum virile*)—
> but simply devours the middles of girls.
> The gods give you back your mind, Philaenis,
> you who think that licking cunt is manly.

This is not a poem about "lesbianism." It is rather a mockery of the antitype, the category of the active woman. Philaenis exercises like a man, eats like a man, and drinks like a man (lines 4–12). These acts are only slightly less absurd than her wish to have sex like a man, that is, with both boys and girls. Like a man, she refuses to be passive/penetrated, whether vaginally, anally, or orally. In her twisted logic, says Martial, this leaves

only tribadism (a parody of vaginal intercourse), attempts at anal violation of boys, and oral sex, cunnilingus. What Philaenis fails to realize is
that cunnilingus is equally passive, equally an act of being penetrated.

Deviate Sexual Acts and the Scale of Humiliation

Thus, contra Foucault, the Romans did indeed divide sexual acts into the
approved and the forbidden.[18] Since a man is defined as a penetrator,
there are exactly three things he can do sexually: he can penetrate someone (male or female) in the mouth, anus, or vagina. Equally, there are exactly three things he is forbidden to be: a *cinaedus*, a *fellator*, or a *cunnilinctor*. A woman, on the other hand, is forbidden to *act* at all—her only
acceptable role is to be passive. And here we can see the massive power
of the list, of systems of knowledge, for all other possible sexual activities
become opaque to the culture. If "active" is defined as penetrating with a
penis, "passive" is therefore any role that is not phallocentric, in which a
man does not insert his penis in an orifice. Not only are being penetrated
and servicing a woman orally passive, but any erotic activity that does not
culminate in intercourse runs the danger of being labeled "passive" because someone is not being fucked. So Catullus (16) is attacked as a passive for confining his descriptions of sex to kissing. "Writing such soft
stuff, Catullus must be soft himself, and sexually effeminate. Catullus
threatens to prove his masculinity on them in person"[19] . . . *pedicabo ego
vos et irrumabo*.

Further, contra Foucault (1986: 114–15), the Romans did not treat the
aphrodisia as an aggregate. There is a demonstrable hierarchy in the desirability of each of the three sexual acts and in the degree of victimization that corresponds to it. The Roman created what we may call "the
scale of humiliation": vagina, anus, mouth. Being fucked in the vagina is
simply normal for a woman; it is not as degrading as being fucked in the
anus. The most humiliating thing to suffer, as it is the most enjoyable to
inflict, is to be fucked in the mouth.[20] For a man, any penetration is humiliating, but the same scale applies: being fucked in the anus is bad,
more humiliating still is being fucked in the mouth.[21] Not only were
some actions imposed and some forbidden, some were more forbidden
than others.

Anomalous People and Willing Victims

Since every sexual act is based on the distinction between active and passive, every sexual act encodes power relations: dominator and dominated,
each carries a burden of aggression or humiliation, power or powerless-

ness. The dominant ideology is the ideology of domination. Though a woman cannot be active, the act of penetration has not only literal but also symbolic and connotative meanings. The symmetry of the system demands that the slots for passive men and active women be filled in; the cultural schema demands antitypes. The grid accordingly constructs two monstrosities: the passive man and the active woman.

The active side is normal, that is, a *vir* will *futuere*, *irrumare*, and *pedicare* indiscriminately on whatever body he chooses. The category *vir* subsumes the labels *fututor*, *pedico*, and *irrumator* (see the table above). *Vir* exists as the level of emic, cultural type; that is, a *vir* may take pleasure in all of these actions. Similarly, in our culture, a heterosexual male may describe himself as an "ass-man" or a "leg-man" while still remaining a normal manly man.

On the other hand, each of the passive acts shows a distinct tendency to be objectified and embodied as a separate entity. Though the labels *cinaedus* and *pathicus* can subsume the other categories of passive male, there is also a distinctive sexual ontology of *pathicus/cinaedus* (anal), *fellator* (oral), and *cunnilinctor* (vaginal). Each of these will perform the actions of another, but each seems to have a stated preference. What remains constant, though, is the distinction between active and passive (Hallett 1989a: 223); a *cinaedus* cannot become a *pedico*, a *fellator* cannot become an *irrumator*, a *cunnilinctor* cannot become a *fututor*.

The reified victim (pathic male and even "normal female") is an object of contempt. Having been created, these creatures are then despised. Yet, in part to absolve the aggressors from guilt, the passive victim is rewritten as active: one who actively desires to be hurt, humiliated, fucked and fucked over. We see what we may call "the creation of the willing victim." Women enjoy being penetrated, enjoy being raped (Ov. *Ars Am.* 1.673: *grata est vis ista puellis*; Joshel 1992; Richlin 1992e), as do ontologically passive men. The *irrumatus* (grammatically passive) is a *fellator* (grammatically active), who enjoys being fucked in the mouth; the *pedicatus* is the *cinaedus*, who enjoys being fucked in the ass and will nearly commit rape in order to be raped (Petron. 21, 23–24). Similarly, the **fututus* is the *cunnilinctor*, who derives his sexual pleasure through his tongue. Thus, the passive orifices can be assimilated to a vision of oral aggression. "Hungry" vaginas can actively desire to be used (*Priapea* 83 Oxford). Anuses are voracious (Catull. 33.4; Mart. 2.51.6).

The Normal Male

We can begin by examining the unmarked cases: the active man (*vir*),[22] and the passive woman (*femina*). The normal man is constructed according to the Priapic model as delineated by Richlin (1992a). He will penetrate anyone in any hole; he takes pleasure; he seeks and hunts (Veyne 1985: 29). The *vir* is not the same thing as our "heterosexual," not least because a *vir* will have sex with (fuck) other males. This act violates our very definition of "heterosexual." More important still, to have sex with other males may be the *proof* of his status as a *vir*, a manly man. So Catullus 16 and the famous taunt of Valerius Asiaticus when accused of effeminacy (*mollitiam corporis*) by P. Suillius Rufus (Tac. *Ann.* 11.2.2): "Ask your sons, Suillius," he said, "they'll tell you I'm a man (*virum*)."

There may be men who are interested mostly in women, and it is possible to create nonce and humorous terms for them (*ancillariolus*, Mart. 12.58; *mulier-osus, -ositas*, Plaut. *Poenulus* 1303; Afranius *com.* 371; Cic. *Fat.* 10, *Tusc.* 4.25; Gell. 4.9.12; cf. *Anth. Pal.* 5.49), but none of these imply exclusive interest in women, and none are emic categories, that is, primary terms of the discourse. That a man is interested only in women does not define an ontological category; it is a personal idiosyncrasy. The emperor Claudius is possibly the only man singled out as exclusively interested in women in all of Roman history—even Ovid (*Ars Am.* 2.683–84) merely expresses a preference.[23] Suetonius writes, "He was of an extreme lust towards women, completely lacking in experience of males" (*libidinis in feminas profusissimae, marum omnino expers, Claud.* 33.2). The very vocabulary is significant. Suetonius cannot call Claudius a *vir*, not even *mulierosus*; these terms do not describe the exclusivity he finds remarkable. Suetonius has no word for "heterosexual"; it is not a category he can readily label. Instead he has to *describe* this peculiarity of taste to his readers.

Rome, then, totally ignores our distinction. And to call the Romans or Greeks "bisexual" just repeats the error (so Cantarella 1992). It's not that they fall on this side of the line, or that side, or in the middle. The point is that *the line doesn't exist*. We in turn completely ignore the Roman distinction. The active/passive distinction, though it has many emotional ramifications for us, does not determine sexual types. A man who practices cunnilingus (passive to the Romans) is still (by our definition) a heterosexual. A man who receives fellatio (active to the Romans) from another man is still (by our definition) a homosexual. The concepts of *vir* and "heterosexual" are structurally completely different.

The Normal Female

The normal woman is passive (Veyne 1985: 30). This is true on the most literal of levels. The good wife doesn't move (Lucr. 1268–77; Mart. 10.68.10; Plut. *Conjugal Precepts* 18). A wife who does is the subject of frequent jokes: she is an adulteress who has learned her moves elsewhere (Mart. 11.104, 7.18; Ov. *Am.* 1.10.36, 2.10.35; Tib. 1.9). The *femina* is penetrated in any hole; she gives pleasure; she is sought and hunted. And here we can see clearly the anomalous nature of feminine sexuality in, as it were, action. The cultural equation of "passive" with "pathic" causes "normal" feminine sexuality to be viewed as contemptible (Richlin 1992a: 174). It also runs into practical difficulties, where it conflicts with the ambiguous desires of individual men. Not only do lovers (e.g., the elegiac poets) prefer sexually active, loving women to cold fish, but so do some husbands (e.g., Mart. 7.91; 10.35, 38 on the second Sulpicia; H.N. Parker 1992b; Hallett 1992b; Richlin 1992g). Feminine passion, to satisfy cultural expectations, must be simultaneously active (hence the sexual meaning of *morigera*, "actively pleasing the man," Adams 1982: 164) and passive, still under the control of the husband (Mart. 10.47.10). It is Plautus's Alcmene who strikes the mean; she prays for desire, but moderate desire (*sedatum cupidinem, Amph.* 840).

The Abnormal Male

Now let us look at the abnormal. The *pathicus* (passive man), as constructed at Rome, is the antitype to the *vir*, serving to define him. The *pathicus* inverts the values of the *vir*. He will desire to be penetrated. Now, just as the Roman classification recognizes nothing like our heterosexual, so it recognizes nothing like our homosexual. This is not to say that men who loved men exclusively might not have existed, though again they are surprisingly hard to find. Galba is about the only possible candidate. He, however, is an instructive case. Suetonius says of him, "In sexual matters, he was more inclined to males, and then none but the hardbodied and those past their prime" (*libidinis in mares pronior et eos non nisi praeduros et exoletosque, Gal.* 22). Note here that Galba is the active partner, not the passive; that even he has merely a *preference* for males; and that what is odd about him is a liking for adult men rather than soft boys. Suetonius, therefore, is not describing a "sexual orientation"; he is commenting on a peculiarity of taste on the part of a manly man. Galba appears to be the only case in Roman history where a man is specifically stated to prefer adult males. Galba may be the closest thing to a "homosexual" in our sense (Richlin 1993b: 532), but even so, to apply the term to him is misleading. Vergil, too, is a possible "homosexual" in our sense, though again, he is said merely to be *libidinis in pueros pronioris*, "sexually more inclined to boys" ([Suet.] *Verg.* 9), and the *Life* of Vergil records the rumor of an affair with Plotia Hieria, which she is said to have denied (10). That is, Vergil is described as a normal man in Roman terms, with an idiosyncratic preference for just one type of partner.

There indeed may have been men who were "homosexual" in our sense (primarily or exclusively attracted to men), but they would not have known themselves to be such or have been recognized as such. Instead, those whom we label "homosexuals" would have been filed under the labels of either *viri*, "normal men" (such as Galba), or *pathici* (such as the objects of Martial's or Juvenal's scorn), entirely on the basis of what they did with those other men. The *pathicus*, then, was simply not our "homosexual"; the structural descriptions differ profoundly. Several features, which have generally been missed in previous discussions, make this clear.

First, there is no mutuality, no exchange of pleasures: a *pathicus* will never wish to *futuere*, *pedicare*, or *irrumare*; he will not even desire to have his penis touched.[24] He derives pleasure not through his penis, but solely from being used in his mouth or anus. The *pathicus*, if anything, approaches more closely our concept of the masochist than of the homosexual. Our phrases "love between men" or "same-sex love" imply a mutuality that is completely lacking from the Roman sexual scheme. Though an adult male could express love for a boy, in Roman culture a man penetrates another adult almost exclusively as a punishment or a mark of contempt.

Second, just as the *vir* is indifferent to the sex of the object he uses, so the *pathicus* is indifferent to the sex of the subject who uses him. The *pathicus* will delight not only in being the victim of men, being penetrated by a penis in the anus or mouth, but also in being the victim of women, primarily by providing cunnilingus but also by being used, as it were, as a dildo with his penis (Mart. 5.61). Martial (4.43) insists he did not call a man a *cinaedus*; he called him something worse, a cunt-licker (*cunnilingum*; and cf. 2.84). This is the point of Martial 10.40:

> Since people were always telling me
> that my Polla was spending time in secret with a *cinaedus*,
> I broke in on them, Lupus. He wasn't a *cinaedus*.

Perhaps few things show the differences between our sexual system and the Romans' more vividly than these three lines. For us the only "natural" deduction to be drawn is that the speaker found them having intercourse; if he's not a "homosexual," then he must be a "heterosexual." For Martial's audience the deduction is quite different. If he's not a *cinaedus* (someone who enjoys being fucked in the ass), then he must be "much worse" (Ker 1968, 2: 185). He could not have suddenly become active, and so could not possibly be having intercourse; instead, he's a *cunnilinctor*.[25]

The *pathicus* will not desire to penetrate, but he may be forced to do so by the raw facts of anatomy. Hence we find throughout Martial various jokes about passive men being forced by poverty or a type of oral impotence to have intercourse (Mart. 6.33, 11.85, 11.87; cf. esp. 11.47: cunnilingus in order to avoid intercourse).[26] Further, though this leads us off into gender roles rather than sex roles per se, the passive man is effeminate in all the metaphorical senses. The man weak (as women are weak) in self-control, in resisting pleasures, will be pathic; the texts reveal a complex of overindulgence in wine, food, and sex. Thus, paradoxically from our point of view, the man obsessed with women is passive; hence the well-known picture of the *cultus adulter*, for whom we have our own curiously ambiguous phrase: "ladies' man."[27]

The *pathicus*, then, does not correspond to our society's construction of the "homosexual" at all. The two differ both etically (that is, their structural descriptions are markedly different) and emically (that is, they occupy different positions in a system of opposites). The two types do share certain features, but this is because each is the antitype of the unmarked normal "man." But just as the *vir* who has sex with boys (Tac. *Ann.* 11.2.2) or men (Catull. 16) to prove his manhood is hardly our heterosexual, so neither is the *cinaedus* our "homosexual." Naturally, if one wishes to be penetrated, a man's the best thing, and nobody gives humiliation like a man. But the *pathicus* violates our very definition for "homosexual," since he will be used by men and women indifferently.

Third, there is a point that I have not seen made in any discussion of ancient sexuality, though it raises itself instantly in the course of an anthropological survey. And this is simply that *cinaedi* do not have sex with *cinaedi*. In our system, "homosexuals" (by definition) have sex only with other "homosexuals." But *cinaedus* is not a reciprocal relation. *Cinaedi* have (or want to have) sex with normal men, with manly men. Two *cinaedi* in the Roman scheme is a ridiculous situation: two men, neither of whom wishes to penetrate. If there were men who loved other men, Rome would ask only, "Who's fucking whom?" (cf. the case of Galba above: he's the man). Thus the *cinaedus* simply does not correspond to our construction of the "homosexual." Nor does the Roman hatred of the *pathicus* correspond to "homophobia," though again they do share some features. Each is an expression of the fear and hate that the dominant group in any society expends on the "Other," the group or groups that define the power elite by negation and exclusion, whether the group exists (e.g., Jews) or not (e.g., witches; see below).

The Abnormal Female

In the same way, the active woman, the *virago*, *tribas*, or *moecha*, will invert the values of the *femina*. She will desire to penetrate, but cannot be truly (phallically) active. It is clear, then, that any woman who enjoys sex is by definition abnormal and masculine. The sexually active woman is the prostitute or the adulteress, who inverts the values of the society. She hunts and seeks out men to give her pleasure and uses them as toys. So the pictures of Sallust's Sempronia, or Cicero's Clodia or Sassia, or Catullus's Lesbia. Such a woman is a monster who violates boundaries. This is given an outward and visible symbolism in the *toga*, the sign that marked adulteresses and prostitutes. The role within the grid of this remarkable feature of Roman public semiotics is clear: the active (phallic) woman is denoted by male dress, marked out as one who crosses boundaries, as a violation of the norm.

The monstrous sexuality of the active woman is built on the model of aggressive male sexuality, to the point where the active woman may prefer a woman as victim. A woman cannot fuck a man except by forcing him into cunnilingus. Thus, even as there are no homosexuals, so the Roman sources know nothing of lesbians in our sense. Rather, they construct the *tribas*, the subject of an article by Judith Hallett (1989a, reprinted in this volume). The *tribades* practice a type of fake intercourse: either they rub their vulvas together or one uses a dildo on the other (Sen. *Controv.* 1.2.23; Mart. 1.90, 7.35, 7.67, 70; Juv. 6.304–13). Thus even *this* sexuality is phallocentric: we hear only once of licking (Mart. 7.67, quoted above); there is even an explicit denial of the practice (Juv. 2.47–48). We hear nothing of mutual masturbation. Rather, the women have to perform a parody of intercourse. Even when women become active, a woman is still the passive object of fucking.

Further, this monstrous sexuality has a physical incarnation. The sexually active woman (whether she seeks men or women) is endowed with a monstrous clitoris (*landicosa*, CIL 4.10004; *Priapea* 12.14; cf. the implications of Phaedrus 4.16.13). Their sex is masculinized: Juvenal's Messalina has a uterine hard-on (Juv. 6.129); Fulvia has a monstrous clitoris (*CIL* 11.6721.5; Hallett 1977). In Laqueur's phrase, "Destiny is anatomy" (1990: 25–62). The *pathicus* is only threatened with castration (Mart. 9.2.14); no doctor ever suggests castration as a cure for sexual excess or deficiency. But clitoridectomy is a carefully described operation to correct a phallic clitoris (Aët. 16.105; Paul of Aegina 6.70; Mustio 2.26). Systems of knowledge and power are inscribed not only with the pen but also with the scalpel.

Thus the Romans were not "before sexuality."[28] A man in active public life was under constant attack (and constantly attacking his enemies) as having been a *puer delicatus* as a youth, a *cinaedus* as an adult, a *cunnilinctor*, ruled by women, or a woman himself (Richlin 1992a: 97–98, 140; Edwards 1993: 63–97). Nor are women "before sexuality." The sexually active woman is a monster (Veyne 1985: 30, 33). She may escape censure only by being passive (or by a careful manipulation of the symbols of passivity; so Cornelia, "the Mother of the Gracchi"). Likewise, the active woman is under constant attack as man, whore, adulteress, or virago. The reverse is also true: the anomalous woman, the woman active in any sense, is attacked as sexually active and hence monstrous (Sempronia, Fulvia, Lesbia, Messalina), and this characterization serves to feminize her men.

Materiality

For Roman sexuality our only sources are public male posturings. Even elegy and epitaph fall into this category. We may never be able to recover the reality of what people did in the privacy of their rooms, much less what people felt in the privacy of their hearts. The public system of classification is purely a matter of matter; it has nothing to do with emotions, with affect, with love. It is concerned with bodies, with orifices, with power.

Yet such public systems of roles and expectations have enormous power to affect individuals, not only in how they act, but even in how they feel and conceive of themselves. We may not believe in or follow our society's script for male or female behavior—the readers of this collection are perhaps the least likely to do so—but it affects us all profoundly. A trivial example may show this best. Societal expectations not only guarantee I will never wear a dress, they guarantee I will never wear a *small watch*.

The *cinaedus*, it is clear, was good to think with. The category was useful as an antitype for delineating acceptable behavior and attacking enemies. The question now arises, was it anything more? In short, were there any *cinaedi*, really?

Three different questions are frequently mixed together when we look for gay people in antiquity (Boswell 1980; 1990a: 137 with n. 8), and they must be carefully distinguished. First: Did the concept/classification/category "homosexual," as we construct it, exist? Here, as I hope I have shown, the answer is simply, "No." The search for "gays" in antiquity is pointless. Equally, we must stop assuming that the main culture was "straight." To put the matter bluntly, heterosexuals have no claim on antiquity either. Second: Did "homosexual" men and women, as *we* define them, exist in antiquity? Here the answer is a highly qualified, "Yes." There were probably men and women primarily or exclusively attracted to the same sex. The point is that this fact was not particularly important, to them or to their society (Wiseman 1985: 10). Rather, depending entirely on what sexual acts they enjoyed with those of the same sex and how they enjoyed those acts, they were defined by their culture as normal or abnormal.

These first two questions mistakenly confuse our categories with those of Rome. However, a third question can still be meaningfully asked (Richlin 1993b). Not, "Did 'homosexuals' (as we define them) exist?" but "Did *cinaedi*, as the *Romans* defined them, exist?" That is, was there anybody there?

Our immediate answer is, "Of course, they existed." When Juvenal and others attacked *cinaedi*, they were attacking real people, not an anthropological abstraction. But this is not necessarily the case. Let's take the useful example of the witch. In numerous societies (Medieval and Renaissance Europe, Navajo, Bantu), one can mock witches, warn people not to become witches, even kill people as witches, without the need for any real supernatural witches. We can restate the matter in terms of set theory. The set {cinaedus} clearly existed and was in constant use, but were there any members in the set? That is, were cinaedi antitypes like Jews, who, however misrepresented, do actually exist; or were they antitypes like witches, who, however often represented, do not?

When we ask the question, "Were there any real cinaedi in Rome?" we are asking about a stereotype, and the reality behind a stereotype, when we have nothing but the stereotype. The inquiry into materiality therefore must be formulated rigorously, for we are in constant danger of begging the question. If we ask, "Were there cinaedi?" we must also ask, "And in whose terms?" The answer to this, of course, is: "In the terms of those who control the discourse, the dominant group." If we ask, "Were there cinaedi?" we are employing a term defined by the power elite. So Richlin (1993b: 524) rightly defines cinaedi in normal Roman terms as "those who liked to be sexually penetrated by other men," and, I would add, sexually used by women (cf. ibid.: 533). We are asking, we are forced to ask (at least at first), "Were there really any men who depilated themselves, scratched their head with one finger," and all the other dead give-aways (Richlin 1992a: 258 n. 3). "Were there really men who enjoyed being humiliated, buggered, raped in the mouth, or faute de mieux, performing cunnilingus?" The answer, I think, is, "Yes." Some men like that did, perhaps, exist.

Thus when Richlin and others raise the question of the materiality of the cinaedus—and, let us not forget, the materiality of the normative vir, of the femina, and of the other categories as well—I think it likely that these roles did indeed affect behavior. For we are dealing here with the extraordinary power of cultural roles to mold individual actions. I think it extremely likely, therefore, that men avoided scratching their heads, so that others would not take them for cinaedi, and satire is full of secret cinaedi aping the signs of viri. For men doing exactly the opposite, a single example must suffice. Seneca, no friendly witness, provides a portrait of Mamercus Scaurus (Ben. 4.31.3–5; Richlin 1992a: 281–82):

> Didn't you know that he used to take the menstrual blood of his female slaves in his gaping mouth?[29] Did he even pretend it wasn't true? Did he even want to seem pure [i.e., orally uncontaminated]? I'll tell you his own story about himself, which I remember was being circulated and laughed at even when he was present. He had once used an obscene word to Annius Pollio, who was reclining at dinner, and then said that he was going to do what he preferred to suffer, and when he saw Pollio's frown, he said, "If I've said anything bad, on my own head be it!" He used to tell this story himself.

That is, Scaurus, in response to something Pollio had said, offhandedly remarked, "Fuck you."[30] He then changed it around by adding, "But I'd prefer you to fuck me." Here we have a picture of a man who is attacked as a *cunnilinctor*, and who presents himself as a *cinaedus*, who makes a joke of one of the worst of Roman insults. But we must remind ourselves, it is still a picture by an enemy. Men attacked their enemies as *cinaedi*. We have no words directly from anyone who identifies himself as a *cinaedus*.

Cultural types can and do influence behavior. Does this mean, however, that the constant depiction of *cinaedi* points to men who constantly depicted themselves as *cinaedi*? Does this qualify as a sub- or counterculture? I do not believe the evidence is sufficient to say, though the example of Scaurus points to a way in which the cultural type of the *cinaedus* might have been deployed for individual self-fashioning.[31]

Tacitus in Ohio

Let me make clearer the kinds of potential error that reoccur in discussing the sexualities of another culture and the materiality of a stereotype. An ancient ethnographer, Tacitus say, is transported here. He begins to describe our society, particularly our sexual customs. At first he is simply appalled. On our streets perverted *pathici* openly flaunt themselves, wearing T-shirts that boast of their disgusting oral submission to women ("Muff-Diving Instructor," "Free Mustache Rides"); they advertise their loathsome services in the personals columns of newspapers. Then he is bewildered. On the other hand, we treat as the vilest of criminals perfectly normal men whose only crime is the perfectly normal action of buggering boys. Some *pathici* we persecute, others we allow in public. Some *viri* we consider normal, others we incomprehensibly incarcerate.

Tacitus begins his fieldwork. He asks us, "Do you have any perverts?" We respond, "Yes." He then asks, "Are there men who like to be buggered?" Again, we respond, "Yes." He then records in his *de America* the presence of *cinaedi* and the universality of the active/passive split. This is the first error in fieldwork: assuming that the emic categories of your culture must be found everywhere. Later, however, he begins to realize that many of us, gay or straight (in our terms), are sometimes active and sometimes passive (in his terms). He will not, however, solve his problem by creating the additional category of "bi-actives." He has still utterly missed what makes a difference. If he insists that nevertheless everyone is "really" either active or passive, and that our categories of "homosexual" and "heterosexual" often filter or obscure information necessary to answer questions of interest to Roman researchers about sexual orientation, we will eventually get tired of trying to explain things to him.

Let us now suppose that after some time he finally realizes that his categories of *vir/cinaedus* do not match up with our categories "homo/heterosexual." He avoids falling into the ethnocentric error of assuming that his emic category of *cinaedus* is a human universal. So, as a good scholar, he asks, "Do you have any 'homosexuals'? By that I mean what your own primary sources reveal: men who want to be women, and have limp wrists and a cunning talent for interior decoration. Do you have any 'lesbians'? By that I mean diesel dykes, who think they can use their clitorises like penises," etc., etc. We would be forced to answer: "Yes. There actually are men and women who fit that description." And then we would add, "But really, it's just a stereotype."

And this raises the further question: Would we (gay or straight) recognize ourselves or assent to these descriptions, or would we not say, "I am not that name"? We may not know for certain if there were any *cinaedi*, in any terms, but we can use groups we do know exist. If an anthropologist asks of ancient Rome or modern America, using the terms of the dominant culture, "Were there 'women'? By which I mean sexually insatiable (or alternately frigid) air-heads, obsessed with clothes and gossip," etc., etc. (read Juvenal or watch television), we'd be forced to say: "Yes, there are such women, but I am not that name."[32] If she asks, "Were there any 'men'? By which I mean promiscuous, treacherous, rapists all" (read Ovid or watch television), we'd be forced to answer, "Yes, but I am not that name."

Thus "*cinaedus*" represents a real category, in that people were willing to assign others to it. We do not know if anyone called a *cinaedus* would have accepted that name, or how he would have acted. We know nothing of what "love between men" might have been. Our sources do not speak of love. And yet we must go beyond what we are told, even if (as in the case of Rome) it is only a single speculative step. We must become resisting readers.

Notes

1. In brief: emic (also called experience-near) categories in a culture correspond to the phon-*emic* level of analysis, vs. etic categories (experience-far), which correspond to the phon-*etic* level. Emic categories, like phonemes, are those which are of significance (literally make a difference) within the culture itself, specifically those systems of classification which are used to divide the universe of discourse. Much-studied examples are kinship, color, disease, and species terminologies. There are two important points. First, emic categories may differ greatly between cultures. For the Romans, *patruus* and *avunculus* are emic terms; "uncle" is not. Second, within an individual culture, emic terms occupy a higher level in the organization. In our own sexual system, "heterosexual" and "homo-

sexual" are emic terms; "ass-man" or "leg-man" are not. For this important distinction, see Pike 1967 and Holland and Quinn 1987. In this article, I will be outlining Roman *emic* concepts, that is, the discourse of the culture as a whole. A history of exceptions, reactions, and rebellions can only be written against the background of this system.

2. Foucault 1980; Greenberg 1988; Halperin 1990a; McWhirter, Sanders, and Reinisch 1990. J. Katz 1995 is especially refreshing.

3. Gender may not appear at all, or only as a secondary feature. Even when it does, the axis of same vs. other may be irrelevant to the definition of sexual categories. See Herdt [1981] 1994, 1982, 1984 (with Whitehead 1985); Gilmore 1990, esp. 146–68 and 201–19.

4. Martin and Voorhies 1975: 84–107.

5. Housman 1931: 408 n. 1 (= 1972: 1180 n. 2); Dover 1978: 16, 81–91, 168–70; 1984: 143–57, esp. 148–49; Richlin 1992a, esp. 131–39; Veyne 1985: 26, 29–30; Foucault 1985: 46, 84–86, 210–11; Wiseman 1985: 10–13. Even Boswell: "This 'penetration code' . . . was clearly not related to a dichotomy of sexual preference, but to issues of power, dominance, and submission" (1990b: 72).

6. E.g., Veyne 1985: 30.

7. A failure consistently to make the vital distinction between active and passive severely weakens the usefulness of many works, including Boswell 1980; MacMullen 1982; Lilja 1983; Rousselle 1988, 1989; Cantarella 1988, 1992. Richlin 1983 forms the basis for this and all subsequent studies.

8. E.g., Carrier 1980, 1995; Fry 1985; Lancaster 1988; R. Parker 1985; Tapinc 1992; W. Williams 1986.

9. A point already made by Kinsey, Pomeroy, and Martin 1948: 656.

10. So Boswell 1990b: 76–77: "These primary modern rubrics [hetero- vs. homo-] were of little import or interest to ancient and medieval writers, and the categories the latter employed (e.g., active/passive; sinful/holy) often filter or obscure information necessary to answer questions of interest to modern researchers about sexual 'orientation.'" Boswell assumes that "sexual orientation" (i.e., our hetero- vs. homo-) is a natural given and seems peeved at the ancients for not knowing what they really meant.

11. Wiseman 1985: 10–13, for a beautifully succinct statement.

12. I.e., a "kisser" is not a separate sexual being on the same level as a *fututor*, any more than "breast-man" is a category to rank with "heterosexual."

13. An observation of Judith Hallett and Marilyn Skinner; see also *Oxford Latin Dictionary* s.v. 3a; H. N. Parker 1993: 321.

14. Varro *Sat. Men.* 205; Sall. *Cat.* 13.3; Cic. *Phil.* 2.86; Tac. *Ann.* 11.36.5; Petron. 9.6; *Priapea* 45; Sen. *Ben.* 4.31.4; *Dig.* 3.1.1.6 (Ulp.); see Richlin 1992a: 14; Adams 1982: 189–90.

15. Contra Adams 1982: 120–22; see Hallett 1983: 106. The sense of power is never wholly absent, and is often primary.

16. Hor. *Sat.* 1.2.132–33; Mart. 2.49, 2.60, 9.67; Apul. *Met.* 9.27–28; with a radish or fish: Catull. 15.19; Juv. 10.314–17; cf. Richlin 1992a: 215.

17. Cf. the jokes and innuendoes in Cic. *Dom.* 25, 47, 83, where Clodia uses Cloelius as an oral dildo; Richlin 1992a: 99.

18. Foucault 1985: 53, 92–93, 114 (cf. 38, 138); 1986: 124; H. N. Parker 1992a: 97–98.

19. Wiseman 1985: 123; see Fitzgerald 1992.

20. Cf. *Priapea* 35; Mart. 4.50, 9.4, 9.40, 9.67, 11.40, 11.46, 12.79. For fellatio as especially the job of a slave or prostitute, cf., for example, in literature: Mart. 3.75, 9.4, 11.40, 11.61.5, 12.55; Lucil. 334–35 (Marx); *Anth. Pal.* 11.328.9–10; and in real life: *CIL* 4.1969 (Diehl 467), 2028, where the price is specified, or 4.2259, 2268, 2273, 2275, 2278, from a brothel, etc. Cf. also, where the social status of the woman is not directly stated: Mart. 1.72, 1.94, 4.50, 4.84, 8.87, etc.; *CIL* 4.1388, 1389 (Diehl 657), 1510, 2292 (Diehl 658), 4192 (*fellatrix*); 1427 (Diehl 660), 1651, 2402, 2403, 2421, 4158, 4185 (Diehl 659), 4434, 5095, etc. (*fellare*); 1425 (Diehl 649) (*lingit*).

21. *Priapea* 35, 44; Mart. 2.84, 9.4, 9.40, 11.40, 11.43, 11.45–46, 12.35, 12.85 (also Gallus *Anth. Pal.* 5.49; Dio Cass. 62.13.4; Suet. *Ner.* 35.4; see MacMullen 1982: 492–93 and n. 27; Veyne 1985: 30–31).

22. E.g., Mart. 7.58.10; Suet. *Vespasian* 13. See Walters, this volume.

23. Suetonius does not consider this a mark in Claudius's favor. Clodius Albinus is a similar case; S.H.A. *Clod.* 11.7 merely says *aversae veneris semper ignarus et talium persecutor*, "He was always ignorant of the back-to-front Venus [anal intercourse] and a persecutor of such."

24. The only cases I know of where there is said to be turnabout are Suet. *Calig.* 36.1 and perhaps Sen. *Ep.* 99.13 (Richlin 1993b: 540).

25. Rightly Richlin 1992a: 246 n. 36 (as against 222 with 258 n. 6). See also Veyne 1985: 33. The same joke is behind Mart. 12.38 (contra Shackleton Bailey 1993, 2: 363).

26. Mart. 7.58 (Galla, who keeps marrying her *cinaedi*), and cf. also cases of *pueri delicati* forced to service both master and mistress: Mart. 6.39.13–14, the pictures of Giton (e.g., Petron. 24, 108, 113), and Trimalchio himself (63.3, 69.3, 75.11). Further, it is a common joke that the chief of such services will be cunnilingus; cf. Mart. 3.81, 4.43, 11.47; cf., too, Auson. *Epigrams* 78 (cited above).

27. The phrase is Ovid's (*Tr.* 2.499); see Richlin 1992a: 136–39; Foucault 1985: 84–86; H. N. Parker 1992a: 98–99. Cf. the portraits at Mart. 3.63, 10.65; Juv. 6.O.1–34; Lucil. 1058 (Marx): *barbati moechocinaedi*; Petron. 126–27 (Encolpius as a male prostitute for women); and Mart. 7.58, 9.2 (where the man who is totally ruled by his mistress is a pathic who ought to be castrated), 10.40, 10.65, 12.34, 12.49 (a troop of *cinaedi* in the service of a woman).

28. Foucault 1980: 105–7, 152–53, 156; 1985: 1–6; Halperin, Winkler, and Zeitlin 1990b: 5–6; Gleason 1990, esp. 390 n. 2, 411–12.

29. Note that the purpose of cunnilingus is not the pleasure of the woman but the humiliation of the performer, increased by the fact that he is humiliating himself with his slaves.

30. What he probably said was *te irrumabo*, "I'll fuck you in the mouth" (Richlin 1992a: 281–82).

31. See also Barton 1994.

32. Richlin (1993b: 531 and n. 22) points out the parallelism of the problems of definitions of *cinaedus* and "woman," citing Riley 1988.

THREE

UNSPEAKABLE PROFESSIONS: PUBLIC
PERFORMANCE AND PROSTITUTION
IN ANCIENT ROME

Catharine Edwards

ACTORS, gladiators, and prostitutes in ancient Rome were symbols of the shameful. Their signal lack of reputation was reflected and reinforced in the law, which, in the late Republic and early Principate, classified them as *infames* (*infamis* may be translated as "lacking in reputation," *fama*). Even those among them who were Roman citizens (as opposed to free noncitizens or slaves) were subject to a range of legal disabilities. The legal sources (compiled later than the period under consideration here) are fragmentary and hard to interpret; the principal text, Justinian's *Digest*, was compiled in the early sixth century c.e., when the attitudes of Rome's ruling elite had been transformed by Christianity. Literary and epigraphic texts can offer more immediate perspectives on earlier periods. It seems that those who followed infamous professions were generally not permitted to speak on behalf of others in a court of law. Under most circumstances they were not permitted to bring accusations against others. They were debarred from standing for election to magistracies. Their bodies might be beaten, mutilated, or violated with impunity.

The legal position of those who followed shameful professions under the Republic is often difficult to determine. I shall not attempt to examine the origins of *infamia*, which may well have developed in quite different ways for the different professions under discussion here. But it is clear that even from an early period, some disabilities did apply, in par-

I am most grateful to Amy Richlin for encouraging me to develop my ideas for this piece when we first met in 1990, for allowing me to see work of her own at that time unpublished, and for her stimulating comments on an earlier draft. The editors of this volume have also prompted me to rethink some important issues. In addition, I would like to thank Thomas Wiedemann and Kathleen Coleman, who offered perceptive criticisms. Michael Crawford and Jane Gardner kindly helped me to negotiate some legal questions. Any remaining faults are, of course, my own.

ticular to actors. As the sphere of Roman power and the number of Roman citizens grew, legal prescriptions proliferated. The rigidification and codification of the social hierarchy under Augustus confirmed and demarcated the position of the flagrantly humble. *Infames* may not have constituted an entirely coherent legal category until the second or third century C.E., but it still makes sense to scrutinize what it was that, in earlier periods, too, caused certain professions in ancient Rome to be marked out as infecting their practitioners with an indelible stain.

The legal status of those who followed these stigmatized professions was in most respects equivalent to that of soldiers dishonorably dismissed or convicted criminals. Yet for convicts, this status and the legal disabilities that it entailed were not necessarily permanent. For actors, gladiators, and prostitutes, by contrast, *infamia* was an inescapable consequence of the way they earned their living. While disgraced soldiers and criminals, marked with shame, withdrew from public life (even if they could not entirely escape public notice), actors, gladiators, and prostitutes took on their degraded status when they embarked upon their public roles.

Those who followed professions associated with public performance and prostitution were utterly devoid of honor—that precious commodity that was thought to inhere most fully in those who governed Rome. But so conspicuously did they lack honor that they played a vital part in the processes by which honor was constructed. Actors, gladiators, and prostitutes were paraded as examples of what those who sought officially sanctioned *dignitas* ("social standing") should at all costs avoid. Paradigms of the antithesis of honor, they occupied a crucial place in the symbolic order.

Why were these particular professions so shameful? And why should shame bring legal stigma? In exploring these questions, I shall try to set out what these professions had in common, the logic underlying a categorization that might at first seem bizarre. My tentative answer involves Roman attitudes toward pleasure, as well as toward honor and public life. In the theaters, arenas, and brothels of Rome, the infamous sold their own flesh (in the case of actors, gladiators, and prostitutes; and the flesh of others, for pimps and trainers of gladiators were also stigmatized). They lived by providing sex, violence, and laughter for the pleasure of the public—a licentious affront to Roman *gravitas*. But at the same time, the life of vulgarity and excess that they stood for was as authentically Roman as the consulship, triumphs, and temples to the gods.

In Michel Foucault's account of sexuality in the Greco-Roman world, the experience of pleasure is presented as becoming increasingly problematic as one moves from the time of Plato to the time of Plutarch.[1] Excessive indulgence in pleasure threatened the public profile of the elite male citizen in the early first century C.E. (when lack of self-control was associated with an inability to govern others). By the second century C.E., in Foucault's account, such indulgence tended rather to challenge the elite male citizen's self-image.

Volumes 2 and 3 of *The History of Sexuality* offer a wealth of provocative insights into a number of ancient texts.[2] But in concentrating so closely on male members of the elite, Foucault gives little consideration to those against whom the new forms of self-constitution served to define these individuals.[3] It may well be the case that the texts that survive from the ancient world allow us to engage only with those of the male elite class from which virtually every one of their authors came. But we cannot hope to understand the construction of elite male identities without considering those who were excluded from this category and the processes by which they were excluded.

The specific associations of those pleasures from which the philosophically inclined reader is encouraged by his preceptors to draw away receive little attention from Foucault. Underlying the texts he examines, however, is a notion of low sensual pleasure, dangerous, at least in part, because its power, its appeal, is universal. Self-control and discernment regarding sensual pleasures were traditionally the markers of masculinity and social refinement. Immoderate pursuit of low pleasure was associated with women, slaves, and the poor—those who had to be controlled by others if they were not to fritter away their lives in self-indulgence. Thus, to enjoy vulgar pleasures—the pleasures of eating and drinking, sex, gambling, going to the games—was to risk one's identity as a cultured person.[4]

My aim in this essay is to examine the position of public performers and prostitutes in ancient Rome in the context of Roman constructions of pleasure, sexuality, and social hierarchy. Some similar issues have been explored by Amy Richlin in her study of the figure of the *cinaedus* (a Roman term for an adult male who allows himself to be penetrated); *cinaedi*, like those who followed the professions to be examined here, were stigmatized as *infames*.[5] Richlin's suggestive study also stresses the interdependence between Roman constructions of sexuality and Roman social hierarchy. Carlin Barton's recent work dramatically emphasizes the powerful fascination the figure of the gladiator exercised over Roman society.[6] The parallels she observes between gladiators and actors are worth investigating further, as is the association between public performers and prostitutes. An exploration of what Romans felt these professions had in common can cast light on the reasons they were felt to be especially shameful. It is surely no coincidence that all professions that incurred *infamia* were associated with transgressive sexuality. These figures were the objects of other people's desires. They served the pleasure of others. They were tarnished by exposure to the public gaze.

The final part of my essay will look briefly at the relationship between those who, because of their professions, were branded with dishonor by the law and those whom the law marked out as conspicuously honorable, the senatorial and equestrian elite, and, in particular, Roman emperors and their families.

Debarred from official public life, actors, gladiators, and prostitutes were nevertheless conspicuous public figures, made more so by the stigma that attached to them. Hand in hand with official stigmatization went the increasing allure that surrounded these professions. In the first century c.e. in particular, some members of the senatorial and equestrian orders, the juridically defined elite of Rome, are said to have deliberately embraced these infamous professions for themselves. And Roman emperors are to be found, in the pages of ancient writers at least, prostituting upper-class matrons, fighting in the arena, and appearing onstage. The conceptual link between actors, gladiators, prostitutes, and their associates is strikingly illustrated by texts that deplore elite participation in these activities.

Infamia

Infamia, "lack of public honor," was the opposite of *existimatio*, "reputation," and *dignitas*, "social standing."[7] An *infamis* had, as a consequence of moral turpitude, lost the status of a full citizen. There were several ways in which a person could become *infamis*. *Infamia* was a consequence of conviction in some civil and all criminal trials. Some forms of sexual behavior might entail *infamia*; a woman caught in adultery, even if not convicted of the crime, was *infamis*, in the view of some jurists.[8] As we have seen, a man who allowed himself to be penetrated by another man was also termed *infamis*.[9] *Infamia* was also a consequence of participation in the professions that form the subject of this essay.

A.J.H. Greenidge, whose monograph on *infamia* was published in 1894, defined *infamia* as follows: "Special disqualifications based on moral grounds from certain public or quasi-public functions."[10] The term is not used only of disqualifications; it often appears in ancient texts in a less technical sense, meaning the degraded moral state that might or might not be recognized with the stamp of *infamia* by the law.[11] Cicero, referring to the *infamia* that is imposed on convicted criminals, draws a distinction between *infamia* that arises from condemnation for an offense and *ipsa infamia*, "true *infamia*," which arises from committing the offense, regardless of whether legal stigma is imposed (*Leg.* 1.90.50–51).[12] Elsewhere, Cicero speaks of the *infamia* suffered by a man who is waiting to be tried

(*Att.* 1.16.2). And we should not necessarily assume that when the satirist Juvenal describes one of his victims as *infamis* he is referring to the man's legal status (for instance, *Sat.* 2.2). This ambiguity is disconcerting.

There are a number of legal sources relevant to the study of *infamia*. The most extensive is Justinian's *Digest*, compiled as a codification of current law in the early sixth century c.e. from the commentaries on the law of earlier jurists (mostly composed in the second century c.e.). Not surprisingly, this work cannot always be relied on as an accurate guide to the law of several centuries earlier. It is often difficult to discover to what extent the texts of earlier jurists have been altered by the later compilers. We glimpse the contours of the pagan world obscurely through the pages of the Christian *Digest*. Some important changes may be inferred. Since gladiatorial games were banned under the Christian emperors, it seems highly likely that some references to gladiators have been omitted (even if, in practice, the games continued to take place).[13] In general, we should not expect the passages preserved in the *Digest* to be complete. This may explain some of the disparities between lists of infamous persons.

Some sources have not been subject to Christian emendation and can provide a useful check on material in the *Digest*. An inscription known as the *Tabula Heracleensis*, probably from the time of Julius Caesar, records legislation relating to local government, sometimes referred to as the *lex Iulia municipalis*. This includes lists of categories of persons whose participation in local government is restricted. Among those barred from standing for local magistracies are anyone "who has or shall . . . have been hired out for the purpose of fighting as a gladiator . . . or who has or shall have prostituted his person; or who has been or shall have been a trainer of gladiators or actor; or who shall run <or shall have run> a brothel" (*queive depugnandei caussa auctoratus est erit fuit fuerit . . . queive corpor<e> quaestum fecit fecerit; queive lanistaturam artemve ludic<r>am fecit fecerit; queive lenocinium faciet <feceritve>*, (lines 112–23, trans. Crawford).[14] This provides important confirmation that these professions were legally stigmatized even in the time of Julius Caesar.

I shall look at some of the different legal forms of *infamia* in a little more detail below. First, though, one might note one of the conclusions of Greenidge's study. He doubts that "a definite and uniform conception of *infamia* existed under the republic or even under the principate."[15] Instead, he suggests, *infamia* was a portmanteau term that appeared relatively late. The range of disqualifications that are often termed *infamia* were not directly connected in the period before Hadrian, when it seems that the current version of the praetor's tralaticiary edict (the *edictum perpetuum*) came to be regarded as providing the definitive list of *infames*, as of many other legal categories.

Scholars of Roman law have traditionally placed a premium on the pursuit of system and coherence in the object of their study, a pursuit that may run up against insuperable obstacles in the study of *infamia*. Yet for the historian, the diverse meanings attaching to the term (as well as the range of terms that are often treated as parallel to it) in legal and non-legal texts can be suggestive rather than frustrating. Cicero's reference to the ambiguity of *infamia* in the *De legibus* suggests that Romans saw the different applications of *infamia* as significantly related. These applications might not always cohere with one another. The law might not always be an accurate index of the moral censure with which certain activities and persons were regarded. Particular applications of the law might be open to contestation. Yet those who expounded and administered the Roman legal system were brought up on Cicero and may well have read the works of Juvenal or Seneca. Their moral world was partly constituted by, and indeed helped constitute, these and other literary texts.

An additional difficulty with attempting to explore the legal disabilities imposed on those who followed infamous professions in the late Republic and early Principate is that these seem to have varied considerably in the course of this period.[16] However, it is worth sketching roughly the different kinds of legal disability that might be imposed as a consequence of an individual's profession, before going on to look briefly at the chronological development of the law.

Different forms of legal disability, which might be referred to as *infamia*, could be imposed by several different mechanisms. Legislation was one means of imposing disqualifications on the infamous. Those who followed shameful professions were not permitted to bring criminal accusations under some laws.[17] The infamous were also banned from sitting on juries. The *lex Acilia repetundarum* of 122 B.C.E., for instance, prescribed a jury of 450 equestrians. Specifically excluded were men who had hired themselves out to fight as gladiators, as well as convicted criminals.

Under the Republic, the censors were charged with reviewing the social and moral standing of Roman citizens, in particular the senatorial and equestrian elite, every five years (in theory—tenure of this office was sporadic in the late Republic). It was they who excluded individuals considered unfit from the army, the senate, and the public assemblies. Actors were certainly excluded from the Roman army. The *Digest* prescribes capital punishment for soldiers who appear on stage (48.19.14; 49.16.4.1–9).[18] Gladiators, too, were not permitted to become soldiers (though many may have served as soldiers before entering the arena). The oath gladiators swore when they embarked on their profession is regularly represented in ancient texts as a counterpart to—a shameful parody of—the oath of allegiance sworn by soldiers.[19] We may think of military service as a burden rather than a privilege, but it was a significant element in full citizenship (especially in a state such as Rome, which represented itself as composed of citizen-soldiers), denied to those who earned their living on-stage or in the arena.

We may assume, too, that practicing a disgraceful profession was one of the many possible grounds for dismissal from the senatorial and eques-trian orders.[20] The censors were also responsible for assigning citizens to tribes for the purpose of voting in elections. Actors, it seems, were not assigned to a tribe and were thus unable to vote. This was already the case in the fourth century B.C.E., according to Livy (7.2.12).[21] Censors might ban individuals from standing for magistracies on the grounds that they were not morally worthy. Actors, gladiators, and prostitutes were banned from standing for local magistracies in the legislation recorded on the *Tabula Heracleensis*. They were also banned from standing for magistracies in Rome.[22] The Christian writer Tertullian, in his homily on the evils of the pagan games written in the second century C.E., remarks that the pagan Romans themselves felt public performance to be disgraceful and banned performers from participating in state functions (*De Spect.* 22):

> etenim ipsi auctores et administratores spectaculorum quadrigarios, scaeni-cos, xysticos, arenarios illos amantissimos . . . ex eadem arte qua magnifaci-unt, deponunt et deminuunt, immo manifeste damnant ignominia et capitis minutione, arcentes curia, rostris, senatu, equite, ceterisque honoribus om-nibus simul et ornamentis quibusdam.

> Even those who finance and administer the games, while they celebrate the art of the charioteers, actors, athletes, and gladiators (whose appetite for love outdoes that of any other men) . . . at the same time degrade and stig-matize them for that same art. Indeed, they condemn them to public dis-grace and civil dishonor, banning them from the council chamber, the ros-tra, the senate, the equestrian order, all other public honors, and a good many distinctions.[23]

Tertullian's list is more extensive than those to be found in the law codes; athletes and charioteers are generally not subject to the same legal dis-abilities as are imposed on other performers (though this was a source of debate among the jurists). It seems all public performers were excluded from state honors.[24]

Due to accidents of preservation, a great deal less is known of the im-position of *infamia* by the censors than of praetorian *infamia*. *Infamia* as imposed by the praetors seems to have related largely to legal procedure. The praetor's edict, as it appears in Justinian's *Digest*, preserves a later form (the Julian redaction of the *edictum perpetuum*, dating from the reign of Hadrian) of what was probably the earliest codification of *infamia*. The rights of several categories of person are circumscribed by this edict, one of the objectives of which seems to have been the preservation of the dignity of the praetor's court. Thus the edict sets out lists of persons who may not represent others in legal actions before the praetor (women, the blind, and those who were *in turpitudine notabiles*, "infamous due to the shamefulness of their lives") and persons who may represent others only under exceptional circumstances (including *omnes qui edicto praetoris ut infames notantur*, "all those who are branded as *infames* in the praetor's edict"). Those *in turpitudine notabiles* include *qui corpore suo muliebria passus est*, "a man who has allowed his body to be treated like that of a woman," and those who have hired out their services to fight with wild beasts (gladiators may have been included in this category in the pre-Christian period).[25] Those who have been convicted of certain crimes are also included here. The second category (i.e., those who may represent others only in exceptional circumstances) covered actors and pimps, besides soldiers who had been dishonorably dismissed, bigamists, those who had failed to obey certain rules relating to mourning, and those convicted of certain crimes. These persons were also banned from appointing others to represent them in court.[26]

The praetor's edict imposed restrictions on male prostitutes, wild-beast fighters, pimps, actors, and probably gladiators (women engaged in any of these professions were already banned on the grounds of their sex from representing others). These restrictions may not seem particularly severe in themselves. Yet they are an indication of the impotence of such individuals in all legal situations. Judges were advised by legal authorities to trust witnesses in accordance with their social and moral standing (*Dig.* 22.5.2; 5.3 pr.).[27] Of course, prejudice will affect the application of the law in any system. But it is striking that the law in ancient Rome specifically encouraged judges and juries to disregard the words of those whose way of earning a living was thought shameful. One jurist advised that the word of gladiators and similar persons should be trusted only if they were under torture (*Dig.* 22.5.21.2).

One of the most striking aspects of the legal situation of those labeled *infames*, which emerges from a few incidental references in literary texts and the law codes, is their liability to corporal punishment. An important step in the development of the Roman Republic (according to the mythical account cherished in later centuries) was the successful struggle on the part of the plebs to achieve protection from a magistrate's arbitrary use of his *virgae*, the rods that were a symbol of his power. The tribune of the plebs was their protector, and they might make an appeal to the people of Rome (this right was later superseded by that of appeal to the emperor).

Protection from corporal punishment was one of the hallmarks of Roman citizenship. Cicero, speaking in defense of Rabirius, claimed that the infliction of beating and death on a citizen amounted to an attack on *libertas* (*Rab. Post.* 12). Similarly, in his denunciation of Verres, he speaks with horror of corporal punishment inflicted on a Roman citizen by Verres while he was governor of Sicily (*Verr.* 2.5.161ff.). Freedom in Rome was primarily conceived of in terms of the right to protection from arbitrary use of power. This protection marked off Roman citizens from noncitizens (who could not appeal against the arbitrary use of force by, for instance, a provincial governor), and, in particular, it marked them off from slaves. Liability to corporal punishment was one of the most vivid symbols of the distinction between free and slave in Rome.[28] The distinction between free and slave with regard to corporal punishment continued to be invoked by the classical jurists in their arguments even after it was effectively blurred in the second and third centuries C.E., as low-ranking free persons became liable to a wide variety of forms of corporal punishment.[29]

Public performers, even if Roman citizens, were traditionally liable to corporal punishment even in the late Republic. Suetonius includes the following in his list of Augustus's measures relating to the theater: "He curbed the power allowed the magistrates by an ancient law of punishing actors anywhere and everywhere, restricting it to the time of the games and to the theater" (Suet. *Aug.* 45). The power of the magistrates is restricted but not wholly removed. The biographer goes on to describe how an actor was beaten with rods through the three theaters of Rome because of his association with a wellborn Roman matron.

The jurist Paulus, commenting on the *lex Iulia de vi*, writes that magistrates are to be punished under this law if they inflict corporal punishment on a Roman citizen who attempts to appeal to the emperor. Some citizens, however, are not covered by this protection (*Sent.* 5.26):

> hac lege excipiuntur, qui artem ludicram faciunt, indicati etiam et confessi et qui ideo in carcerem duci iubentur, quod ius dicenti non obtemperaverit quidve contra disciplinam publicam fecerint.

> Excluded from this law are those who appear onstage, so long as they have been accused and have confessed their guilt, and have been sent to prison on the grounds that they failed to obey the magistrate or did something contrary to public order.

The magistrate's power to inflict corporal punishment is hedged about with restrictions—but then, so was a master's power of life and death over his slave.

Private individuals were permitted to exact violent revenge for their offended family honor from those who followed infamous professions (and some other categories of humble persons, including slaves, the family's freedmen, and men condemned in a court of law). This was not allowed against more respectable citizens. Augustus's legislation on punishing adulteries included the following provision (*Dig.* 48.5.25[24] pr. Macer):

> hac lege cavetur, ut liceat viro deprehensum domi suae ... in adulterio uxoris occidere eum, qui leno fuerit quive artem ludicram ante fecerit in scaenam saltandi cantandive causa prodierit.

> For it is provided by this statute that a husband is permitted to kill a man whom he catches in adultery with his wife in his own house ... if the [paramour] is a pimp or if he was previously an actor or performed on the stage as a singer or dancer. (Trans. Watson)

Other jurists, writing with reference to the same legislation, offer slightly different lists of persons whom the injured husband may attack with impunity.[30] The inconsistencies between these lists, originally derived from the same law, illustrate the degree of variation that might be introduced in the course of several transcriptions.

The jurist Callistratus, writing in the first half of the third century c.e., presented it as a tradition of Roman law that those without reputation were to be punished more severely than the respectable (*Dig.* 48.19.28.16). Though only stage performers are subject to corporal punishment by magistrates, all those who followed infamous professions were to some degree left more vulnerable than other citizens by the law. Moral turpitude corroded the citizen's legal armor.

So far I have referred rather loosely to infamous professions. The lists of persons subject to various disabilities do not always correspond exactly. In part, this may be due to the haphazard way in which the legal prescriptions have been preserved. But the question of exactly which professions were to bring infamy on their practitioners was certainly a matter of some dispute among the jurists. Chariot drivers, some jurists argued (presumably against others who wished to penalize them), were pursuing honor rather than gain and should not be classed as *infames*.[31] In general, chariot drivers do not seem to have been subject to legal disabilities (though they are included in Tertullian's list of those excluded from magistracies). To some extent, their exemption from the penalties inflicted on other performers may be explained in terms of the historical associations of chariot driving. The elder Pliny refers to the participation of aristocratic Romans in the circus games (chariot races) in the early days of Rome (*HN* 21.7). When Tacitus describes Nero's desire to participate in the games, he presents chariot driving as considerably less shameful than appearing onstage (*Ann.* 14.14). It was perhaps also because the bodies of chariot drivers were so much less the focus of the public gaze than those of actors or gladiators.

A further difficulty was the question of whether one had to be paid for one's performances in order to count as an actor, beast-fighter, or gladiator. The *Digest* includes a lengthy discussion by the jurist Ulpian, who concludes that only the man who has hired out his services to fight wild beasts in a public show is to be *notatus* (3.1.1.6). The jurist Labeo (who wrote under Augustus) emphasized the importance of the public nature of the spectacle (*Dig.* 3.2.2.5).[32] A disagreement over the relevance of pay is also attested with regard to prostitutes. Ulpian suggests that a woman who is openly promiscuous should be classed as a prostitute, even if she does not accept money (*Dig.* 23.2.43.3).[33]

Other professions, besides those associated with public performance and prostitution, were sometimes stigmatized to a certain extent. Usury was forbidden by the Twelve Tables but was subsequently legalized, after which it brought no more disqualification than other trades.[34] The *Tabula Heracleensis* lists a number of professions that are incompatible with holding a local magistracy, in addition to those associated with public performance and prostitution (lines 104–7). This may well have been because they involved paid work for local government, so that holding a local magistracy could have involved a conflict of interest.[35]

Those who followed infamous professions were systematically limited in their civil rights. Legal disqualifications were justified with reference to the moral shortcomings of the persons stigmatized—the ways in which they earned their living were incompatible with being a full Roman citizen. Actors, gladiators, and prostitutes were treated like condemned criminals, as profoundly untrustworthy. Those who sold their bodies for the pleasure of others forfeited the protection Roman law accorded to the bodies of other citizens.

Infamous License

Legal and literary sources repeatedly group these professions together. One striking feature of the legal position of the infamous is their assimilation to slaves, in particular, as regards their liability to corporal punishment. The legal texts that have been examined so far relate only to those actors, gladiators, and prostitutes of free-citizen status. Probably the majority of those who followed these professions were slaves or free noncitizens. But this does not explain the legal stigma attaching to those who were Roman citizens. Many Roman citizens worked alongside slaves as builders, agricultural workers, shopkeepers. What made the infamous like slaves was that they too served the pleasures of others, they too had no dignity, their bodies too were bought and sold.

It is important not to blur differences. The half-starved prostitute who sold her body among the tombs of the via Appia no doubt had little in common with the star gladiator of the emperor Titus's games or the actor who dared to make a joke about Nero's murder of his mother in front of a huge audience—and got away with it (Suet. *Ner.* 39). Yet, those who followed these professions, in addition to their déclassé legal status, shared an association with various forms of sexuality constructed as deviant in ancient Roman texts. I shall explore the particular associations of each profession in turn before going on to consider how these varieties of sexual "deviance" relate to the social and legal marginalization of these categories of people.

Gladiatorial shows were originally given only as part of the funeral celebrations of important public figures, which were provided by their heirs. From the time of Augustus, however, such games were regularly given by the emperor without the excuse of a funeral and came to be expected as manifestations of imperial generosity. Wild-beast fights, at first part of the circus games, were included among the shows in the arena under the Principate.[36] Emperors monopolized the provision of gladiatorial games in Rome itself. Though they were held on only a few days each year, the cultural significance of these immensely popular shows was vast. The games were volatile occasions, for the crowd might take advantage of the emperor's presence to voice protests.[37] While emperors risked their popularity, gladiators risked their lives.

Gladiators will be discussed only briefly here, since they have been the subject of several thorough and suggestive studies in recent years.[38] Professional gladiators of free status seem to have been found in Rome from the third century B.C.E. Even in the time of Plautus, the term "gladiator" could be used in a metaphorical sense.[39] If they were free men rather than slaves, gladiators, in return for money, took an oath, undertaking to suffer branding, being bound in chains, beating, or death by the sword.[40] They thus surrendered their bodies to indignities normally experienced only by slaves. These men regularly fought one another to the death, though a popular gladiator might be spared (on the decision of the man providing the games rather than his fellow fighter) to compete another day. A few gladiators survived long enough to retire from the arena, but probably most met their deaths at the hands of their fellows, a source of entertainment to the Roman people.[41]

Gladiators were celebrated as heroes.[42] Under the Principate, in an age when most Roman citizens had no personal experience of warfare, they were a reminder of the virtue (*virtus*, "military courage," "manliness") that had made Rome great.[43] But they were also despised. For cultured Romans, the gladiator was the epitome of the thug—a man who earned his living through brute force. Politicians alleged to have used violence to get their way were regularly compared to gladiators.[44]

Emblems of an aggressive masculinity, gladiators were thought to be overpoweringly sexually potent and attractive to women.[45] Tertullian, in a passage quoted above, refers to them as "gladiators, whose appetite for love outdoes all others, to whom men surrender their souls and women their bodies, too" (De Spect. 22). Juvenal describes a senator's wife who abandons her family to follow a gladiator (6.103–12):

> qua tamen exarsit forma, qua capta iuventa
> Eppia? quid vidit propter quod ludia dici
> sustinuit? nam Sergiolus iam radere guttur
> coeperat et secto requiem sperare lacerto;
> praeterea multa in facie deformia, sicut
> attritus galea mediisque in naribus ingens
> gibbus et acre malum semper stillantis ocelli.
> sed gladiator erat. facit hoc illos Hyacinthos;
> hoc pueris patriaeque, hoc praetulit illa sorori
> atque viro. ferrum est quod amant.

So how did he look, this man who set Eppia on fire? Was it his youthful charm? What did she see in him to make it worth the sobriquet of "gladiatress"? Her darling Sergius was no spring chicken, past middle age, retirement on the cards with that wounded arm. Besides that, his face was a sight, scarred from his helmet, a large sore on his nose, his infected eye always weeping. But he was a gladiator. That makes them all Adonises. This was what she set above her children, her homeland, her sister, and her husband. The sword is what they love.

The insatiable sexual appetites of wellborn females are the object of frequently expressed disapproval on the part of Roman moralists.[46] Lust causes these women to disregard social hierarchy, drawing them to the lowest of the low. Stripped of the social and cultural paraphernalia that give identity and status to most men, the gladiator is naked, defined only by his weapon. He is all sword.[47]

The ambivalence some elite Romans felt toward gladiators and those who fought wild beasts may seem one of the more understandable features of these horrific spectacles. But the suspicion with which actors were viewed is for us more puzzling. Actors seem to have been subjected to the widest range of legal disqualifications, to judge from the surviving sources (though we should remember that gladiators are likely to have been omitted from some legal texts by Christian compilers, while female prostitutes would already have been subject to legal disqualifications qua women). This was perhaps a consequence of an actor's potential for unorthodox social mobility.[48] While most actors were humble figures, stars could earn large sums of money (though this is also true of gladiators).

Performers in general, but actors in particular, are regularly alleged to have become the friends of emperors.[49] The suspicion with which actors were regarded is perhaps also due to their public voice—an opportunity to command the attention of the Roman people, otherwise denied to all but the political elite. But actors were explicitly in the business of trickery and illusion. While all those who sold their bodies for entertainment thereby undermined the trust one might place in their words, the speech of actors was paradigmatically false.[50]

Acting was associated with political challenge. Magistrates and even emperors could find themselves the objects of subtle or not so subtle mockery in the theater. Tiberius expelled actors from Italy, Tacitus writes (*Ann.* 4.14), on the grounds that

> multa ab iis in publicum seditiose, foeda per domos temptari; Oscum quondam ludicrum, levissimae apud vulgum delectationis, eo flagitiorum et virium venisse, ut auctoritate patrum coercendum sit.

> they frequently fomented sedition against the state and stirred up debauchery in private houses; the old Oscan farce, once the light entertainment of the common people, had attained such extremes of immorality and power, that it had to be contained by the authority of the senate.

The intertwining of sexual and political license in the description of the crimes of actors attributed to Tiberius reflects the characteristic preoccupations of Roman representations of stage players.[51]

Actors' ability to arouse laughter seems to have been considered particularly disturbing. What was regarded as "low" comedy was especially disapproved of by moralizing critics.[52] Martial (9.28) plays on this association, making an actor boast that he could have made Cato and "the stern Curii and Fabricii" (archetypes of old-fashioned sobriety) laugh. The Atellan farce was a long-established tradition of Roman comedy. Under the Principate, the form of drama known as mime, which also seems to have been a kind of farce, became increasingly popular, too. Juvenal's excoriation of members of the elite who appeared onstage focuses particularly on the shame aroused by their comic gestures and vulgar jokes (see the passage from *Satire* 8 quoted below).

The Christian Tertullian inveighs against the indecency of the theater (*De Spect.* 17), describing it as

> privatum consistorium impudicitiae, ubi nihil probatur quam quod alibi non probatur. ita summa gratia eius de spurcitia plurimum concinnata est, quam Atellana gesticulatur, quam mimus etiam per muliebres res repraesentat, sensum sexus et pudoris exterminans, ut facilius domi quam in scaena erubescant, quam denique pantomimus a pueritia patitur ex corpore ut artifex esse possit.

the proper home of all unchastity, where nothing is admired unless it is elsewhere disapproved of. Its greatest charm is above all contrived by its lewd-
ness—the lewd gestures of the comedian in the farce, the lewd performance
of the actor playing a woman, stamping out all sense of sex and shame, so
that they are more likely to blush at home than onstage, and finally the obscene experiences of the pantomime actor, who must suffer sexual humiliation from his youth, if he is to become a performer.

The sexual ambiguity of male actors was disturbing. Their ability to imitate women is the object of Juvenal's indignation, too (3.95–97).[53] So
closely are deviant sexuality and the stage associated for Tertullian that he
represents the experience of being penetrated as a necessary part of an
actor's professional training.

Actors were often represented as highly desirable to both men and
women.[54] The dictator Sulla had a lengthy affair with an actor called
Metrobius, according to Plutarch (*Sull.* 3.3). Augustus's associate Maecenas was said to have been in love with the actor Bathyllus (Tac. *Ann.*
1.54). The wives of the emperors Claudius and Domitian allegedly had
affairs with actors.[55] As was noted above, the depravity of high-ranking
women is often signaled in Roman texts by the baseness of the men they
desire. A slave girl in Petronius's *Satyricon* criticizes the low tastes of her
mistress (*Sat.* 126):

> quod servum te et humilem fateris, accendis desiderium aestuantis. quaedam
> enim feminae sordibus calent, nec libidinem concitant, nisi aut servos
> viderint aut statores altius cinctos. harena aliquas accendit aut perfusus pul-
> vere mulio aut histrio scaenae ostentatione traductus. ex hac nota domina est
> mea: usque ab orchestra quattuordecim transilit et in extrema plebe quaerit
> quod diligat.

> When you admit you are a base slave, you set her desire alight. For some
> women lust after common filth and cannot feel aroused except when they
> see slaves or serving men with their tunics hitched up. Gladiators set some
> of them on fire, or a muleteer covered in dust, or an actor disgraced by ap-
> pearing onstage. My mistress is one of those: disdaining the first fourteen
> rows, she looks to the back of the crowd, seeking out a man to love among
> the lowest plebs.

Seating arrangements at the theater were a vivid representation of Roman
social hierarchy: the senatorial elite sat in the front rows, equestrians sat
in the fourteen rows behind the senators, the poorest citizens, those who
could not afford a toga, sat at the back.[56] For the licentious woman (in
the view of Roman moralists), those outstanding for their lowliness and
disgrace were the most attractive.[57]

Actors and actresses were regularly assumed to be prostitutes.[58] We should not deduce that this was because many actors and actresses sold their sexual services. Rather, the way in which they made their living, exposing themselves to public view, their bodies objects of fascination and desire, was perceived to be analogous to the way in which prostitutes made their living. Like prostitutes, their bodies had to please—as did those of gladiators. The very sight of these performers was thought to produce sexual pleasure—*Ledam molli saltante Bathyllo / . . . Apula gannit / sicut in amplexu, subito et miserabile longum*, "As she watches the pantomime Bathyllus playing the role of Leda . . . all at once Apula moans in drawn-out ecstasy, as if in a man's embrace" (Juv. 6.63–65).

The prostitute, in particular the female prostitute, was an evocative figure in the literature of ancient Rome.[59] Venal, shameless—but also alluring and persuasive—she was regularly invoked as a metaphor for corrupt literary style.[60] Prostitutes were marked out by their clothing. Expensive courtesans, we are told, wore dresses of gaudy and transparent silk. Prostitutes were also distinguished for wearing the toga, that uncomfortable garment otherwise worn only by male Roman citizens—a blatant display of their exclusion from the respectable social hierarchy. The female prostitute was antithetical to the male Roman citizen.

It seems likely that prostitute status had to be legally registered. Tacitus relates the case of Vistilia, the daughter of a senatorial family who registered as a prostitute, allegedly to avoid prosecution for adultery: *licentiam stupri apud aediles vulgaverat, more inter veteres recepto, qui satis poenarum adversum impudicas in ipsa professione flagitii credebant*, "She had registered her license to commit adultery among the aediles, in accordance with the custom of our ancestors, who believed that public disgrace was sufficient punishment for abandoned chastity" (*Ann.* 2.85).

Despite the probable existence of such a register of prostitutes, scholars often suggest that the boundary between prostitutes and "respectable" women was less than clear.[61] Certainly Roman writers regularly attribute meretricious attributes to women of every social class. Propertius and Ovid harp on the venality of their mistresses. Propertius, for instance, suggests that a common prostitute would be less grasping than his loved one (2.23). This preoccupation seems as much an indication of the fascination exercised by the figure of the prostitute as a reflection of the means by which the female associates of the literary elite made their living. When Cicero describes Clodia, a wealthy widow who was the sister of his enemy Clodius, as a *meretrix*, we would be rash to deduce that she made her living by selling her body (*Cael.* 47–50). Cicero's mode of attack here is parallel to his use of the term *gladiator* in his attack on Roscius's senatorial opponent (*Rosc. Am.* 3.8, 6.17). This is not to say that members of Rome's elite never engaged in such activities (there is some evidence that they did, as we shall see below), but we must beware of taking the metaphors of invective or elegy at face value.

Prostitution, for many Roman writers, represented the most degrading form of female existence imaginable. One of the elder Seneca's rhetorical exercises presents as a particularly grotesque and lurid case a dispute over whether a woman who had been kept in a brothel could subsequently become a priestess. One part of the argument runs: "It is not without reason that a lictor attends a priestess: he removes a prostitute from her way" (*Controv.* 1.2.8). As a priestess moved through the city, her attendant would drive away prostitutes (and other disgraceful persons) so that they would not pollute her sight. Priestesses were public figures symbolizing purity; prostitutes, also public figures, represented the depths of impurity. Plautus in the *Curculio* makes one of his characters distinguish between inaccessible objects of desire—freeborn boys, girls, and matrons—and accessible ones. He uses a simile, contrasting fenced-off land with the public road. Respectable women and children are the property of individual men. The prostitute is the *publica via* (33–38)—what everyone treads underfoot. The extreme lowness of prostitutes is also reflected in their frequent association with dirt (Prop. 2.23, for instance, singles out as the prostitute's defining attribute her *immundo . . . socco*, "filthy slipper").[62]

Men as well as women lived by selling their sexual services. A calendar from Praeneste, dating from early in the first century C.E., records a holiday for male prostitutes (on the day following that for the female prostitutes).[63] They often appear in the legal texts examined above. Generally, male prostitutes receive less attention than female ones in literary texts, though Juvenal's ninth satire takes the form of a dialogue between the satirist and one, Naevolus, who lived by selling his sexual services.

Prostitutes and public performers were not the only individuals to be subject to *infamia* as a result of their professions. Pimps and trainers of gladiators were also stigmatized. *Lenones* (keepers of brothels) often, though not invariably, owned the prostitutes whose services they hired out. "Procuring is no better than prostitution," observes the jurist Ulpian (*Dig.* 23.2.43.6). A *lanista* was the manager of a troupe of gladiators. If they were slaves, he was their owner. If they were free men, it was to him (usually) that they swore their oath, binding themselves to submit to branding, being bound, and dying by the sword. *Lenones* and *lanistae* regularly appear as a pair,[64] often cropping up, for instance, as the hangers-on and supporters of those of Cicero's opponents whom he wishes to present as most disreputable.[65] For some, these people were even more degraded than the prostitutes and gladiators from whom they earned their living.[66] Seneca refers to the pander and the trainer of gladiators as "the most despised of men," *contemptissimo cuique* (*Ep.* 87.15).[67]

Dangerous Pleasures

Actors, gladiators, and prostitutes, and those who hired out their services, were regarded with profound ambivalence by their fellow citizens (as well as by the law). They were all associated with forms of transgressive sexual behavior. Yet this association does not explain the suspicions with which they were regarded or their relegation to the category of *infames*. It is rather another manifestation of the struggle on the part of those laying claim to moral and legal authority to marginalize these threatening persons. But why were they perceived as threatening?

One explanation might be that they were associated with pleasures, and pleasures of a very dubious kind. Cicero, discussing which professions might be appropriate to an honorable man, remarks on the shamefulness of earning one's living by ministering to the pleasure of others (*Off.* 1.150):

> minimeque artes eae probandae, quae ministrae sunt voluptatum:
>
> > cetarii, lanii, coqui, fartores, piscatores
>
> ut ait Terentius; adde huc, si placet, unguentarios, saltatores, totumque ludum talarium.

> Least respectable of all are those trades which serve the sensual pleasures:
>
> > "Fishmongers, butchers, cooks and poulterers, and fishermen,"
>
> as Terence says. Add to these, if you will, perfumers, dancers, and all the cabaret.

These pleasures, *voluptates*, are pleasures of the senses.[68] Cicero refers explicitly to purveyors of luxury foods and perfumes and to dancers. His remarks seem obviously applicable to those professions legally stigmatized as well, although he does not directly refer to them. They were perhaps too low, too troubling to be openly discussed in this context—unspeakable as well as infamous.

The entertainment to be derived from watching actors or gladiators perform might not seem to the twentieth-century reader to have much in common with sexual pleasure. But the term *voluptas* is regularly used of the experience of watching the games, as well as of the more commonly recognized pleasures of the flesh.[69] Livy speaks of the pleasure, *voluptas*, of watching gladiators in the arena (41.20). Tertullian exhorts Christians to abjure the pleasures of the shows, *spectaculorum voluptates*, warning against the force of these pleasures, *voluptatium vis* (*De Spect.* 1). The sensual nature of these pleasures is repeatedly emphasized (*De Spect.* 13, 14, 17). Augustine, too, warns against the pleasure, *voluptas*, of watching gladiators fight (*Confessiones* 6.8).[70]

We might wish to identify some Roman *voluptates* as sadistic, in contrast to straightforward sensual pleasures, but this distinction is not made by Roman writers. Rather, they regularly imply a strong connection between susceptibility to the *voluptas* associated with attending the games and susceptibility to other kinds of "low" pleasure. In the writings of the literary elite, it is often slaves who dream of such delights, along with gambling and the food and drink purchased in *tabernae*.[71] In one of Horace's *Epistles*, for instance, a master upbraids his slave for desiring the low pleasures of the city: *ludos et balnea*, "the games and the baths," and *fornix et uncta popina*, "the brothel and the greasy tavern" (1.14.14ff.). These were the pleasures of those whose base natures prevented them from enjoying the refined pleasures of the mind—or so it was conveniently believed by the educated elite.

Some kinds of pleasure, or indeed, pleasure in general, might be described as *infamis*. Seneca describes *voluptas*, in the strictly Stoic sense, as a *res infamis*, "shameful thing" (*Ep.* 59.2). Quintilian quotes an emotive aphorism that he classifies as belonging to the hortative department of oratory: *virtus facit laudem . . . at voluptas infamiam*, "Virtue brings praise . . . but pleasure brings disgrace" (*Inst.* 5.10.83). Excessive indulgence in low pleasures was alleged to be inimical to a life of public duty. The life of virtue and the life of pleasure were often contrasted in Roman texts.[72] Orators repeatedly castigate their opponents for their low tastes.[73] To be physically implicated in the provision of such pleasures was to pose an obvious danger to the stability of Roman society. Seneca's exposition of the evil allurements of pleasure is particularly revealing (*De vita beata* 7.3):

> virtutem in templo convenies, in foro, in curia, pro muris stantem, pulverulentam, coloratam, callosas habentem manus; voluptatem latitantem saepius ac tenebras captantem circa balinea ac sudatoria ac loca aedilem metuentia, mollem, enervem, mero et unguento madentem, pallidam aut fucatam et medicamentis pollinctam.

> Virtue you will find in the temple, in the forum, in the senate house, standing before the city walls, dusty and sunburnt, her hands rough; pleasure you will most often find lurking around the baths and sweating rooms, and places that fear the police, in search of darkness, soft, effete, reeking of wine and perfume, pallid or else painted and made up with cosmetics like a corpse.

Pleasure is embodied in the figure of the prostitute, associated with darkness, filth, softness, artifice and death—the antithesis of what it is to be a true and vigorous man, committed to the public good.

What is especially shameful is the public presence of this figure, visible—as the term prostitute (derived from the Latin *prostare*, "stand out") suggests. Seneca elsewhere speaks of the bodies of prostitutes exposed *publico . . . ludibrio*, "for public humiliation" (*QNat.* 1.16.6). Similarly, what is shameful about professional gladiators is not that they fight, but that they do so for money and in public.[74] And other Romans derived pleasure from these spectacles of degradation. Augustine explicitly lists public performers and prostitutes as the lowest form of humanity, again emphasizing the public nature of their disgrace (*De fide et operibus* 18.33).

All these professions are disgraceful, but perhaps that of the prostitute most vividly symbolizes the shame of the infamous. The commodity of the prostitute, sex, serves as a metonymy for the sensual pleasure purveyed by all those Romans labeled infamous, hence the erotic associations of actors and gladiators. Those who sell their bodies for public exhibition in the theater or arena are assumed to be sexually available. All these bodies are the objects of uninhibited public gaze. Subordinated to the desires of others, these infamous persons are assimilated to the feminine and the servile, unworthy to be fully Roman citizens.

Aristocrats of Infamy

The final part of my essay will look briefly at the involvement of the elite—and of the imperial family—in infamous activities. My aim here is to suggest the paradoxical glamour of the conspicuously disgraced and to confirm the parallels that, according to my argument, Romans perceived between professions labeled infamous.[75] The alleged participation of members of the senatorial and equestrian elite in public performance and prostitution reflects, too, the role played by the archetypically dishonorable in constructions and contestations of the honor members of Rome's elite were thought, above all, to possess.

Actors, gladiators, and prostitutes were paradigmatically lacking in honor in ancient Rome. How better, then, to humiliate the honorable elite than by compelling some of its members to take on these conspicuously shameful roles? Historians relate the scandalous degradation of senators, equestrians, and their female relatives, forced by perverted autocrats to entertain with the spectacle of their humiliation the Roman people whom their ancestors had governed.

Yet it seems, too, that some members of Rome's elite *voluntarily* took on the roles of actor, gladiator, and prostitute. The motives usually ascribed to them are financial necessity consequent on a profligate lifestyle or, in the case of women registering as prostitutes, an attempt to escape the legal sanctions their sexual misbehavior would normally attract. It seems puzzling, though, that such people should choose precisely the most shameful means of escaping from their predicaments. Rather, these stories are the most striking demonstration of the peculiar glamour of infamous professions.

The juridically honorable perhaps felt envy at the freedom brought by the total lack of *dignitas* of those who followed infamous professions.[76] Rigorous exclusion from the social and political hierarchy liberated the infamous from some of the preoccupations of those who had access to legitimate honor—preoccupations (with attaining the emperor's favor, above all) regularly likened to servitude by ancient authors.[77] Public performance and prostitution were associated with license and disorder, with pleasures that escaped the control of official authority. At the same time, ostentatiously degraded senators and equestrians may be seen as taking advantage of the potential offered by public humiliation to parade their disempowerment under the autocratic regime of the emperors.[78]

The appearance of members of the senatorial and equestrian elite onstage and in the arena is first attested under the dictator Julius Caesar. Suetonius, in his biography of Caesar, records that in his games of 46 B.C.E., two equestrians (one of them a former senator) fought in a gladiatorial contest in the forum, and another equestrian, the playwright Laberius, was forced by Caesar to appear onstage (39.1).[79] Equestrians are alleged to have fought as *bestiarii* in 41 or 40 B.C.E. (Dio Cass. 48.33.4). The first known occasion when a senator fought as a gladiator was at the dedication of the temple of Julius Caesar in 29 B.C.E. (Dio Cass. 51.22.4).

Several emperors reputedly compelled members of the elite to appear in the public games or to take on the role of prostitute. This humiliation of the rich and privileged was said to be a source of enormous pleasure to the common people (Dio Cass. 56.25.8).[80] According to Suetonius and Dio Cassius, the emperor Caligula opened a brothel in his residence on the Palatine, staffed by the wives of the foremost men and the children of aristocratic families (Suet. *Calig.* 41.1; Dio Cass. 59.28.9). Nero's amusements for the people involved every variety of humiliation for Rome's upper classes. The entertainment of 64 C.E. included the prostitution of elite women and children.[81] On another occasion, men and women of the senatorial and equestrian orders are said to have appeared in plays, while a well-known equestrian rode a tightrope-walking elephant (Suet. *Ner.* 11.2).[82]

Tacitus emphasizes the degradation these appearances brought Nero (*Ann.* 14.14):

> ratusque dedecus molliri, si pluris foedasset, nobilium familiarum posteros egestate venalis in scaenam deduxit; quos fato perfunctos ne nominatim tradam, maioribus eorum tribuendum puto. nam eius flagitium est qui pecuniam ob delicta potius dedit quam ne relinquerent. notos quoque equites Romanos operas arenae promittere subegit, donis ingentibus, nisi quod merces ab eo qui iubere potest vim necessitatis adfert.

Thinking he might lessen his own disgrace, if he polluted others, too, he brought onstage the descendants of noble families, made venal through their poverty. They are dead now and I shall not relate their names, from respect for their ancestors. And the fault lay rather with him who gave them money not to dissuade them but to encourage them to do wrong. He also induced some well-known Roman equestrians to appear in the arena, by means of huge bribes; the money of one who may resort to force can itself be compelling.

Luxury has ruined these scions of the nobility, but the bribes of an autocrat are peculiarly irresistible. Compulsion, the desire for financial reward, and the wish to win imperial favor are here indistinguishably intertwined.

But sometimes dishonor itself seems to have been actively sought out by aristocrats. Juvenal vividly expresses disgust at the appearance of patrician Romans as actors and gladiators (8.183–92):

> consumptis opibus vocem, Damasippe, locasti
> sipario, clamosum ageres ut *Phasma* Catulli.
> Laureolum velox etiam bene Lentulus egit,
> iudice me dignus vera cruce. nec tamen ipsi
> ignoscas populo; populi frons durior huius,
> qui sedet et spectat triscurria patriciorum
> planipedes audit Fabios ridere potest qui
> Mamercorum alapas.

When you had run through your family fortune, Damasippus, you hired yourself out for the stage, to act in that noisy play, Catullus's *Ghost*. Lentulus was a star as the crucified bandit (a performance worthy of real crucifixion in my opinion). The audience shares in the disgrace. They sit there without a blush, looking on at the gross buffooneries of patricians, listening to the farces of barefoot Fabii, laughing at the slapstick of the Mamerci.

Part of Juvenal's point is that these men chose to undergo this humiliation. It has not been forced on them by an exigent emperor, *nullo cogente Nerone*. The satirist's disapproval focuses especially on the laughter aroused by the patrician comedians. The shame of this spectacle is exceeded only by the appearance as *retiarius* of another nobleman, Gracchus, who was a member of a distinguished priesthood.[83]

Some emperors attempted to prevent members of the senatorial and equestrian elite from embracing these forms of conspicuous degradation. Up to the end of the first century c.e., there are numerous references to legislation against their taking on shameful roles.[84] In 38 b.c.e., "an act was passed preventing any senator from acting as a gladiator" (Dio Cass. 48.43.2–3).[85] A more extensive restriction, banning senators' descendants and probably equestrians, too, was imposed in 22 B.C.E. by Augustus (Dio Cass. 54.2.5).[86] Several equestrians are recorded as appearing onstage or in the arena, nonetheless. The ban seems to have been temporarily raised as regards equestrians in 11 C.E.[87] Dio Cassius comments (56.25.7–8):

> The equestrians—surprisingly—were permitted to fight as gladiators. This was because some were making light of the dishonor imposed as punishment. Since, then, forbidding it had proved useless and those who had taken part seemed to deserve a greater punishment, or else because it was thought that they might be dissuaded, permission was given for them to participate in the contests. And so they met death instead of dishonor, for they continued to fight as much as ever, encouraged by the eagerness of the crowds looking on.

Dio Cassius seems almost to imply that it was the prospect of incurring *atimia* that had prompted some equestrians to enter the arena—lifting the ban might discourage equestrians from fighting. The imposition of degraded legal status contributed to the frisson aroused by the spectacle of Rome's most honorable citizens engaging in one of Rome's least honorable professions.

In 19 C.E., under Tiberius, a law was passed imposing severe penalties on members of the senatorial and equestrian orders who attempted to evade the ban on their appearances onstage or in the arena by deliberately incurring *infamia* through condemnation in a public court (thus losing their status as senators or equestrians, and so no longer being subject to the ban). The text is preserved in a fragmentary inscription from Larinum in the south of Italy.[88] Presumably, an earlier piece of legislation (not attested) had prescribed punishment more severe than *atimia* for members of the senatorial and equestrian orders who so appeared.[89] The last attested piece of legislation against public performance by the elite is listed by Tacitus among the measures of Vitellius in 69 C.E. (*Hist.* 2.62).

Suetonius, in his life of Tiberius, lists measures to prevent elite women taking on the role of prostitutes alongside measures to prevent the appearance of members of the elite onstage and in the arena (*Tib.* 35.2):

> feminae famosae, ut ad evitandas legum poenas iure ac dignitate matronali exsolverentur, lenocinium profiteri coeperant, et ex iuventute utriusque ordinis profligatissimus quisque, quominus in opera scaenae harenaeque edenda senatus consulto teneretur, famosi iudicii notam sponte subibant; eos easque omnes, ne quod refugium in tali fraude cuiquam esset, exsilio adfecit.

> Notorious women, who had registered themselves as procuresses in order to escape prosecution under the adultery law (to which, as matrons, they would otherwise be liable), and those most profligate young men of the senatorial and equestrian orders, who had sought out the legal stigma consequent on

criminal conviction in order to evade the law banning persons of their orders from stage and arena, he punished with exile, so that no one should find refuge from the law by such trickery.

The legislation on appearance onstage and in the arena is presumably the same as that recorded in the inscription from Larinum. It seems highly unlikely that the same law covered the registration of high-ranking *matronae* as prostitutes, but Suetonius's juxtaposition of these measures suggests a parallel between the conspicuous disgrace associated with stage appearances and that associated with prostitution. The measure against prostitution is also referred to by Tacitus, who reports that it was specifically aimed at women of senatorial and equestrian families (*Ann.* 2.85).[90]

The emperor's position as legitimate ruler was underwritten by the ordered nature of the rest of the social hierarchy. The first emperor, Augustus, by legislating to enforce lines of demarcation between senators, equestrians, and the rest, indirectly enhanced his own position at the top.[91] It was by part of the same process that the legal status of those at the bottom of the hierarchy of citizens, those who were branded as *infames*, became more rigidly defined and circumscribed. The greater formality of the social hierarchy, the tighter control exercised over it, reflected well on its guarantor, the emperor—so long as he remained in control. But disregard for social hierarchy—especially on the part of those who appeared to have most to gain from its reinforcement, senators and equestrians—was a challenge to the emperor's authority and, indeed, might be seen as undermining the legitimacy of his own position.

Some emperors are praised for taking seriously their moral responsibilities and attempting to limit the disruption to the symbolic order wrought by aristocratic renegades. Others displayed their power over the Roman social hierarchy by themselves disrupting it—or at least, so their subjects alleged. Hence emperors are themselves represented as *lenones* and *lanistae* profiting by traffic in the bodies of Roman citizens—worse, of Roman aristocrats. As we have seen, Caligula was said to have kept a brothel on the Palatine, and Nero, too, was alleged to have provided elite women and children for the sexual gratification of the people of Rome. These emperors and others are said to have amused the people by engaging the services of senatorial and equestrian actors and gladiators, submitting them to the most public humiliation in the heart of Rome. If the emperor was the crucial figure on whom the whole edifice of public honor depended, he was in the best position to destroy it. There is no need to be convinced of the literal truth of these stories to see them as illustrations of the powerful associations of public performance and prostitution.

Under the Principate, the family of the Caesars became a public institution. Just as the emperor was supposed to exemplify male virtue, his female relatives were to incarnate the virtues proper to Roman womanhood. Insofar as any women had access to public honor in Rome, they did. The emperor's womenfolk were assimilated to Vestal Virgins (Dio Cass. 49.38).[92] The unprecedentedly public role taken on by female members of the imperial family is also to be detected in the ascription to some of them of a very different—but also public—role, that of prostitute. Augustus's daughter Julia sold her sexual favors by the statue of Marsyas in the forum, according to Seneca (*Ben.* 6.32). Claudius's wife Messalina is alleged to have taken on the prostitutes of Rome at their own game—and outdone them (Juv. 6.115ff.). The body that gave birth to Britannicus bared to the world, the emperor's insatiable wife demands cash for sex. Messalina's disgrace is summed up in Juvenal's oxymoron *meretrix augusta*, "imperial whore."[93] A figment of the satirical imagination, perhaps, but one that can cast light on the perceived extremes of the Roman social hierarchy.[94]

And emperors themselves appeared onstage and in the arena—or so historians tell us. Nero's appearances onstage, described by Tacitus and Suetonius, are presented as among his most shocking deeds.[95] A soldier involved in a conspiracy against the emperor is made by Tacitus to explain why he abandoned his previous loyalty: it was when the emperor was revealed as parricide, matricide, and actor. The emperor Commodus is said to have been assassinated when he planned to be inaugurated as consul for 193 C.E. dressed as a gladiator.[96] Emperors were making a mockery of the whole social hierarchy, by themselves taking on the roles of the most degraded members of Roman society. Only their elimination could restore order.

Whether or not emperors and their families actually took on these infamous roles, they were nevertheless powerful categories of analysis for those trying to make sense of their rulers. Emperors should be sources of order and authority, incarnations of *gravitas*. Represented as embracing the positions of the lowest citizens, those whose lives were so base they scarcely counted as citizens at all, emperors could most clearly be seen to cause chaos. As category distinctions collapsed, so social order was radically destabilized. These aspects of imperial behavior are presented by ancient accounts as emblematic of transgressive rule—a clear indication that activities that appear to be socially marginal may at the same time occupy a central position in the symbolic order.[97]

Notes

1. Foucault 1985, 1986.
2. Though for some of the problems with Foucault's approach, see Richlin 1991.
3. This deficiency is partially remedied by a number of recent studies of the

sexually marginal in the ancient world, such as Winkler 1990: chap. 2; Halperin 1990a; and Richlin 1993b.

4. For a more detailed exploration of this, see Edwards 1993: chap. 5, "Prodigal Pleasures."

5. Richlin 1993b.

6. Barton 1993.

7. The fullest discussion of *infamia* is Greenidge 1894. Richlin 1993b makes a number of perceptive observations about *infamia*. Gardner 1993: chap. 5, "Behaviour: Disgrace and Disrepute," provides a clear account of the practical consequences of being *infamis*. For a detailed exploration of the associations of *dignitas*, see Pöschl 1989.

8. Cf. *Dig.* 23.2.43.12 and 13 (Ulp.).

9. For a full discussion of this kind of *infamia*, see Richlin 1993b, esp. 554–69.

10. Greenidge 1894: 8. Cf. Paulus *Sent.* 1.2.1.

11. Other terms are sometimes used as equivalent to *infamia* or the adjective cognate with it, *infamis*. Parallel nouns include *probrum* and *ignominia*. As adjectives, one might find *famosus, turpis, probrosus*, and sometimes *infamia notatus* (discussed by Kaser 1956). The use of cognate terms in a wide variety of contexts inevitably affects usage of the technical legal term.

12. Greenidge 1894: 5. Cf. Richlin 1993b: 555–61.

13. Greenidge 1894: 70. Cf. Ville 1981: 340; Wiedemann 1992: chap. 4.

14. Newly edited Latin text and English translation in Crawford 1996, 1: 355–91.

15. Greenidge 1894: 35. Cf., too, criticisms of previous scholars in Kaser 1956 regarding their attempts to find a single definition of the term covering all instances of its use.

16. Greenidge 1894: 20.

17. Ibid.: 163ff. Cf., e.g., *Dig.* 47.23.4, 48.2.4. Women were only permitted to bring accusations in cases concerning themselves or their immediate families.

18. On the construction of acting and fighting as antithetical activities, see Edwards 1993: 101–2.

19. Sources discussed by Ville (1981: 246–55).

20. Cf. Greenidge 1894: 88ff.

21. Ibid.: 34 and 106ff. Cf. Tert. *De Spect.* 22, quoted below, and Cic. *ap.* August. *De civ. D.* 2.13).

22. Greenidge 1894: 67–68. Engaging in any kind of trade seems to have been regarded as a disqualification. It seems likely that those following particularly disgraceful professions were subject to a ban that continued in force even after the profession in question was abandoned.

23. In the case of passages from the *Digest* I have used the translation edited by Alan Watson (1985). In all other cases translations are my own, except where otherwise indicated.

24. The earliest attestation of this in a legal text is a rescript of Severus and Antonius in the early third century C.E. (*Dig.* 1.7.5[4].1).

25. On these categories, see Richlin 1993b: 558–59, 561; and Greenidge 1894: 121.

26. Greenidge 1894: 159–60; Gardner 1993: 110–18.

27. See Garnsey 1970: 231 for a discussion of the importance of the moral standing of witnesses.

28. See Saller 1991, esp. 151–55.

29. Ibid.: 154.

30. Paulus *Sent.* 2.26.4; *Mosaicarum et Romanarum legum collatio* 4.3.1ff. Cf. *Dig.* 48.5.39.9.

31. Greenidge 1894: 124.

32. Ibid.: 198. Cf. Cic. *Off.* 1.150. Roscius, the famous actor of the late Republic, was granted equestrian status by the dictator Sulla. This is surely to be connected with his refusal of payment for subsequent public performances (Cic. *QRosc.* 23). Nevertheless, Roscius's new status was felt to be highly problematic, an exceptional instance of preferment that vividly demonstrated the exceptional power of Sulla (cf. Edwards 1993: 130–31).

33. See Gardner 1986: 132ff. on jurists' definitions of prostitutes.

34. Greenidge 1894: 70. It was, however, again subject to penalty under the later empire (*Codex* 2.11 [12] 20, 290 c.e.).

35. Gardner 1993: 130–34; Crawford 1996: 383–84.

36. *Bestiarii*, wild-beast fighters, were perhaps less glamorous than gladiators (Ville 1981: 335). They have a much lower profile in literary texts, though they are regularly mentioned in legal prescriptions. They continued to be tolerated by Christian emperors long after gladiatorial fights were banned. Beast fighters are sometimes treated as a category separate from gladiators in the legal and literary texts examined above. Often, though, they are assimilated.

37. Cameron 1976; Yavetz 1969; Bollinger 1969; Nicolet 1980: chap. 9; Hopkins 1983: chap. 1; Clavel—Lévêque 1984; Edwards 1993: chap. 3.

38. In particular, those of Ville 1981; Hopkins 1983; Wiedemann 1992; and Barton 1993.

39. "Le gladiateur professionel fait déjà parti du paysage psychologique de Rome" (Ville 1981: 47).

40. Ville 1981: 246–55 discusses the gladiator's oath in detail. Cf. Barton 1993: 3, 14–17.

41. Barton 1993: 12ff. effectively evokes the horror of such spectacles.

42. On the glamour of gladiators, see Ville 1981: 334–39, and Barton 1993: chap. 1.

43. Cf. Wistrand 1992; Wiedemann 1992: chap. 1; and Hopkins 1983: 2, which quotes Pliny *Pan.* 33. Cicero also emphasizes the exemplary nature of the spectacle of gladiatorial courage (*Tusc.* 2.17.41).

44. Cic. *Cat.* 1.29, 2.24; *Rosc. Am.* 3.8, 6.17. Cf. Velleius Paterculus on Egnatius Rufus (2.91.3). For discussion, see Ville 1981: 342–43; Wiedemann 1992; chap. 1; Barton 1993: 18 n. 21, 48. In the late Republic, political figures sometimes seem to have used bands of gladiators to terrorize their opponents (Ville 1981: 270–71).

45. See Ville 1981: 303, 330–31, on the numerous sexual conquests regularly attributed to gladiators in graffiti as well as literary texts. Barton (1993: 47–49) makes some perceptive observations about the paradoxical association of gladiators with both discipline and wantonness.

46. No doubt this in part reflects an anxiety that the ranks of the elite might be penetrated by children of base fathers (cf. Juv. 6.76–81), though such fears do not often find explicit expression (Edwards 1993: 49–54).

47. See Hopkins 1983: 22. Cf. Adams 1982: 19–22. Ville also refers to the link between violence and eroticism in Roman culture (1981: 343, with additional material contributed by Paul Veyne). Most gladiators seem to have been renowned for their excessive masculinity. But one type of gladiator, the *retiarius*, who fought with a net and trident, seems to have been regarded as effeminate. Perhaps the entrapping, engulfing net was felt to be a particularly feminine accessory. On the different varieties of gladiator, see Ville 1981: 306ff.; on *retiarii*, ibid.: 227–28, 310. For the terminology, see Housman 1904.

48. See Levick 1983: 108.

49. See Dupont 1985, and Edwards 1993: 123–34, for more detailed discussion of the position of actors in ancient Rome.

50. Actors were regarded as totally lacking in *fides*. This is suggestively, though sometimes misleadingly, discussed by Dupont 1977.

51. Cf. Tac. *Ann.* 1.16; *Dial.* 40.1.

52. See Richlin 1992a: chap. 1, on Roman sexual humor in general.

53. The epitaph of an actor named Vitalis celebrates his ability to impersonate women (*Anth. Lat.* 487a).

54. On effeminacy, see Richlin 1992a, esp. chap. 4, and 1993b; Gleason 1990 and 1995; and Edwards 1993: chap. 2, "*Mollitia*: Reading the Body."

55. Tac. *Ann.* 11.28 and 36; Suet. *Dom.* 3 and 10.

56. On seating, see E. Rawson 1987, esp. 106–10.

57. For women desiring actors and gladiators, see also Suet. *Aug.* 45, and Juv. 6.60–113, part of which is quoted above.

58. For the identification of actors with prostitutes, see, e.g,. Tac. *Ann.* 1.72; of actresses, Stat. *Silv.* 1.6.65ff. T. C. Davis 1991 explores the assimilation of actresses to prostitutes in nineteenth-century London. This was not because many actresses were prostitutes but rather because, "like prostitutes, actresses were public women; their livelihood depended on their attractiveness and recognizability" (139).

59. Surprisingly little has been written on prostitution in Rome. Abundant material is collected by Herter (1960). However, much of it—in particular references from Roman comedy and the writings of the early church fathers—is highly tendentious. Herter treats as pertaining to his study of prostitution all references to women perceived to be sexually available. Krenkel (1988) is more reliable, though very brief. McGinn (1989) offers a sensitive approach to some aspects of prostitution. He is working on a full-length study of prostitution in Roman society (McGinn, forthcoming).

60. For instance, Tac. *Dial.* 26; Sen. *Helv.* 6.2ff.; Plut. *Mor.* 142. On effeminate literary style, see Gleason 1995: 103–30.

61. See, e.g., J. Griffin 1986: 28. Veyne (1988: chaps. 5 and 6) suggests that the apparently fluid social status of the elegists' mistresses should be seen as another aspect of the literary game-playing so characteristic of Roman love elegy.

62. Cf., too, Sen. *De vita beata* 7.3 (quoted below); Juv. 6.131–32.

63. Degrassi 1963: tab. 43. For discussion of male prostitution in ancient Rome, see Kroll 1933: 160ff.; Griffin 1986: 22–26; MacMullen 1982: 484–502; and especially Richlin 1993b.

64. E.g., Sen. *Controv.* 10.4.11; Sen. *Ep.* 87.15; Juv. 6.216–18; [Quint.] *Declamationes* 287.

65. For instance: *Verr.* 2.1.33; *Phil.* 2.58; *Cat.* 4.17.

66. Cf. Ville 1981: 272ff., 341, 343.

67. Cf. Juv. 6.216–18.

68. In another Ciceronian treatise (*Fin.* 2.4.13), the character named Cicero is made to set out two meanings of *voluptas*, one cerebral, the other sensual: *laetitiam in animo, commotionem suavem iucunditatis in corpore.*

69. The term *voluptates* is used to refer to organized public entertainments by a number of writers, e.g., Cic. *Mur.* 74; Stat. *Silv.* 1 pr.; Tac. *Hist.* 3.83; *Ann.* 3.6, 4.62; Suet. *Tib.* 42.2; Apul. *Met.* 4.13; *CIL* 8.11340.

70. On the erotic pleasure some Romans seem to have felt at spectacles of cruelty, see Barton 1993: 47ff.

71. It is intriguing that those women who worked in such taverns are regularly assimilated to prostitutes in legal texts, e.g., *Dig.* 23.2.43.9, 4.8.21.11 (Ulp.). Does this indicate merely an overlap of personnel, or perhaps also a conceptual overlap?

72. For example, Ter. *Ad.* 863ff.; Cic. *Off.* 1.106. For a fuller discussion of this, see Edwards 1993: chap. 5. Barton (1993: chap. 2, "Desire") explores Roman anxieties about the dangers posed to the state by the desire for sensual pleasure on the part of its citizens.

73. Cf. Wiedemann 1992: chap. 1, on excessive interest in the games as a subject for criticism in classical invective.

74. Cf. Ville 1981: "Ce qui est infamant dans la gladiature n'est pas l'activité meurtrière elle-même, mais le caractère public de l'exhibition: il en était de même des comédiens" (270).

75. Gladiators appear most often, and their symbolic significance is well emphasized by Barton (1993). Although she gives little consideration to acting and prostitution, texts discussing elite participation in these activities go some way toward supporting her argument for the obsession of the Roman elite with abasement.

76. Remarked on by Plutarch (*De tranq. anim.*13). Cf. Barton 1993: 12, 25–40.

77. E.g., Tac. *Ann.* 1.2; Epictetus *Dissertationes* 4.1.6ff.

78. Cf. Barton (1993: 25–40) on the essential ambiguity of the aristocratic gladiator's position under the Principate. She draws attention to the role of the gladiator as a model for the collusion necessary to elite success in this period.

79. Cf. Dio Cass. 43.23.5; Macrob. *Sat.* 2.7. Ville (1981: 256) suggests they were all relieved of the *infamia* that would normally attach to public performances of this kind. This is explicitly stated with regard to Laberius.

80. As Barton (1993: 35–36) emphasizes with reference to gladiatorial games, the higher the status of the performers, the greater the gratification for the audience.

81. Dio Cass. 62.15.2ff.; Tac. *Ann.* 15.37; Suet. *Ner.* 12, 27.

82. This was a family tradition, according to Suetonius, who describes games given by an earlier Domitius Ahenobarbus when he was praetor under Augustus (*Ner.* 4). The youth games (*Iuvenalia*) initiated by Nero are severely disapproved of by Tacitus (*Ann.* 14.15). Ville (1981: 267–70) suggests, however, that these games, which were open only to young amateurs, did not bring the same disgrace on participants as regular public spectacles but were rather a source of prestige for those who performed well in them.

83. See note 47 above on the *retiarius*. Ville (1981: 142–43, 262) suggests that Juvenal is hinting that Gracchus appeared in the arena dressed in the insignia of the priesthood.

84. See Levick 1983.

85. It is quite probable that this covered the stage as well (ibid.: 106).

86. Levick (ibid.) sets out a highly plausible emendation that would make the ban cover equestrians, too.

87. See the discussions by Levick (1983: 107ff.) and Ville (1981: 257). Ville sees this as an attempt on the part of legislators to encourage members of the elite to appear onstage and in the arena, thereby adding glamour and interest to the games, now largely given by the emperor himself. See Suet. *Aug.* 43.2–3 for games given by the emperor involving members of the elite.

88. For an extensive discussion of problems of interpretation, see Levick 1983. The text has recently been reedited by Lebek (1990).

89. See Levick 1983: 112–13, for a discussion of the technical difficulties.

90. Cf. *Dig.* 48.5.10.2, discussed by Gardner (1986: 133). Some difficulties with the text are discussed by Levick (1983: 111).

91. Cf. Wallace-Hadrill 1981: 46–47.

92. On the public role of imperial women, and in particular of Augustus's wife Livia, see Purcell 1986.

93. Dio Cass. 60.31.1 also refers to Messalina's activities as a prostitute, adding that she compelled other women of the highest rank to follow her example.

94. See further Joshel, this volume.

95. Tac. *Ann.* 15.33 (Nero's stage debut in Neapolis), 15.40, 15.67, 16.4; Suet. *Ner.* 21.2–3. Nero's acting is discussed in detail in Woodman 1993 and Edwards 1994.

96. Hdn. 1.14–17; Dio Cass. 72.19–22. See Wiedemann 1992: chap. 5, for a discussion of examples of other emperors practicing as gladiators. So long as this was done in private, it is not presented as deserving criticism.

97. As Babcock notes (1978: 32).

PART THREE

GENDER SLIPPAGE IN LITERARY CONSTRUCTIONS

OF THE MASCULINE

FOUR

DINING DEVIANTS IN ROMAN

POLITICAL INVECTIVE

Anthony Corbeill

OVEREATING, naked dancing, telling jokes—three activities guaranteed to curtail any young Roman's political aspirations. The connection between moral profligacy and extravagant feasting constitutes a stock charge in invective texts from the late Republic. In this essay I explore the foreboding environment of the banquet room to examine those features recurring most frequently in Roman representations of perverted feasters. The discussion will of necessity be schematic, and the conclusions will apply only to a particular area within this type of invective: many elements inform the illicit character of convivial excess, and a single explanation for all these elements would necessarily oversimplify. I shall not, therefore, consider the standard explanation for the danger represented by excessive banqueting, namely that banquets reflect a Greek or Eastern way of life that will slowly infiltrate and destroy Roman *gravitas*. Without doubt, this explanation contributes much to understanding why banqueting themes are so prevalent in moral critiques written by Roman authors from the late Republic.[1] In fact, Greek loan words dominate the very vocabulary of the banquet, thus creating the impression of "a way of life imported as a package."[2] Yet these alleged origins fail to explain fully the Romans' perverse fascination with banqueting practices. The power in the rhetoric of banqueting invective lies not simply in a clever manipulation of xenophobia, but in Roman concerns about the nature of the masculine self.

The effeminate male actively participates in the banquet's debauchery. In political invective directed at the feast, the Roman orator consistently fastens upon specific, externally visible traits to indicate to his audience

This essay is condensed from the fourth chapter of my book *Controlling Laughter: Political Humor in the Late Roman Republic* (Princeton: Princeton University Press, 1996), in which I examine the role public humor plays in simultaneously defining and enforcing social norms. All translations from Latin and Greek authors are my own.

the effeminate character of an opponent. These external signs serve a double function: physical traits or affectations of a person not only reveal past involvement in an immoderate feast, but also presage future affiliation with a convivial setting. An analysis of these external indicators reveals their distinctly Roman significance: the stigma of convivial excess stems from anxiety over what constitutes—and what deconstitutes—Roman masculinity.

The effeminate banqueter does not inhabit only rhetorical invective; the combination of food, dance, and effeminate or sexually submissive behavior occurs in comedy and epigram as well.[3] The generic character of these effeminate feasters tempts modern readers to attribute to them a purely literary existence, one that the Romans have simply borrowed from Greek antecedents. This scholarly tendency, originating from a compulsion to rid Roman society of the slightest traces of male homoeroticism, is best exemplified by certain modern attitudes toward the homoerotic poems of Catullus and Horace: their expressions of love for young boys derive not from real affection, some scholars claim, but from literary influence.[4] Such assertions promise to be replaced by more balanced assessments; rather than reflecting a debt to literary ancestors, the poets seem instead to be responding to the very real Hellenization of their society.[5] Indeed, villas discovered outside the city of Rome have revealed owners who emulated Greek luxury almost to the exclusion of Roman elements.[6] And the possibility that life imitates art, at least in part, should not be ignored out of hand. Recent research into the role of spectacle in Roman society demonstrates that the Romans tended to blur, rather than highlight, this distinction between life and art.[7] Such practices strengthen the possibility that the invective topos of deviant dining, a topos that has been traced back to Babylonian wisdom literature, helped shape the identity of an already existing subculture.[8] Hence a process of cultural transmission is operative here that is more complex than a simple matter of literary influence. The effeminate banqueter represents not simply a literary inheritance, but the hybrid product of social realities and imaginative forebodings.

A further consideration encourages us to use invective texts as a gauge of actual Roman behavior. Orators use invective to construct an ideology that necessarily entails a certain level of complicity on the hearers' part. In the particular process of defining and enforcing the importance of masculinity, public speakers found an easy target for their insecurities in the person of the effeminate male.[9] Since the effectiveness of an orator's persuasive ability depended in large part upon his credibility, one would expect the orator to form in his invective as coherent and realistic a picture as possible. Thus we would be extremely credulous to believe that a Roman audience would allow constant references to practices entirely alien to its experience, especially when these practices are mentioned only to be censured. Hence the rhetorical power of invective against banquets and effeminacy, a power attested to by its frequency—if by nothing else—virtually ensures that some reality supports these hostile accusations. Recent scholarship has begun to clarify the relationship at Rome between political ideology and actual sexual practices, confronting the evidence at face value rather than simply explaining it away.[10] If this approach is applied to the effeminate banqueter, he is found to occupy a liminal world between literature and reality: his literary aspect allows the orator to employ caricature, thereby ensuring that an audience will recognize the figure he describes, while the element of reality allows the real threat of this figure to be felt. In the following discussion, I recreate a context within which this particular mode of invective alternately appealed to and appalled its hearers. I begin by bracketing questions of historicity, focusing instead on how the banquet and its attendant vices are constituted in our extant texts as a reality directly opposed to proper Roman behavior. These observations will then allow me to concentrate on why this counterreality was construed as an already present threat to society. Finally, the qualities associated with the effeminate male lead to a consideration of the nature of male homoerotic behavior at Rome. Extant evidence strongly supports the notion that our constructed effeminate male constitutes a real category of person to whom distinguishing and distinctive codes of behavior can be ascribed.

Feasting Words

On both a moral and a semantic level, Romans linked gluttony with ineffective self-management. The popular vocabulary of bankruptcy and financial profligacy derives from words that describe excessive indulgence in food and drink: a person who squanders wealth "devours" it (*comedo, devoro*); to declare oneself bankrupt is to "overcook" or "boil away" (*decoquo*), and so a bankrupt person is an "overcooker" (*decoctor*).[11] It is not difficult to discover the relationship between the financial and convivial domains: wasting away time and money in the sensual pleasures of food prevents a person from maintaining control of an estate. This equivalence provides a paradigm for humorous invective. The elder Cato, for example, exploited the similar semantics of gluttony and financial mismanagement. Macrobius preserves one instance (*Sat.* 2.2.4):

> sacrificium apud veteres fuit quod vocabatur propter viam. in eo mos erat ut, siquid ex epulis superfuisset, igne consumeretur. hinc Catonis iocus est. namque Albidium quendam, qui bona sua comedisset et novissime domum quae ei reliqua erat incendio perdidisset, propter viam fecisse dicebat: "quod comesse non potuerit, id combussisse."

Among the ancients there was a sacrifice called "beside the road." In this type of sacrifice it was the custom to consume by fire anything left over from feasting. From this practice comes Cato's joke. When a certain Albidius had squandered his own goods and had recently lost in a fire his only remaining house, Cato said Albidius had conducted a "sacrifice beside the road": what he couldn't squander/devour (*comedo*), he burned up.

Cato literalizes the bankruptcy metaphor: since Albidius cannot "eat away" his whole estate, he conducts the sacrifice appropriate for one setting out on a journey (Festus p. 229 [Mueller])—what cannot be eaten is set on fire. A similar connection between the glutton and the spendthrift underlies a joke of Cato preserved by Plutarch (*Cato Mai.* 8.7):

τὸν δὲ πεπρακότα τοὺς πατρῴους ἀγροὺς παραλίους ὄντας ἐπιδεικνύμενος προσεποιεῖτο θαυμάζειν ὡς ἰσχυρότερον τῆς θαλάττης, "ἃ γὰρ ἐκείνη μόλις ἔκλυσεν, οὗτος," ἔφη, "ῥᾳδίως καταπέπωκεν."

Pointing to a man who had sold the seaside estates of his ancestors, [Cato] pretended to marvel that the man was stronger than the sea. "For what the sea washed away with difficulty," he said, "this man has easily drunk down."

Katapinō ("drink down") presumably translates the Latin verb *ebibo*, another word from the domain of the feast that the Romans metaphorically applied to financial profligacy.[12] These two remarks of Cato do not represent merely cheap jokes. In fact, the attribution to Cato attests to their profoundly Roman character.[13] Another pair of anecdotes preserved by Plutarch conveys his feelings about preserving patrimony: he once remarked that one of his three regrets in life was to have been intestate for an entire day (Plut. *Cato Mai.* 9.6); on another occasion he notes that to lessen patrimony befits not a man but a widowed woman, whereas to increase patrimony reveals a godlike paragon (Plut. *Cato Mai.* 21.8). The importance Cato placed on the proper management of finances helps to explain his humorous abuse of gluttonous spendthrifts.[14]

Cato's conceptual matrix of gluttony, financial profligacy, and the proper role of a man (as opposed to a woman) reemerges in the time of Cicero with explicitly political connotations. The activities of the immoderate feaster come to occupy a position opposed to that of a proper Roman statesman. In his speech *Pro Sestio*, the orator highlights the questionable morality of the former consul Gabinius by referring to his penchant for feasting and sex (*Sest.* 26):

me ipsum ut contempsit helluo patriae! nam quid ego patrimoni dicam, quod ille tum cum quaestum faceret amisit.

How this consumer of the fatherland (*patriae*) spurned even me! For why should I say [consumer] of his "father's land" (*patrimoni*), something he lost when he was out selling his favors (*quaestum faceret*)?

The abuse reveals an interesting thought progression. After alluding to Gabinius's inability to govern the state (*belluo patriae*), Cicero segues into remarks on the inability to control financial affairs. The relationship becomes more concrete through the etymological link Cicero exploits with his pun on *patriae* and *patrimoni*. Abandoning the *fatherland* and squandering a *father's estate* expose similar faults of character. Catullus's lampoon of Mamurra in poem 29 depends on similar associations. Mamurra's treatment of his inheritance anticipated his exploits as governor: "First his father's property was ripped to shreds" (29.17). After enumerating Mamurra's plundering of the provinces, Catullus encapsulates all these exploits in one phrase: "What can this man do other than devour a well-oiled patrimony?" (*aut quid hic potest / nisi uncta devorare patrimonia?* 29.21–22). Like Gabinius, Mamurra recapitulates in a corrupt public career his incapacity in private affairs.

These short outbursts by Cicero and Catullus against their political opponents reveal a close correspondence between representations of the public and the private, a concern one finds reflected in legal texts that treat financial prodigality.[15] As has been noted, Cicero translates the charge of gluttony into a danger to the state (*belluo patriae*); Catullus uses the corresponding verb form to characterize Mamurra's actions (*helluatus est*, 29.16). A similar association between Gabinius's immoderate private life and his neglect of state matters occurs elsewhere. Cicero describes him in *In Pisonem* as "that whirlpool and glutton, born for his belly, not for praise and glory"—praise and glory constituting, of course, traditional goals of the Roman aristocrat.[16] The passage from *Pro Sestio* also shows the orator ridiculing Gabinius for wage-earning, an activity deemed beneath the dignity of a statesman.[17] The phrase he uses, however, contains a double entendre and thereby adds another dimension to the complex of charges levied: *quaestum facere* (literally, "to profit") can stand as an abbreviated form of *quaestum* [*corpore*] *facere* ("to profit from one's body"). Cicero implies not only that Gabinius had to support himself financially but that he did so through prostitution.[18] The connection in invective between financial and sexual profligacy also occurs in Catullus's attack (29.7, 13–14, 16). One may trace this motif in Roman political discourse back to at least the middle of the second century.[19] Yet another element of Cicero's attack here will recur in the invective connected with feasting: Gabinius's reputation as a catamite points to the sex of his clientele, thereby further degrading the former consul as being something less than a man.[20] All these charges characteristic of political invective—gluttony, financial mismanagement, political ineptitude, and sexual profligacy (especially between men)—intersect in the dark and mysterious arena of the banquet.

It is often difficult to distinguish among the precise activities to which the speaker could refer in his invective against the feast. The description of the activities is often as obscure as the shadowy settings in which these activities allegedly occur.[21] The confusion stems in part from the orator's stance as an upright man (*vir bonus*): were he able to describe in detail what happens at these private feasts, he could potentially implicate himself in the activity. The obscurity resulting from this necessary ignorance increases the efficacy of the motif: the allusiveness of many of these descriptions titillates the listeners' imagination and encourages them to envision the precise details of the occasion that the orator presents in bare outline. In this way the speaker allows his audience to play the voyeur, to satisfy its fascination with the forbidden: "The speaker should manipulate the description of reality so that the audience imagines more than it sees."[22] Nevertheless, in spite of this mannered ambiguity, certain themes emerge with consistency.

Five areas of activity commonly surface in association with the immoderate feast: excessive eating, drunkenness, the telling of jokes, dancing and singing (including poetry recitation), and various forms of sexual intercourse.[23] Constructed as vices, these activities frequently occur in combination: Cicero describes his enemy Gabinius in a largely asyndetic series as "done in by wine, eating-houses, pimping, and adultery" (*vino ganeis lenociniis adulteriisque confectum*, *Sest.* 20). Often the practices are alluded to even more elliptically: Piso's teachers of philosophy—who also arrange his banquets (*conditores instructoresque convivi*)—instruct their student that every part of the body should always be involved in some sort of pleasure or sensual stimulation (Cic. *Red. Sen.* 14–15). Vague lists of intertwining vices abound in invective of this type. Yet despite the frequency of these sorts of allegation, any attempt to differentiate between the activities of the feast proves not only impossible but misguided, since their confusion and conflation are precisely the point. The rhetorical handbooks instruct that if an opponent can be shown to be guilty of one vice, it is then possible to implicate him in any others.[24] Therefore, rather than attempting to distinguish between these activities artificially, I shall be considering their common features. In particular, I shall concentrate on the most prominent guest figured in the Ciceronian representation of the feast: the dancing, effeminate, male.

The Dancer Is the Dance

The dance characterizes the feast so well that it is mentioned in Roman invective only in a banqueting context. Yet the abuse directed at dancing feasters could not be wielded simply at random. The orator needed to provide a substantial and verifiable foundation for his accusations. To be effective in accusing an opponent of connections with the immoderate feast, the speaker had to present evidence visible to his audience. Believing requires seeing.

In the midst of a typical account of the breakdown of morality in the Republic, Cicero in *De legibus* attributes moral decline in part to the seductive tendencies of music and dancing (*Leg.* 2.39):

> illud quidem video, quae solebant quondam compleri severitate iucunda Livianis et Naevianis modis, nunc ut eadem exultent et cervices oculosque pariter cum modorum flexionibus torqueant. graviter olim ista vindicabat vetus illa Graecia, longe providens quam sensim pernicies inlapsa in civium animos malis studiis malisque doctrinis repente totas civitates everteret.

> I do see one thing in particular: that those same people who at one time were accustomed to be filled up with a pleasurable feeling of austerity at the measures of Livius and Naevius are nowadays jumping around and twisting their necks and eyes in time with the changing measures. In the past, ancient Greece punished severely that kind of behavior, for it foresaw well in advance how this source of destruction, gradually creeping into the minds of citizens, would suddenly overturn entire states through its evil pursuits and teachings.

As Roman civilization declined from the period when its oldest poets were writing, Cicero recognizes in dancing a vice that conspires with other base activities for the potential destruction of the state. This moralizing opinion of dance also informs invective from the century preceding Cicero. In a fragmentary piece of invective written by the second-century B.C.E. satirist Lucilius, dancing and effeminacy appear to be associated: "Like a fool you went dancing with the *cinaedi*" (Lucil. 33 [Warmington]). A later grammarian, commenting on this passage from Lucilius, remarks that "among the ancients, dancers or pantomimes were called *cinaedi*" (Non. p. 5 [Mercerus]). Indeed, this grammarian's statement is confirmed by a contemporary of Lucilius, Scipio Aemilianus. Scipio complained how the freeborn young Romans of his day "are learning to sing, something our ancestors wanted to be considered disgraceful to the freeborn; they go, I say, to dancing school, freeborn girls and boys among the *cinaedi*" (Macrob. *Sat.* 3.14.7 = *ORF* 21.30). Part of the stigma of the dance derives from its associations with the passive role in male-male sexual encounters since, in ancient Greece and Rome, male-male homoerotic behavior was figured as nonreciprocal, involving a virile penetrator and a passive, penetrated partner.[25] *Cinaedus*, in fact, eventually became a standard word to describe the penetrated partner in such a relationship.[26] The dance, it seems, indicated commitment to a specific, predetermined lifestyle.

It is not surprising, therefore, to encounter the charge of dancing in public invective. In a speech accusing Murena of electoral corruption in

63 B.C.E., the younger Cato alleged that the defendant was a dancer (*salta-tor*). In defending Murena from this accusation, Cicero maintains that dancing constitutes a vice incapable of existing in isolation, "for almost no one dances while sober—unless perhaps he is insane—neither while alone nor in a moderate and honorable banquet. The dance is the final accompaniment to an early banquet, a pleasant locale, and many luxurious activities" (*Mur.* 13).[27] Cato has not accused Murena of any of dancing's attendant vices. Therefore, Cicero maintains, the accuser can only be incorrect in calling Murena a dancer.

Cicero's rhetorical strategy here reveals his audience's assumptions. Both orators presume their audience will agree that associating Murena with dancing will implicate him in the attendant vices Cicero later lists—disgraceful banqueting, sex, revelry, lust, and excessive expenditure. And if Cato can succeed in establishing his opponent's associations with the feast, he will all the more easily prove Murena guilty of electoral corruption, as this charge will be construed as consistent with Murena's immoral character. Such a belief in the association between personal immorality and political corruption informs the historian Sallust's famous description of the conspirator Sempronia: her skills in the dance, poetry, and witty conversation clearly foreshadow her eventual disservice to the state (Sall. *Cat.* 25). Yet the younger Cato's single accusation of dancing does not suffice here. The dance presupposes a broader context of corruption, a context that Cato has failed to delineate.

To be sure, in his own invective Cicero also relies upon the multiple negative associations the dance conjures up in his audience's mind.[28] Yet the orator is not simply hypocritically or opportunistically using a weapon he himself has condemned. Rather, his own use of the charge is quite different from Cato's attack, as Cicero represents it in his speech *Pro Murena*.

In his second oration against Catiline, Cicero muses on the military efficacy of the more luxuriant members of Catiline's group of revolutionaries (*Cat.* 2.23):

> quo autem pacto illi Appeninum atque illas pruinas ac nives perferent? nisi idcirco se facilius hiemem toleraturos putant, quod nudi in conviviis saltare didicerunt.

> But how will they stand that frost and snow in the Appenines? Maybe they think they'll tolerate winter more easily since they've learned to dance naked at banquets.

Earlier in the speech, Cicero had invested a great amount of energy in proving that Catiline's men, when not stirring up political unrest, devote their lives to feasting (see especially *Cat.* 2.22, cited below). Dancing, then, serves to cap an already well-delineated characterization. The naked dancing of the Catilinarians, an activity conspiring to overthrow Roman morality, has been falsely construed by the rebels, Cicero humorously conjectures, as a type of training designed to overthrow the Roman military. In light of Cicero's own use of the charge of dancing in the Catilinarian orations, the inadequacy of the attack on Murena becomes clear. Cato has not verified his accusations of dancing, as Cicero does, by pointing to any other signs of Murena's connection with immoderate feasting. Hence Cicero needs simply to question the truth of Cato's charge of dancing to show that it represents slanderous abuse (*maledictum . . . maledici conviciatoris, Mur.* 13).

Cicero rebuts Cato by indicating the absence of corroborative evidence for his charge. To be effective, the topos of the immoderate feast requires a type of external signal that can indicate, even when the accused is separate from the activity, the implicit probability of involvement. Such a signal would provide a powerful rhetorical tool, for the passages discussed above have demonstrated that proof of involvement in merely one vice can implicate an individual in all the sordid components of the feast. Indeed, these signals were available. They derive from the ways in which the luxurious atmosphere of the banquet was thought to alter the physical appearance and affectations of its male participants.

The Conception of the Roman Male

Orators of the late Republic conflate the phenomena of the immodest banquet and the effeminate male. Each situation normally suggests the other, and both embody a potential threat to the state. Attendance at a feast, I have noted, anticipates political inefficacy. The Romans speak of effeminacy in similar terms. In late 44, B.C.E., Quintus Cicero writes despairingly to Tiro of the consuls-designate, Hirtius and Pansa: "I know them thoroughly—full of lusting and lounging of the most effeminate nature. If they don't yield the helm, there's the greatest danger of everything being shipwrecked" (*Fam.* 16.27.1). This picture of the effeminate feaster of the late Republic, a strangely androgynous glutton of food and sex, contributes to the modern reader's despair over whether one can glean any truth from Roman invective.[29] Yet this unstable figure can be used to advantage: the danger it represents contributes to an understanding of Roman masculine self-definition.

An effeminate man threatened the Roman male. As suggested earlier, the fear of Hellenic or Eastern influence may explain in part what the Romans of this time were wary of—namely, the infusion of different ways of thinking about government and society. Modes of thinking that the Romans perceived as being at odds with their own became associated with Eastern manners and dress. Yet this formulation does not answer why Roman society fixated on the fear of effeminacy. One possible explanation lies in the Roman male's conception of self and of the natural features that he felt separated him from a woman.

Medical writers of the second century c.e. reiterate theories of sex differentiation that date back 700 years to the works of Empedocles. According to these writers, conception involved the intermingling of warm male semen and cool female semen.[30] The net temperature resulting from this interaction determined the sex of the child: "Males were those fetuses who had realized their full potential" by amassing the greatest amount of heat while still in the womb; insufficient accumulation of heat, on the other hand, produced a female.[31] The theory found support in empirical observation: as a result of her cooler body temperature, a woman has a softer, moister physical makeup than a man. This theory of the differing amount of heat in the sexes seems to have had currency in the late Republic: Varro, for example, affirms in his treatise on agriculture that dry plants are relatively infertile, as opposed to those that are "looser and [therefore] more fertile, as the female is [looser and more fertile] than the male."[32] The formulation of this assertion, in which the statement that the female is looser (*laxiora*) than the male is supplied as a given, implies a consensus among Varro's readers concerning what properties constitute the male as opposed to the female. Further evidence for the widespread application of this idea can be found in the rhetorician Quintilian, who conjectures that the voices of young boys are weaker than those of men because boys still retain "dampness" (*propter umorem, Inst.* 11.3.28).

Aside from the apparent parallelism of thought in Varro and Quintilian, there are additional reasons for supposing that this caloric theory of sex differentiation was part of the collective knowledge of a late Republican Roman. First, Galen was a compiler whose work "summarized all that was worthy in the medical tradition of the classical world."[33] That he does not indicate that this theory of sex differentiation had been recently contested may indicate its acceptance in the late Republic. Second, Lucretius's account of conception in book 4 of *De rerum natura* harmonizes with the theory propounded by Galen.[34] Finally, the philosophical conception of pleasure (and hence vice) as fluid, whereas virtue is dry and hard, also accords with this split in the characterization of the sexes.[35] The warm, dry male and the cool, moist female of Republican invective offered a familiar dichotomy.

An interesting consequence arises from the perceived role of heat in a human being's conception: according to Galen, if the heat of a male were to subside at any point during the course of his lifetime, he might risk blurring his sexual identity. "No normal man might actually become a woman; but each man trembled forever on the brink of becoming 'womanish.'"[36] These words describing Roman male anxieties during late antiquity apply equally well to the late Republic. For behind the humorous invective of effeminacy there continually lurks the possibility of a man undergoing a behavioral transformation. This potential threat to the socially constructed natural order, whereby the biological male is expected to exhibit specific masculine traits, becomes recapitulated via public humor into a threat to political order.

If Galenic theories of sex differentiation had legitimacy for these Romans—and the treatises of Varro and Quintilian indicate channels by which these theories may have found wider and even more practical applications—then invective against effeminacy emerges as something more than mere slander. The orator who accuses an opponent of feminine characteristics—or indeed, alleges that his adversary has actually undergone some form of sexual transformation—now can be construed as not merely degrading a person's social standing. That is, in comparing a man to a woman, the attacker does not simply suggest that his opponent has the social value of a woman. Rather, a preponderance of effeminate qualities in an adversary would allow an opposing speaker to assert that an opponent not only violates the boundaries of social propriety but represents a failure within nature itself. In late Republican oratory, effeminate qualities imply passive homoerotic activity, and this construct came to be represented as a marked failure in a man with political pretensions.

The belief that a lapse from the natural order informs the social danger of effeminacy finds direct expression in a text from 142 B.C.E., wherein Scipio Aemilianus inveighs against Publius Sulpicius Galus (Gell. 6.12.5 = ORF 21.17):

> nam qui cotidie unguentatus adversus speculum ornetur, cuius supercilia radantur, qui barba vulsa feminibusque subvulsis ambulet, qui in conviviis adulescentulus cum amatore cum chiridota tunica inferior accubuerit, qui non modo vinosus, sed virosus quoque sit, eumne quisquam dubitet, quin idem fecerit, quod cinaedi facere solent?

> For if someone, drenched daily in perfumes, adorns himself before a mirror, shaves his eyebrows, walks about with his beard plucked and thigh hairs pulled out; who, as a young boy with his lover, wearing a long-sleeved tunic, was accustomed to lie in the low spot at banquets; who is not only fond of wine, but fond of men also; then would anyone doubt that he has done the same thing that pathics (*cinaedi*) usually do?

Galus openly flaunts effeminate traits; he wears perfumes, depilates face and body, once banqueted with older lovers, and as an adult betrays a fondness for other men. Aemilianus depicts Galus's natural sex struggling against the socially constructed norms of Roman masculinity. In Aemilianus's formulation, a proper Roman observer can construe this behavior as nothing other than a perversion of nature. Galus, one must conclude, is pathic.

A Man for Every Woman, a Woman
for Every Man

No man in the late Republic ever actually became a woman—at least so far as we know.[37] A man could, however, approach this transformation when certain characteristics commonly identified as feminine began to affect his behavior. In invective, an orator most frequently associates the manifestation of effeminate traits in an opponent with a presumed role as the penetrated male in a homoerotic relationship; the dominant partner does not ever seem to have been the direct object of abuse for playing the active role.[38] Rhetorical invective against the sexually submissive male finds a parallel in the threats of anal rape (*pedicare*) and oral rape (*irrumare*) that recur in graffiti and invective poetry.[39] These two sexual threats serve similar purposes of degradation. At their most basic level, they make the opponent into an object of sexual violence, or at least into the plaything of another's sexual whims, and so expose the opponent as not having control over his own body. This rigid distinction between active and passive roles accounts for part of the expressions of repugnance toward cunnilingus one finds repeatedly in Roman texts. For a Roman, subservience to a woman's desires implies sexual passivity—and even ambiguity—in the male.

Accusations of womanish behavior occur in a well-known passage from Cicero's *Second Philippic*. In an earlier speech, now lost, it seems Antonius claimed that Cicero had once been his teacher. Cicero replies that in fact the young Antonius had never availed himself of the orator's instruction (*Phil.* 2.3):

> ne tu, si id fecisses, melius famae, melius pudicitiae tuae consuluisses. sed neque fecisti nec, si cuperes, tibi id per C. Curionem facere licuisset.

> If you had in fact done that, you would have served your reputation and chastity better. But you didn't do it and, even if you were wanting to, Gaius Curio wouldn't have let you.

Cicero implies that Antonius's role as Curio's beloved, a role he refers to elsewhere in the speech (*Phil.* 2.44–45), explains in part his present moral profligacy. Antonius's passive sexual position corresponds to an inability to control his own moral upbringing. This formulation from 43 B.C.E. explains the point of a joke dating from the previous century. Cornelia, the mother of the Gracchi, had been slandered for having adulterous relations. Her son Gaius defended her from one attack as follows (Plut. C. Gracch. 4.4):

ἐπεὶ δὲ διαβεβλημένος ἦν εἰς μαλακίαν ὁ λοιδορηθείς, [ὁ Γράγχος] "τίνα δὲ" εἶπεν "ἔχων παρρησίαν συγκρίνεις Κορνηλίᾳ σεαυτόν; ἔτεκες γὰρ ὡς ἐκείνη; καὶ μὴν πάντες ἴσασι 'Ρωμαῖοι πλείω χρόνον ἐκείνην ἀπ' ἀνδρὸς οὖσαν ἢ σὲ τὸν ἄνδρα."

And when a man was hurling invective who was customarily accused of effeminacy, [Gracchus] replied: "What boldness of speech allows you to compare yourself with Cornelia? Did you give birth as she did? And besides, everyone in Rome knows that she spends more time in the absence of a man than you do, [although you are] a man."

Gracchus's barb implies that his unnamed opponent abandons features of his masculinity by preferring to adopt the female role in his intercourse with men. As a result of this denial of his true nature, he is less worthy of respect than a woman. Other passages from the late Republic also show a speaker relegating an opponent to a subservient status by alluding to his submissive role in sexual situations.[40]

The invective of effeminacy strives to equate an opponent's status with that of a woman or even, as in the example just cited, with that of a failed woman. The abuse could go still further: humor often arises from depicting the opponent as threatening to become literally transformed into a woman. For example, Cicero portrays the relationship between Antonius and Curio as a kind of marriage wherein Antonius rejects his maleness (Phil. 2.44):

sumpsisti virilem, quam statim muliebrem togam reddidisti. primo vulgare scortum; certa flagiti merces nec ea parva; sed cito Curio intervenit, qui te a meretricio quaestu abduxit et, tamquam stolam dedisset, in matrimonio stabili et certo collocavit.

You donned the toga of an adult male, which you immediately turned into a woman's. At first [you were] a common whore; there was a fixed price for a trick—and not a small one. But Curio swiftly intervened and took you away from the prostitute's trade, settling you in a calm and stable marriage just as if he'd given you a wedding gown.

The ultimate degradation of the passive partner resides in equating not only his behavior but also his sex to that of a woman; later in the same speech, Curio is described as Antonius's husband (vir, Phil. 2.50). Other prominent Romans are described as women on account of their alleged intercourse with men: Bibulus publicly dubbed Julius Caesar the "Bithynian queen" for his relations with Nicomedes (Suet. *Iul.* 49), Cicero called the younger Curio "Curio's little daughter" (*filiola Curionis, Att.* 1.14.4), and Clodius became "the people's female Appuleius" (*illa populi Appuleia, Att.* 4.11.2).

Public charges of effeminacy, however, never entirely negate the masculine vices of the accused. This type of invective often charges the opponent with the seemingly oxymoronic combination of passive, effeminate subservience and violent, male lust. The ambiguous halfway point between male and female provides the accuser with the unique opportunity of charging his opponent with the worst vices of both "sexes." In this case, the danger is that the accused's physical makeup confuses distinctions that must remain clear. The effeminate male cannot recognize that the biological and social construction of maleness must coincide.

According to Suetonius, the elder Curio wished to show Caesar's reputation for both adultery and sodomy when he described Caesar in a public speech as "a man for all women and a woman for all men" (Suet. *Iul.* 52.3), a charge that echoes one Cicero had made about Verres (*Verr.* 2.2.192).[41] Parallel examples depict men engaging in both dominant and subservient sexual roles without any notion on the accuser's part that the charge seems to raise logical problems.[42] This realm of androgyny does not, however, simply indicate that there is "no consistency" on the part of the accuser.[43] Rather, the theoretical possibility that a man could lose his gender has opened up a legitimate space for invective. The "androgynous man" does not represent a breach of logic so much as a potential threat always inherent for the male.

It now remains to consider how the orator attempted to convey to his audience the truth behind these charges of effeminacy. I mentioned earlier that legitimate invective requires external, visible means of verification. And in fact, extant texts from the Republic and other periods, including those writings outside oratory, reveal an awareness of a consistent set of features that were thought to characterize a dissipating masculinity.

The Category of the Effeminate Male

Effeminacy does not represent, as may first appear, a charge available at the whim of any accuser. Cicero's corpus contains no evidence that he was himself so charged, nor does the accusation enter the list of Vatinius's many vices. In the case of Piso, it is applied only vaguely, chiefly through his affiliation with Gabinius. Yet in Cicero's treatise on humor in the second book of *De oratore*, we find a mockery of effeminacy from the mid-second century B.C.E. that at first appears to advise without reservation the use of such abuse (*De Or.* 2.277):

> cum Q. Opimius consularis, qui adulescentulus male audisset, festivo homini Egilio, qui videretur mollior nec esset, dixisset "quid tu, Egilia mea? quando ad me venis cum tua colu et lana?" "non pol" inquit "audeo, nam me ad famosas vetuit mater accedere."

> The former consul Quintus Opimius, a man who'd had a bad reputation as a young boy, once had said to the witty Egilius—since he seemed rather effeminate (*mollior*) and [yet] was not—"What do you say, Egilia my girl? When are you coming over to my house with your distaff and wool?" Egilius replied, "I don't dare, by Pollux, since my mother has forbidden me to go near women with bad reputations."

Cicero relates this episode to demonstrate the attractions of wittily turning a charge back on an opponent. It is significant, however, that the narrator has taken care to provide his reader with background on each of the participants in the anecdote. This background is essential for understanding the rhetorical advice being offered. The anecdote requires that the joke's audience know in advance about Opimius's notorious youth (*qui adulescentulus male audisset*). The hearers, then, must have some sensitivity to the truth of the charges being brought before them. Hence Opimius does not fail because his remark was not funny—this factor is not relevant to Cicero's discussion. Rather, the humiliation of Opimius offers a clear warning to the potential orator that the substance of a charge must be verifiable. Opimius relied too much upon the signs of Egilius's effeminacy, signs that the joke's introduction reveals to be deceptive: Egilius only seemed effeminate. Egilius, accused by a speaker who lacks a proper regard for visible evidence, can then overcome the insult by referring to Opimius's infamous past.

Opimius cannot be faulted for thinking that Egilius's external appearance would incriminate him. In the late Republic, orators repeatedly appeal to specific external indicators—or groups of indicators—to demonstrate a male opponent's internal, effeminate character. For example, Cicero preserves the following "slight play on words" (*parva verbi immutatio*) that the elder Cato made in response to an anonymous opponent: *si tu et adversus et aversus impudicus es*, "If both from the front and from behind you are a shamelessly effeminate (*impudicus*) male" (*De Or.* 2.256). With the accusation of being "shameless from behind" (*aversus impudicus*), Cato mocks his opponent as a submissive partner to male lovers. *Adversus* ("from the front"), in contrast, is usually taken to refer to the adversary's shameless way of speaking.[44] A passage from Gellius, however, supplies a more satisfactory explanation—oral penetrability (Gell. 3.5.1–2; cf. Plut. *Mor.* 126a, 705e):

> Plutarchus refert Arcesilaum philosophum vehementi verbo usum esse de quodam nimis delicato divite, qui incorruptus tamen et a stupro integer dicebatur, nam cum vocem eius infractam capillumque arte compositum et oculos ludibundos atque inlecebrae voluptatisque plenos videret: "nihil interest," inquit, "quibus membris cinaedi sitis, posterioribus an prioribus."

> Plutarch relates that the philosopher Arcesilaus used strong language concerning a rich man [who was] exceedingly effeminate, but was said to be untainted and free from vice. For when [Arcesilaus] perceived his broken speech and artfully arranged hair and his playful eyes filled with charm and desire, he said, "It doesn't matter what parts you pathics (*cinaedi*) use, those in back or those in front."

For Arcesilaus, the reputation of the rich man had no relevance; his exterior betrayed his true nature. The similarity between the witticisms of Cato and Arcesilaus may not be accidental. Other passages from Cato's writings show the censor's familiarity with Greek aphorisms.[45] The "front parts" (*membra priora*) of the Arcesilaus episode and the "frontal shamelessness" (*adversus*) of Cato most likely refer, then, to the same feature: the use of the mouth in fellatio. At the same time, however, Cato, like Arcesilaus, must have had to find proof for these charges of effeminate behavior in his opponent's very appearance: the man's exterior indicates to an onlooker his hidden vice. The voice, hair, and eyes of the rich man necessarily mark his effeminacy. This pair of anecdotes teaches an important lesson. It does not matter how well immorality lies concealed—one's true character will inevitably emerge in external signs.

A writer from the early Empire offers explicit testimony to a Roman belief in the validity of external indicators. In one of Seneca's *Epistulae*, the philosopher teaches Lucilius how to distinguish unexamined adulation from true and considered praise. There is a difference, Seneca affirms, between approval gained in the theater and at school. And how to determine the character of a critic? As in all areas of life, a clear estimate of an individual's character arises from external factors (Sen. *Ep.* 52.12):

> omnia rerum omnium, si observentur, indicia sunt, et argumentum morum ex minimis quoque licet capere: inpudicum et incessus ostendit et manus mota et unum interdum responsum et relatus ad caput digitus et flexus oculorum; improbum risus, insanum vultus habitusque demonstrat. illa enim in apertum per notas exeunt.

There are all types of indicators for all things, provided they are attended to, and one may obtain evidence for character from even the smallest details: you can tell an effeminate man (*inpudicus*) from his walk, from [the way] he moves his hands, from sometimes [even] a short reply, from [the way] he brings his finger up to his head, and from his eye movement. Laughter betrays the wicked man, expression and bearing the insane one. For those [qualities] come out into the open through signs.

When properly scrutinized, appearances do not deceive. Seneca seems to pass on a lesson he learned from his father, whose *Controversiae*—in form a handbook by the elder Seneca for his three sons—includes a diatribe against the youth of his day that shares all the same features of the effeminate male, except for the reference to peculiar eye-movement (Sen. *Controv.* 1, praef. 8–9, 10):[46]

somnus languorque ac somno et languore turpior malarum rerum industria invasit animos: cantandi saltandique obscena studia effeminatos tenent, [et] capillum frangere et ad muliebres blanditias extenuare vocem, mollitia corporis certare cum feminis et immundissimis se excolere munditiis nostrorum adulescentum specimen est. quis aequalium vestrorum quid dicam satis ingeniosus satis studiosus, immo quis satis vir est? . . . ite nunc et in istis vulsis atque expolitis et nusquam nisi in libidine viris quaerite oratores.

Sleep and laziness and something more disgraceful than sleep and laziness—a passion for wicked deeds—have attacked their souls: obscene passion for singing and dancing has a hold on these effeminates. The model for our youths is in curling the hair, lightening the voice to the caressing sounds of a woman, competing with women in physical delicacy, and adorning themselves with unrefined finery. Which of your contemporaries is—how shall I say?—talented or studious enough? No; which is man enough? . . . Go on, look for orators among those [who are] depilated and smooth, in no way men except in lust.

This passage from the moralizing and conservative elder Seneca provides an important link between his son and the invective texts I have been considering. All the features that he describes as associated with effeminacy are found in representations of the late Republican banquet—singing, dancing, curled hair, womanly voices. As I proposed at the outset, late Republican invective against effeminacy tended to be conflated with fears of the immoderate feast.

I have argued that the effeminate banqueter is not simply a literary fiction, a composite figure patched together from the groundless anxieties of the orator's audience. Instead I presume that invective's efficacy requires at least some degree of correlation between the charges raised publicly and the realities of contemporary society. It is now time to consider the corollary to this claim: to what extent can the effeminate male be said to constitute a specific category of person?

During the past two decades scholars concerned with Greek antiquity have been attempting to clarify Greek attitudes toward male-to-male sexual conduct.[47] Recent debate has centered in particular on the distinctions between ancient and modern notions of male-male sexual activity, for, according to prominent researchers on sexuality, especially Michel Foucault, it is only since the late nineteenth century that male homoerotic behavior has played an integral role in the social definition of an individual. The societies of ancient Greece and Rome did not, they argue, attribute the same degree of importance to an individual's sexuality as does modern society. Preference for one type of erotic experience over another was "not a matter of typology involving the individual's very nature, the truth of his desire, or the natural legitimacy of his predilection."[48] Hence for the Greeks, at least, it is claimed that activity we in the twentieth century would label "homosexual" was simply a "set of acts" in which the sex of the person penetrated is irrelevant. Thus the sex of one's sexual partner did not occupy the same privileged position that it has in our culture in defining an individual's essence: "It is not immediately evident that differences in sexual preference are by their very nature more revealing about the temperament of individual human beings, more significant determinants of personal identification, than, for example, differences in dietary preference."[49] An individual's choice of sexual partner was not, according to this line of reasoning, considered an integral part of that person's character.

Debate continues over the validity of this Foucauldian model for ancient Greece.[50] For the Roman world, Foucault's treatment is regrettably sparse and difficult to evaluate.[51] Certainly his assertion that, until recent centuries, the "sodomite" was not defined by "a kind of interior androgyny, a hermaphrodism of the soul" finds clear refutation in the exegesis of Seneca quoted above, as well as in many of the texts I have cited throughout this section.[52] For both Seneca's account and invective texts from the late Republic are predicated on the notion that the signs by which an observer may judge another person originate from the subject's internal makeup—the identifiable traits, says Seneca, "come out into the open" (*in apertum . . . exeunt*). The vigor with which oratory constructs a stance diametrically opposed to the activities of the effeminate banqueter strongly suggests the existence of the figure in Roman reality.

The gestures, movements, speech, and dress of the effeminate male of late Republican invective cannot, as I have shown, be separated from the banquet and its attendant sexuality. On the contrary, the male beloved is both delimited and delineated by these very characteristics. Effeminacy connotes a specific sexuality. The precision with which the Romans defined the sexually passive male may best be shown by returning once again to the letter of Seneca cited above. The polysyndeton of Seneca's formulation (*et . . . et . . . et . . . et . . . et*) makes it clear that he envisages all the different elements of his list as jointly characterizing the effeminate male. Seneca provides a systematic formulation of the different features that cohere in defining the sexually passive male. It is surely no accident that these characteristics correspond to elements found in Ciceronian invective. Of course, it would be misguided to use these outward signs to define the precise nature of this group's sexuality. Yet our inability to do so does not thereby erase the group's existence.[53] Similarly, I do not wish to claim that frequent victims of this form of abuse, such as Marcus Antonius or Publius Clodius, were necessarily consciously aligned with a specific group of effeminate men. Yet the rhetorical power of the invective would seem to depend on the theoretical possibility that these people existed as a category of human beings. Once this is accepted, the next step, that there were actual persons who belonged to this category, does not seem so difficult to take.

Standards of discretion and a desire for deniability affect the orator's choice of expression. If the orator uses too much detail in describing the sexual escapades of an opponent, he risks losing his own respectability.[54] Hence there arose an alternative to the explicit description of homoerotic acts, an alternative that, as we have seen, was already widely accepted in the second century B.C.E.: would anyone doubt but that a man displaying the typical characteristics "has done the same thing that pathics usually do" (Scipio Aemilianus in Gell. 6.12.5)? The speaker has access to a set of signs that allow him to raise specific charges, but to do so indirectly. Reference to these signs does not constitute mindless abuse; rather, the signs provide the audience with recognizable indications of immorality. The use of sexual discourse for political ends does not erase the possibility that the discourse depends on physical and sexual relations. We may never learn what precisely male-male sexual contact meant in Roman society, but unless we simply assume a gullible audience willing to be duped by a skillful orator, we must expect there to be some truth behind these constructions of effeminacy. The Roman orator constructs beliefs not out of whole cloth, but out of prejudices and biases already present in his society. A recognition of this process revives a reader's confidence in the relation between Roman beliefs and the orator's constructed reality, thereby increasing respect for the judgment of the Roman audience. In the remainder of my discussion, I concentrate on public invective texts—texts that refer to real persons—using other texts only to support my conclusions. In these oratorical passages the depictions of the effeminate male are meant to persuade. Are we to believe that an artistic construct entirely divorced from reality could be so convincing?

Effeminate Signs

The indicators of effeminacy that the Roman orator employs fall into three basic categories: dress, adornment, and physical movement and gestures. The categories of course overlap; as I have observed earlier, such fluid boundaries enable the orator to incriminate his opponent in seemingly different vices, while at the same time allowing deniability. Each individual item of visual evidence provides sufficient proof of deviance.

The mockery of effeminate dress at Rome has a heritage dating back to our earliest extant texts. In Plautus's *Menaechmi*, men who crossdress change their sexual identity together with their clothing. Menaechmus I, for example, addresses himself as Ganymede, Jupiter's boy lover, while wearing a woman's *palla* (*Men.* 143). Later in the same play, the parasite Peniculus accuses Menaechmus's twin of being the one who had sported woman's clothing. Menaechmus II responds threateningly (*Men.* 513–15):

> vae capiti tuo.
> omnis cinaedos esse censes, tu quia es?
> tun med indutum fuisse pallam praedicas?

> Watch what you say.
> Do you think all men enjoy being penetrated because you do?
> Do you claim that I put on a woman's cloak?

The notion being mocked in this episode—that if a man puts on women's clothing it means he has feminine tendencies in sexual matters—has Greek precedents in both Old Comedy and oratory.[55] By the time of the late Republic, although this type of joke still occurs in the ridicule of effeminate men, it depends no longer upon a man wearing women's clothing per se, but upon his wearing a type of clothing not normally worn by a Roman male. Long, flowing tunics, reaching to the ankles (*talaris tunica*) and wrists (*manicata tunica*), marked the effeminate male. In fact, the state of being "loosely belted" (*discinctus*) became the metaphorical equivalent to having an effeminate lifestyle.[56] As a result of these associations, Horace need merely describe a man as wearing "low-hanging tunics" for his reader to understand the implied sexual connotation.[57] In choice of dress, the orator found a readily available—and socially recognized—sign of deviance.

Cicero concludes his second oration against Catiline with a list of six different groups of people at Rome from which the conspirator has composed his forces (*Cat.* 2.17–23). At the bottom of the orator's catalogue resides the lowest form of humanity (*Cat.* 2.22):

postremum autem genus est, non solum numero, verum etiam genere ipso atque vita; quod proprium est Catilinae, de eius dilectu, immo vero de complexu eius ac sinu; quos pexo capillo nitidos aut imberbis aut bene barbatos videtis, manicatis et talaribus tunicis, velis amictos, non togis; quorum omnis industria vitae et vigilandi labor in antelucanis cenis expromitur.

And finally there is the group [that is] last not only in my enumeration but also in its very character and way of life. It's Catiline's own group, coming from his levy—or should I say from his close embrace. You see them, glistening with their coiffed hair, either without beards or with long ones, wearing ankle- and wrist-length tunics, and cloaked in sails, not togas. The entire drive of their life and sleepless labor is used up in predawn feasting.

The phrase "from his close embrace" (de complexu eius ac sinu), combined with the mention of the long, flowing clothing, alludes to the effeminate tendencies of this last group. These followers of Catiline hardly represent a physically violent threat; it is their way of life that endangers the state.[58] The description continues by delineating still further their androgynous character—"In these packs roam ... all adulterers, all the unchaste and pathic. These boys, so sleek and delicate, have learned ... to love and to be loved" (in his gregibus ... omnes adulteri, omnes impuri impudicique versantur. hi pueri tam lepidi ac delicati ... amare et amari ... didicerunt, Cat. 2.23)—and finally concludes with the previously cited joke about their infatuation with dancing. The familiar amalgamation of feasting, assorted sexual activity, and the dance resurfaces. Cicero points explicitly to the visual cues for these vices with the direct address to the audience, "You see" (videtis). Most prominent among these visual markers is clothing. The conspirators wear clothes that can only be compared to something not belonging to a proper wardrobe—a ship's sail. They do not wear the proper mark of the Roman male, the toga.[59] External garb betrays internal intention.

Distinction in dress also informs Cicero's ironic rebuttal to Clodius's charge that the orator, being born in Arpinum, is a non-Roman (In Clodium et Curionem 22):

rusticos ei [Clodio] nos videri minus est mirandum, qui manicatam tunicam et mitram et purpureas fascias habere non possumus.

I shouldn't be surprised that I seem rustic to Clodius, since I can't wear a tunic that reaches to the wrist and a headband and purple garlands.

Cicero turns Clodius's accusation back upon his opponent. The orator claims before the senate that Clodius thinks that to be Roman means to sport exotic and effeminate clothing.[60] Through obvious irony, Cicero implies that anyone with such a skewed notion of appearance represents a less acceptable Roman than a provincial such as himself.

Cicero's abuse of Clodius's clothing presents a special case on account of the *Bona Dea* affair of 62, in which the future tribune masqueraded as a woman to penetrate religious rites traditionally restricted to Roman matrons. The disguise allowed Cicero to call into doubt his opponent's masculinity on numerous later occasions: in the speech *De Domo sua*, Cicero applies a familiar formulation to Clodius, calling him "contrary to what is right, often both a woman among men and a man among women" (*contra fas et inter viros saepe mulier et inter mulieres vir*, *Dom.* 139); he was murdered not because Milo had ambushed him but because "a woman had fallen upon men" (*Mil.* 55). Elsewhere, Cicero jokes that Clodius was acquitted of impiety because the jury had decided a man (*vir*) had not witnessed the rites (*In Clodium et Curionem* 4; cf. *Schol. Bob.* p. 86, 23–27 [Stangl]). By the time of Cicero's later invective, Clodius has become a male prostitute, pimping himself for the most prominent politicians of the day.[61] Effeminacy did not, however, prevent Clodius's still-male physique from practicing the worst manifestations of lust: Cicero's many jokes about Clodius's incestuous cravings for his sister are well known, and the orator twice refers to a double vice of Clodius, who engages in sex with matrons at the *Bona Dea* rites while dressed as a woman.[62] Clodius's character exposes him to a twofold attack that reveals his double threat. A man's taking on effeminate dress does more than provide an indication of sexual character; it can also, when the occasion demands, create that character.[63]

Closely allied to dress as an indicator of effeminacy is cosmetic adornment, which can include depilation, the wearing of perfumes, and fastidious concern for the hair.[64] All three features occur in both Scipio's abuse of Galus (*cotidie unguentatus . . . supercilia radantur . . . barba vulsa feminibusque subvulsis*) and Cicero's description of Catiline's "lowest class of humanity" (*pexo capillo, nitidos*). Similarly, the elder Seneca rebukes the tendency among the youth of his day "to primp themselves with unrefined finery" (*immundissimis se excolere munditiis*, *Controv.* 1, praef. 9). The connections between such adornment and the feminization of the male are clear. The descriptions all recall the feast, together legitimating the associated charge of effeminacy.

Adornment of the hair leads to effeminate gesturing. The younger Seneca included among the indications of sexual submissiveness "bringing the finger to the head" (*relatus ad caput digitus*, *Ep.* 52.12). Public figures in the late Republic also appeal to this mysterious sign in order to degrade an opponent. Pompey provided an especially attractive target. Plutarch relates that in the year 56 B.C.E. Pompey neglected public affairs to spend time with his new, young wife. His eventual reappearance in the forum prompted Clodius to lead a group of supporters in the following taunt (Plut. *Pomp.* 48.7):

"τίς ἐστιν αὐτοκράτωρ ἀκόλαστος; τίς ἀνὴρ ἄνδρα ζητεῖ; τίς ἐνὶ δακτύλῳ κνᾶται τὴν κεφαλήν;" οἱ δὲ [πολλοί], ὥσπερ χορὸς εἰς ἀμοιβαῖα συγκεκροτημένος, ἐκείνου τὴν τήβεννον ἀνασείοντος ἐφ᾿ ἑκάστῳ μέγα βοῶντες ἀπεκρίναντο "Πομπήιος."

"Who is the licentious general? What man is looking for a man? Who scratches his head with one finger?" As Clodius pulled up his toga and shook it, the mob, just like a chorus well trained in responsion, answered each time with a loud shout: "Pompey!"

Clodius, it seems, prompts the crowd's response by improvising his own drag show: he pulls up his toga to match the stereotypic dress of the effeminate man. The added conceit of scratching the head with one finger enjoyed wide popularity.[65] According to one functionalist interpretation of the gesture, the effeminate man scratches with a single finger so as not to disturb a carefully prepared hairstyle.[66] Other sources support this hypothesis. A letter of Cicero reveals that he, too, had concerns about Pompey adopting a foppish demeanor, and contemporaneous images of the general show his desire to emulate the windblown hairstyle of Alexander the Great.[67] A remark of Cicero further supports this connection between gesture and fastidious appearance. The orator once remarked that he had not thought Julius Caesar capable of overthrowing the Roman state, since he used to see Caesar "having such exquisitely arranged hair and scratching himself with one finger" (Plut. *Caes.* 4.9). The same collocation of an effeminate male's nice hairstyle and habit of headscratching occurs in Lucian (*Rhetorum praeceptor* 11). A fastidious concern for the hair harmonizes well with the Roman stereotype of the effeminately adorned male.

The womanlike walk constitutes another physical affectation that invited ridicule. A joke of Cicero demonstrates that the Romans associated a certain stride with each sex (Macrob. *Sat.* 2.3.16):

Cicero . . . cum Piso gener eius mollius incederet, filia autem concitatius, ait filiae "ambula tamquam vir."

Since his son-in-law Piso walked rather daintily, whereas his daughter walked with too much bustle, Cicero said to his daughter "Walk like a man—*your* man."

Women were expected to walk slowly and softly, whereas men should move with quick determination.[68] The joke centers on the unexpected force of *vir* ("husband"); the word's normal meaning, "man," cannot apply to Piso's unvirile delicacy. Other Roman authors explicitly associate effeminate males with a specific manner of movement and carriage of the body that they describe with forms of the verb *incedere* (Juv. 2.17; Sen. *Ep.* 52.12; *QNat.* 7.31.2). The long, flowing tunics worn by the alleged effeminate may have forced him to affect a slow, swaying gait in the manner of a woman (see Hor. *Sat.* 1.2.25), but it is more likely that, as was the case with a person's physical appearance, a womanly stride supplied physiological evidence that a man was undergoing an internal transformation. This transformation, consequently, revealed itself in external traits.

One particular passage in which Cicero derides an opponent's walk brings us back to the dance. After mocking Clodius's dress in the invective speech *In Clodium et Curionem* (22, cited above), Cicero continues his abuse as follows (ibid.):

> tu vero festivus, tu elegans, tu solus urbanus, quem decet muliebris ornatus, quem incessus psaltriae, qui effeminare vultum, attenuare vocem, laevare corpus potes.

> But you alone are pleasant company, charming and witty. A woman's dress and a music girl's walk become you, a man who can adopt a womanish expression, speak in a high voice, and lift lightly the body.

Womanly garb fits Clodius, who puts on a new sex together with his new clothing. The mention of the "music girl" (*psaltria*) and the phrase "to lift lightly the body" (*laevare corpus*) recall dancing, which further implicates the now-effeminate Clodius in immorality by associating him with the immoderate feast.[69] Gabinius participates in the same figural banquet as Clodius. In the speech *In Pisonem*, Cicero describes Piso as emerging from a shadowy drinking hall with Gabinius, "that coiffed dancing girl" (*cum illa saltatrice tonsa*, *Pis.* 18).[70] I have already presented a number of passages in which Cicero alerts his audience to Gabinius's passion for men; the reference to his love of dancing reaffirms this characterization.

The Roman orator could use a number of external indicators to implicate his opponent in effeminacy. Two signs listed by Seneca in his letter to Lucilius remain: the pitch of the voice and eye movement. Voice quality, a sign that betrays the effeminate male in the physiognomic writers as well, receives occasional mentions in the late Republic as a sign of effeminacy.[71] In the passage just cited, Clodius's metamorphosis into a dancing girl includes the thinning out of his voice (*In Clodium et Curionem* 22). The orator Hortensius, in responding to an attack on his own masculinity, alters the tone of his voice as a way of impersonating an effeminate, dancing male (*voce molli atque demissa*, Gell. 1.5.3). This form of mimesis seems to have been a practice common among other public speakers of the period. Quintilian records how voice inflection played a role in *prosopopoeia*, a rhetorical technique in which the orator impersonates an absent or imaginary speaker (*Inst.* 11.1.39). Orators undoubtedly employed still more vocal tricks that are difficult, if not impossible, to detect in our written texts. Eye movement, so far as I can discover, is not the subject of mockery in our extant public speeches. Cicero does, however, frequently bid his audience to consider the eyes (*oculi*) of his opponent, but without specifying what type of eyes signifies what type of character. For this information, one can turn to the writers on physiognomy, whose findings often correspond with the categories of Ciceronian invective.[72]

The illicit banquets decried in Roman invective provide an effective counterpoint to the activities of a proper Roman citizen. The verisimilitude of these descriptions should not concern us any more than it did the Roman orator. In order not to implicate himself in the very vices he intends to attach to his opponent, the speaker must stand at a safe distance, certain of the banquet's corruption but unclear on any details that may betray personal involvement. This precarious position explains the rhetorical convergence of the effeminate male and convivial excess. The effeminate male displayed an easily defined appearance; his internal character emerged through his dress, adornment, and physical movement. By latching on to these available signs, the speaker conjured up an illicit world within which his opponent operated, a world of fluctuating gender and ambiguous sexuality. The realm of the banquet may escape precise description, but its chief participant, under the scrutiny of a properly informed jury, stands ready to be exposed.

Notes

1. See Edwards 1993: 186–88.
2. MacMullen 1982: 486–87.
3. E.g., Plaut. *Men.* 197–98; *Miles gloriosus* 666–68; *Poenulus* 1298, 1317–18; *Stich.* 769–72; Catull. 29.1–5, 47.3–6 (cf. the chart in Richlin 1988: 362).
4. For Horace, G. Williams 1962: 39–42; for Catullus, Arkins 1982: 106–7.
5. Griffin 1976: 88 offers an excellent survey of how "Roman life, and particularly the life of luxury and pleasure, was so strongly Hellenistic in colouring and material that no simple division into 'Greek' and 'Roman' elements is possible."
6. Zanker 1988: 25–31; cf. Cic. *Rab. Post.* 26–27.
7. Dupont 1985: 119–23 (theater); Barton 1993: 54–65 (the Roman games); Versnel 1970: 371–97 (the Roman triumph). For modern parallels, see Rogin 1987, especially chap. 1, "*Ronald Reagan:* The Movie" (1–43), and the further remarks of Greenblatt (1987: 263–72).
8. Weeks 1981 discusses the effects that social representations of homosexuals have had on actual practitioners of homoerotic behavior. Richlin 1993b analyzes the possibility of a homosexual subculture in ancient Rome. For Babylonian precedents, see Burkert 1991: 12–13.
9. I disagree with the claims of Boswell (1990b: 70–72) that "'sexual identity' had little to do with expected social roles in the community" (71). This assertion is said to apply broadly to "Mediterranean city-states of the ancient world (ca. 400 B.C.–400 A.D.)" (70).
10. See most recently Richlin 1993b; Cantarella 1992: 120–41. Discussion in

MacMullen 1982 covers the "exceptions, contradictions, and tensions" (485) in trying to posit a "Roman attitude" toward male homosexuality, uncovering along the way "various pressures to conform and counter-pressures which obliged people to conceal a part of themselves" (496).

11. *Comedo*: Plaut. *Pseudolus* 1107; Catull. 29.14; Cic. *Phil.* 11.37; Hor. *Epist.* 1.15.40; Mart. 5.70.5; *Thesaurus linguae Latinae* 3: 1767.25–72. *Devoro*: Catull. 29.22; Cic. *Phil.* 2.67; *Verr.* 2.3.177; [Cic.] *Invectiva in Sallustium* 7.20; Quint. *Inst.* 8.6.25; Macrob. *Sat.* 3.13.6; *Thesaurus linguae Latinae* 5.1: 876.21–50. *Decoctor*: *Thesaurus linguae Latinae* 5.1: 197.65–198.7; Crook (1967: 375–76) agrees that in situations of debt, *decoquere* must mean "to squander," in spite of the scholiast to Cic. *Cat.* 2.5 (*Scholia Gronoviana* p. 281, 7–10 [Stangl]), who claims that a *decoctor* is one who "cooks away" a debt, as opposed to a patrimony.

12. *Ebibo*: Plaut. *Trinummus* 250; Hor. *Sat.* 2.3.122; *Dig.* 5.3. 25.16 (Ulp.). Edwards 1993: 175 cites a similar use of *effundo* and *profundo* ("pour out").

13. The elder Seneca speaks of Cato as an oracle of morality (*Controv.* 1, praef. 9); see further Edwards 1993: 1–2, 139, 177.

14. The connection between gluttony and poverty was also exploited before Cicero's day; see Cic. *De Or.* 2.265.

15. Edwards 1993: 180–83.

16. Earl 1967: 11–43 discusses the importance of *laus* and *gloria* in the late Republic.

17. Cic. *Off.* 1.150–51 (discussed by Finley 1985: 35–61) is the *locus classicus*. The Romans did not, however, disdain the accumulation of wealth so much as the means of accumulation: see *Off.* 1.92, 2.87; D'Arms 1981: 20–24.

18. See further Cic. *Red. Sen.* 11. For the phrase *quaestum facere* signifying prostitution, see *Dig.* 23.2.43 (Ulp.); *CIL* 1. 593.122–23 (*Tabula Heracleensis* referring to male prostitution); Plaut. *Poenulus* 1140; Ter. *Haut.* 640; and perhaps Cic. *Quinct.* 12.

19. *ORF* 21.19 = Gell. *NA* 6.11.9; see also Sall. *Cat.* 14.2.

20. Cicero also alludes to Gabinius's reputation at *Red. Sen.* 11–12; *Sest.* 18; *Pis.* 20.

21. See, e.g., Cic. *Rosc. Am.* 134; *Cat.* 2.22; *Sest.* 20; *Pis.* 18, 53, 67; *Prov. Cons.* 8; *Cael.* 69. It is a proverb that the frequent banqueter is unaccustomed to daylight; see Cic. *Fin.* 2.23; Otto 1890: n. 1662.

22. Cic. *De Or.* 2.242; see Barton 1993: 85–106.

23. I do not discuss the following examples: Cic. *Verr.* 2.5.92–94, 137; *Pis.* 42; *Phil.* 2.104–5; Sall. *Cat.* 13.3; Livy 39.15.9; Suet. *Gram.* 15.

24. Cic. *Inv. Rhet.* 2.33; cf. 2.50 and *Rhet. Her.* 2.5.

25. The ancients generally—and in invective apparently always—perceived of male homoerotics as nonreciprocal: the beloved in a relationship would always play the passive role within that relationship and was portrayed as receiving little or no physical pleasure from the arrangement; see Dover 1978: 16 and 100–109 passim, and more recently Halperin 1990a: 30–38, which compares this polarization of sex roles to the larger social structure in Athens. On Rome, see Veyne 1985: 29–30, 33; Richlin 1992a, esp. 55–56; and Edwards 1993: 74–75, which discusses how "accusations of effeminacy may be seen as diluted threats of rape." For additional moral judgments on dancing from the late Republic, see Macrob. *Sat.* 3.14.9 = *ORF* 8.114–15 (the elder Cato); Cic. *Off.* 1.150, 3.75 (cf. 3.93); Nep.

Epam. 1.2; Sall. *H.* 2.25 (cf. Val. Max. 9.14.5; Pliny *HN* 7.55). My discussion of effeminacy concludes with a reconsideration of the invective against dancing.

26. Using archaeological and literary evidence, Colin 1952–53: 329–35 explores the semantic development of *cinaedus.* See also Winkler 1990: 45–70 (classical Athens); Gleason 1990: 396–99 (second century c.e.).

27. For the opprobrious associations of a banquet held early in the day, see, e.g., Cic. *Verr.* 2.3.62; Catull. 47.5–6. Catiline's men provide a special case; they begin their feasts before dawn (Cic. *Cat.* 2.22).

28. In addition to *Cat.* 2.23, cited in the text, see Cic. *Verr.* 2.3.23 (Verres' son); *Planc.* 87 and *Pis.* 22 (both of Gabinius).

29. See, for example, Syme [1939] 1956: 149–50; Nisbet 1961: 192; Richlin 1992a: 102.

30. For the common belief in female semen during antiquity, see Blayney 1986: 230.

31. The quotation comes from Peter Brown (1988: 9–10), who cites Aretaeus 2.5 in support; cf. also Gal. *De usu partium* 14.6–7; *De semine* 2.5. Galen appears to follow Empedocles (Arist. *Gen. An.* 764a1–6; cf. 723a24–25; Aët. 5.7.1). Brown's discussion of sexuality in late antiquity first prompted many of the connections I make in my own argument between male anxiety and invective against effeminacy.

32. Varro *Rust.* 1.41.4; I understand *femina* and *mas* to refer to male and female animals (or human beings) as opposed to plants. A similar dichotomy occurs in Polemo's treatise on physiognomy (1.194.11 [Foerster]).

33. Scarborough 1969: 49.

34. Lucretius does not specifically treat the problem of sex differentiation (R. D. Brown 1987: 322–23).

35. See Edwards 1993: 173–74, which cites in particular Sen. *Dial.* 7.7.3.

36. P. Brown 1988: 11, citing Gal. *De semine.* 1.16; Gleason 1990 has a similar discussion of sex types in the second century c.e. (see especially 390–92). Quintilian advises the orator to maintain physical strength (*firmitas corporis*), lest "the voice be thinned out to the frailty of a eunuch, woman, or sick person" (*Inst.* 11.3.19). Laqueur 1990: 126–27 describes Renaissance accounts of how a sudden increase in heat could change women into men.

37. Plin. *HN* 7.36 does, however, consider cases in which women turned into men, a passage cited with approval by Aulus Gellius (9.4.13–15); see further Hallett 1989a: 221–22 (reprinted in this volume). For a modern discussion, see Bloom's account of female-to-male transsexuals (1994), which contains many fascinating insights into the nature of a person's inherent gender.

38. The only possible exception I know of is the obscure pun at Cic. *Phil.* 2.62. Active lovers can be derided for their excessive preoccupation with boys (although I know of no certain example from the late Republic). For the evidence, see MacMullen 1982, esp. 488, 490 n. 21, 498; and Richlin 1992a, esp. 220–26 and index s.v. "Pederasty." In this case, however, it does not seem to be the sex of the partner that is faulted, but the lover's enslavement to physical pleasure.

39. See the discussion in Richlin 1981b and 1992a, passim; Adams 1982: 124–30; Parker's contribution to this volume. Krenkel 1980: 77–80 provides a compendium of the meanings of *irrumatio* throughout Roman life.

40. Examples include Cic. *De Or.* 2.265; *Verr.* 2.3.159, 2.4.143; Suet. *Iul.* 49 (cf.

Aug. 68; *Otho* 2.2); Plut. *Cic.* 7.7 = *Mor.* 204–5. For visual evidence, see Zanker's discussion of Octavian's propaganda campaign against Antonius (1988: 57–65).

41. For the sarcastic use of *vir* ("man") in these two passages and its stark contrast with *mulier* ("woman"), see Santoro L'hoir 1992: chaps. 1, 2.

42. Cic. *Sest.* 20 (the pathic Gabinius is a frequent adulterer); *Har. Resp.* 42 (Clodius; cf. also *Pis.* 65; *Har. Resp.* 59); *Phil.* 14.9; [Cic.] *Invectiva in Sallustium* 9 (Sallust cannot refrain from men; cf. 15, where all husbands are angry at Sallust's adultery); Catull. 57.1–2, 8–9; Livy 39.15.9 (male celebrants at Bacchanalia); Sen. *Controv.* 1, praef. 9; and, perhaps, the tantalizingly brief Lucilius 1048 (Warmington): *inberbi androgyni, barbati moechocinaedi.* Carson 1990: 154 n. 39 cites comparable Greek examples. Sen. *Controv.* 2.1.6 offers an interesting possibility: young men act effeminate to attract women.

43. The quoted phrase is from Richlin 1992a: 98, whose brief but well-documented account of rhetorical invective has been very helpful in shaping my discussion, which I see as refining rather than substantially disagreeing with her own.

44. So Monaco 1968 ad loc., following Turnebus.

45. Astin 1978: 187–88.

46. Eye movement is discussed by Cicero in his rhetorical works as an indicator of temporary, not permanent, character, and seems to be employed that way in his speeches (*Orat.* 60; *De Or.* 3.221–23). I find the following links between the remarks of the two Senecas (the relationship within these pairs will be elaborated in the text through parallels from the late Republic): (1) *incessus . . . et manus mota* (*Ep.*) = *saltandi . . . studia* (*Controv.*); (2) *unum interdum responsum* (*Ep.*) = *ad muliebres blanditias extenuare vocem* (*Controv.*); (3) *relatus ad caput digitus* (*Ep.*) = *capillum frangere* and *immundissimis se excolere munditiis* (*Controv.*). I shall also discuss a fourth element in the elder Seneca's text—depilation (*in istis vulsis atque expolitis*)—a practice that the son, being concerned only with gesture and movement, does not include in his own list. Quintilian (*Inst.* 5.9.14) also acknowledges the possibility of appealing to external signs of the effeminate male. He specifically mentions depilation (*corpus vulsum*), a mincing gait (*fractus incessus*), and feminine dress (*vestis muliebris*). In the anonymous Latin work *De physiognomonia*, the signs of the *effeminatus* correspond well to the categories mentioned by the younger Seneca (2.75–76 [Foerster]; see also 1.276, 1.415, 2.123; Arist. *Phgn.* 808a.12–16).

47. Serious consideration of the subject began with Dover 1978. The subsequent wide-ranging survey by Boswell (1980) has received much criticism for its contention that "gay people" have existed throughout the history of Western society; see the bibliography in Halperin 1990a: 161 n. 32 and Boswell's own restatement of his views (1990b). Patzer's 1982 study attempts to trace pederastic behavior to military ritual; see Halperin's critique (1990a: 54–61).

48. Foucault 1985: 190; see his entire discussion at 187–203, and Halperin 1990a: 15–40.

49. Halperin 1990a: 26, following Foucault; cf. Winkler 1990: 4. In a review of Halperin and Winkler, Thornton (1991) argues that their work has "seriously oversimplified Foucault's ideas" (182). Richlin 1993b: 524–28 offers a detailed critique of the positions of Halperin and Winkler.

50. See, e.g., Thorp 1992: 58 (focusing on Plato's *Symposium*), who is re-

sponding to Halperin 1990a: 18–21; also Boswell 1990b: 77; Golden 1991: 338. Even Winkler admits that "*kinaidos* was a category of person, not just of acts," at least insofar as the *kinaidos* displayed deviant behavior (1990: 46). D. Cohen 1991a: 171–202 uses legal and biological texts to qualify Foucault's claims, assessing legal attitudes toward pederasty in the context of the law of *hubris* (175–82).

51. Richlin 1992a: xv–xvi discusses Foucault's neglect of Roman sources. See also Edwards in this volume.

52. Foucault 1980: 43; cf. 1985: 19, where, after discussing stereotypes of effeminacy in the ancient world, he asserts that it is "completely incorrect to interpret [these traits] as a condemnation of . . . what we generally refer to as homosexual relations." His contention that the ancients had no conception of an "interior androgyny" is also belied by Roman attitudes toward female-female sexual behavior (a subject he neglects), to which activity our extant sources "attribute male activities and apparatus" (Hallett 1989a: 221, reprinted in this volume).

53. Starting from the known strictures on reclining at Roman banquets, Booth (1991) conjectures about the extent and nature of male homoerotic activity on these occasions; see esp. 112–13.

54. See the discussion in Richlin 1992a: 13–26.

55. On Aristophanes, see Geffcken 1973: 83–84; for oratory, Dover 1978: 75–76.

56. *Discinctus* seems to have come to indicate loose morals by contrast with the "well-girt" soldier (*praecinctus*): see *Thesaurus linguae Latinae* 5.1: 1316.59–66, Richlin 1992a: 92; 1993b: 542 n. 45.

57. Hor. *Sat.* 1.2.25 (*tunicis demissis*) and Rudd 1966: 143. Cicero puns on the effeminate associations of the *tunica manicata* at *Phil.* 11.26 (cf. Shackleton Bailey 1982: 225–26). See also Sen. *Ep.* 92.35, 114.6 (Maecenas). Quintilian explicitly states that a tunic worn below the knees is feminine (*Inst.* 11.3.138). Bremmer 1992: 19 and n. 11 catalogues similar associations in the Greek world.

58. The description of Catiline's band by the historian Sallust contains the same elements of censure. His group includes "whichever pathic, glutton, and gambler had destroyed his patrimony with hand, stomach, or penis" (*quicumque impudicus ganeo aleator manu ventre pene bona patria laceraverat*, Sall. *Cat.* 14.2).

59. For the loose toga as a mark of excessive refinement, see the comments of K. F. Smith (1913) on Tib. 1.6.40, and Tracy 1976: 60. For the converse case of the stern Roman in a scanty toga, see Hor. *Epist.* 1.18.30, 1.19.15.

60. The wearing of purple occurs as an element of invective at Cic. *Clu.* 111; *Cat.* 2.5; and *Cael.* 77 (where the prosecution apparently used this charge against Caelius). Tracy 1976: 60 lists other disreputable colors.

61. Cic. *Sest.* 39, 46, 48, 52; *Har. Resp.* 1. Skinner 1982: 202–3 discusses these passages in the context of Catull. 79.

62. Cic. *Har. Resp.* 8; *In Clodium et Curionem* 23; Geffcken 1973: 82 discusses at greater length the significance of Clodius's apparel.

63. For legislation curtailing what clothes a Roman man might wear, see Manfredini 1985: 260–71; Dalla 1987: 18–23. The notion that changing dress can alter sexual desire has been common throughout the history of Western culture; see Garber 1991, passim.

64. Colin 1955: 10–13 provides a long list of passages from the late Republic concerning perfumed men; see J. Griffin 1976: 93 for additional examples. The indicators listed in the text are those I have found in the extant works of late Republican authors. The list is not, however, necessarily complete: Isidorus cites a passage from a speech of Gaius Gracchus to show that in the second century, the wearing of more than one ring betokened effeminacy (*Etym.* 19.32.4 = *ORF* 48.58). I know of no similar example from the late Republic of this sign, but see Hor. *Sat.* 2.7.9; Sen. *QNat.* 7.31.2; Quint. *Inst.* 11.3.142. The passage from Seneca also refers to males depilating themselves and using feminine adornments.

65. For the application of this abuse to Pompey, see also Calvus *FPL* 18 (Morel); Plut. *Mor.* 89e, 800e; *Pomp.* 48.7; Amm. Marc. 17.11.4.

66. Courtney 1980 on Juv. 9.133; cf. Suet. *Aug.* 68. Onians (1951: 138) attributes this association to an ancient notion that the head contained "the generative soul," which had an "itching" whenever sex was desired. This explanation, however, fails to account for why all our sources emphasize the use of only *one* finger (Seneca does not specify "one," but does use the singular *digitus*) and why this gesture indicates homoerotic tendencies, as opposed to general sexual desire.

67. Cic. *Att.* 2.3.1; for Pompey's hairstyle, see Plut. *Pomp.* 2.3; Poulsen 1936: 18 (coins), 42 (bust).

68. Gleason 1990: 392–93 describes perceptions of walking for later antiquity.

69. Through references to passages from New Comedy, Geffcken 1973: 86 connects the *psaltria* and the dance.

70. Nisbet (1961 ad loc.) thinks *tonsa* refers to Gabinius's fastidiously well-trimmed hair, which is elsewhere described as unusually long. As I have noted, such a concern for hairstyle does indeed match the character of a Roman *effeminatus*.

71. For the physiognomic treatises, see Polemo 1.162.4; Anon. *De physiognomonia* 2.135.3 (Foerster). Gleason 1995: 82–121 provides a full survey of the importance of the voice both in rhetorical treatises and in a Roman's daily regime and self-presentation.

72. For references to the eyes in Cicero's rhetorical writings, see n. 46 above. The anonymous Latin compiler of physiognomy, following Polemo (see Gleason 1995: 32), spends twenty-four Teubner paragraphs discussing the meaning of various kinds of eyes, calling the eye "the most important part of all physiognomical science" (*summa omnis physiognomoniae*, Anon. *De physiognomonia* 2.31 [Foerster]). Nevertheless, he still claims to have hardly exhausted the subject (2.61).

FIVE

EGO MULIER: THE CONSTRUCTION

OF MALE SEXUALITY

IN CATULLUS

Marilyn B. Skinner

IN MEMORY OF JACK WINKLER

What is the position of the woman who identifies with men
who identify with women?
(Jane Gallop, *Thinking Through the Body*)

THE ROMAN medical and philosophical discourses that figure so
prominently in the third volume of the *History of Sexuality* present a "model of sexual austerity," according to Michel Foucault,
in which a behavioral regimen grounded on reason constrains desire in
order to promote sober cultivation of the self (Foucault 1986: 39–68). Yet
such prescriptive documents afford only glimpses of the affective currents
roiling beneath ideology. Imaginative literature—which, properly analyzed, can offer pregnant insights into *mentalité*—produces a contrasting
impression of chaotic anxiety, called forth, it appears, by disturbances in
traditional gender roles. Texts of the late first century B.C.E. are notorious for the phenomenon of "gender dissonance": in virtually every literary genre, boundaries between "male" and "female" as essential categories
of psychosexual identity fluctuate wildly and eventually break down.

For the implied male reader, such gender indeterminacy encourages,

This study is a revised and shortened version of an essay that first appeared in *Helios* 20.2
(1993): 107–30, and is reprinted here with the kind permission of the editor of *Helios*,
Steven M. Oberhelman. All translations are my own. I appreciate the help and suggestions
of numerous colleagues, including William W. Batstone, Brenda Fineberg, David Fredrick,
Ernst Fredricksmeyer, Micaela Janan, Victoria Pedrick, Richard Thomas, the anonymous
referee of *Helios*, and the readers for Princeton University Press. I also owe a deep intellectual debt, and an even greater debt of friendship, to Judith P. Hallett and Amy Richlin.
The strengths of the argument, such as they are, are due to others; its flaws remain my
sole responsibility.

first and foremost, a sympathetic engagement with fictional portrayals of the other sex, to a degree that allows even the sacrosanct values of epic to be called into question. Thus Roman poets of the Republican and Augustan periods invite audiences to revisit sagas of heroic adventure, now viewing events from the perspective of the woman who has suffered at the mythic protagonist's hands (Gutzwiller 1992). Variations on the predicament of this "neoteric damsel in distress," who makes her debut in the tense final years before the collapse of the Roman Republic, come to dominate the arts: Ariadne and her abandoned sisters are featured in both Ovid's *Heroides* and third- and fourth-style Pompeian wall-painting (Fredrick 1995). Another example of assigning primary expressive capacity to the female figure may be found in theatrical performances—namely, a vogue for transvestite mimes in which men danced the parts of nefarious tragic queens (Newman 1990: 348–66; Richlin 1992e). Love lyric and elegy, however, appear to invert patriarchal power relations to a much greater degree than does mythological narrative or even mime. The erotic scenario of those two genres, which involves an *amator*, or poet-lover, in thrall to his capricious mistress, has recently given rise to the hypothesis that an actual shift in emotional attitudes occurred among educated young men of the late Republic. Pragmatic notions of marriage as an alliance of propertied families and extramarital liaisons as commercial transactions gave way, so it is claimed, to the wish for a reciprocal "whole love" between equal partners (Lyne 1980: 1–18).

Ignoring its suspicious resemblance to themes found in modern mass entertainment, critics impute that romantic mystique to Roman writers on the basis of empirical readings of the ancient sources. Yet a substantial body of anthropological research warns us not to take the content of such sources at face value. Sexual discourses, anthropologists advise, are infused with meanings that resonate to a profound degree with other spheres of activity nominally detached from sex. The aggregate of values and practices embraced under the term "sexuality" is constantly pressed into service as a code for the articulation of notions more immediately associated with public manifestations of rank and authority (Ortner and Whitehead 1981; Caplan 1987). Semiotic fields structured upon the putatively natural polarity of "male" and "female" must therefore be treated as products of cultural systems whose sexual protocols are implicated in a broader nexus of directives dealing with social status.[1] Hence the peculiar meanings assigned to a reversal of gender postulates can be determined by interrogating the specific cultural context in which they are embedded. Finally, radical gender anomalies, thus decoded, provide analytic clues to the symbolic structures fundamental to a given culture. Whenever norms are violated, the nebulous ideological convictions permeating them respond by assuming contours much more sharply defined.

Applying those methodological principles, I propose to undertake a detailed investigation of gender dissonance in the poems of C. Valerius Catullus (87–54 [?] B.C.E.) in order to arrive at some tentative conclusions about the Roman construction of male sexuality. Catullus's writings mirror the feverish atmosphere of the decade immediately preceding the outbreak of civil war between Pompey and Caesar in 49 B.C.E. As John Boswell notes, they are an acknowledged "sociological gold mine" of sexual mores because of their outrageously frank references to a spectrum of licit and illicit activities (Boswell 1980: 75). Elsewhere I have argued that Catullus's graphic sexual images lend metaphoric weight to charges of financial profiteering on the part of leading politicians (Skinner 1979, 1982, 1989). I shall now attempt to demonstrate that the poet expresses a corollary social alienation by inverting standard gender arrangements in both his narrative compositions and his erotic verse.

For over half a century, ever since E. A. Havelock first remarked on the "strong dash of the feminine" in Catullus's personality (Havelock 1939: 118), scholars have been intrigued by a palpably androgynous inflection in that literary voice. In the large cycle of poems dealing with Catullus's ill-fated love for his mistress "Lesbia," transsexual motifs are all-pervasive (Adler 1981: 129–66). Programmatically for the Lesbia cycle (Wiseman 1985: 152–55), the speaker of poem 51 adopts a female literary persona, inscribing his private declaration of passion into three renowned stanzas by Sappho. The sense of personal violation he feels as he grapples with Lesbia's repeated betrayals of faith is confessed in language very similar to that put in the mouth of Ariadne, the castaway heroine of poem 64 who mourns her forfeited innocence in a thrilling aria (64.132–201).[2] In poem 68, memories of a tryst with Lesbia are inextricably fused with the legend of Laodamia's tragic union with her husband Protesilaus: the overlay "entails that the more passive and suffering part in love, normally thought of as feminine and here embodied in Laodamia, is transferred on to Catullus" (Macleod 1974: 83). Throughout a long series of epigrams, the speaker betrays an unmanly weakness of will as he sinks deeper into obsessive lust; poem 76, the pivotal text in this sequence, has been proclaimed "an exercise in applying to a man the feminine sensibility" (Newman 1990: 338). Finally, in the last two stanzas of poem 11, Catullus denounces Lesbia as a degenerate monster who exhausts her lovers and compares his doomed love to a flower cut down by a passing plough—a harsh transposition of the hallowed epithalamic association between ploughman and bridegroom, flower and virgin bride. This reversal of sex roles amounts to nothing less than a symbolic repudiation of masculinity (Duclos 1976; Sweet 1987; Forsyth 1991).

Catullus's Lesbia cycle seems a promising point of departure, then, for investigating literary gender flux and thereby unearthing the psychological substrate of Roman constructions of sexuality. As we proceed, though, we must guard against falling into a dangerous trap. In antiquity, expected audience response to a text was predicated on subjective identification with its narrative voice, presumed to be one with the voice of the author (Tompkins 1980: 202–6; Konstan 1991). The rhetorical devices of first-person erotic lyric and elegy encouraged the male listener or reader to project himself fully into the speaker's role so as to share vicariously in an experience realized through the medium of art.[3] Later in this study, we will unpack the functional connection between the mode of psychosexual subjectivity culturally prescribed for Roman men and the emotive participation dynamic imposed upon those men as consumers of erotic verse. Here we need only point out that modern readers, no less than their ancient counterparts, are liable to be seduced by such textual strategies into assimilating themselves to the perspective of the speaker and, in the process, automatically adjusting that perspective to fit a contemporary frame of reference (Gutzwiller and Michelini 1991: 77–78). This would explain why twentieth-century critics have habitually resorted to Freudian models of sexual development in order to account for the Catullan lover's ostensible feminization.

Biographical speculation runs rampant in this type of study: the poet is invested with Oedipal difficulties arising from, for example, the traumatic loss of a mother's love in childhood, and his subsequent attachment to Lesbia is diagnosed as a symptom of neurosis.[4] In all those facile applications of psychoanalytic theory, it is further assumed without argument that the sexual drive is invariable in configuration, shaped by universal human experience and therefore uniform across time and space. But that methodological presupposition cannot be reconciled with anthropological evidence, surveyed above, that points to a basic cultural construction of sexuality. Nor does it tally with historical data on the organization of the ancient upper-class Roman or Italian family.

Orthodox Freudian doctrine holds that the adult subject's erotic impulses are molded in infancy by family dynamics. But, by the same token, if constitutive patterns of emotional interaction between children and parents differ markedly from one society to another, adult eroticism must necessarily take on different inflections and modalities. Now, the social makeup of the elite Roman household, including children's relationships to parents and primary caretakers, was in no way comparable to that prescribed, at least as an ideal, for the modern European nuclear family. As a general rule, the mother of the household (*materfamilias*) did not even nurse her infant or deal with any of its physical needs; she saw relatively little of her children in their early years and, if divorce took place, was permanently separated from them, since custody belonged to the father (Dixon 1988: 13–40 and 104–40). The labor of child care was delegated to slaves of both sexes, who also gave the baby whatever early emotional nurturing it received (ibid.: 141–67; Bradley 1991: 13–75). Paradoxes of social domination and dependence implicit in such caretaking arrangements must have imbued their affective texture with considerable ambivalence (Joshel 1986). Sexual subjectivity originating in such an emotional ambiance arguably would not resemble any form of subjectivity produced in the present-day nuclear family, and the plot of the so-called Oedipal romance would also be structured differently—if, indeed, it obtained at all. Mechanical Freudian readings of Catullus based on the abstract triangle of father, mother, and child ignore one crucial issue, the actual circumstances of Roman family life. They thus preclude investigation of other kinds of linkage between the private sexual behavior of Roman men and the larger system of social relations.

To discover what Catullan gender reversal does entail, then, we should begin with a text less immediately accessible than a love poem, one that bewilders or shocks us—for, as the cultural historian Robert Darnton notes, researchers gain their fullest glimpses into past symbolic worlds by "picking at the document where it is most opaque," and so most indicative of an unfamiliar point of view (Darnton 1985: 5). Catullus 63 would surely meet criteria for an "opaque" document. Its sensational account of Attis, a Greek youth who castrates himself out of fanatic devotion to the goddess Cybele, fascinates and repels modern readers, who possess no cultural analogue for the protagonist's act of self-mutilation and are at a loss to understand his motives. Yet, on some rudimentary level, Attis's religious frenzy seems to parallel the erotic obsession of the Catullan *amator*: the same sequence of passion, self-destruction, and remorse narrated as mythic event is reenacted as putative autobiography in the love poems.[5] Approached as a source of information about ancient gender ideology, poem 63 may illuminate the studied use of gender dissonance throughout the Lesbia cycle. Since it will turn out to address large social issues, it may help us place subversions of gender, as a literary phenomenon, within their historical context. Finally, a fuller understanding of the cultural and political meanings attached to the speaker's relations with his mistress casts light on yet other facets of the semiotic transactions between sexual activities and distribution of power in a surprisingly large group of Catullan texts.

Within the ancient sex/gender system, certain assumptions are especially relevant to Catullus's presentation of Attis; the fact that they are largely at odds with our own notions of gender assignment may account for widespread critical disquiet over the poem's tone and content. The scheme of gender relations prevailing in the contemporary West posits "woman" as the conceptual antithesis of "man." In theory, the two sexes are symmetrically opposed. As duBois (1988: 10–17) makes clear, though, woman's place is biologically subordinate to man's, for in orthodox Freudianism, as it is institutionalized within our culture, absence of the male sex organ is deemed an ontological lack. Belief in woman's physiological inferiority can be traced back to fourth-century B.C.E. Greek philosophic thought, since Aristotle's notions of the female as "deformed male" and mere passive recipient of semen are the undeniable precursors of later European views (Horowitz 1976; Lloyd 1983: 94–105). Yet ancient myth and ritual preserve elements of another sex/gender system in which the female is ontologically prior to the male. In that alternative scheme, a fertility goddess gives birth to a son who becomes her consort but survives only long enough to inseminate her, thus insuring the succession of the next generation. The son-lover's primary symbolic relation to the goddess is that of the individual as distinguished from the species; but, insofar as he incorporates the principle of masculinity, the myth also reflects upon the relatively limited role of males in the reproductive process (Burkert 1979: 99–122 and 1983: 81). Neither of the two sex/gender systems, it must be emphasized, is a literal description of the natural order.[6] Each is the product of intense cultural elaboration of select biological data. Together they offer complementary stylizations of human procreative activity.

In classical Greece both of these systems were in force concurrently. Hesiod's *Theogony* gave canonical status to a reworking of the myth of the goddess and her son-consort in which the latter obtains supreme cosmic power by breaking the biogenetic chain of succession (Detienne and Vernant 1978: 57–105; Sussman 1978; Arthur 1983). Variants that preserve the original plot enter the mainstream literary tradition somewhat later and in disguised form, with the male partner reduced to a mortal lover.[7] Although the Asiatic cult of Cybele had spread to Athens by the fifth century B.C.E., her companion Attis does not turn up in Greek literary or archaeological records until the Hellenistic period (Vermaseren 1977: 13–37; Burkert 1979: 102–5). The silence of earlier sources may perhaps be explained by the explicitness of this sacred tale: in contrast to the more nuanced fates of his legendary counterparts Endymion, Tithonus, Phaon, and Adonis, Attis's tragedy demonstrates the precariousness of virility in a particularly forthright way.

Contemporary sexual ideology also proclaims that children develop a core intrinsic gender identity soon after their earliest recognition of biological difference between the sexes. Once stabilized in early childhood, that identity thereafter remains constant throughout life. Ancient gender identities seem to have been more dubious, at least in the case of men. "Masculinity in the ancient world," Maud Gleason remarks, "was an achieved state, radically underdetermined by anatomical sex" (1995: 59). The uncertainty surrounding "maleness" as a descriptive category is explained by its conceptual tie to hegemony. As Foucault has famously shown, Greco-Roman sexual relations are organized as patterns of dominance-submission behaviors that ideally replicate and even confirm social superiority or inferiority (1985: 38–52; cf. 1986: 4–36). True masculinity, the sexual posture of the dominant erotic agent or penetrator, is attained only at maturity, after an adolescent has passed through the stage of erotic passivity and objectification (i.e., feminization) triggered by the onset of puberty. As a prerogative restricted to the head of a household, the status of citizen male is predicated upon control—control of wife and children, of slaves, of one's external circumstances, and, above all, of self. To maintain that status, constant physiological and psychological vigilance is required. Any loss of physical vigor due to infirmity or overindulgence in carnal pleasure, any analogous lapse of moral resolve, or any diminution of social standing, can weaken the bulwarks of masculinity and cause reversion to a passive "womanish" condition (Foucault 1985: 82–86; cf. Giacomelli 1980). In the end, the debilitating onset of "shameful" old age robs even the most robust and austere male of active manhood.[8] Ancient masculinity is thus always provisional and intrinsically at risk, but never so much as in the presence of the sexually experienced female, whose erotic energies are presumed to be boundless and whose erotic demands are correspondingly insatiable (Carson 1990).

Although invested with a contrary set of expectations, the sexuality of adolescent Greek and Roman boys creates social dilemmas as perplexing as those involving grown men. From the perspective of an adult male, boys are legitimate objects of sexual pleasure. Yet the freeborn youth's future responsibilities to the civic community preclude his identifying with the passive role (Foucault 1985: 215–25). Roman society attempted to surmount this problem by forbidding relations with citizen boys; thus the literary *puer delicatus*, "boy-favorite," is normally a slave or ex-slave, often of foreign extraction (Verstraete 1980; MacMullen 1982; Lilja 1983; Richlin 1992a: 220–26). In classical Greek pederastic literature, conversely, the beloved is a youth of good family. He is stereotyped, however, as emotionally and physically impassive, initially unmoved by the pleas of his admirer and finally compliant out of gratitude, not desire (Dover 1978: 52–53; Foucault 1985: 223–25). Like a well-brought-up maiden, he is modest in demeanor and discomfited by references to sexual matters (D. Cohen 1991a: 195). Conflation of gender roles is reinforced by the ascription of secondary sex characteristics that assimilate him physiologically to a girl. One effect of this romantic stereotype may have been to make a real-life boy's metamorphosis from feminine passivity to fully active male sexuality psychologically difficult—more difficult, at least, than the comparable passage from boyhood to adult manhood experienced in our own culture. The intense hostility discharged against the figure of the effeminate pathic (*kinaidos*, Latin *cinaedus*) supports such a conjecture, for phobic revulsion at superannuated *erōmenoi*, "objects of desire," may have been a cultural mechanism for compelling grown youths to abandon the passive role and take up the privileges and burdens of adult masculinity.[9] Whatever the emotions felt by young men (emotions no historian, of course, can ever recover), Greek sources regularly depict male adolescence as a liminal stage characterized by sexual ambiguity (Vidal-Naquet 1986: 106–28) and portray the passage from youth to adulthood, the "ephebic transition," as a period of great psychosexual risk, especially for renowned beauties.[10] Roman writers, though more intent upon the moral dangers besetting young men, are no less worried about this time of life.[11]

How do those ancient protocols of manhood help to explain Attis? In poem 63 the frame of reference is Greek throughout (Syndikus 1990: 76–80), a circumstance that must strongly color a Roman audience's attitude toward its protagonist. In his own homeland, Attis had been the conventional *pais kalos,* "lovely boy"—the toast of the gymnasium, acclaimed by suitors who thronged his doors and decked his house with garlands. His great central soliloquy poignantly juxtaposes shocked recognition of present circumstances with nostalgia for a glorious but now sadly vanished past (62–73):

> quod enim genus figuraest, ego non quod obierim?
> ego mulier, ego adolescens, ego ephebus, ego puer,
> ego gymnasi fui flos, ego eram decus olei:
> mihi ianuae frequentes, mihi limina tepida,
> mihi floridis corollis redimita domus erat,
> linquendum ubi esset orto mihi sole cubiculum.
> ego nunc deum ministra et Cybeles famula ferar?
> ego Maenas, ego mei pars, ego vir sterilis ero?
> ego viridis algida Idae nive amicta loca colam?
> ego vitam agam sub altis Phrygiae columinibus,
> ubi cerva silvicultrix, ubi aper nemorivagus?
> iam iam dolet quod egi, iam iamque paenitet.

For what state of being have I not assumed? I a woman, I a young man, I a stripling, I a boy, I the choice of the gymnasium, I the pride of the wrestling ground: for me the doors were crowded, for me the threshold warm, for me the house wreathed with flowered garlands when it was time at daybreak for me to leave my bed. Shall I now be called the gods' servant and Cybele's handmaid? Shall I be maenad, half myself, a seedless man? Shall I frequent green Ida's uplands chill with snow? Shall I lead life with the woods-dwelling deer, the forest-ranging boar, beneath tall Phrygian peaks? Now, now I rue, now, now I wish undone what's done.

Accordingly, it seems appropriate to recall a suggestion advanced by Kenneth Quinn over twenty years ago but unaccountably ignored in subsequent critical discussions.[12] Quinn read Catullus 63 as a character study of a young man who found that he "could not make the transition society demanded from the role of *puer delicatus* to that of husband" (1972: 250). Given the maturational scheme of Greco-Roman masculinity outlined above, that insight seems intuitively correct, for it offers a rationale for the protagonist's act that would in fact conform to the mental world of a Roman audience.[13]

Two passages in the text lend strong support to Quinn's interpretation. After castrating himself, Attis exhorts his comrades to proceed to Cybele's shrine, reminding them of their common motive for self-emasculation: *et corpus evirastis Veneris nimio odio*, "You have unmanned your bodies from too much loathing of Venus" (17). *Odium* is a striking word, connoting a decided antipathy to sex; and the qualifying adjective *nimius*, though glossed as the mere equivalent of a superlative by commentators, may contain an authorial intimation that preadult asexuality has exceeded its chronological limits.[14] Again, as we have already seen, the monologue of the repentant protagonist looks back, with somewhat disquieting vanity, to his earlier career as celebrated *erōmenos*: *ego gymnasi fui flos, ego eram decus olei* (64). Here the language betrays a narcissistic fascination with one's own desirability culturally imputed to youths as passive sexual objects.[15] These touches characterize Attis as fastidiously averse to the active sexual role. Through self-mutilation, then, he attempts to remain fixed at the passive stage, in defiance of biological impulses to growth and development. By such drastic means, he hopes to avoid the painful struggle for psychosexual autonomy required to effect his transformation into a fully functioning adult male.

Thus poem 63 is preoccupied with the personal and social consequences of an aborted ephebic transition. Attis's failure is overdetermined, taking place simultaneously on two narrative planes, each with its own distinct logic of causality. On the mythic plane the outcome is preordained, for in a female-oriented cosmos, masculinity is by definition ephemeral; on the dramatic plane the outcome of misguided human choice confirms the fears encapsulated in psychosexual ideology. Attis is portrayed as a handsome Greek boy whose head has been turned by too much praise. Wishing to remain a passive object of admiration, he sacrifices his burgeoning manhood to the female life-principle, only to discover that, through this repudiation of biological necessity, his short-lived personal identity will again be swallowed up in the morass of the undifferentiated. The two story lines converge, each reinforcing the other. If sexual ideology regards the status of the male penetrator as constantly endangered by the female, it is precisely because myth, which operates at a greater psychic depth than prescriptive tenets, employs the inescapable, all-embracing womb of the sinister goddess-mother to figure the abyss of personal annihilation. *Ego mulier* (63) is both a mythic and a psychosexual oxymoron.[16]

Through Attis's rash act, the conceptual category of the masculine is destabilized. Its weakening is most conspicuous on the lexical level, where grammatical gender distinctions meld into the epicene. Attis castrates himself in the poem's fifth line. In the ensuing narrative, s/he is morphologically marked as female, stigmatized as a *notha mulier*, "pseudo-woman" (27), by feminine constructions.[17] Throughout the protagonist's central monologue, self-referential terms vacillate frenetically between genders—contrast, for example, *miser* (51) with *furibunda* (54). If masculine terminations finally prevail, it is only to emphasize that Attis is no longer an authentic male: in awarding her apostate the courtesy of his/her former sex (*hunc*, 78; *qui*, 80), Cybele is being sardonic. When the normal passage from feminized adolescence to adult male independence is arrested in progress, one catastrophic effect is a meltdown of linguistic gender.

Since masculinity is the category of the culturally prized, its loss entails the concomitant disappearance of a broad continuum of related values. Scholars have long been aware that the entire semiotic field of Catullus 63 is aligned around gender polarities, with the prime dichotomy of "male" and "female" subsuming other elementary antitheses, those of culture and nature, human and animal, rationality and madness, freedom and slavery. The most comprehensive account of this gender-based taxonomy is provided by Carl A. Rubino (1974), who follows the structuralist method of Claude Lévi-Strauss in charting the syntax of symbolic oppositions uncovered in the poem. As Rubino finally concedes, however, that organic scheme of oppositions "turns out to be a false dialectic" (170). Attis's self-mutilation suppresses the male pole, which exists from that moment only in retrospect, while the "awesome divine power of the female" takes control of the narrative, making an equable resolution of its tensions impossible. Defying the mandates of structuralist logic, poem 63 refuses to allow for the eventual mediation of its range of cultural contradictions.

The anomaly in Catullus's handling of the doomed god/failed ephebe paradigm becomes more evident when compared with the formal treatment of the same mythic pattern in archaic and classical Greek texts. For the Greeks, too, gender polarity served as a basic axiological framework for organizing a complex array of social values analogically—values encoded in artistic and literary renditions of myth, in a liturgy of seasonal rituals, and in accompanying ensembles of folk customs and beliefs (Lloyd 1966: 15–85; duBois 1982). In the androcentric Hellenic cosmos, man is predictably designated the avatar of the rational, civilized public order, and woman is identified with the chaotic domain of nature, those messy private aspects of human existence tied to recurrent biological processes. Yet any reductionist arrangement in which masculinity is made to stand for the good in human life and femininity for its evils at length breaks down, proving a mere temporary alignment on the metonymic grid. Within the comprehensive Greek symbolic scheme, antithetical categories interpenetrate and mutually reinforce each other, thereby stabilizing the social fabric. Consequently, the premature death of an Adonis or the misfortunes of such ephebic types as Melanion and Pentheus turn out to be liminal aberrations that ultimately serve the larger purpose of reestablishing a balance of forces.[18]

Catullus, in contrast, transforms Attis's rejection of his adult sexual role into an irrevocable abdication of male cultural responsibility. In embracing a permanent state of feminine subjugation, the protagonist leagues himself with all that must be painfully eradicated from the public sphere, from the marketplace and the assembly of freely deliberating citizens. As Newman observes, he deeply offends "the code which guards civilization itself" (1990: 217). Human society accordingly disappears from the world of the poem. After their celebratory orgy, Attis's companions vanish, leaving him first alone with his remorse and then defenseless against the primal energy embodied in Cybele's lion. Even his reason, that which qualifies him to claim membership in the human community, is perishable. His fatal act of self-mutilation was the fruit of a violent impulse that seized him at the very moment of his arrival on Phrygian soil (2–5):

> Phrygium ut nemus citato cupide pede tetigit
> adiitque opaca silvis redimita loca deae,
> stimulatus ibi furenti rabie, vagus animis,
> devolsit ili acuto sibi pondera silice.

As he eagerly touched the Phrygian grove with quickened foot and approached the Goddess's dense shaded grounds wreathed by forests, there and then, spurred by raging madness, his mind reeling, he severed the weight of his groin with a sharp flint.

Like masculinity, like the social order, reason itself is tenuous. Cybele inflicts madness where she will, and in the end the narrator can do no more than beg her to send it elsewhere (92–93):

> procul a mea tuos sit furor omnis, era, domo;
> alios age incitatos, alios age rabidos.

Lady, far be all your fury from my house; drive others frenzied, drive others crazed.

Oblivious to the minor accidents of culture and intellect, nature reasserts itself as an overpowering urge to give up the daily battle for rational consciousness, to slide back down into an inert condition of permanent enslavement to the life force. The mythic motif of the "failed ephebe" has been stripped of its prior symbolic capacity to mediate between cultural polarities. In Catullus's poem, we shall find it assuming a completely different function—that of externalizing the social anxiety caused by a stringent reduction in political autonomy.

Freudian-inspired critical commentary, as I have argued, tends to bind the poet rather too intimately to his fictive creation Attis. Yet another school of criticism goes to the opposite extreme by dismissing the text as a mere display piece, a clever exhibition of artistic dexterity.[19] For its part, that approach ignores the probable effect of the narrative upon a contemporary reader. If ancient masculinity was as brittle as I believe it was, members of Catullus's original audience might well have been caught up imaginatively in this mythic account, feeling Attis's experience of sexual slippage analogous to a loss of elite male social identity. Alliteration, assonance, hypnotic repetition, above all the pounding galliambic rhythm—such verbal and metrical effects must have evoked something of the frenzied delirium infecting Cybele's followers. A reader's sense of estrangement would have been intensified by Attis's foreign origins and by the desolate surroundings in which he finds himself. Alone in savage Asiatic terrain, in a region brought under Roman sway only a few years before poem 63 was composed, the Greek protagonist epitomizes the subjugated oriental. Emotive affinity with Attis would bring a Roman male to see himself in his mind's eye as both feminized and colonized, reduced to an ethnic as well as a sexual Other.[20] As alien as he may seem, however, Catullus's antihero is still meant to be representative of the norm, incorporating in his maimed body a complex of gripping cultural insecurities.[21] Further examination of the poem will reveal it to be a repository of covert political comment, symptomatic of the malaise affecting Catullus's contemporaries at that historical moment. Meanwhile, if Anglo-American critics press for a grotesque, theatrical, even absurdist strain in 63, they may be suspected of distancing the poem too far, not only from its author and first readers, but also from themselves. Modern masculinity, its radically different protocols notwithstanding, is still not quite as stable as modern man would like it to be.

The anxieties generated by Catullus's version of the Attis story would not have been limited to matters of sex. Ancient sexual ideology favors the conversion of discourses nominally concerned with erotic behavior, actual or fantasized, into a matrix for addressing larger power issues. Because varieties of sexual practice were so drastically reduced to a single master plot, an active/passive confrontation in which the submissive partner was feminized, sex itself could function as a primary symbolic counter—the most privileged application of those gender categories commonly used to encode Greco-Roman political relations (MacAlister 1992). Whatever was assigned to the "female" side of the sexual equation would then operate, through representational extension, as a mark of deviation from the norm. As such, it would oscillate vehemently between the polar extremes of positive and negative, "same" and "different" (Hallett 1989b), especially when implicated in religious, political, and economic undertakings among the elite, or between the state and its citizens (Stehle 1989; Hillard 1989; Kampen 1991). Accordingly, a reciprocal synecdochic bond between sex and power would have permitted Romans writing during the troubled first century B.C.E. to depict constitutional turmoil within their society by ringing changes on the arresting theme of gender anarchy, allegorizing political crisis as a jarring disruption of natural gender roles (Fitzgerald 1988; Oliensis 1991). Because transpositions of sex and power are in themselves so central to the Attis myth, it may be enlightening to read Catullus 63 as a response to political conditions. Let us try.

At the time Catullus composed his Attis poem, fascination with the cult of Cybele, under her Roman name of "Magna Mater," was running high. Approximately ten years earlier, M. Terentius Varro had published the Menippean satire *Eumenides*, which contained a scene, apparently set in the goddess's temple, involving an encounter between the narrator and her eunuch priests. That satire, strongly topical in its religious and social content, must have made a vivid impression upon Catullus, for the language of fr. 142 C (= 133 B), *apage in dierectum a domo nostra istam insanitatem*, "Be off straightaway with that madness of yours from my house," is patently recalled at 63.92, *procul a mea tuos sit furor omnis, era, domo*, "Far be all your fury from my house" (Cèbe 1977: 653–58). The Republican polymath also displayed a scholarly curiosity about Cybele: Augustine (*De civ. D.* 7.24) summarizes Varro's exegesis of the symbolism attached to her image, although Attis, we are explicitly told, received no mention there. Lucretius's famous description of a procession in her honor at 2.600–660 seems to enter polemically into an intellectual debate raging among the writer's peers.[22] In Catullus 35, an otherwise unknown Caecilius is encouraged to complete an epyllion entitled "Magna Mater." A generation later we find Maecenas trying his hand at galliambic verses on Cybele (fr. 5 and 6 M). Finally, Ovid (*Fast.* 4.179–372) provides readers with what was surely the most exhaustive aetiological treatment of her rites. Widespread interest in a divine figure so intimately associated with religious emasculation, monstrous sex-role transformation, and orgiastic frenzy would suggest that, for contemporary Romans, the myth and cult of Magna Mater must have possessed profound symbolic meanings.[23]

Now, the isomorphism of ancient social and sexual relations induces Foucault (1986: 81–95) to posit a causal connection between changes in Roman political conditions and new modes of subjectivity. Tighter restrictions on freedom of action in the public sphere and graver risks for both large and small players in the political game resulted, he argues, in a more intense absorption with oneself as ethical subject, ultimately leading to modifications in sexual values and practices. This trend emerges "starting from the moment when new conditions of political life modified the relations between status, functions, powers, and duties" at the beginning of the imperial epoch (ibid.: 85). If we follow Foucault in assuming a necessary connection between the public world and private consciousness, we can postulate in turn that the perilous realities of Roman political life in the decades preceding Octavian's consolidation of authority—decades of civil disturbance, brutal power struggles between dynasts, and occasional bloody proscriptions—also affected individual subjectivity, and in a far less subtle way.[24] When he pleads the evils of the times to explain his withdrawal from public life (*Cat.* 3.3–5; *Iug.* 4.3–49), the contemporary historian Sallust need only appeal to his readers' collective memory of past events.

I submit, then, that the monstrous inversion of gender relations contained in the asymmetrical partnership of *minax Cybebe*, "threatening Cybele," and her emasculate consort Attis reflects elite alarm over perceived restrictions on personal autonomy and diminished capacity for meaningful public action during the agonized death throes of the Roman Republic. It hints at despair in the face of historical changes that, as a practical consequence, were repeatedly exposing upper-class men, their property, and their families to the haphazard evils of civil war and domestic tumult. Attis's tragedy is the triumph of chaos, in which male civic virtue, exhibited in the ordered activities of *foro, palaestra, stadio et gymnasiis*, "forum, wrestling-ground, stadium and gymnasia" (60), is swept away into the *furor* seething outside the civilized enclave. As the pathetic victim of such *furor*, Catullus's Greek youth becomes a surrogate for his own intended readers—enterprising young men born, like the poet himself, to influential Italian and Transpadane families, highly educated, talented, groomed for success at Rome, yet unforeseeably marginalized and, worse, suddenly endangered. Fears for personal safety, coupled with the chagrin of political defeat, could readily be subsumed under Attis's horrified repudiation of adult male sexuality. Thus in Catullus 63 a contemporary narrative of political impotence is retold as a myth of self-destructive estrangement from the male body.[25]

Cybele's literary popularity is coextensive with that of the "lady mistress" (*puella domina*) of Roman elegy, another occurrence of a poetic transfer of power to the female side. Like Attis, the elegiac lover opts for *mollitia* or "softness" as he neglects military duty to wallow in despair over the cruelty of his beloved. While the representational function of elegy remains one of the most debated issues in contemporary criticism of ancient texts (Veyne 1988; Kennedy 1993), compelling cases have lately been made for considering the erotic scenarios of Propertius, Tibullus, and Ovid to be implicated in ideological issues. Thus Wyke defines elegy as metaphoric political discourse that seeks "to portray the male narrator as alienated from positions of power and to differentiate him from other, socially responsible male types" (1989b: 42). Building upon her earlier, highly influential, classification of this genre as "countercultural," Hallett identifies valued aspects of "sameness" as well as "otherness" in Propertius's representation of Cynthia and certain of her female counterparts; such constructions of "woman," she argues, inevitably call Augustan social and moral precepts into question (Hallett 1973 and 1993: 62–65). Gold (1993a) adds that indeterminacy in elegiac sex-role assignment subverts the very category "female," muddling traditional Roman signifying practices and, by extension, Roman cultural values. Finally, even in the absence of straightforward allusion to political and topical matters, the elegiac lover's distinguishing *mollitia* makes him an obvious counterweight to edifying discourses aimed at reinstating a civic virtue grounded on male self-mastery.[26] The presence of latent political undertones in quasi-autobiographical erotic verse is, after all, not surprising, given the homology of sex and power embedded in the ancient dominance-submission model of erotic relations.

Like Roman elegy's "confessional" narratives, the Lesbia epigrams mingle topical commentary with their love story, expressing political concerns far more overtly than elegiac convention would subsequently permit. Ever since Richard Reitzenstein noted the presence of a "language of party politics" in Catullus, critics have been puzzled by the incongruous connotations of such recurrent expressions as *fides* ("credibility"), *foedus* ("compact"), *officium* ("service"), *pietas* ("dutiful respect"), and especially *amicitia*—the speaker's own term for his liaison with his mistress, disconcertingly redolent of pragmatic Roman power alliances.[27] Ross subjects that political terminology to searching philological analysis (1969: 80–95; 1975: 8–15). Catullus, he contends, employs it to draw a tacit analogy between his own adulterous affair and a general moral bankruptcy stemming from the dishonorable behavior of the Roman ruling class. The eroticized metaphor of *amicitia* or political friendship is an evocative means of speaking about "more universal, more characteristically Roman concerns" (1975: 15) in relation to a particular set of events in the poet's own life.[28]

In a brief thought experiment, let us interchange tenor and vehicle of the metaphor. When approached from the outset as political statements, the Lesbia epigrams cease to track the rupture of an intimacy that would later become, almost fortuitously, a trope for corrupt practices. Viewed from the warp side, they focus instead upon such practices, depicted as components of a disastrous love affair. The slipperiness of erotic language and the perceived gap between declaration and hidden intent on the part of the beloved reflect the debasement of a civic discourse divested of its old religious and moral sanctions (Janan 1994: 92–95). As it recounts Catullus's vain attempt to establish a lasting erotic *foedus* through an act of adultery (Rubino 1975), the epigrammatic scenario shows the ethical confusion generated by a breakdown in communal *fides* and *pietas*. Since the unfaithful wife and mistress is a highborn Roman *materfamilias* (68.143–46, 79.1–2) and her paramour only a *domi nobilis*, or member of the provincial elite, their affair is tantamount to a client relationship, with Lesbia playing the de facto role of patron and Catullus occupying the subordinate place of lesser *amicus*.[29] In its inherent power asymmetry, then, the ill-fated association involves a breach of patronage etiquette: we observe the rules governing dealings between the ruling class and its municipal clients, encapsulated in the language of political and social alliance, violated for the sole benefit of Lesbia, the more advantaged partner.[30] One thematic objective of the Lesbia poems, it would seem, is to connect the frustration of ambition among Catullus's peers with aristocratic venality by encoding exploitative manipulations of the patronage system within the most privileged circles as a noblewoman's greedy pursuit of sexual adventures.

As we delve into the allegorical message of the epigrams, however, we should not become deaf to their emotive content. Throughout these verses, the Catullan speaker revels in pious martyrdom even as he voices his grievances. In poem 75, for example, he declares that his conscience has bankrupted itself through dedication to duty (*mens . . . se officio perdidit ipsa suo*, 1–2), and in the next poem, 76, he extrapolates from personal injury to cosmic moral chaos (Dyson 1973: 141–42). Appeals to ethical principles serve not only to exculpate his earlier surrender of will but also to verify his credentials as a steadfast adherent of *mos maiorum* in a vicious world. Thus, with a rhetorical finesse no later elegiac imitator ever quite attained, our bruised speaker intimates that corruption within society, as well as the pain of the Lesbia affair, can be transcended through formation of a new *foedus amicitiae* between poet and (male) reader (Adler 1981: 41; Fitzgerald 1995: 212–35; for Augustan parallels, see Oliensis, this volume). The consolations of reciprocal, homosocial literary friendship might appear to have displaced his former political preoccupations.

Yet the Catullan lover's very affective state, his longing for the absent beloved as a supplement to the incomplete self, charged with equal parts of self-loathing and self-righteousness, is, from a gender-oriented standpoint, idiosyncratic—because that oddly familiar nexus of sentiments inscribed here into a male subjectivity is elsewhere regarded as quintessentially feminine. It is, to be precise, the posture of the "abandoned woman," one of the most semiotically dense icons of Western literature, whose characteristic set-piece, a bitter tirade against the faithless lover, may have received its definitive shape in a lost episode of Callimachus's *Aetia* (Puelma 1982: 237–38). In his exhaustive investigation of this figure, Lawrence Lipking observes that she is herself an intrinsically politicized construct (1988: 11–14). Insofar as her plight embraces the suffering of socially muted groups, the forsaken heroine laments for injured humanity everywhere; her song "flourishes wherever those who hear it are reminded of their own subjection and alienation, of everything that is missing from their lives" (11). The angry remonstrances of Catullus's own Ariadne, to cite one immediate example, may be taken as an indictment of false military values, fraught with apprehension of impending civil war (Konstan 1977: 75–84; Newman 1990: 220–21). Drawing on that long tradition of female complaint, the reproaches of the Catullan lover still convey messages of political disenfranchisement even when construed as erotic pronouncements.

Once we have raised it to the surface, that subtext ought not to disappear after we return to reading the Lesbia cycle in a more conventional fashion. We must realize that in any Catullan poem the affliction of the male or female speaker will carry political implications. But its most immediate surface appeal will nevertheless be erotic: vulnerability endows his distraught characters—Ariadne, Berenice's Lock, "Catullus" himself, even Attis—with poignant charm. Yet these passive figures are presented to the reader not as titillating objects of lust, as would be the case in present-day pornography, but as alternative subject positions permitting scope for emotive fantasy.[31] Although their passions were gendered "feminine," a male reader was expected to discharge his own repressed feelings through sentimental involvement in the character's predicament.

Cravings to experience the victim's state of mind were a basic ingredient in the construction of ancient male sexuality. In the Greco-Roman world, power, as we have seen, was openly eroticized—so openly and so thoroughly as to undermine biological identity. If the dynamics of social hierarchy are given concrete expression in terms of gender relations, a man vexed by social disadvantage will be at liberty to immerse himself, if only provisionally, in a synthetic "female" sensibility. At first glance, assumption of such a passive posture might seem acutely degrading. Paradoxically, however, as I argue elsewhere (Skinner 1991, 1993), it supplied a channel for imaginative escape. This was, after all, the sole literary venue conceded to ancient men for voicing a forbidden sense of inferiority. Identification with emotionally prodigal figures, such as outcast girls and feckless lovers, must have afforded a fleeting relaxation of stringent psychic controls, a relatively harmless foray into voluptuous self-pity.

When we read his poetry in this light, we note at once how skilled Catullus is at articulating the conflicts within Roman male subjectivity. His texts bear witness to the existence of a pathetic—one might well call it "pathic"—impasse built into the cultural injunction to maintain staunch self-control. Through its ruthless denial of personality traits branded "womanish" and associated with the despised *cinaedus*, the elite adult male role gave rise to its own frustrations. Homology of sexual and social dominance so extreme as to result in conceptual fusion made psychic virility extraordinarily sensitive to the slightest lessening of *dignitas*, "prestige," while stigmatizing failure as effeminate. Insecurities engendered by the political upheavals of the first century B.C.E. could therefore be vented only through "playing the other," to use Zeitlin's phrase (1985: 80–81)—through recourse to erotic or mythic fantasy in which the reader vicariously shared in anguish voiced through a counterfeit feminine persona. In manipulating literary strategies employed by Roman culture to appropriate and reintegrate traits expelled from the masculine psyche, Catullus's poems, though hardly unique, are singular in their intensity and so reflect the strained conditions under which they were composed.

Of course, male escape into a female subject position does nothing to alleviate real power imbalances between the sexes. Thus Richlin finds "no exit from gender hierarchy" in cross-sex identification with oppressed heroines: insofar as the female remains the "site of violence," the fantasy reinforces male claims to domination (1992e: 173–78). Gutzwiller and Michelini in fact contend that Catullus and the elegists indirectly reassert a male ethos through their rhetorical exploitation of a "posture of subservience" (1991: 76–77). It would be unduly optimistic to assume that an inherent cultural instability in Roman gender roles and an ambiguity in the construction of social masculinity would have had positive consequences for women as a group. The most one can say is that individual women may well have used those uncertainties in the sex/gender system as leverage in negotiating advantages for themselves.

In analyzing Roman gender dissonance, however, my object was not to investigate its influence upon the material conditions of women's lives but to demonstrate its cultural specificity by linking it to a coherent set of sexual protocols. The erotic posture adopted by the Catullan elegiac speaker has been shown to parallel the construction of masculinity in the Attis myth: despite their strangeness, both are reflexes of prevailing sexual ideology. Although much of what it meant to be a Roman man—to *be* Catullus or a member of his immediate audience—will forever escape us, an informed grasp of ancient sexual constructs consequently allows us to project ourselves into a mode of male subjectivity foreign to us.

Moreover, even if it contributes little to our understanding of actual dealings between the sexes in antiquity, to read Catullus within the framework of Roman gender expectations is nevertheless an instructive experience. Audience responses programmed into his texts remove contemporary cultural blinkers by troubling the "natural" connection between biological and social manifestations of masculinity that underpins our own sex/gender system, thereby permitting the researcher to gain a firmer purchase on her own ingrained assumptions. For a woman like me to identify with the Roman man who identifies with women is thus to occupy an intermediate place within our nexus of genders, one distanced from prevailing sexual dimorphism and perhaps at one remove from ideology.

Notes

1. I speak as a social constructionist who regards human sexual activity as so mediated by culture, even at the most rudimentary level, that isolating any purely biological and supposedly universal component of sex or gender relations is an impossible task. The three volumes of Foucault's *Histoire de Sexualité*, first appearing in English translation in 1978, 1985, and 1986 respectively, are widely considered to offer the definitive paradigm for a constructionist approach to sexual behavior both modern and ancient. For an overview of the current debate over Foucault and constructionism in the field of classical studies, see now Skinner 1996.

2. On parallels between the language of the epigrams and passages in Ariadne's lament, see Adler 1981: 146–48.

3. For Roman audience empathy with the first-person speaker, see Richlin (1992a: 32–56), who contends that it is a precondition for the appreciation of both erotic poetry and its antithesis, satire. Expected responses programmed into Catullan texts are well analyzed by Adler (1981), Selden (1992), and Fitzgerald (1995: 34–58). Pedrick (1986) remarks that "Catullan poetry is striking in its eagerness not simply to engage readers but actually to control their reactions to the text and hence, their understanding of it" (187–88).

4. The most egregious example of this approach is Rankin 1962; see also Mulroy 1977–78.

5. The line of interpretation that makes Catullus 63 into a fictive reprise of the Lesbia affair begins with Harkins 1959 and is continued by Genovese 1970, Forsyth 1976, and Sienkewicz 1981. Bagg 1965: 83–88 and Putnam 1974 concentrate upon the parallel between the allegorical destruction of Catullus's manhood in 11.21–24 and Attis's self-emasculation. Although Wiseman (1985: 198–206) hypothesizes that poem 63 was a hymn commissioned for the Megalesia, he is nevertheless convinced that "the experience of Catullus the lover is acted out on the opera-stage of myth and legend" (182) and that the poet may therefore have had "his own reasons for accepting the commission" (206).

6. Contra Paglia 1990, who insists that the female-dominant mythic scenario encapsulates the raw truth of nature.

7. On the mythic pattern itself, see Boedeker 1974: 64–84, and Stehle 1990: 88–125.

8. In the fifth century C.E., the African physician Caelius Aurelianus pronounces that boys and old men are alike in inclining toward passive anal sex (*De morbis chronicis* 4.9.137; text in Drabkin 1950: 904). The active role must therefore be understood as only a temporary stage in the adult male life-cycle.

9. For the *kinaidos* as an emblem of deviant masculinity, consult Winkler, 1990: 45–70 (= Halperin, Winkler, and Zeitlin 1990a: 171–209). In the Athenian polis, Winkler contends, sexual surveillance was applied only to politically active elite males. By the second century C.E., however, any individual, male or female, was liable to scrutiny for signs of gender deviance (Gleason 1995: 55–81). On Roman antipathy toward the *cinaedus*, see the definitive study by Richlin (1993b).

10. Golden (1984) argues that certain conventions of Athenian pederasty distinguished freeborn youths from partners of lower status, such as slaves and women, and so minimized the risks during the transitional period of sexual subordination. But Aristotle (*Eth. Nic.* 7.5, 1148b27–31) notes that those who have suffered sexual penetration from boyhood (*tois hubrizomenois ek paidōn*) may through habit develop a taste for it and become lifelong pathics, and the author of [Arist.] *Pr.* 4.26 also warns of inclination to passivity arising from repeated penetration.

11. To cite just one famous example, Cicero (*Cael.* 10) makes a strong appeal to public moral sentiment when he describes youth as *illud tempus aetatis quod ipsum sua sponte infirmum, aliorum autem libidine infestum est*, "That time of life that is suggestible of its own accord and, moreover, vulnerable to the lust of others." For ingenuousness and sexual ambiguity as significant elements in Roman literary portraits of adolescent males, cf. Nugent 1990.

12. One exception is Näsström (1989: 25–26), who rejects Quinn's reading of 63 because he allegedly typifies Attis as a "homosexual," a category that did not exist in antiquity. Quinn, however, never applies the term "homosexual" to Attis, but instead refers to him throughout as a *puer delicatus*.

13. Clay 1995, which appeared shortly after the original version of this essay was published, offers an independent reading of Catullus 63 that agrees with many of the conclusions presented here.

14. Fordyce 1961: 265 glosses *nimio* as *maximo*. Kroll (1968: 133) comments "wohl einfach = *magno*," but cites Hippolytus's rejection of Aphrodite as a parallel for Attis's state of mind. Baehrens (1885: 342) remarks that this use of *nimius* "accedit ad notionem eius quod modum iam excedit."

15. The salient example is Ovid's Narcissus (*Met.* 3.339–510). Like Attis, he is repulsed by sexual contact: *sed fuit in tenera tam dura superbia forma, / nulli illum iuvenes, nullae tetigere puellae* (3.354–55; note the reminiscence of Catull. 62.44).

16. Amy Richlin's insight, expressed in private correspondence.

17. On this exceptional use of feminine forms in Catullus 63, see Fordyce 1961: 264, and Quinn 1973: 286–87. Several feminine agreements, like *adorta* (11) and *allocuta* (49), are metrically guaranteed. Mynors's O.C.T., followed by Fordyce, accepts Guarinus's substitution of the feminine for MSS. *ipse* (45) and Lachmann's corrections *excitam* (42), *teneramque* (88), and *illa* (89).

18. The structuralist analysis of Adonis by Detienne (1977) is well known; for criticisms of his approach, however, see Winkler 1990: 198–202, and Stehle 1990: 94–100. On Melanion, see Vidal-Naquet 1986; for Pentheus, Hippolytus, and

other tragic manifestations of the "failed ephebe," consult Segal 1982: 164–68. Add now Clay 1995: 145–46.

19. The wish to divorce Catullus from emotional involvement with his text seems to inform Elder's surmise that he composed it to "indulge his own virtuosity" (1947: 396) and likewise to underlie Hutchinson's claim of finding "an exhaustive Ovidian ingenuity in the exploration of the paradoxical calamity" (1988: 313).

20. Once more I am obligated to Amy Richlin for drawing my attention to the fact that "Attis' very Greekness," as well as his self-castration, makes him "the embodiment of what any Roman male would fear for himself" (private communication). Differing perspectives on the Roman tendency to associate pederasty, and male homoerotic relations generally, with Greece and the Greek East are proffered by MacMullen 1982; Hallett 1988: 1272, and Edwards 1993: 92–97. To discredit hostile Greek witnesses from Asia Minor, Cicero in his speech *Pro Flacco* baldly appeals to Roman prejudice against the "effete oriental": see especially 51, where the leitmotiv of perjury is skillfully intertwined with insinuations of sexual depravity.

21. Anxiety over the male body itself emerges as a dominant theme in later Roman medical writings. See especially Rousselle 1988: 5–23. Peter Brown (1988: 10) observes: "In the Roman world, the physical appearance and the reputed character of eunuchs acted as constant reminders that the male body was a fearsomely plastic thing." My thanks to Jody Rubin Pinault for this reference.

22. A digest of the learning displayed in this passage is provided by Bailey 1947: 898–909.

23. Stehle 1989: 153–56 persuasively argues that Roman adoption of the Asiatic cult of Cybele in the second century B.C.E. would have reaffirmed key elements of public political and social ideology. My concern here, however, is with those refractory attributes of the foreign goddess that evaded this legitimating framework.

24. The impact of political upheaval on private consciousness has recently been observed by other Roman historians. Analysis of the obsession with gladiators and human freaks during the late Republic and early Empire leads Barton to conclude that cultural fascination with such figures was a compensatory mechanism for relieving "an enormous sense of loss of status and identity" caused by civil disruptions and the onset of the monarchy (1993: 187–89). In a corollary vein, Edwards 1993 establishes that lurid charges of vice and dissipation among the aristocracy constituted a discourse of self-definition and a means of regulating tensions over authority and social standing.

25. In later generations of Latin authors, physical impotence becomes an explicit topos: cf. Hor. *Epod.* 8 and 12; Tib. 1.5.39–44; Ov. *Am.* 3.7; the Priapean poem *"Quid hoc novi est?"* (*App. Verg.* pp. 151–53 O.C.T. = 83 Bücheler); and Petron. *Sat.* 132. Though all of the above passages deal frankly with sexual dysfunction, the real issue at stake is not the speaker's loss of virility per se but its humiliating proof of the body's capacity to refuse the demands of the will. For impotence as a priapic motif, see Richlin 1992a: 116–20.

26. On *mollitia* as a "feminizing" trope, see Kennedy 1993: 31–34.

27. Lyne (1980: 25–26) denies that this terminology is specifically political,

maintaining that it belongs instead to a "language of aristocratic commitment and obligation" widely applicable to all manner of contractual situations among the Roman elite. While the latter claim is true, Lyne's refusal to concede that contemporary political circumstances have any bearing on the lover's dilemma leads him to dismiss the epigrams as unsuccessful literary experiments. Fitzgerald (1995: 114–39) argues more convincingly that, even as it dramatizes the peculiar nature of poetic discourse and the isolated position of its speaker, Catullus's appropriation of this language of obligation adumbrates the "increasing fragility of aristocratic political and social relations in the closing years of the Republic" through "a fantasy of absolute commitment possible only in some other world" (134).

28. Wiseman (1985: 101–15) rightly calls attention to Catullus's conservative background and moral outlook.

29. That a patronage relationship between a noblewoman and a man of lesser rank was permissible in Roman society is indicated by the case of Sextus Roscius, who, threatened with a prosecution for parricide, appeals to Caecilia Metella as his hereditary protector (Cic. *Rosc. Am.* 27). On this and other instances of elite female patronage, see Dixon 1983.

30. Contrary to Ross's view that *foedus*, when used of political alliances, "always refers to a relationship of *amicitia* between equals" (1969: 85), Vinson (1992) establishes that such alliances, though seemingly egalitarian, normally contain hidden power imbalances. A structural asymmetry of this kind, she argues, is inscribed into Catullus's romantic *foedus amicitiae*. On the conversely unequal "patronage" relationship between the poet/lover of elegy and his textualized *domina*, see now Gold 1993b.

31. Here I expressly differ from Richlin (1992e), who, though allowing for possible momentary reader identification with Ovid's raped heroines, ultimately defines them as pornographic objects.

SIX

THE EROTICS OF *AMICITIA*: READINGS IN TIBULLUS, PROPERTIUS, AND HORACE

Ellen Oliensis

T HE SUBJECT of this essay is the conjunction, within Augustan poetry, of two relationships: lover and beloved, and client and patron.[1] These relationships are hinged together by the figure of the poet, who typically casts himself both as a lover and as a client—a double role that begets some interesting complications, as I hope to show.

Let me begin by noting that the lover and the client intersect not only in the person of the poet but also in the ideologically charted space of the city. A man who happened to be out and about near daybreak in first-century B.C.E. Rome might witness this intersection, a kind of "changing of the guard": disheveled young men staggering home after a night spent on the doorstep of a beloved, while toga-clad clients scurry toward a patron's door in anticipation of the morning reception. If our early riser followed the same path each morning over a period of months, noting the size of the throng at each door and plotting its rate of growth or decline, he might learn quite a bit about the current state and future direction of Roman erotics and politics. So Horace can needle a fading beauty by describing the desertion of her door, now left to its own devices (*amatque / ianua limen, Carm.* 1.25.3–4); Catullus's Attis recalls, with nostalgic pride, waking to find his doors thronged and sills warmed (*mihi ianuae frequentes, mihi limina tepida*, 63.65) by the bodies of his ardent admirers; and Cicero remarks, with mixed feelings, that his morning reception is of late "even more thronged than usual" (*etiam frequentius quam solebat, Fam.* 7.28.2). The throng at the door both indicates and enhances the authority of the inhabitant, and attendance at the door may be described as a central duty of both lovers and clients, a duty that identifies them as such.[2]

This essay has accumulated many debts in the course of its protracted gestation. Thanks are due here to W. S. Anderson, John Bodel, Wendell Clausen, Cynthia Damon, David Konstan, Daniel Mendelsohn, Pavlos Sfyroeras, John Shoptaw, Gordon Williams, the Princeton University Press readers, and the editors of this volume for their suggestions and criticisms. All translations are my own.

If the paths of the lover and the client cross near dawn, this crossing is not accidental but symptomatic of what Mario Labate (1984: 214) terms a "profound homogeneity." In the pursuit of their disparate goals, the client and the lover are represented as displaying similar virtues (constancy, discretion, eloquence) and encountering comparable obstacles (the machinations of rivals, the fickleness of patron or beloved). Indeed, Horace's advice to would-be clients in his first book of *Epistles* is duplicated, almost point for point, by the amatory teachings of the elegists. As Labate has demonstrated, accommodation (*obsequium*), the chief virtue of underlings, is central to both didactic schemes. Both the client and the lover are instructed to suit their mood, conversation, and interests to those of the patron or beloved. Both should be ready to provide an escort wherever and whenever the patron or beloved chooses. Both should beware of succumbing to the charms of the patron's or beloved's slaves. Both should set aside their own business if the patron or beloved (naturally a *puer*, in this case) chooses to go hunting. Both should know how to keep a secret. In short, to borrow the terminology of a later age, both should study the arts of the courtier.[3]

And yet the seeming symmetry of the two pursuits is, in crucial respects, a cultivated illusion. First, within the dominant ideology of Rome, the client is a respectable, the lover a disreputable, figure. If some amorous dalliance may be forgiven the young, a mature Roman is expected to devote his energies, as a client or a patron or both in turn, to the network of relations between men that constitutes the fabric of Roman society.[4] The very names we associate with the lover's and the client's characteristic forms of attendance, the *paraklausithyron* and the *salutatio*, are redolent of their differences: night, pleasure, and Greek frivolity on one side, daylight, business, and the profoundly Roman *mos maiorum* on the other. By presenting his amours as the equivalent of a public career, a love poet pretends to a certain (mock) legitimacy. But even the elegists will often concede that love is properly a prelude or interlude, subordinate to the overriding concerns of public life.

Second, there is an ineradicable difference in the distribution of power within the two relationships. Whereas patrons by definition rank higher than their clients, the beloved celebrated in Latin poetry is generally represented as ranking below her or his admirers.[5] Moreover, although the rhetoric of love poetry tends to insist that the lover is vanquished, crushed, enslaved by his all-powerful beloved, the ease with which the poet-lover typically deploys this rhetoric suggests that his abjection is less than absolute. The poet plays the slave within a fiction of his own masterful making. In this sense, the power of the beloved is always his gift, and dependent on his willingness to keep playing.[6] She (it is most often she)[7] falls into the rhetorical control of the pleading poet, who uses her for his own poetic purposes. In the last analysis, it is the poet who makes her yield in certain poems and refuse in others; it is he who endows her with beauty, and takes it away, or even kills her off, as and when he likes, thereby begetting a poetic corpus forever associated with her name—not, of course, her proper name, but the name he has given her, the name that bespeaks his poetry: Lesbia, Delia, Cynthia, Laura, Stella. . . .[8] By contrast, the poet cannot simply do what he likes with a Messalla, a Maecenas, or an Augustus. The patron, who always bears his own name, can never be as pure a variable in the poetic equation as the *puella*.

Even if we grant that the beloved's conventional pseudonym masks a real woman (or boy) who exercises real power, psychosexual if not sociopolitical, over the poet, the use of the pseudonym licenses the poet to treat the beloved as a prop of his poetry. Chameleonlike, she blends right into the verse in which she appears. By contrast, the patron's proper name, never quite assimilated, joins a fictive world, where the poet is theoretically omnipotent, to a world in which his power is relative and limited.[9] The presence of the patron's name makes the poem a public and consequential act, one closely if indefinably related to its extraliterary counterpart. A poem can be a pledge of allegiance or a notice of divorce, an excuse or an accusation, a piece of flattery or a disillusioned disavowal. The lover may dramatize these gestures as episodes in an ongoing tumultuous affair, but the client needs to be more circumspect. Although it may be true that the power of a patron is nothing more than the sum total of others' regard, and that the client, like the lover, can, and no doubt often did, abandon his patron's door, such an abandonment is likely to have significant ramifications. The paraklausithyron may serve, then, as a kind of compensation: one can get up and leave *this* door with impunity—even if one never does. The hyperbolic fiction of erotic enslavement enables the poet both to represent and temporarily to escape the complex reality, at once literary and extraliterary, of subordination to a patron.

The superficial resemblance between the lover and the client masks, then, a radical difference: the one feigns subjection, the other experiences it. The client's subordinate status aligns him finally not with the lover but with the beloved, not with the masculine subject but with the feminine or effeminate object of desire. Horace makes the point with venomous clarity in *Epistles* 1.17, where a social climber who fancies himself the very type of virile fortitude[10] discovers his true image in the mercenary courtesan. A man who accompanies his patron on a trip should not be forever complaining about the road, the weather, and the robbers, Horace warns, since such behavior "recalls the old tricks of the courtesan" (*nota refert meretricis acumina, Epist.* 1.17.55) who laments the theft of her jewelry once too often. The analogy recurs at the beginning of the next epistle, to Lollius (*Epist.* 1.18.1-4):

Si bene te novi, metues, liberrime Lolli,
scurrantis speciem praebere, professus amicum.
ut matrona meretrici dispar erit atque
discolor, infido scurrae distabit amicus.

If I know you, my most outspoken Lollius, you'll be worried that you may wear the appearance of a parasite, when you have set up as a friend. As a matron will be different in kind and color from a courtesan, so a friend will differ from a faithless parasite.

The analogy seems apt. Like a virtuous wife, a true client looks beyond immediate material gratifications to the spiritual and social benefits of a lasting friendship. Like a courtesan, by contrast, a debased client is a fair-weather friend, who sells his services—his visible presence at the door and in the great man's retinue, his adulation, his vote, his poetry—in return for a patron's material support.[11] The association between client and prostitute culminates in the wry envoy to *Epistles* 1, where Horace personifies his book as a pretty slave-boy foolishly eager to market his charms on the street corners of Rome. True, there is a vast difference between a freeborn and wealthy *amicus* such as Horace and the shameless self-prostituting character that he attributes to his book. Still, while it may be easy enough to distinguish a *matrona* from a *meretrix*, it is notoriously difficult to tell a flatterer from a friend;[12] no public ceremony, no style of dress, no social formula or legal record sets the one apart from the other, and the difference between them may be only a matter of degree. It is worth pointing out, moreover, that the analogy heading the epistle to Lollius casts every dependent *amicus* as a woman—the worse sort as a courtesan, the better sort as a wife, but a woman in either case.

To complicate matters further, this casting comes dangerously close to typecasting. A client's subordination to his patron may itself be suspected of having a sexual component. *Amicitia* and *amor* are not only cognate, they also share the same hierarchical structure, since what counts, in the sexual ideology of Rome, is less the gender of the participants than their respective roles: active or passive, penetrating or penetrated, dominant or submissive.[13] Penetration is the prerogative of free men, penetrability the characteristic condition of slaves and women; sexual intercourse is an enactment and reflection of social hierarchy, and, conversely, social subordination always implies the possibility of sexual submission. Hence the common storyline linking sexual passivity to social mobility. For example, according to the Suetonian *Vita*, the playwright Terence, brought to Rome as a slave and freed at an early age "on account of his talent and good looks" (*ob ingenium et formam*), was alleged by some to have used his body to endear himself to Scipio and Laelius (*quibus etiam corporis gratia conciliatus existimatur*). The success of the freeborn could be explained in the same way, and eminent citizens were regularly accused of sleeping their way to the top.[14] Any asymmetrical relation between Roman men is conceivably also a sexual relation, in which the superior (more powerful, more eminent, older, wealthier) takes pleasure from the inferior. The *obsequium* of a freeborn client can always be maliciously misconstrued as a readiness to perform any service, including sexual service.

As the orator Haterius famously observed, sexual submission (*impudicitia*) is "necessity for a slave, duty (*obsequium*) for a freedman" (Sen. *Controv.* 4, praef. 10). The sexual liability of society's lower orders is a common theme of the "lower" genres of Latin literature.[15] But the convergence of social and sexual subordination also leaves traces (and not only in the predictable form of invective) on the upper strata of Roman society and poetry. The rest of this chapter will focus on the cross-fertilization of friendship by sexual love, *amicitia* by *amor*, in the poetry of Tibullus, Propertius, and Horace.[16] My aim is to begin to explore how these poets deflect, acknowledge, exploit, or otherwise manage the erotic potential of the *amicitiae* in which their poems participate.

Patron and beloved make an almost simultaneous entrance onto the stage of Tibullan elegy (1.1.53–58):

> te bellare decet terra, Messalla, marique,
>   ut domus hostiles praeferat exuvias:
> me retinent vinctum formosae vincla puellae,
>   et sedeo duras ianitor ante fores.
> non ego laudari curo, mea Delia: tecum
>   dum modo sim, quaeso segnis inersque vocer.

> It becomes you, Messalla, to wage war on land and sea, so that your house may sport enemy spoils; as for me, the chains of a beautiful girl hold me fast, and I sit guard outside an unyielding door. I don't care about glory, my Delia: so long as I'm with you, I'm happy to be called a sluggard and a do-nothing.

Declining to accompany Messalla on campaign, Tibullus paints himself as a faithful lover but an unreliable client. And yet by publicizing Messalla's military excellence, Tibullus pays tribute to his patron as only a poet can. It is no accident that Messalla is named and apostrophized first in this poem, before Delia. The direct address implicitly privileges Messalla above the generic *puella* who is the third person in this triangle. (Consider how different the effect would be if Tibullus had written something like: "It is fitting for me to stay at your door, Delia; let my powerful friend wage war against Rome's enemies.") Delia, moreover, makes a graceful excuse; Messalla might well have been offended if Tibullus had pleaded a prior engagement not to a pseudonymous *puella* but to another eminent *amicus*. The imperious *puella* who intervenes between *te* and *me* is thus herself subordinate to an overarching decorum that privileges *amicitia* over *amor*. Nor does Tibullus aspire to parity with his great friend. Although *te* and *me* are formally parallel, they function quite differently within the syntax of their respective couplets. Whereas Messalla is a conquering hero, Tibullus, far from triumphing in the field of love, is merely the spoils of Delia's erotic campaign, a decoration for her door. Tibullus is not only no match for his heroic friend, he is also the slave of a woman, hence (the story goes) doubly unmanned.[17]

This twofold subjection causes some interesting problems in the fifth elegy, where Tibullus makes the mistake of bringing Messalla and Delia together. In this account of his latest disappointment, Tibullus describes how he devoted himself to Delia's cure during a dangerous illness. Now Delia is well, and another man enjoys her favor. A disillusioned Tibullus recalls his fantasy of a blissful country life spent with Delia. As the fantasy develops, Delia assumes more and more power until Tibullus dwindles away to invisibility: "She would rule everyone, she would take thought for everything; as for me, I'd take pleasure in being a nobody in the house" (*illa regat cunctos, illi sint omnia curae: / at iuvet in tota me nihil esse domo*, 1.5.29–30). It is at this point that Messalla is invited to join the happy couple in their country retreat, with predictable results (1.5.31–34):

> huc veniet Messalla meus, cui dulcia poma
>   Delia selectis detrahat arboribus:
> et tantum venerata decus, hunc sedula curet,[18]
>   huic paret atque epulas ipsa ministra gerat.

Hither will come my Messalla, for whom Delia will pluck sweet apples from choice trees; in reverence for his greatness, she'll tend him sedulously, she'll prepare and serve his dinner with her own hands.

The vacuum left by Tibullus is filled by Messalla. But the great Messalla is not to be imagined as courting Delia. Rather, it is Delia who assumes the posture of the suitor: she courts Messalla with apples, reveres him as if he were a god, and waits on him as if she were his slave. "Sweet" apples from "choice" trees: the qualifications signal Tibullus's sympathetic participation in Delia's humble wooing.[19] It is as if Tibullus meant to say that all his poetic resources, including Delia, were at his patron's service.

Still, the implications are troubling. In this all-too-familiar triangle, drawn straight from the elegiac repertoire, the poet's rich friend is typecast as the rich lover, the perennial rival of the elegist.[20] As Messalla's faithful client, moreover, Tibullus is impotent to contest this usurpation; he can only watch as events take their inevitable course. It is no wonder, then, that the image of Delia serving Messalla punctures Tibullus's daydream, returning him to the unhappy present, of which it is a mirror. Tibullus goes on to rewrite the story so that the villains are not Messalla and Delia but rather an unnamed "rich lover" (*dives amator*, 47) and "clever bawd" (*callida lena*, 48) who have conspired to corrupt his beloved. But the shade of Messalla lingers, influencing the rhetoric of Tibullus's final plea (1.5.61–64):

> pauper erit praesto tibi semper: pauper adibit
> primus et in tenero fixus erit latere,
> pauper in angusto fidus comes agmine turbae
> subicietque manus efficietque viam.

A poor man will always be there for you: a poor man will be the first to approach and to affix himself to your delicate side; a faithful escort in the narrow column of the crowd, he'll give you a hand and clear you a path.

This is recognizably the language of *clientela*, if of a distinctly servile variety; this lover's plea reads equally well, if not better, as a client's self-advertisement.[21] But the resemblance only underscores the contrast between amatory and clientary codes. Although Tibullus may grovel before Delia, he would never publish his willingness to offer such obsequious attentions to Messalla. Unlike the lover, the client is not cushioned by a residual masculine superiority; when he humbles himself before his patron, there is nothing between him and the ground. Moreover, the client who grovels effectively reduces his own value; gestures of excessive deference are self-defeating.

Propertius is much readier than Tibullus to flirt with the erotic possibilities of *amicitia*.[22] In his *propemptikon* or "bon voyage" poem to Tullus, the dedicatee of his first book of elegies, Propertius, like Tibullus in his first elegy, declines to accompany his friend on a trip to the east on the grounds that he is detained by the love of a girl, held fast by her words (*verba*, 5)—her prayers (*preces*, 6), laments (*queritur*, 8), and threats (*minatur*, 9). If Propertius were to embark, Cynthia would batter him with her own reproachful propemptikon, countering the lure of "cultured Athens" (*doctas . . . Athenas*, 13) and "Asia's riches" (*Asiae . . . divitias*, 14) with an irresistible rhetorical display: "She would score her face with mad hands and say that she owes kisses to the adverse wind, and that nothing is harder than a faithless man" (*insanis ora notet manibus, / osculaque opposito dicat sibi debita vento / et nihil infido durius esse viro*, 16–18).[23] Propertius will not risk the storm of Cynthia's anger, and the energetic Tullus should set off on his mission, abandoning his friend to his life of erotic indolence.

At this point, the poem takes a famous final turn. While Tullus journeys to "soft Ionia" (*mollis . . . Ionia*, 31) or to "Lydian fields" (*Lydia . . .*

arata, 32), Propertius will be suffering back home: "If perchance there comes to you an hour not unmindful of me, you will be sure that I'm living under a hard star" (*tum tibi si qua mei veniet non immemor hora, / vivere me duro sidere certus eris*, 35–36). It is now Tullus who enjoys a "soft" luxurious life while Propertius heroically endures his "hard" star.[24] And it is no longer Cynthia who comes between the friends, but two other ladies, Ionia and Lydia[25]—fair temptresses who have seduced Tullus from Propertius's faithful side. There is more than a hint of pathos in the phrase *non immemor hora*. Is Tullus, then, so likely to forget his long-suffering friend? Taken as a whole, the poem replicates, in a milder tone, the strategy of Cynthia's *verba* and *preces*. Propertius has transformed a client's excuse into a beloved's reproach: the problem is not that Propertius is staying behind, but that Tullus is leaving.

Propertius's poems to Gallus, whom he addresses not as a patron but as a peer, offer a more intoxicating blend of *amor* and *amicitia*. As the first poem of the series opens, Propertius is trying to get an unnamed busybody off his back: "Envious man, will you at long last check those annoying comments of yours and let the pair of us continue on our course?" (*Invide, tu tandem voces compesce molestas / et sine nos cursu, quo sumus, ire pares!* 1.5.1–2). Perhaps the man wants to experience Propertius's passion firsthand (*meos sentire furores*, 3)? If so, Propertius warns, he will regret it; crushed by love, he will end by fleeing to Propertius's door (*mea . . . ad limina curres*, 13). At this point we might expect Propertius to bar his door against his addressee and to enjoy a superior laugh at his expense. But Propertius is not out for revenge; the poem does not present us with the conventional seesaw, which elevates one man at the expense of another (e.g., Hor. *Epod.* 15.23–24; Prop. 2.9.1–2). Instead, the passion the two men share for a woman Propertius now terms, with a suggestive poetic plural, the first of several in this poem, "our girl" (*nostrae puellae*, 19), only brings them closer together. Propertius will open his door and his arms to his unfortunate comrade, offering him what solace he can: "Equally wretched in the love we share, we will be driven to weep mutual tears on each other's breast" (*pariter miseri socio cogemur amore / alter in alterius mutua flere sinu*, 29–30). If there is no reciprocity to be found in loving a haughty *puella*, the lovers may at least exchange tears over her withheld body.

In the course of the poem, Propertius has transformed his rival into a mirror image of himself: pale, thin, tongue-tied, helpless, ridiculous. Out of an envious ill-wisher he has constructed an ideal friend, a perfectly sympathetic alter ego. It is not just that misery loves company. The mutual embrace of these twinned lovers is charged with the energy of their thwarted passion, as *amor* is channeled back into *amicitia*. This diversion of *amor*, which I take to be the central project of the poem, is ostentatiously signaled by the transfer of the quality of "parity" from Propertius and his *puella*, who are represented as a pair (*ire pares*, 2) in the poem's opening lines, to Propertius and his rival, imagined as "peers in amorous misery" (*pariter miseri*, 29) as the poem closes.[26] The *puella* of 1.5 is little more than a device for producing this erotically heightened mutuality.[27]

Only at this point, after the poem has arrived at what seems to be its final destination, does Propertius name both his girlfriend and his friend: "And so stop asking, Gallus, what my Cynthia can do: not without exacting a penalty does she come when invoked" (*quare, quid possit mea Cynthia, desine, Galle / quaerere: non impune illa rogata venit*, 31–32). The tacked-on couplet, with its two proper names, seems to be the punchline to what is revealed in retrospect to be a joke. It is tempting to speculate that this joke had a literary flavor, with "Cynthia" designating not only Propertius's girlfriend but also the poetry in which she is celebrated, and "Gallus" naming not just an inquisitive friend but a famous elegiac poet.[28] It is as if the senior elegist had kindly inquired on the progress of Propertius's little book, perhaps even asking for a sample. What Propertius offers Gallus is both a text and a woman—two "Cynthias" endowed, moreover, with equivalent powers of seduction. When Propertius envisions the friends exchanging tears, *mutua flere*, he may have in mind not only lovers' tears but also the fluent laments of elegy.[29] The elegiac fiction of amorous abasement renders all lovers equal, and the medium of poetry, like the mediating *puella*, allows friends to enjoy the pleasures of perfect reciprocity—in turn exuding tears and absorbing them, giving and receiving, writing and reading.[30] This concluding fantasy may be modeled on Catullus's famous account of his own eroticized poetic encounter with Licinius Calvus (Catull. 50), where the two poets, having "agreed to be dainty" (*ut convenerat esse delicatos*, 50.3; the adjective is typically applied to the effeminate *pueri* who are the conventional objects of male desire), reciprocate each other's verses (*reddens mutua*, Catull. 50.6). Indeed, whether or not Propertius's Gallus is the famous Gallus, his contact with Cynthia effectively transforms him into a poet capable of reciprocating Propertius's elegiac tears.[31]

In 1.10, Propertius returns to Gallus, and this time the friends are sharing not amorous misery but amorous conquest. The tears shed by Gallus and his new girlfriend are an index of pleasure, not grief (1.10.1–3):

> O iucunda quies, primo cum testis amori
> affueram vestris conscius in lacrimis!
> o noctem meminisse mihi iucunda voluptas.

O delicious repose, when I witnessed your love's birth and was privy to your tears! O what delicious pleasure to remember that night.

It is not by chance that the ecstatic tone anticipates the opening of 2.15 (*o me felicem! o nox mihi candida*, etc.), where Propertius celebrates his own sexual felicity; the spectacle of Gallus in his mistress's arms affords Propertius scarcely less pleasure than the sexual act itself. Embedded as it is in this scene of sexual intercourse, *testis* in line 1 bears a trace of its anatomical meaning; it is as if Propertius had been transformed into an adjunct of Gallus's lovemaking equipment. The merging of two male bodies into one is given a mythological precedent in 1.13, a poem commemorating the same evening, where Propertius invokes the image of Neptune "mingling" with the river Enipeus so as to make love to Tyro (*non sic Haemonio Salmonida mixtus Enipeo / Taenarius facili pressit amore deus*, 1.13.21–22)—an apt emblem of Propertius's vicarious participation in Gallus's sexual act. If in 1.5 Gallus was an envious onlooker (*invide*, 1), in 1.10 and 1.13 Propertius is thoroughly gratified by what he sees (cf. *vidimus* at 1.10.6, *vidi ego* at 1.13.14 and 15). In return for this pleasurable viewing, Propertius offers Gallus his considerable skills as a doctor of love. Whereas in 1.5 the poet warned that he was powerless to help another (*non ego tum potero*, 27), in 1.10 he says emphatically the opposite (1.10.15–17):

> possum ego diversos iterum coniungere amantis,
>   et dominae tardas possum aperire fores;
>   et possum alterius curas sanare recentis.

I have the power to rejoin parted lovers, I have the power to open a mistress's sluggish door, I have the power to cure another's fresh pains.

Gallus's potency begets an answering potency in Propertius, a moment of mastery over both himself and his *puella*. Here as earlier, the two friends fall and rise together.

By the time we reach 1.13, however, the friends' fates have diverged. Two relationships are askew in the poem's opening lines. Propertius is doubly deceived, both in his *amicus* and in his *amor*: "You will as usual be pleased by my misfortune, Gallus—that my love has been stolen away, leaving me bereft and alone" (*Tu, quod saepe soles, nostro laetabere casu, / Galle, quod abrepto solus amore vacem*, 1–2). Propertius, by contrast, sides with fidelity, both in friendship and in love: he won't imitate Gallus's treachery by wishing upon him the kind of erotic betrayal he himself has suffered (*at non ipse tuas imitabor, perfide, voces: / fallere te numquam, Galle, puella velit*, 3–4). These contiguous relationships come to be emotionally if not logically intertwined. Although Propertius says nothing more about the betrayals he has suffered, he has plenty to say about those Gallus has perpetrated. For Gallus is, it emerges, by nature a philanderer (*dum tibi deceptis augetur fama puellis,* 5), a perfidious lover as well as a treacherous friend. It is because Gallus's various girlfriends represent Propertius that Propertius is so intent on proving that Gallus, for all his denials, really is desperately in love with the *puella* of 1.10. By subjecting him to one all-absorbing passion, this *puella* will punish Gallus for his mistreatment not only of his prior girlfriends but also of his friend. Propertius's memory of the marvelous first night of love described in 1.10 is accordingly colored in 1.13 by vengeful anger. Where in 1.10 Gallus was pleasurably dying, sighing, and murmuring in his girlfriend's arms, in 1.13 he is burned up by her heat like Hercules on his funeral pyre (23–24; the image colors the otherwise conventional *faces* at 26 and *ardor* at 28). Sexual union is now less a pleasure than a torment. As in 1.5, a powerful *puella* reduces Gallus to impotence, restoring the parity between friends that Cynthia's infidelity disrupted.

The last poem addressed to Gallus, 1.20, snaps the narrative thread loosely linking the three earlier poems. But while there is no mention here of Gallus's *puella* (or, for that matter, of Propertius's), the rhetoric of the poem is familiar. As in 1.10, Propertius offers Gallus advice on keeping a beloved (in this case not a girl but a boy): "Here's my advice for you, Gallus, in token of our [or: in the interests of a] lasting love" (*Hoc pro continuo te, Galle, monemus amore,* 1.20.1). There follows the cautionary tale of Hylas, the beloved boy whom Hercules lost to the nymphs, and the poem concludes by circling back to its opening: "Thus advised, Gallus, you will keep possession of your love" (*his, o Galle, tuos monitus servabis amores,* 51). As in 1.5, a framing repetition draws attention to the slippery relation between *amor* and *amicitia.* In the opening line of the poem, "love" is most readily understood to refer to the relation between Propertius and Gallus; in the penultimate line, it unmistakably denotes Gallus's beloved "Hylas." Like the girlfriend of 1.5, the boyfriend of 1.20 is the medium for an erotic exchange between men, a triangulation imaged here in Zetes and Calais's joint assault on Hylas (25–28; the episode seems to be Propertius's invention). If Propertius's Gallus is the elegist Gallus, and if (as argued by Ross [1975: 75–81]) this poem is replete with echoes of Gallus's poetry, then Propertius's sympathetic involvement with Gallus may include textual as well as sexual affairs. What better figure for this confluence of passions than Hylas, the boy who, as Vergil famously complained (*G.* 3.6), is on every poet's lips?

But there are other ways of configuring the tumbling triangles of this kaleidoscopic text. In his admonitory role, Propertius is doubled by a certain Ascanius, named at the start of the poem: "Misfortune often overtakes a reckless lover; so Ascanius, cruel to the Minyae, could report" (*saepe imprudenti fortuna occurrit amanti: / crudelis Minyis dixerit Ascanius*, 3–4). Who is this Ascanius? Not the son of Aeneas, but a river in whose neighborhood Hylas disappeared. It is to "untamed Ascanius," we are told, that Hercules wept after losing Hylas (*indomito fleverat Ascanio*, 16). A few lines later, Hercules is termed the "unconquered youth" (*invicti iuvenis*, 23), but this is before he is "conquered" by the loss of Hylas. Another conquest is suggested here: lovesick Hercules weeping before indomitable Ascanius looks like a vanquished elegiac lover weeping before his arrogant beloved. Hovering between the role of adviser and the role of beloved, the personified river represents Propertius's double relation to Gallus. And Ascanius is not the only body of water within this poem to conceal a human form. There is also the Hellespont (*Athamantidos undis*, 19), where Athamas's daughter Helle fell from the back of the golden ram, and of course the fatal spring, haunted by Hylas's reflection and by the rapacious nymphs. These fluid bodies are alluring but dangerous: Hylas, who stretches out his hands to draw water out (*plena trahens*, 44), is himself drawn in and under (*facili traxere liquore*, 47). The watery mirror that seduces Hylas with *blandae imagines* (42) may be read as a figure for the glittering surface of the Propertian page, a text that seduces Gallus—perhaps with the images of his own poetry.

The most extensive documentation of the erotics of the patron-client relation is to be found in the poetry of Horace. It is clear from his early poetry that Horace experienced his relation to Maecenas as a potential threat to his manhood (Fitzgerald 1988; Oliensis 1991). In the odes, however, Horace turns the implicit erotics of *amicitia* to the good.[32] Moreover, though we do not know how (or if) Calvus responded to Catullus or Gallus to Propertius, we are fortunate in having some scraps of Maecenas's poems to Horace, which let us glimpse the other side of this erotic/lyric exchange.

That the two men did engage in such an exchange is argued by Emily A. McDermott (1982), who remarks that a good number of Horace's poems to Maecenas, and both of Maecenas's surviving poems to Horace, are cast as responses to an expressed desire—for poetry (*Epod.* 14; *Carm.* 2.12; *Epist.* 1.1), for reassurance (*Carm.* 2.17; Maecenas fr. 2, fr. 3), for company (*Epist.* 1.7). This recurrent feature suggests that the friends engaged in what McDermott terms "an extended poetic dialogue in somewhat the same tradition as the single evening's entertainment engaged in by Catullus and Calvus" (McDermott 1982: 217). It is certainly possible that Maecenas had the Catullan model in mind. The opening of one of his poems to Horace—"If I don't love you more than my very insides, Horace" (*Ni te visceribus meis, Horati, / plus iam diligo*, fr. 3 Courtney)— mimics the opening of Catullus 14: "If I didn't love you more than my eyes, my most delightful Calvus" (*Ni te plus oculis meis amarem, / iucundissime Calve*, 1–2). In this instance at least, Maecenas played Catullus to Horace's Calvus. Whether the two friends actually carried on a poetic dialogue or just enjoyed the fiction of it, it is clear that each aimed at implicating the other within the net of his verse.

Consider *Odes* 2.12, a coy *recusatio* responding to Maecenas's request for a poem in celebration of Caesar's victories. Horace's opening gambit is to claim that he knows Maecenas better than Maecenas knows himself: "*You* wouldn't want" (*nolis*, 1) "hard" (*durum*, 2) martial themes to be matched with the "soft" (*mollibus*, 3) strains of the lyre. In the third stanza, Horace provokingly suggests that Maecenas tackle the job himself, in the form of a prose history (9–12), a suggestion calculated, as Jasper Griffin (1984: 195–96) has pointed out, to make Maecenas's neoteric heart sink. Having reminded Maecenas of their shared disinclination, Horace shifts to describe the poetry that he is ready to compose. Horace will obey his muse instead of Maecenas and will sing not of savage Numantia but of amiable "mistress Licymnia" (*dominae . . . Licymniae*, 13), whose heart is "truly faithful in mutual love" (*bene mutuis / fidum pectus amoribus*, 15–16). Licymnia's pastimes, elaborated in the ode's fifth stanza, are a placid answer to the warlike themes enumerated in earlier stanzas: suited not to war but to simulated strife (*certare ioco*, 18), she stretches out her arms (*dare bracchia*, 18) not in surrender to an enemy but toward the maidens who are her dancing partners.

We might expect the poem to end with this announcement of Horace's preferred theme. Indeed, the descriptive fifth stanza, which consists of a relative clause (*quam nec ferre pedem . . .*) stemming from the previous stanza's proper name, would make a characteristically Horatian close.[33] If the poem ended here, moreover, its numerical center would be strongly and appropriately marked by the juxtaposition of its two other key proper names: Caesar and Maecenas (*Caesaris, / Maecenas*, across what would be the central line break of 10–11). Instead, Horace appends two extraordinary stanzas, inviting Maecenas to appreciate not only his aesthetics but "mistress Licymnia" too. The chaste image of Licymnia among the maidens is supplanted by a much spicier vignette (21–28):

> num tu quae tenuit dives Achaemenes
> aut pinguis Phrygiae Mygdonias opes
> permutare velis crine Licymniae,
>   plenas aut Arabum domos,
> cum flagrantia detorquet ad oscula
> cervicem aut facili saevitia negat
> quae poscente magis gaudeat eripi,
>   interdum rapere occupet?

Surely you wouldn't be willing to take the property of rich Achaemenes or the Mygdonian wealth of fertile Phrygia or the treasure-laden houses of the Arabs in exchange for a lock of Licymnia's hair, when she twists her neck away for blazing kisses or refuses, with compliant fierceness, kisses she, more than the one who demands them, relishes when they are snatched, and sometimes is beforehand in snatching?

Who is delivering these "blazing kisses"? When Licymnia is named as the subject of Horace's poetry in the third stanza, we tend to assume that she is Horace's mistress. In that case, the final stanzas must be understood as offering Maecenas a tantalizing glimpse of his friend's erotic bliss, inviting Maecenas to take Horace's place, if only in imagination, in Licymnia's arms: "If you were in my shoes, surely you wouldn't trade that happiness for all the wealth of the east?" And yet it seems unlikely that Horace would offer his own pleasure as an excuse for his refusal to comply with his patron's demand. If, as seems more probable, Licymnia is not Horace's mistress but Maecenas's, then the closing stanzas require the reader to correct his earlier assumption and to transfer Licymnia, as it were, from one man to the other. Horace would then be buying Maecenas off with a substitute poem: "Wouldn't you really prefer a poem celebrating your seductive Licymnia?"[34] Still, Horace's intimate knowledge of Licymnia's sexual style remains disconcerting; the stanzas in question seem too heated to constitute acceptable praise of another man's mistress. However one reads the scene, the "other man" hovers very close by the entwined lovers. Whoever Licymnia may be, within this poem she triangulates the desires of two men.[35]

This triangulation does not, however, make the two men peers. The logic of the *recusatio* identifies Horace not with Maecenas but with Licymnia. This may be one reason why Licymnia reciprocates (albeit with a provocative delay) her lover's attentions, as the "mutual love" of the fourth stanza heats up into the twinned infinitives, passive and active (*eripi, rapere*), of the final stanza. Exploiting the inherent dynamics of this conventional literary gesture, Horace has reformulated the *recusatio* as a sexual tease.[36] As the coy poet at once withholds and grants the desired poem, so Licymnia, with her *facilis saevitia*, at once resists and invites the kisses her lover demands (*poscente*, 27)—a double movement nicely encapsulated in the expression *detorquet ad*, "twists away toward." In this scenario, the wealth of "Lydian" Maecenas counts for nothing, since a single lock of Licymnia's hair, like the slender ode that advertises it, holds more pleasure than all the riches of the east. As Horace's seductive rhetoric insists (*nolis, num . . . velis*), Maecenas gets what he really wants. In one of his poems to Horace, Maecenas seems to agree (fr. 2 Courtney):

lucente<s>, mea vita, nec smaragdos
beryllos neque, Flacce mi, nitentes
nec percandida margarita quaero
nec quos Thynica lima perpolivit
anellos nec iaspios lapillos.

> Darling, I'm not interested in brilliant emeralds or shining beryl, my Flac-
> cus, or bright white pearls, or rings polished smooth by Bithynian file, or
> jasper gems.

It is significant that Maecenas addresses Horace, in a meter favored by Catullus, as *mea vita*, an erotically colored endearment (as noted by Courtney 1993: 277) used by Catullus of Lesbia. Maecenas's priamel seems to
lack only its romantic conclusion: "All I want is you." Like a good elegiac
lover, Maecenas would rather stay home with his beloved Horace than
travel the world in quest of exotic riches.[37]

It is not only the elegiac lover but also, and indeed especially, the
beloved who is called upon to resist the lure of wealth. In *Odes* 3.16, Horace confirms his fidelity to Maecenas by rejecting the advances of another, richer man. It is only in the fifth of its eleven stanzas that the poem
announces its addressee and arrives at the familiar themes—the disad-
vantages of wealth, the superior pleasures of the retired life—which will
form its subject (17–20):

crescentem sequitur cura pecuniam
maiorumque fames. iure perhorrui
late conspicuum tollere verticem,
   Maecenas, equitum decus.

> As wealth increases, so does anxiety and the desire for more. I've done right
> to shrink from raising my head high for all to see, Maecenas, ornament of
> the knights.

The poem begins elsewhere, with a series of exempla illustrating the evil
effects of money, not on the rich man, but on the objects of his nefarious
designs. The most elaborate of these exempla is the first: eight lines detailing the measures taken by Acrisius to preserve the virginity of his
daughter Danae, measures that availed him nothing against Jupiter and
Venus, who knew that "there would be a safe and open path for the god
transformed into cash" (*fore enim tutum iter et patens / converso in pretium
deo*, 7–8). The flavor of this exemplary tale is something less than
Olympian: "Acrisius is assimilated by implication to the typical husband
of Augustan love poetry who resorts to locked doors to protect his wife's
virtue; Jove, well-known for his adulterous affairs, to the typical man
about town who knows how to bribe his way past any door" (Quinn

1980: 273). Unlike the elegiac lover, Jupiter will sing no mournful paraklausithyron; the king of the gods has other, more effective means of gaining entrance.

How does this little story, and the other illustrations of the corrupting power of gold that follow it, relate to Horace's championing of virtuous poverty in the rest of the poem? It is not enough to gloss over the rift with a paraphrase—for example, "No matter how great the power of wealth may be, its possession involves so many evils that it is not worth striving for" (Syndikus 1973: 162). Such a paraphrase erases the specificity of the opening *exempla*, which have to do not simply with the power of wealth in general, but with its power in particular to corrupt. The poem reads as a refusal—pointedly oblique, intentionally obfuscated—of a proffered gift, a gift that Horace feels would compromise his integrity.

Although Horace's immediate addressee is Maecenas, he seems to be glancing, as if over Maecenas's shoulder, at someone else. After detailing the dignified modesty of the life he enjoys on his Sabine farm—no Calabrian honey, no expensive wine, no foreign estates, but no sordid poverty either (33–37)—Horace hastens to add that this absence of luxuries is a sign not of the patron's stinginess but of the client's preference: "Nor, if I wanted more, would you refuse to give it" (*nec, si plura velim, tu dare deneges*, 38). The pronoun *tu* should perhaps receive a mildly contrastive stress, in opposition to an unmentioned other—possibly, as Tenney Frank (1925) suggested long ago, Augustus: "If I want anything more, I can get it from you, Maecenas, without recourse to anyone else." In his biography of Horace, Suetonius quotes a letter from Augustus to Maecenas that reveals that Augustus once wooed Horace for himself: "Before now I could take care of my correspondence with my *amici* myself; now, seeing that I am extremely busy, and in ill health, I wish to steal (*abducere*) our Horace away from you. He will come, then, from that parasitic table of yours to my 'royal' (= patronal) table and will assist me with my correspondence." In this wittily couched request or command, Augustus implies that he and Maecenas are rivals for Horace's services. As Augustus indicates, moreover, with a jocular hyperbole, the entertainment provided by a mere parasite such as Maecenas can hardly compete with that offered by the *princeps*, patron of patrons. And yet the future tenses of Augustus's letter were, as it turned out, overly optimistic. Horace declined the invitation. Nor, Suetonius adds, was Augustus angry at the refusal (*ne recusanti quidem*), which Horace justified, as in many a poetic *recusatio*, by pleading unfitness, in this case ill health. Read in this light, *Odes* 3.16 appears to be an extended deflection of the implications of the opening identification of Danae and Horace on the one hand, Jupiter and Augustus on the other. It is instructive to compare Ovid's elegiac Danae (*Am.*

3.8.29–34), who is a prototype, not surprisingly, of the mercenary *puella* seduced by a *dives amator*. Horace's Danae, by contrast, represents not the poet's beloved but the poet himself, who, unlike Danae, modestly resists the blandishments of an importunate *dives amicus*.

In *Odes* 2.17, Horace comes close to envisioning the kind of passionate symmetry imagined by Catullus and Propertius. The poem is framed as a response to Maecenas's reiterated complaints (1–4):

> Cur me querelis exanimas tuis?
> nec dis amicum est nec mihi te prius
>   obire, Maecenas, mearum
>   grande decus columenque rerum.

Why do you wear me out with your complaints? It is not the gods' will nor mine for you to perish first, Maecenas, great glory and stay of my fortunes.

The word used for Maecenas's complaints, *querelae*, often designates the "plaint" of the elegiac lover in particular.[38] Perhaps Maecenas has been imagining Horace failing to mourn his death, as Propertius (1.19, 2.8) imagines Cynthia failing to mourn his. With Horace's response to Maecenas's *querelae*, the silence of the elegiac beloved is broken. And this beloved, though careful to signal his respect for his eminent protector (*decus columenque*, 4), has his own erotic complaint to make. If Maecenas fears that a forgetful Horace will outlive him, his expression of these fears threatens Horace's life, generating the poem's opening counterreproach: "Why do you dis-spirit me?" (*cur me . . . exanimas?* 1). Maecenas's breathed suspicions of his own death take Horace's breath away. This breath, figured in both the sound and the sense of *exanimas*, is exhaled in the exclamatory, swooning *a*, replete with neoteric eroticism, which broaches the second stanza (5–9):

> a! te meae si partem animae rapit
> maturior vis, quid moror altera,
>   nec carus aeque nec superstes
>   integer? ille dies utramque
> ducet ruinam.

Ah! if you, part of my soul, are snatched away by a premature force, why tarry I, the other half, neither as precious nor surviving whole? That day will mean the destruction of us both.

Two men who share a single *anima* cannot but live and die together. The surviving Aristophanic half, severed from its mate, will not survive for long.[39]

The stylistically effeminate and grammatically feminine *a* not only opens the stanza, it echoes through it, most resoundingly in *altera*, a feminine adjective prominently placed at the end of line 6 in apposition to the subject of _moror_, Horace. The reader will supply _pars_: if Maecenas is "part" of Horace's soul, then Horace may be described, reciprocally, as "part" of Maecenas's. Even so, the feminine adjective startles. It is not only Horace, moreover, but also Maecenas who is depicted in a feminine posture, as the direct object of Death, here conceived, in terms suggestive of sexual assault, as an alien "force" that "carries off" its passive victim. As if reanimating both himself and his friend, Horace goes on to proffer a more manly pledge (9–12):

> non ego perfidum
> dixi sacramentum: ibimus, ibimus,
> utcumque praecedes, supremum
> carpere iter comites parati.

The oath I have taken will not be forsworn: we will, we will be on our way, whenever you lead the way, comrades ready to speed on the final journey together.

Hierarchy and Roman virility are at once reasserted, as Horace swears allegiance to his commanding officer in the battle not of love but of life, a battle in which they are no longer passive victims of death but aggressive actors, "seizing" (_carpere_, 12) the road, not skirting it. But the erotic color of the preceding stanzas spills over onto this martial scene. Like Vergil's Nisus and Euryalus, these friends, who will fight and die together, are imaged both as warriors and as lovers.[40] Two months after the death of Maecenas in 8 B.C.E., Horace did in fact follow his friend on his "last journey"; he was buried near him on the Esquiline hill.

In _Sexual Symmetry_ (1994), David Konstan associates "symmetrical or reciprocal love" exclusively with the Greek romantic novels, arguing that all other genres in antiquity are premised on a hierarchically structured desire. The convergence of social and sexual subordination in the poems discussed in this chapter may be taken to support Konstan's claim. It is clear that the client could experience his social subordination as a threat to his manhood; the presence of Messalla, for example, seems to render Tibullus impotent in relation to Delia. This structural "femininity" could also be turned into an asset, as when Propertius flirts with Tullus, or when Horace teases a pleading Maecenas. But some of these poems offer us glimpses of another mode of desire, one involving pleasurable reciprocity if not perfect symmetry. In their different ways, Propertius's poems to Gallus and Horace's poems to Maecenas enter into a kind of exchange that circumvents the seemingly rigid opposition between penetrating and being penetrated, having the phallus and lacking the phallus.[41]

When two friends trade poems, the one-way act of penetration yields to a series of interactions in which each man plays each part alternately. This intercourse may take place only on the page, but the pleasure it yields is lasting and real.

Notes

1. I use the terms "client" and "patron" (where a Roman would speak of "friends") to distinguish the partners in an asymmetrical friendship. For an overview of the Roman patronage system, see Wallace-Hadrill 1989a.

2. On the lover at the door, see Copley 1956; on the client at the door, Bramble 1974: 133, 151. If lovers were wont to lie prostrate at the door, clients could at some houses avail themselves of outdoor benches set up for their convenience; see Wallace-Hadrill 1988: 55.

3. See Labate 1984: 175–226; White 1993: 88–91.

4. Cf. Hor. *Ars P.* 166–67 (on the "ages of man"): "Attaining the age and spirit of manhood, he changes his pursuits, seeks wealth and connections (*amicitias*), and pays heed to status."

5. I am simplifying a difficult issue here; on the anomalous status of the elegiac beloved, see Konstan 1994: 151–59.

6. As the grumpy conclusion of a Horatian paraclausithyron suggests: "Not forever will these ribs of mine put up with threshold and downpour" (*non hoc semper erit liminis aut aquae / caelestis patiens latus, Carm.* 3.10.19–20).

7. I use the feminine pronoun frequently in this chapter to stand for both the male and the female beloved.

8. On Propertius's textual manipulations of Cynthia, see Wyke 1987; Gold 1993a: 87–90.

9. Similarly Gold (1993b: 293): "Male patrons always possess (or at least are given by their poet/clients) an identifiable, stable character and a power external to the poetry," whereas Propertius's Cynthia "is wholly a creature of the poet."

10. If (as argued by G. Williams 1968: 14–17) Scaeva is not a fictional character, then Horace's irony is aimed at his own epistolary persona—here, that of an expert and officious parasite.

11. On the debased *amicus* as prostitute, see Skinner 1982; on sexual and clientary hierarchies in Catull. 10, see Skinner 1989.

12. See, e.g., Cic. *Amic.* 94–95 and, more pessimistically, 99.

13. On Roman (homo)sexuality, see Richlin 1993b and C. A. Williams 1995; a good summary of the (limited) acceptability of male homosexual activity is found in Hallett 1988: 1266.

14. On this species of invective, see Hallett 1977; Richlin 1992a: 86–104; Edwards 1993: 73–97. The ultimate perversion decried in Juv. 2 and 9 is the simultaneous inversion of sexual and social hierarchies: the aristocrat Gracchus taking a horn player for his husband, Virro the *mollis avarus* counting over his gifts on the Matronalia. On Juv. 2, see Konstan 1993.

15. Abundant documentation may be found in Lilja 1983 and Richlin 1992a.

16. On the other side of the story, the contamination of *amor* by *amicitia*, see Ross 1969: 80–90 (on the language of *amicitia* in Catullus's poems to Lesbia/Clodia); Gold 1993b: 286–93 (on Cynthia's "patronage" of Propertius).

17. At the end of the poem, with Messalla safely *hors du combat*, Tibullus reclaims his virility, transforming himself from a vanquished doorkeeper into a soldier of love (*dux milesque bonus*, 75) who is ready to break down the beloved's door (*frangere postes*, 73).

18. I follow Goold's Loeb edition in reading *decus, hunc* for the (semantically and metrically) implausible *virum, hunc* of the manuscripts.

19. As Marilyn Skinner points out to me (in correspondence, 1 Aug. 1991), Delia stands here not only for the elegiac lover but also for the client "welcoming Messalla to her rustic home, as Horace offers Maecenas the fruits of his Sabine farm."

20. See Van Nortwick 1990: 116–17.

21. Similarly White 1993: 88.

22. In part, this is because the *amici* he addresses in the poems discussed here are less eminent than Tibullus's patron. Tullus was a junior member of the Volcacii, "a Perusine family of consular standing" (Syme [1939] 1956: 466; Propertius's tone would be quite different, one suspects, if he were addressing not the nephew but the proconsular uncle); and whoever Gallus may be, Propertius addresses him as a peer.

23. On this embedded propemptikon, see Cairns 1972: 12–13.

24. See Stahl 1985: 93–96. On *mollis* and *durus* as generic markers of the feminine/erotic and the masculine/military, see Kennedy 1993: 31–32. As Gordon Williams has remarked to me, *mollis* is also literally appropriate here; Tullus apparently enjoyed life in the luxurious east so much that he stayed on (Prop. 3.22).

25. Although *Lydia* turns out to be an adjective, modifying *arata*, it (she) first appears to be another nominative singular place-name, parallel to *Ionia* (cf. earlier *doctas Athenas* and *Asiae*). The allure of riches tests the fidelity of both lover and beloved (see further below).

26. Contra Moritz 1967, referring *pares* at 2 to Propertius and Gallus.

27. On the erotic triangle as a conduit of male desire, see Sedgwick 1985: 1–27. The friends' loving embrace transmutes potentially sexual elements (tears, *sinus*); see Adams 1982: 90, 142.

28. In support of the identification, which must remain doubtful (it is dismissed by White [1993: 250]), see Cairns 1983; J. King 1980; Ross 1975: 67–68, 83, 95 n. 3 (pointing to possible echoes of Gallus's poetry at 24 and 28). Propertius may have added the final couplet (thus retroactively dedicating the poem to the poet Gallus) to an already completed poem.

29. For tears as a hallmark of elegy, see, e.g., *flebilibus modis* (Hor. *Carm.* 2.9.9, to the elegist Valgius), *flebilis . . . Elegia* (Ov. *Am.* 3.9.3).

30. On the "sexual positions" of author and reader, see Habinek 1992: 194–200 (on Seneca); Kennedy 1993: 59–63 (on Ovid); Selden 1992: 487–88 (on Catullus).

31. On such appropriations, see Hallett 1989b: 64–65. An effeminate style may be valuable precisely because it violates the norm; on *mollitia* as a means of achieving distinction, see Kennedy 1993: 38–39.

32. Armstrong (1989: 25) remarks that it is to Maecenas that Horace addresses

"his versions of the commonplace topics and phrases that other ancient poets thought suitable for addressees who could be labeled 'family members' or 'long-term loves.' "

33. Cf., e.g., *Carm.* 1.4, where Lycidas, introduced in the penultimate line, generates the concluding relative clause (*quo calet iuventus* . . . , 19); see further Esser 1976: 76–91.

34. So Santirocco 1980: 230.

35. On Licymnia, see Nisbet and Hubbard 1978: 180–83, suggesting (without pursuing the indecorous consequences) that Horace "leaves it to the initiated to suspect that he is talking about Maecenas' love rather than his own." G. Williams (1968: 299–302) proposes that the poem was written on the occasion of Maecenas's marriage with Terentia; against the identification of Licymnia with Terentia, see G. Davis 1975.

36. On "the aesthetics of teasing" in Catullus, see Fitzgerald 1995: 35–44.

37. Cf., e.g., Tib. 1.1.51–52: "Better that all the world's gold and emeralds perish than that any girl weep at my travels!" (*o quantum est auri pereat potiusque smaragdi / quam fleat ob nostras ulla puella vias!*). Maecenas's poem also bears comparison with a Ciceronian epigram elaborated by Pliny (*Ep.* 7.4.6), which publishes not only Cicero's affection for Tiro but Tiro's effeminate subordination. On Pliny's response to Cicero, see Fitzgerald 1995: 44–46. Richlin (1992a: 281) points to Augustus's parody of Maecenas's bejeweled lines (Macrob. *Sat.* 2.4.12: *Cilniorum smaragde, iaspi Iguvinorum,* etc.). If Horace is Maecenas's "jewel," Maecenas in this spoof is Augustus's.

38. See the (elegiacally tinged) erotic *queror/querela* at *Epod.* 11.12 and *Carm.* 2.9.17–18, 2.13.24, 3.11.52, and 3.27.66.

39. The interdependence is underscored by the echo of *a te meae* in *parte animae, maturior,* and *moror altera.* Horace may have had in mind Cicero's discussion of ideal friendship in *De amicitia.* Near the treatise's end, Laelius describes the birth of friendship in Platonic and erotically charged terms: "When Virtue lifts herself up and shows her light and sees and recognizes the same light in another, she moves toward it and receives it from the other in turn, from which springs the flames of what may be called love or friendship (*ex quo exardescit sive amor sive amicitia*); for both words are derived from 'loving'" (*Amic.* 100). It is the abstraction *Virtus,* the essence of manly excellence, who warms to "her" light in another; consider how different the effect would be if the players in this scene were not twin *Virtutes* but Orestes and Pylades or Scipio and Laelius. On the parallels between elegiac *amor* and Ciceronian *amicitia,* see Alfonsi 1945.

40. Cf. Syndikus 1972: 458, on the erotic charge of Horace's declaration.

41. Edwards (1993: 84) points out that we do not actually know "how far the roles actually adopted in homosexual relationships were exclusively 'active' or 'passive.' "

SEVEN

READING BROKEN SKIN: VIOLENCE

IN ROMAN ELEGY

David Fredrick

Let the captive girl go sadly before, hair undone,
    body all white—if her beaten cheeks would allow it.
A bruise pressed in by my lips would have been more fitting,
    her neck marked by the caress of my teeth.
                    (Ovid, *Amores*)

OVID is not simply being flippant when, in *Amores* 1.7, he suggests an amorous bite as the alternative to beating his mistress. Torn dresses, pulled hair, scratches, and bruises are scattered throughout Roman elegy, often in association with lovemaking. If this genre employs the female body as a metaphor for its Alexandrian poetic qualities, how should this broken skin be read? Does violence betray its attempts at "taking the woman's part," confirming that it is an "obstinately male" genre?[1] This essay situates elegiac violence in the context of two distinct ways of representing the mistress: erotic description, which fashions an incomplete but aesthetically perfect body as poetic metaphor (*candida puella*); and jealous suspicion, which produces a degraded body liable to verbal or physical aggression (*dura puella*). These modes converge in the genre's often professed (but rarely obtained) goal of intercourse with the *puella*, where Callimachean metaphor apparently becomes penetrable flesh. Such an approach points toward the reclaiming of epic as a genre closely associated with elite masculinity. But masculinity, as defined through political and social competition, was at the end of the first century B.C.E. an increasingly hollow form of theater, "a loathsome and bitter burlesque," as Carlin Barton has put it.[2] Its recu-

I would like to thank the editors for their patient and helpful criticism. Thanks also to Stanley Lombardo, Martha Malamud, and Amy Richlin for their responses to earlier versions of this argument. Unless otherwise noted, the translations here are my own.

peration in elegy is therefore parodic, but not simply funny; for its male authors, elegy's wounds are ambiguous metaphors for the transformation of elite masculinity into text.

Fascination and Anger: Scopophilia and Voyeurism

> haec sed forma mei pars est extrema furoris;
>   sunt maiora, quibus, Basse, perire iuvat:
> ingenuus color et multis decus artibus, et quae
>   gaudia sub tacita ducere veste libet.
>   (Propertius 1.4.11–14)

> me iuvenum pictae facies, me nomina laedunt,
>   me tener in cunis et sine voce puer;
> me laedet, si multa tibi dabit oscula mater,
>   me soror et cum quae dormit amica simul:
> omnia me laedent: timidus sum (ignosce timori)
>   et miser in tunica suspicor esse virum.[3]
>   (Propertius 2.6.9–14)

Elegy frequently oscillates between fascination and suspicion. Since either posture can be read as "feminine" or "masculine," the genre's gender identification is unstable. It is plausible to argue that laudatory erotic description seeks to endow the *amator* with Callimachean *mollitia* (softness), which the *servitium amoris* confirms; it is equally plausible to argue that such descriptions objectify the mistress, and so express male discursive mastery, which the *amator's* anger confirms.[4] But if gender cannot be unambiguously assigned to the fascinated or jealous *amator*, the two poses present clear contradictions in the type of female body each constructs.

The "fascination versus jealousy" pattern is familiar from Western representations of women alternatively as virgins or whores, and a useful critical model is provided by Laura Mulvey's "Visual Pleasure and Narrative Cinema."[5] Mulvey assigns each half of the dichotomy, as it appears in mainstream cinema, a distinct representational strategy: "fetishistic scopophilia" (= virgin) and "sadistic voyeurism" (= whore). The two are not interchangeable. Scopophilia presents the woman as a collection of desirable fragments that suggest but still conceal the anatomical difference between the sexes; it "builds up the beauty of the object, transforming it into something satisfying in itself." Voyeurism, on the other hand, presents sexual difference as the woman's castration, constructing a plot to expose her crime and justify the penalty: "Pleasure lies in ascertaining guilt ... asserting control and subjugating the guilty person through punishment or forgiveness."[6]

Mulvey emphasizes that scopophilia and voyeurism are contradictory in their approach to narrative time and space:

> [The fetishized woman] tends to work against the development of a story-line, to freeze the flow of action in moments of erotic contemplation. . . . One part of a fragmented body destroys the Renaissance space, the illusion of depth demanded by the narrative; it gives flatness, the quality of a cut-out or icon, rather than verisimilitude, to the screen.[7]

Mulvey's analysis is apposite to elegy's fascination and its suspicion. Each pose constructs its own map (or metaphor) for the female body according to different assumptions about her anatomy, and correspondingly different rules of narrative time and space. For the *candida puella* as slender poetic icon, from whose description genitals are significantly lacking, time stops and space is collapsed into a gratifying visual presence.[8] The *dura puella*, on the other hand, is separated from the *amator* by an almost endless series of barriers (doors, rivers, dinner parties, old nurses, voyages abroad, eunuchs). Behind these lies her sexual experience with other men, which makes her "iron," "bloody," and "wild," reintroducing spatial depth and a temporal plot focused on exposure followed by forgiveness or punishment.[9] The *candida puella* is aesthetically pleasing but physically inviolable: "The parts of her body that evoke desire in the poet form a sort of circle around the genitalia ... it is as if there were a blank space in the middle of the woman."[10] This blank space effectively precludes sexual or violent penetration, and, in generic terms, epic. Voyeurism, meanwhile, reinscribes penetrability in the blank space, allowing the representation of physical contact with the *puella*, where, as the epigraph from Ovid indicates, violence overlaps with sex, and military images are frequently used.[11]

Callimachean (Greek) *phthonos* and Lesbia

One of elegy's most important literary models is Callimachus, not only in the avoidance of epic, but in the use of the erotic body—in Callimachus's case, usually an adolescent male—to represent desired poetic qualities.[12] But Callimachus is not always Callimachean. The *pais*, like the elegiac *puella*, both represents programmatic attributes and transgresses them through infidelity; consequently, the poet's persona slides back and forth between opposite sides of envy (*phthonos*), its dew-sipping object in the prologue to the *Aetia*, its angry subject in several erotic epigrams. However, the disfiguring effect of *phthonos* is internalized by the poet, leaving no marks on the body of the *pais*, a strategy that contrasts with the verbal staining or beating of the female body in Catullus and Roman elegy. In *Aetia* fr. 1, the poet complains that the Telchines, "malignant gnomes," are muttering at him again; he condemns them as "a race that understands only how to melt (*tēkein*) its own liver," and tells the "destructive breed of Jealousy (*Baskaniēs*)" to be gone.[13] *Baskania* is virtually a synonym for *phthonos*, and *tēkein* is the Greek verb typically used to describe the effect of *phthonos*. That the Telchines, while muttering against the poet, also melt their own livers is consistent with the double-edged condition of the *phthoneros*: "The malice that is inherent in *phthonos* rebound[s] upon the *phthoneros*."[14] At the end of the *Hymn to Apollo*, *phthonos* itself addresses Apollo, whispering secretly into his ear that he disdains the singer who does not sing as much as the sea; Apollo kicks Envy while replying that the Assyrian River is immense but polluted, and that bees do not bring moisture to Demeter from just any source, but from the pure, high, unmixed, trickling stream. The poet concludes by bidding Blame (*Mōmos*) go where *Phthonos* has gone.[15]

The *phthoneros* is characterized internally by "wasting and emaciation, pallor and sunken eyes; the frowning brow and gnashing teeth of rage; and perhaps physical distortions such as a hunched back," and externally by "the *phthoneros* strangling himself, choking, or bursting, or some clearly visible rendering of the self-inflicted wound or internal torture."[16] A desirable object always stands in opposition to this tortured body. In the *Aetia* prologue and the *Hymn to Apollo*, this object is the Callimachean text itself, characterized by lightness, brightness, delicate wings, and childlike purity. In the erotic epigrams, however, the desired body is represented by a *pais* whom the poet typically loses (*Epigr.* 28 [Pfeiffer]):

> Ἐχθαίρω τὸ ποίημα τὸ κυκλικόν, οὐδὲ κελεύθῳ
> χαίρω, τίς πολλοὺς ὧδε καὶ ὧδε φέρει·
> μισέω καὶ περίφοιτον ἐρώμενον, οὐδ' ἀπὸ κρήνης
> πίνω· σικχαίνω πάντα τὰ δημόσια.
> Λυσανίη, σὺ δὲ ναίχι καλὸς καλός—ἀλλὰ πρὶν εἰπεῖν
> τοῦτο σαφῶς, Ἠχώ φησί τις· "ἄλλος ἔχει."[17]

I detest the Cyclic poems, I'm not happy on the highway that carries a crowd here and there. I hate the boy-love who cheats, and I don't drink from the common well. I'm disgusted at everything public. Lysanias, yes, you are handsome—so handsome—but it's barely spoken when an echo comes back: "Another man has him."

This poem partly conforms to the contrast between the polluted body/text and Callimachus: the clumsy epic poem, the heavily traveled highway, and the public well are all rejected. However, the "boy-love who cheats" has muddied the position of the poet. He detests, hates, and is disgusted at everything public, an accumulation of visceral emotion that contradicts the image of the delicate, dew-sipping cicada. The distorted echo of *kalos kalos* by *allos ekhei* matches the transformation of Callimachus's own persona from *erastēs* to *phthoneros*.

In the fourteen erotic epigrams, *phthonos* persistently attends desire.[18] The object of *Baskania* or *phthonos* in the *Aetia* prologue, the *Hymn to Apollo*, and epigram 21, the poet becomes its subject as the *pais* paradoxically represents Callimachean poetics and betrays them by being beyond the reach of the poet—by implication possessed by someone else. The *pais* shifts abruptly from a metaphor for Callimachean poetics to its opposite, *kalos* but corrupt, attractive but polluted: "I know my empty hands hold no riches, but Menippus, by the Graces don't tell my own dream to me. It's agony to hear this bitter word, dear boy, the most disenchanting (*anerastotaton*) thing you've said" (*Epigr.* 32).

Setting the stage for elegy, Catullus adapts for Latin poetry many of Callimachus's programmatic themes, including the use of the erotic object as a metaphor for desirable literary qualities. Like the Callimachean *pais*, Lesbia is depicted ambiguously: a model of erotic/aesthetic perfection, but sexually corrupt. However, the disfiguring effect of jealousy is projected, through Catullus's invective, onto her body. Unlike Callimachus's epigrams, and in contrast to the poems on the infidelity of the *puer* Juventius (24 and 81), Catullus's attacks on Lesbia focus on specific sexual acts and the anatomy involved (11.15–20):

> pauca nuntiate meae puellae
>   non bona dicta.
> cum suis vivat valeatque moechis,
> quos simul complexa tenet trecentos,
> nullum amans vere, sed identidem omnium
>   ilia rumpens.

Announce to my girl a few words, not so good to hear: May she live and prosper with her adulterers, holding in her embrace three hundred at a time, loving none truly, but bursting their groins again and again.

Catullus 11 is a violent representation, not because it depicts an exchange of blows but because the action it attributes to Lesbia—hundreds of partners with the obvious implication of genital, anal, and oral penetration—is viewed as extremely demeaning in Roman society. Moreover, the poem claims that this is a role she willingly assumes; she is "guilty" because of her uncontrolled desire.[19] Poem 11 shares this insistence on physical detail and specificity with several others, such as poem 58: "Caelius, our Lesbia, that Lesbia, that Lesbia whom Catullus loved alone more than himself and all his friends, now in the crossroads and back alleys slips back the foreskins of the descendants of great-hearted Remus."

In their graphic content, poems 11 and 58 are comparable to the invectives directed at Gellius, Mamurra, and others, which equate the cravings for food, money, and sexual pleasure. The upper and lower strata of the body are confused, producing a "grotesque body," voracious in penetrating and being penetrated.[20] Poem 11 reduces Lesbia to a collection of interchangeable holes, while the use of the stem *vor(ax)*, *vor(o)* ("voracious," "devour") in poems 29, 33, and 80 similarly assimilates the mouth, anus, and genitals, culminating in Gellius's mouth devouring Victor's penis (80.5–8):

> nescio quid certe est: an vere fama susurrat
> grandia te medii tenta vorare viri?
> sic certe est: clamant Victoris rupta miselli
> ilia, et emulso labra notata sero.[21]

There's something going on: does rumor whisper truly that you devour the impressive hard-ons of a man's crotch? It's true: the burst groin of poor little Victor shouts it, and your lips smeared white with milked-out sperm.

As the echo between 11 (*ilia rumpens*) and 80 (*ilia rupta*) suggests, Lesbia is implicated in the larger treatment of the body in Catullan invective; specifically, Gellius's "stain" here will spread to her when she becomes his lover in poem 91. Similarly, Egnatius's habit of drinking his own urine in poem 37 is particularly offensive to Catullus because Egnatius is identified as one of her lovers, in language that echoes the charges made in 11 and 58: "All you great good fellows make love to her, and, what's really ignoble, all you small-time back-alley fuckers, too."

At the same time, Catullus's poetry constructs a Callimachean body (*lepidus, elegans, suavis, mollis, pura*) closely associated with Lesbia and Juventius. This body represents an "aesthetic of slimness."[22] The physical contact allowed to it is oblique; in comparison with the invective poems, the thousands of kisses in poems 5, 7, and 48, like the sparrow in 2 and 3, defer a more substantial meeting of the flesh. This deferral becomes, through metaphor, infinite: more kisses than the sands of the Libyan desert, more kisses than the stars, kisses denser than fields of ripe grain.

Marilyn Skinner has emphasized the dichotomy in Catullus between the "social virility of the iambicist" and the "emotional vulnerability of the *amator*."[23] But the *amator*'s vulnerability, like the iambicist's virility, depends on the penetration of the object. For the *amator* to suffer and forgive, or suffer and attack, Catullus as poet must first represent Lesbia's violation. In addition, anger remains an important constituent of the amatory *ego* in later elegy, where violence steps into the gap left by Catullan invective. Catullus's shift to a female object consequently reflects more than the fact that Greek and Roman males could be indifferent to the gender of those whom they penetrated. It foregrounds sexual difference, rather than promiscuous behavior alone, a difference marked on the body, rather than a difference evident in behavior but unmarked physically (e.g., the penetrability of the *pais*). Callimachus's echo, "Some other man has him," is inscribed on Lesbia's anatomy: some other man has her *qua* "her." The contradiction between peripheral characteristics (face, eyes, breasts, feet) as metaphors for aesthetic perfection and genitals as the site of corruption and loss will be construed in elegy along generic lines, so that the closer one moves from the former toward the latter, the closer one approaches (mock) epic.

As Foucault put it, in the Hellenistic world, "The agonistic game by which one sought to manifest and ensure one's superiority over others . . . had to be integrated into a far more extensive and complex field of power relations."[24] There is no question that competition within and between city-states was subordinated to struggles between Hellenistic kingdoms; moreover, the citizen's physical role in this political game had changed. The hoplite-*kinaidos* opposition fundamental to the classical construction of the male body appealed to widely shared military experience. By the third century B.C.E., however, warfare had diversified beyond the limits of the classical phalanx, and mercenaries were widely used for both heavily armed and lighter armed troops. To put it bluntly, the Hellenistic citizen did not customarily expect to put on the armor and kill or be killed.[25] This suggests a changed relation to the ensemble of institutions inherited from the polis, a slippage of the male body from its prior definition through collective warfare.

One of the institutions affected by this transformation was poetry. Considerable attention has been given to the shift of emphasis in Alexandrian poetry from oral to textual performance, a shift whereby the poets measured, self-consciously, their separation from the cultural past. Cameron has recently taken this view to task as "modern dogma," and he demonstrates convincingly that festivals and symposia continued to be relevant for poetry. However, the issue of "oral versus written" involves more than weighing the Library against traditional venues for composition and reception. It bears on poetry's relation, as one of the avenues through which gender was constructed and performed, to civic life, which had changed dramatically in the area of military service. This change was fundamental politically because of the importance of hoplite warfare in defining the male citizen, and fundamental poetically because of Homer. Cameron is consequently less successful in maintaining that there was no conflict between Callimachus's technique and the oral forms and contexts of the classical period.[26] Most importantly, Callimachus rejected the Homeric combination of narrative realism and military/historical content. Whether its target is epic in general, or Antimachus's use of epic realism in elegy, this poetic rejection is what made Callimachus "revolutionary" for his own day and for later Roman poets (who did read it as a rejection of epic). If, as Cameron claims, "the problem was how to de-epicize elegy," this is essentially connected to the "de-epicization" of the citizen through his increased distance from warfare, a citizen for whom the epic battlefield has faded into text that no longer intersects lived experience.[27]

The self-definition of the Roman male elite was similarly dependent on political competition and military accomplishment, and similarly disturbed when Republican institutions crumbled. In framing their reaction, Roman poets found a convenient precedent in Hellenistic poetry. As Martha Malamud has put it, "The adoption of . . . Callimachean poetics in particular provided [Augustan poets] with a sophisticated mechanism for exploring political and social dissonance."[28] Again, epic functioned as the literary analogue for the construction of masculinity through political and military action. Propertius (3.9), noting that he desires only to be found pleasing compared with Callimachus, declares that he will write epic when Maecenas pulls himself out of the shade and leads armies into battle; Ovid (*Am.* 1.1, 1.15, 2.1) rejects epic together with military, legal, and political pursuits.

The elegiac poets embrace the fragmented aesthetic of Callimachus and repudiate the realistic, linear narrative of epic. However, they employ a female rather than a male erotic object in the great majority of their poems. The *recusatio* of epic is thus mapped onto an idealized circle of body parts and attributes that exclude the mistress's genitals—a process of representation that also suspends temporal movement and spatial depth. Jealousy is also mapped onto the female body in the form of bruises and bites that represent, through displacement, the sexual difference avoided in scopophilic description. The genre's trajectory leads from the intangible wound of the *amator* as he falls under the mistress's charms and so departs from epic narrative, to a second wound, the suspicion of infidelity that breaks the fetishistic spell, to the physical wounding of the mistress, which marks the poet's (always temporary) realignment with both masculinity and epic.[29] The wound on female flesh is thus a blot on the self-representation of the poet, a transgression of his aesthetic principles.

Violent Venus

The process is particularly well illustrated in the first fifteen poems of Propertius's second book. Poem 2.1, in its movement from erotic-poetic fetishism and the *recusatio* of epic to the incurable wound inflicted by the *dura puella*, and then to the representation of sex as war, lays out the themes that will dominate the next fourteen poems.

Lines 1–16 programmatically equate Cynthia and the text. The *amores* are written (*scribantur*) and the book is *mollis*; Cynthia substitutes for Calliope and Apollo, the familiar inspirations of Callimachus and of Vergil's *Eclogues*; if she walks in Coan silk (a probable reference to Philitas), the papyrus scroll (*volumen*) becomes all silk; she plays the lyre with ivory fingers (*digitis . . . eburnis*) that suggest her status as constructed art object. She also plays it with skill (*arte*), implying the familiar programmatic term *docta*, "learned." However, lines 13–14 disturb the equivalence between Cynthia and the Callimachean text: *seu nuda erepto mecum luctantur amictu, / tum vero longas condimus Iliadas*. With her clothing torn away, she struggles nude with the poet, and they "compose very long *Iliads*." The word *nuda* jeopardizes scopophilic poetics by calling attention to the *puella's* genitals, which lack any Callimachean programmatic vocabulary. Moreover, beneath the parodic humor, the violence of epic remains, and by the middle of the poem, infidelity will be its motivation.

The poem continues (17–50) with a *recusatio* of epic addressed to Maecenas and specifically mentioning Callimachus, a progression that would seem to make clear the opposition of Callimachean erotic description to epic narrative. However, the problem of sex as epic violence is raised again in lines 45–50. As the alternative to other subjects, the *amator* claims that he "versifies battles on the narrow bed," but his wish that he alone enjoy his love reveals the potential for aggression behind the military metaphor. He remembers that Cynthia condemns the entire *Iliad* on account of Helen, a reminiscence of the sexual *Iliads* of lines 14–15 with uncomfortable implications for Cynthia's role. By lines 57–78, the *amator* suffers a wound worse than that endured by any epic hero, and finally requests that Maecenas weep over his epitaph: *huic misero fatum dura puella fuit* ("A hard mistress was this poor man's doom"). *Dura* negates the *puella's* Callimachean qualities, and suggests that, as *nuda*, she is something the poet rarely obtains: to do so, he must break through the barriers that both conceal and represent her sexuality with other men.

Oscillation between Callimachean scopophilia and mock-epic voyeurism dominates Propertius 2.2–2.13. In 2.2, the poet declares that he thought himself free, only to be recaptured by the *puella's* beauty, elaborated by a set of mythological comparisons; in 2.3 he scolds himself for his lack of will, and then lists the charms he found impossible to resist. Her face is like white lilies, like snow mixed with vermillion, like rose petals floating in milk; her eyes are like torches and stars; her body glistens in Arabian silk; she dances like Ariadne; she is *docta* in playing the Aganippean lyre; her writings (*scripta*) match those of the poet Corinna. Poem 2.4 underscores the importance of sexual difference for the use of the erotic body as metaphor: *ego* laments the *delicta dominae* ("crimes of the mistress") that compel him to *ira*; he prays that his friends love boys, rather than girls, since the former are persuaded by a single word, while the latter "will scarcely become soft even by blood itself" (*altera vix ipso sanguine mollis erit*).

In 2.5, violence is considered, but found to be poetically incorrect (21–26):

> nec tibi periuro scindam de corpore vestis,
> nec mea praeclusas fregerit ira fores,
> nec tibi conexos iratus carpere crinis,
> nec duris ausim laedere pollicibus:
> rusticus haec aliquis tam turpia proelia quaerat,
> cuius non hederae circuiere caput.

I will not rip the dress from your perjured body, nor will my anger smash down your closed doors, nor will I tear apart, in my rage, your woven coiffure, nor dare to hurt you with my harsh thumbs: let some rustic seek such shameful battles, whose head the ivy does not encircle.

The *amator* chooses the Callimachean alternative: "I will write, therefore, what no age will ever efface, 'Cynthia, a powerful beauty, Cynthia, light in words'—believe me, although you disdain the murmurs of rumor, this verse, Cynthia, will turn you pale." This *scripta puella*, injured by verse rather than blows, recalls in strategy if not in explicit language Catullus's invectives against Lesbia.

Poem 2.6 repeats the theme of jealousy, but ends with a statement of eternal devotion: "You will always be my girlfriend, you will always be my wife." In 2.7, movement away from anger toward reconciliation is confirmed from the outside, as Augustus's marital legislation is withdrawn and the lovers rejoice. However, in 2.8 the pendulum swings back: Cynthia is again "iron" (*ferrea*), and the *amator* claims that he will kill himself, and her, too (25–28):

> sed non effugies: mecum moriaris oportet;
> hoc eodem ferro stillet uterque cruor.
> quamvis ista mihi mors est inhonesta futura:
> mors inhonesta quidem, tu moriere tamen.

But you will not escape: you should die with me; the blood of both will drip from the same sword, although that murder will disgrace me—it may be a disgrace, but you will die just the same.

In lines 29–38, he compares his grief to Achilles' after the loss of Briseis, a *dolor* that "rages" (*saevit*). In poem 2.10, he tries on more epic masks, declaring his willingness to kill and to die fighting his rival, like Polyneices and Eteocles.

Maria Wyke has demonstrated the inseparability of Callimachean metaphor from the description of the *puella* in Propertius 2.10–2.13, poems that contemplate a switch to epic poetry only to be driven back to elegy by the *puella's* beauty.[30] As such they fit the general pattern of poems 2.1–2.9, which alternate between increasingly violent dismay at Cynthia's unfaithfulness (voyeurism) and reassertions of erotic/poetic devotion (scopophilia).

The pattern comes to a generically loaded climax in poems 2.14 and 2.15. Poem 2.14 begins by comparing lovemaking to Agamemnon's victory over Troy—as in 2.1, sex equals the *Iliad*, and Cynthia by implication equals Helen. In line 24, this erotic triumph is worth more than victory over the Parthians: "This my spoils, this my conquered kings, this my chariots will be" (*haec spolia, haec reges, haec mihi currus erit*). In 2.15.1–20, the *amator* presents his moment of triumph in detail, using violent language (*rixa*, "quarrels"; *luctata*, "struggling") to describe lovemaking. His account moves significantly from secondary erotic details (her exposed nipples, her self-concealment, her kisses on his eyelids, their entwined arms, their kisses) to a declaration of the importance of visual pleasure ("the eyes are love's leaders") and complete exposure, appealing to the effect that the nudity of Helen and Endymion had on Paris and the goddess Selene (*nuda Lacaena, nudus Endymion, nudae deae*). The *amator* anticipates resistance and violence (17–20):

> quod si pertendens animo vestita cubaris,
>   scissa veste meas experiere manus:
> quin etiam, si me ulterius provexerit ira,
>   ostendes matri bracchia laesa tuae.

But if you are stubborn, and lie down clothed, with your tunic torn away you will know my hands. Still more, if anger provokes me further: you will show your mother the bruises on your arms.

Movement beyond the limits of Callimachean description toward the "blank space" is matched by movement toward *ira*. The torn-off tunic, as obstacle, stands in for all the other obstacles that define the *dura puella*, whose emotional inaccessibility is matched by so many physical barriers. Full disclosure of sexual difference in the bedroom overlaps with elegy's obsession with discovering the *puella's* guilt, the equivalent of breaking down the doors to find her with another man. Scopophilia is transformed into voyeurism, and looking becomes a blow; the display of sexual difference is transposed into the bruised arms Cynthia shows to her mother.

This shift is not atypical of the genre. The "fascination-jealousy" pattern occupies numerous elegies, and scenes of violent contact, while infrequent, are not for that reason incidental.[31] Ovid gives a particularly clear (to the point of generic self-parody) demonstration of this in *Amores* 1.5 through 1.7. In 1.5, Corinna appears to the poet during a nap on a hot afternoon; the shades are shut, and the (dim) light is just right for the display of "modest girls." As this paradox suggests, everything is halfway in lines 1–10: midday, partly drawn shades, half-light, partly open dress, hair that covers and reveals her neck. The fetishizing technique continues in lines 17–22:

> ut stetit ante oculos posito velamine nostros,
> > in toto nusquam corpore menda fuit.
> quos umeros, quales vidi tetigique lacertos!
> > forma papillarum quam fuit apta premi!
> quam castigato planus sub pectore venter!
> > quantum et quale latus! quam iuvenale femur!

As she stood before our eyes, her dress cast aside, in her whole body there was nowhere a flaw. What shoulders, what arms I saw and I touched! The nipples' shape just right to be pressed! How flat the stomach beneath the perfectly pure breast! Her flank—its size and quality! What a youthful thigh!

At this point he declares, "Why mention the details?" (*singula quid referam*); nude body is pressed to nude body, and "Who doesn't know the rest?" (*cetera quis nescit*). This poem is especially clear in its presentation of the "circling of the look," and representative of the descriptive strategy that transforms the *puella*'s body into an icon, Wyke's Callimachean metaphor.

Menda can be used of a physical blemish, a literary fault, or a slip of the pen—but if there is no flaw, no *menda*, why does the description halt? If the *amator* saw nothing unworthy of praise (*nil non laudabile vidi*), why does one part lack its *laus*? The hint that there is something to be hidden or corrected in this body is confirmed by the use of *castigato* to describe her breasts (*pectore*), which suggests not simply "flawless," but "punished"; the literal meaning of the word is "compelled to be chaste" (*castum* + *ago*). It is important, then, to note the battle over Corinna's tunic in lines 13–16: the poet tears it away (*deripui tunicam*), and although it does not cover much, she battles (*pugnabat*) to keep it on, struggling like someone who wishes to lose. This battle is preceded by a comparison of Corinna to Lais, "loved by many men" (*multis Lais amata viris*).

Amores 1.6 follows with a lengthy appeal to Corinna's doorkeeper, who keeps the door firmly shut in the *amator*'s face, although the latter points out that he does not come as a soldier with an army, but as a lover. Magnifying the less tangible frames of dress and description around her genitals in 1.5, the closed door of the *puella*'s house in 1.6 suggests, as usual, that the mistress is with another man. The *amator* refuses the "epic" action of breaking down the door, but in *Amores* 1.7 he replaces this with a physical assault that disfigures the *puella*'s body and blots the poet's Callimacheanism. The mock triumph in 1.7.35–42 must be cross-referenced specifically with the fetishism of 1.5:

> i nunc, magnificos victor molire triumphos,
> cinge comam lauro votaque redde Iovi,
> quaeque tuos currus comitantum turba sequetur,
> clamet, "io, forti victa puella viro est!"
> ante eat effuso tristis captiva capillo,
> si sinerent laesae, candida tota, genae.
> aptius inpressis fuerat livere labellis
> et collum blandi dentis habere notam.

Go, victor, celebrate your magnificent triumph, wreathe your head with laurel, give thanks to Jupiter, and let the crowd that follows your chariot cry, "Io, a girl has been conquered by a brave man!" Let the captive girl go sadly before, hair undone, body *all white*—if her beaten cheeks would allow it. A bruise pressed in by my lips would have been more fitting, her neck marked by the caress of my teeth.

The description in 1.5 emphasizes its omission of her genitals; here in 1.7, she would be *tota candida* if not for her battered cheeks. Moreover, the poet suggests that even in lovemaking he would have bitten her neck; the resulting bruise (*livor*) would be the proof of sex, the erstwhile goal of the genre, and yet it is discoloring, aesthetically at odds with the pristine appearance of the *puella* as metaphor.[32]

The same basic pattern is found in *Amores* 2.12–15, which move from triumphant sex, to Corinna's abortion, to the *amator*'s description of her from the privileged perspective of her signet ring. In 2.12 the *amator* claims that his lovemaking with Corinna is a triumph that "lacks blood" and is "without slaughter." However, the relation between the Callimachean metaphor and epicized sex (or beating) suggests that the latter displays what the former has left out—female genitals as a wound. Lines 17–24 compare lovemaking to the wars (hardly bloodless) between Trojans and Greeks, Lapiths and Centaurs, Latins and Trojans, Romans and Sabines, using the repeated line-opening *femina* to emphasize that women were the cause. The next two poems describe Corinna's abortion as warfare and gladiatorial combat.[33] Thus 2.15 (1–8):

> Quid iuvat inmunes belli cessare puellas,
> nec fera peltatas agmina velle sequi,
> si sine Marte suis patiuntur vulnera telis,
> et caecas armant in sua fata manus?

> quae prima instituit teneros convellere fetus,
>   militia fuerat digna perire sua.
> scilicet, ut careat rugarum crimine venter,
>   sternetur pugnae tristis harena tuae?

What is the gain for defenseless girls to escape war, and choose not to follow the savage ranks with shields, if without Mars they suffer wounds by their own weapons, and they arm blind hands for their own destruction? Whichever girl first began to tear out tender offspring, she deserved to die in her own warfare. So that your belly may lack reproachful wrinkles, perhaps, is the grim sand scattered for your battle?

These lines fill in the blank space as wound, underscore its opposition to Callimachean description, and associate it generically with epic. While the *amator* describes sex as a triumph without blood, the *nuda puella* remains the site of violent penetration just the same; *Amores* 2.13 and 2.14 are at least as voyeuristic as the poems representing sex or beating. In 2.14.39–40, the *amator* observes that the girl who attempts abortion often perishes, and as she is carried to the pyre, with hair unbound (*resoluta capillos*, 2.14.39 = *effuso capillo*, 1.7.39), all who see her cry out (*clamant*, 2.14.40 = *clamet*, 1.7.38), "She deserved it" (*merito*). There is an equation that runs between the poet's triumph after beating the *puella*, his triumph after making love to her, and this funeral procession after an abortion attempt. Like the husband, guard, and locked door Ovid boasted of overcoming in 2.12.3, abortion is another barrier representing the mistress's independent sexuality, her transgression of Callimachean *mollitia* and the limits of aesthetic fetishism—an "independence" and a transgression constructed for her by the genre.

From the female body as the locus for abortion, *Amores* 2.15 returns immediately to scopophilic description: the *amator* prays to become Corinna's signet ring—a tender burden she could never refuse to bear—so that he can ride on her finger, slip in between her breasts, be moistened by her lips, and accompany her to her bath. Here the description ends, as the sight of *te nuda* would cause the ring to get an erection and play the part of a man.[34] A similar movement from violence back to fetishism is found in 1.7. After wondering why he did not simply scream at the girl and tear away her tunic down to the waist, the *amator* describes how he, "iron-hearted," scratched her face with his fingernail (49–58):

> at nunc sustinui raptis a fronte capillis
>   ferreus ingenuas ungue notare genas.
> astitit illa amens albo et sine sanguine vultu,
>   caeduntur Pariis qualia saxa iugis;

> exanimis artus et membra trementia vidi,
> ut cum populeas ventilat aura comas,
> ut leni Zephyro gracilis vibratur harundo
> summave cum tepido stringitur unda Noto;
> suspensaeque diu lacrimae fluxere per ora,
> qualiter abiecta de nive manat aqua.

She stood stunned, her face white without blood, like marble blocks cut from the slopes of Paros. I saw her lifeless joints and her limbs trembling, as when the wind ruffles the leaves on a poplar, as when a graceful reed whispers gently with the Zephyr, or when wavetops ripple with the warm south wind; her tears hung suspended, then flowed down her face, as water trickles down from melting snow.

The action freezes, and the mistress's body is taken apart into a graceful, trembling, whispering landscape; *aura, leni, tepido, gracilis,* and *manat* all convey, with appropriately Callimachean artifice, a gentle, soothing "nature." As the comparison to Parian marble suggests, the mistress is once again an icon, and the representational mode has shifted back to erotic contemplation. The *amator* is overwhelmed, and falls before her feet.

Ovid's use of landscape to make a Callimachean metaphor of the *puella*'s body in 1.7 offers an interesting comparison with a third elegist, Tibullus. Tibullus's sixteen elegies show the same oscillation between fascination and suspicion, but they have very little description of the charms of Delia or Nemesis, which should make it difficult for them to function as the poetic metaphor suggested by Wyke.[35] However, Tibullus substitutes ekphrases of an idealized countryside for the mistress's body. In the bucolic setting of 1.1, the *parva hostia, exiguum pecus,* and *pura fictilia* are contrasted to excessive wealth, the cause of war; the Golden Age of 1.3.35–48 and the fantasy of Delia in the country in 1.5.21–36 or 1.10.15–24 are also contrasted to the horrors of war and epic.

But if landscape rather than the female body is the *materia* for Tibullus's descriptive passages, the same process makes his landscapes "pastoral" and the elegiac *puella* "Callimachean." The *puella* without *pudenda,* with the blank space in the middle, is a lot like the Golden Age landscape, without labor, disease, greed, or war. The discovery of infidelity parallels the irruption of all of these woes; it amounts to a return to the city and an opportunity for mock-epic violence. At the end of 1.10, the drunken farmer and his wife go back from the rural festival to their bedroom, where their lovemaking reproduces the epicized sex found in Propertius and Ovid. In these "wars of Venus," the woman's hair is torn out and the door is broken down; her cheeks are beaten and the man, as "victor," laments that his demented hands were too strong.[36] Tibullus then condemns the beating, suggesting (61–66),

> sit satis e membris tenuem rescindere vestem,
>   sit satis ornatus dissoluisse comae,
> sit lacrimas movisse satis: quater ille beatus
>   quo tenera irato flere puella potest.
> sed manibus qui saevus erit, scutumque sudemque
>   is gerat et miti sit procul a Venere.

It's enough to tear the thin dress from her body, enough to wreck her elegant curls, enough to reduce her to tears: that man is four times blessed at whose anger a delicate girl can weep. But whoever rages with his fists, let him carry a shield and spear, exiled far from gentle Venus.

What began as rustic rape—the blessings of Golden Age peace end at the shattered bedroom door—shifts to familiar elegiac ground. *Lascivus Amor*, thin dresses, and elegant curls all suggest the urban settings used by Tibullus when the mistress is being unfaithful. Reinforcing the movement from countryside to city, the woman is first called *uxor*, then *femina*, then *puella*.[37] The passage does not state explicitly why the lover beats her, but in elegy unfaithfulness is *the* cause of anger. Tibullus, like Propertius and Ovid, condemns outright beating, but recommends tearing off the girl's dress, wrecking her hair, and making her cry; not only is this permissible, it brings the greatest pleasure. However, even this ideal of limited violence is transgressed here, as it is elsewhere in elegy.

With one significant exception: Sulpicia, whose poems are the only surviving evidence of what elegy often suggests, that women were interested readers and not infrequently writers of this genre.[38] Sulpicia's corpus resembles male elegy in some respects. Her lover's name, Cerinthus, has associations with bees, wax, and writing, which suggests that he is, like the *puella*, a metaphor for Callimachean poetic composition—a *scriptus vir* (or *puer*?).[39] Poems 4.7 and 4.12 also portray their lovemaking as delayed, though in the latter poem the cause is Sulpicia's own fear of revealing the strength of her desire, not the interposition of a rival. In poem 4.10, however, Sulpicia as female lover accuses Cerinthus of being preoccupied with a prostitute, while she herself is *Servi filia Sulpicia*. The reassertion of her superior name and status is perhaps comparable to the male elegists' reconsideration of epic in the face of their mistresses's infidelity.

Sulpicia's poems do not contain scopophilic lists of Cerinthus's attributes; they do not contain the military language consistently present in the male elegists, nor is there any reference to bites or blows. However, by associating their object with Callimachean text (Cerinthus = writing tablet), the poems imply elegy's scopophilic mode of erotic description. Cerinthus is not only written upon, he is the means through which Sulpicia exposes her poetic self to the readers' gaze, as a public rather than a private text (4.7.7–9):

> non ego signatis quicquam mandare tabellis,
> *me legat* ut nemo quam meus ante, velim,
> sed peccasse iuvat.

I would not wish to entrust anything to sealed letters, so that no one might *read me* before my lover, but it is pleasing to have erred.

In these closed tablets, Sulpicia's lover would "read" her before anyone else—but she has become an unsealed text. Placed in her lap (4.7.4, *in nostrum deposuitque sinum*), Cerinthus affords a perspective from which to read "Sulpicia" that anticipates Ovid's ring.[40] This produces a similarly contradictory movement between exposure and concealment: while Sulpicia's *ego* would be more ashamed to cover up (*texisse*) than to lay bare (*nudasse*) her love in 4.7, in 4.13 she has left Cerinthus for a night because she "desires to conceal her ardor" (*ardorem cupiens dissimulare meum*).

Sulpicia thus exploits not only an instability of gender intrinsic to elegy, but a confusion of the inscriptive metaphor itself: Callimachean writing, in the male elegists, is an extended disavowal of sexual penetration—which should, according to the metaphor, be analogous to inscription. A *scripta puella* is already wounded, though the male elegists seek to present her as an unblemished surface. But if Ovid as ring portrays a mistress with a blank space in the middle, denying the violence of his own writing, Sulpicia, by casting Cerinthus as tablet and herself as a text to be read, has underscored the ambiguity of the writing metaphor itself: in the center, for herself and for the male elegists, there is both text (wound) and pen.

The problem confronted by the male elegists (the status of the body when elite competition had ceased to provide a reliable definition for it) is not irrelevant for elite women. The stereotypical expectations for elite women—early, arranged marriage and childbirth; chastity; careful management of the household; discipline in the raising of children—were, like those of men, tied to political competition. Women were not emancipated from these expectations during the late Republic, but their meaning was placed in doubt, no less than the meaning of being a senator or a consul.[41] For Sulpicia to offer "herself" to be read (in the act of inscribing her lover/text Cerinthus) seems no less a metaphor for this vulnerability, both political and corporeal, than for Propertius or Ovid to write elegy.

Wyke's emphasis on metaphor establishes a clear break from reading elegy's mistresses as real. However, this point can be granted without allowing the word "metaphor" to neutralize differences between the *candida* and the *dura puella*. Alongside the cheeks like snow and the eyes like stars there are torn dresses, bites, bruises, and abortions. Elegy consistently portrays sex not only as violent penetration, but also as the violation of its own poetic values; the mistress's wound is made a metaphor for epic. But what kind of "metaphor" is this, particularly in the context of Augustan Rome? Is the *ira* that produces elegiac violence itself completely semiotic, as Veyne's reading suggests?[42]

The very notion of bodies used as texts seems a central problem here. The oscillation between Callimachean metaphor and (mock) epic wound strongly suggests an oscillation between the ideal and the "real." If the former turns flesh into idealized text, then the latter, by restoring narrative realism, should make text back into flesh; if the circle of positive attributes is constructed by denial of the "real" of sexual difference, the blank space must be where that "reality" is revealed. But elegy consistently textualizes its violence by presenting it as mock epic, a transgression of Callimacheanism that is nevertheless not "real" violence (i.e., violence offered for straightforward identification). At the end of *Amores* 1.7 the *amator* declares, "Put your recomposed hair back in place" (*puella, pone recompositas in statione comas*), suggesting that the poem has been a transparent play on the extremes of the genre; its violence, like its fascination, was only a surface effect. This does not remove the aggression, but it does complicate its meaning.

Augustan Rome did not enjoy an easy relation with the real, particularly with respect to the elite male body. As Walters argues in this volume, the upper-class *vir* was defined by his freedom from penetration, sexual or violent, in all contexts except military service. This was the guarantee of his social reality, distinguishing independent political action from an empty show under compulsion. As Cicero glumly observed in 55 B.C.E. (*Fam.* 1.8.1–4):

> Commutata tota ratio est senatus, iudiciorum, rei totius publicae; otium nobis exoptandum est, quod ii qui potiuntur rerum praestaturi videntur, si quidam homines patientius eorum potentiam ferre potuerint; dignitatem quidem illam consularem fortis et constantis senatoris nihil est quod cogitemus.

> The entire nature of the senate, the courts, and the Republic itself has changed. Leisure is what we should hope for, and those in power seem ready to grant it, if certain men were able to bear their power more patiently. We should imagine that the consular dignity of a brave and steadfast senator is nothing.

The *vir*, Cicero not the least, was penetrable indeed; in the Principate, Republican institutions became a palpable fiction. Tacitus (*Ann.* 4.19) remarks of the trial of Gaius Silius under Tiberius: "Therefore with much seriousness, as if Silius were being treated in accordance with the law, as if Varro were a real consul, or *that thing* (*illud*) were a Republic, the senate was collected."

In the transformation of Republic into Principate, confusions of status went hand-in-hand with the blurring of divisions between the stage and reality, which sheds additional light on elegy's disturbing mixture of Callimachean metaphor with sexual violence. Two social categories were confused whose separation had been crucial: senator and actor. The latter's penetrability, as a slave, guaranteed that his public words and deeds, onstage, were not "real," while the former's inviolability gave his words and deeds "proper weight and authority."[43] This confusion was explored theatrically through the appearance of upper-class Romans on the stage or in gladiatorial spectacles, and through "fatal charades" where an actor physically suffered in a supposedly fictional situation (e.g., a condemned Prometheus is really eaten by vultures; a boy-actor Icarus really falls to his death).[44] Such confusions of status and reality are instructive for elegy. Elegy opposes Callimachean metaphor to epic, the generic stand-in for elite masculinity and its privileged relation to the "real" defined as political power. Extravagantly artificial, it assumes the glamorous but shameful status of the act.[45] It simultaneously pursues a sadistic narrative reminiscent of the genre it had seemed to reject and inscribes a wound on female flesh to represent this narrative. When it then says of the wound, "This too is text," elegy exposes the semiotic dilemma of the male body defined by a vanishing capacity for political action.

Notes

1. For the *puella* as Callimachean metaphor, see Wyke 1987, 1989b, 1989c, Keith 1994. For "gynesis" and "taking the woman's part," see Gold 1993a; for the genre of elegy as "obstinately male," see Lowe 1988, and Wyke 1994. Instances of violence in elegy challenge the general impression of the lover as summarized by Wyke (1994: 120): "He submits, not imposes, is weaponless rather than armed, soft not hard, and feminine not masculine."

2. Barton 1993: 46.

3. "But her form is the least part of my madness—there are greater things, Bassus, for which it's a pleasure to die: her natural color, her skill in many arts, and those joys better discussed under silent sheets." "The faces of young men in pictures wound me, their names too, the tender baby in the crib with no voice wounds me; it wounds me if your mother smothers you in kisses, or if your sister or a girlfriend sleeps beside you. Everything wounds me: I'm scared (forgive me) and in torment I suspect that under that dress there's a man."

4. Kennedy 1993, and Wyke 1994, who notes that the Sulpician narrator's "adoption of both masculine and feminine subject positions . . . is not unparalleled elsewhere in the corpus of elegiac poems" (115).

5. Mulvey [1975] 1989. For the debate in film theory provoked by Mulvey's essay, see Fredrick 1995: 270 n. 13. Mulvey's theory was applied systematically to representations of women in visual art by Pollock 1988; for additional uses in art, literary criticism, and classics, see Fredrick 1995: 269 n. 12.

6. Mulvey [1975] 1989: 21–22.

7. Ibid.: 19–20; cf. 26, "The structure of looking in narrative fictional film contains a contradiction of its own premises: the female image as a castration threat constantly endangers the unity of the diegesis and bursts through the world of illusion as an intrusive, static, one-dimensional fetish."

8. An excellent illustration is provided by Prop. 1.3.1–20, lines that consist entirely of the poet's immobile contemplation of Cynthia's sleeping form, summed up in the closing distich: *sic intentis haerebam fixus ocellis / Argus ut ignotis cornibus Inachidos* ("Thus I was frozen, transfixed with intent eyes, like Argus fixed on Io with her unfamiliar horns").

9. E.g., Prop. 2.8.12, *illa . . . ferrea*; 2.17.1–2, *mentiri noctem, promissis ducere amantem, / hoc erit infectas sanguine habere manus*; 2.18c.23, *nunc etiam infectos demens imitare Britannos*.

10. Richlin 1992a: 47.

11. See Cahoon 1988 for an analysis of military metaphors and language in the *Amores*.

12. Keith (1994: 39–40) notes the use of the erotic object to represent the poetic text, but does not observe that this object is, in Callimachus, usually male. Cameron (1995: 303–38) argues that Callimachus does not reject epic per se but rather Antimachus's improper use of epic style in his elegiac *Lyde*.

13. *Aetia* fr. 1.1–17 [Pfeiffer]; translation of *Telchines* by Lombardo and Rayor (1988). For the association between the Telchines and the evil eye, see Hopkinson 1988: 91.

14. Dunbabin and Dickie 1983: 9, cf. 15.

15. See F. Williams 1978 and Hopkinson 1988: 85–91. Cf. *Epigr.* 21 [Pfeiffer], where Callimachus is said to have sang "poems stronger than Spite (*Baskaniēs*)."

16. Dunbabin and Dickie 1983: 19.

17. Downplaying connections between this poem, the highway in the *Aetia* prologue, and the muddy river in the *Hymn to Apollo*, Cameron concludes, "The primary purpose of the poem is surely erotic rather than literary" (1995: 399). It seems unnecessary to insist on one meaning to the exclusion of the other, especially since Cameron's own discussion of the *Lyde* (303–38) demonstrates the use of erotic objects as literary metaphors.

18. *Epigr.* 25, 28–32, 41–46, 52, 63 [Pfeiffer].

19. This accusation is repeated in poem 37, and is implicit in other poems that remark upon her infidelity (70, 72, 75, 76, 85). For the concept of "staining" associated particularly with oral-genital contact, see Richlin 1992a: 26–31.

20. The phrase "grotesque body" comes from Bakhtin; for discussion in connection with Roman literature, see Gowers 1993: 30, 55. Examples: poems 21, 29, 32, 37, 39, 47, 57, 59, 74, 78, 79, 88–91, 110, 114, 115.

21. Catullus presents the image of Gellius fellating himself in poem 88.

22. Gowers 1993: 44. She concludes that the movement in poem 13 from the tangible *cena* to the intangible odor of the *unguentum* "is a guide to the balance of real and insubstantial in Catullus' work as a whole" (240–42).

23. Skinner 1991: 6.

24. Foucault 1986: 95. He adds that the transformations of the Hellenistic period "brought about, in a much more general and essential way, a problematiza-

tion of political activity" (86) that extended into the early centuries of Roman rule.

25. On the hoplite-*kinaidos* opposition, see Vidal-Naquet 1986: 85–156 and Winkler 1990: 45–70. On the movement away from classical hoplite warfare, in both tactics and the use of mercenaries, see Griffith 1935: 1–7, 317–24; Ober 1991: 190–92; and V. D. Hanson 1991a: 253–56. For the reorientation of the *gymnasion* away from the training of future soldiers and toward intellectual and physical pleasure, see Giovannini 1993: 268–74.

26. Cameron 1995: 3–103. For writing and Hellenistic poetry, see Bing 1988: 10–48; Lombardo 1989, and Lombardo and Rayor 1988.

27. Cameron 1995: 407. Lazenby (1991: 106) points out that Homer remained the "Bible" of the Greeks because of the shared experience of hoplite warfare, noting that "hoplites were 'the nation in arms' . . . in states where those who could not afford such service were excluded from full civic rights."

28. Malamud 1993: 156; cf. Gutzwiller and Michelini 1991. For the effect of the "Roman revolution" on concepts of the self among the elite, see Barton 1993; Skinner 1991, 1993; Hopkins 1983. For the importance of competition and status in domestic life (housing, furnishings, dining), see Clarke 1991: 1–24, 369–71; D'Arms 1990; Fredrick 1995; and Wallace-Hadrill 1994: 1–61.

29. See especially Ov. *Am.* 1.1 and 2.1; for the wounding of the *amator* by infidelity, see, e.g., Prop. 2.1.57–70, where the speaker compares his injury to those of Philoctetes, Phoenix, Androgeos, Telephus, and Prometheus, and pronounces it much worse because it is incurable.

30. Wyke 1987, who concludes that this group of poems "re-establishes an allegiance to a politically unorthodox, Callimachean poetic practice" (60).

31. For erotic fascination vs. jealous anger, see Prop. 1.1–1.9, 1.11–1.16, 2.16–2.19, 2.24–2.26, 2.29–2.29a, 2.30, 2.32–2.34, 3.1–3.6, 3.10–3.14, 3.16–3.17, 3.19–3.20, 3.23–3.25; and Ov. *Am.* 1.1–1.10, 1.14, 2.1, 2.5, 2.9–2.11, 2.16–2.19, 3.1–3.4, 3.7–3.8, 3.11–3.12, 3.14.

32. For biting in elegiac lovemaking, see also Tib. 1.6.13–14 and Prop. 3.8.21–22.

33. On these two poems, see Gamel 1989.

34. *Am.* 2.15.25: *sed, puto, te nuda mea membra libidine surgent / et peragam partes anulus ille viri.*

35. E.g., Tib. 1.2, 1.4–1.6, 1.9, 2.3–2.4, 2.6.

36. Tib. 1.10.51–60: *rusticus e lucoque vehit, male sobrius ipse / uxorem plaustro progeniemque domum. / sed veneris tunc bella calent, scissosque capillos / femina, perfractas conqueriturque fores; / flet teneras subtusa genas: sed victor et ipse / flet sibi dementes tam valuisse manus. / at lascivus Amor rixae mala verba ministrat, / inter et iratum lentus utrumque sedet. / a lapis est ferrumque, suam quicumque puellam / verberat: e caelo deripit ille deos.*

37. See Tib. 1.5.47–76, 1.6.1–41, 2.3, 2.4.

38. See Hallett 1992a: 350–51. On Sulpicia in the context of elegy, see Hinds 1987; Lowe 1988; Roessel 1990; Santirocco 1979; and Wyke 1994.

39. Cf. Roessel 1990: 247, "Sulpicia writes on her lover, both figuratively and literally." For Cerinthus there is no masculine counterpart to the epithet *puella*,

although Sulpicia does address him as *mea lux* (4.12.1) and designates herself *tua puella* (4.11.1).

40. Ovid may have had Sulpicia's poem specifically in mind in *Am.* 2.15.15, *idem ego ut arcanas possim signare tabellas*, which partly echoes Sulpicia's line, *non ego signatis quicquam mandare tabellis* (4.7.7).

41. See Bradley 1991: 125–204; Dixon 1988: 41–140, 168–209, and 1992: 36–97; Treggiari 1991: 205–61. For a skeptical view of women's alleged "emancipation" during the late Republic, see Gardner 1986: 257–66.

42. Veyne 1988: 85–115; but Wyke (1989a) questions Veyne's separation of elegy's semiotic code from Rome's social history.

43. Edwards 1993: 85. She there summarizes the actor's position as a paradigm of low status and the implications of Nero's reign as actor-emperor, which "causes everyone to dissemble"; see also Bartsch 1994: 36–62.

44. Coleman 1990.

45. Edwards 1993; she remarks that "acting . . . was seen as incompatible with virtually anything that was admirable in a Roman citizen" (86). This is also the self-proclaimed position of the elegist.

PART FOUR

MALE CONSTRUCTIONS OF "WOMAN"

EIGHT

PLINY'S BRASSIERE

Amy Richlin

A S WE TRY to write the history of Roman sexualities, the sexual experience of women is most difficult to recover, almost unknown at first hand, heavily screened in male-authored erotic and literary texts. The journey you are about to undertake travels through little-known wildernesses of Roman texts in search of the sexual experience of Roman women. These texts are far from erotic, a jumble of encyclopedias and agricultural handbooks. In treating their content as pertinent to women's sexual lives, I have to point out that *Our Bodies, Ourselves* has occasionally been targeted as pornographic and is seen even by its creators as an important step forward in women's sexual freedom.[1] Similarly, the material to be examined here brings us into the everyday world of women's sexual experience, including mundane topics like menstruation, fertility, contraception, abortion, aphrodisiacs, pregnancy, childbirth, and well-baby care. The texts treat having babies as part of having sex, and I will, too; though babies are few and far between in love elegy or invective, in the wholly marriage-centered world of the encyclopedias, babies are everywhere.

The question of women's place in ancient medicine has been the subject of much excellent recent scholarship. Despite this, and somewhat surprisingly, the reader will find most of the Roman material here new. Even so eminent a scholar as Ann Hanson, writing about ancient medical writers, treats Soranus as a Greek along with the Hippocratic writers, and moves to the Middle Ages when she wants to talk about *Gynaikeia* in Latin (1990: 311). The majority of the new feminist work on ancient medicine is Hellenocentric, and many studies are not primarily concerned

Portions of this paper were presented at the Brown University conference on Roman women in 1986, and the research for it was continued thanks to a grant from the National Endowment for the Humanities in 1987–88. Many thanks to Judith Hallett and Marilyn Skinner for their patience, and to Charlotte Furth, Sarah Iles Johnston, Holt Parker, David Soren, and Heinrich von Staden for contributions, criticism, and help. Thanks most of all to San, who always laughs.

Translations throughout are my own, except as noted. The text of Pliny used here is Rackham, Jones, and Eichholz 1938–63.

with rooting the systems they analyze in a broader cultural context.[2] Heinrich von Staden's analysis of Celsus on the female body (1991) is exceptional in its attention to the Roman ideologies behind Celsus's ambivalence. Here I will be relying mainly on the *Natural History* of the elder Pliny (24–79 C.E.), along with the encyclopedist Pompeius Festus (second-century C.E. epitomator of an Augustan work), the agricultural writer Columella (60s C.E.), and other similar writers. Although they often leave us in a murky ancient Mediterranean soup of sources, they can also on occasion tie in their dicta with observed practice in the Italian countryside, or let us know that they are turning to female practitioners or popular belief as their source. These writers are not, properly speaking, medical writers—they have no medical training—but they hold up for our perusal a collage of beliefs from many strata of their society, and they richly repay study.

How were these writers different from medical writers as such? What can they tell us about Roman women that medical writers might not? Again, Pliny himself makes a good starting point. As G.E.R. Lloyd suggests in his brief but pointed overview (1983: 135–49), Pliny has the virtues of his faults. His vast encyclopedia is built along contradictory lines: much of it derives from Pliny's enormous reading, yet he generally recognizes the value of experience, and sometimes turns to his own observations; he often inveighs against magic and superstition, then in the next breath records lists of magical cures, with or without negative comment; sometimes he follows Greek scientific sources almost word-for-word, elsewhere he reports what he has seen in the Italian countryside. Cures using bugs are dubbed almost too disgusting to relate (29.61), while earthworms are acclaimed as so versatile that they are kept in honey for general use (29.91–92). He could never be called a critical reader in any consistent sense; as his nephew innocently remarks of him (*Ep.* 3.5.10), "He read nothing without making excerpts from it; indeed, he used to say that there was no book so bad that some part of it wasn't useful." Although he writes a crabbed and difficult prose, often sounds cantankerous, and was certainly a terrible bigot, the *Natural History* exudes a sort of sweetness, like the monologues of the old codger in *The Wrong Box*. That he was extremely curious is well attested by the manner of his death; the *Natural History* itself shows that he carried this curiosity to the point of gullibility, as for example in his account of the herb doctor he met who told him he could get him a thirty-foot moly root (25.26).

He had the deepest contempt for doctors.[3] In a long tirade (29.1–28) he makes it clear that this contempt is ethnic and class-based. Pliny was a wealthy man, a Roman equestrian, a naval commander, author of a book on cavalry tactics, a book of military history, and a book on rhetoric, as well as a slave-owner, landowner, scientist, encyclopedist, and friend of emperors.[4] For him, doctors and their medicine are Greek and worse than useless to Romans; when he proclaims (29.1) that "the nature of remedies . . . has been treated by no one in the Latin language before this," he ignores Celsus and Scribonius Largus—perhaps because they counted as "no one" to him. Again and again he reviles doctors for making huge profits; this is the contempt of a Roman equestrian for a tradesman. He compares doctors to actors (29.9), persons whose civil status was diminished due to the dishonor felt to adhere to their occupation (see Edwards, this volume). He associates medicine with the luxury and moral corruption that it was a cliche, in Roman oratory, to associate with the Greek East (29.20, 26–27). He repeats seriously what was a standing joke, for example in the epigrams of Martial: that doctors murder their patients (29.11, 13, 18). The Roman people, he says, did "without doctors but not without medicine" for six hundred years (29.11), and he quotes in its entirety a letter of the elder Cato to his son Marcus dismissing Athens, Greek literature, and Greek medicine with loathing (29.14): "A most worthless and intractable race. . . . They have sworn to kill all of us, whom they call 'barbarians,' by their medicine. . . . I prohibit you from all doctors." Cato's authority here is guaranteed, in very Roman terms, by reference to his triumph, censorship, age, public service, and experience (29.13, 15). Pliny goes on to claim that he himself is making use of Cato's own book of home remedies (29.15), and insists that *Romana gravitas* must separate Romans from the practice of medicine, even from the writing of medical books in Latin.

Yet he compiled the *Natural History*. There is thus in his text always a tension between the matter at hand and Pliny's attitude toward it; he writes, not (shudder) as a medical professional, but as a Roman equestrian eager to make useful knowledge available to Romans. (In this he succeeded. Despite its chaotic organization, the *Natural History* proved popular; it was to have a long afterlife, enjoying honor and respect down through the Middle Ages and Renaissance [Chibnall 1975], and it is still in print today after two thousand years.) Pliny's book, despite overlaps, is thus essentially different from the texts produced by Roman medical writers: for example, his coevals Celsus and Scribonius Largus, the second-century doctors Galen and Soranus, and the probably later writer Metrodora.[5]

For one thing, the last three of these writers were Greeks, though Galen and Soranus practiced in Rome; and they wrote in Greek. Soranus looks down on his adopted city: "The women in this city do not possess sufficient devotion to look after everything as the purely Grecian women do" (2.44, trans. Temkin). For another, they are concerned, in their writing, to present a system of health care; a section of Metrodora's work is even arranged by headings in alphabetical order, for ease in consultation. Though Soranus's book is largely concerned with advice to women and midwives, he brings up folk medicine in order to discredit it (1.63, contraceptive amulets; 2.6, why women loosen their clothing and hair during childbirth), or patronizes it: "Even if the amulet has no direct effect, still through hope it will possibly make the patient more cheerful" (3.42, trans. Temkin; but cf. Lloyd [1983: 168–82], who credits Soranus for his willingness to humor his patients). To Pliny, doctors, the Magi, peasants, and his own observations are all grist to the mill; just as Cato wrote a *commentarium* for the use of his wife, son, slaves, and *familiares* (*HN* 29.15), so Pliny is writing one for a larger circle. The medical writers write as outsiders, or from above, as professionals; Pliny writes from inside.

This essay takes its name from a brief remark in the *Natural History* (28.76): "I find that headaches are relieved by tying a woman's brassiere on [my/the] head."[6] The strangeness of this image, outstanding even among Pliny's weird parade, has haunted me since first I read it. Of course it made me laugh; I always think of a man in a toga sitting and working late into the night by lamplight, with a contraption on his head that looks like something Madonna would wear. In fact Roman brassieres probably looked more like Ace bandages; yet the image is still strange, because Pliny does not just mean that a headache is cured by wrapping a stretchy thing around your head. He is talking about the medicinal uses of the female human body, and he seems to believe that something is exuded from women's bodies that would make a brassiere cure a headache. Strange as his belief system may be to us, it seems possible to ask what the experience of it would have been like for women contemporary with Pliny.[7] Moreover, Pliny and his bra may be useful as a symbol embodying the yin and yang of Roman medicine: we can focus on Pliny, and consider what his gynecology, his use of the brassiere, has in common with his status in Roman culture; or we can focus on the woman whose brassiere it was.

Linda Gordon, in an important article (1986), delineated two opposing approaches to the writing of women's history. In one approach, the historian paints women as the victims of an oppressive structure, showing how patriarchy and patriarchs keep women downtrodden. In the other approach, the historian paints women as agents, working out their own strategies to deal with whatever system they find themselves in. This second approach often tries to locate and analyze "women's culture": sets of strategies that women at particular times and places have adopted.[8] Following up on a suggestion I made in an earlier article (1993a: 291–92), I will here argue that the episode of Pliny's brassiere can be used as a starting point for both these approaches. And I will begin with Pliny.

Pliny and the Brassiere

> I thought of that old gentleman, who is dead now, but
> was a bishop, I think, who declared that it was impossible for
> any woman, past, present, or to come, to have the genius of
> Shakespeare. He wrote to the papers about it. He also told a
> lady who applied to him for information that cats do not
> as a matter of fact go to heaven, though they have, he added,
> souls of a sort. How much thinking those old gentlemen
> used to save one! How the borders of ignorance shrank back
> at their approach! Cats do not go to heaven. Women
> cannot write the plays of Shakespeare.
> (Virginia Woolf, *A Room of One's Own*)

What does it mean when Pliny puts a brassiere on his head? Why do we laugh? Partly, at least, because of who he is. He's a man in a toga; the brassiere doesn't suit his dignity. What's a man like that doing with a bra on his head?

The relation between Pliny the scientist and the brassiere on his head might be taken as a symbol of the way Roman medicine colonizes the female body. Pliny's *Natural History* includes a major section in book 28 on the medical uses of the female human body; this section has a lot to say about menstrual blood, about which there is also a section in book 7.[9] In addition, there are a great many other bits about the female body dotted throughout the text, and other writers, as well, talk about the issue—not medical writers, but agricultural writers like Columella, and encyclopedists like Pompeius Festus.

The point is not only that these writers view the female human body as raw material for medicines, but also why they think this would work. Evidently the female body itself is intrinsically powerful—both harmful and helpful; almost uncanny, evidently due to its special processes, not only menstruation but also childbirth and lactation. Anne Carson (1990) has talked about the symbolic properties attributed to Greek women's bodies in literary texts; in Roman encyclopedic writing we see similar attitudes given practical form. Indeed, the Roman texts provide a perfect example of the kind of ambivalence suggested by Thomas Buckley and Alma Gottlieb as the paradigm for menstrual "taboos."[10] Moreover, as we look at the Roman texts, it is useful to contrast them with studies of attitudes toward the female body in other Mediterranean cultures, especially those influenced by Christianity, Judaism, or Islam. Rome has nothing to compare with the theological basis for menstrual disgust in the

Turkish village culture studied by Carol Delaney (1988), nor is there any mention of prohibitions concerned with religious ritual.[11] The beliefs attested in the encyclopedic texts are secular and practical in their area of concern; while they use evaluative language, like *tantum malum* ("so great an evil") or *monstrificum* ("monstrous"), there is apparently no theological or cosmological reason for it.

Sometimes just the female body itself, even the sight of it, can be dangerous. Describing the frankincense trade in Arabia, Pliny notes that those who trade in this precious commodity cannot let themselves "be polluted (*pollui*) by any meeting with women or with funeral processions" (12.54).[12] The appearance of a woman as a bad omen or pollutant is not uncommon; Pliny describes what he calls "the rustic law on many Italian farms," whereby care is taken to keep women from walking down the road using a spindle, or even carrying one in the open, since such a sight would "blight all expectations," especially for the crops (28.28). While the ostensible source of the problem here is the spindle, the virtual identity between women and spinning/weaving is surely in play.

Often the power of the female body is associated directly with menstruation. Its powers to help are awesome, almost frightening, and are noted with a certain ambivalence; as Pliny says, "Many say there are remedies, too, in such an evil." Hailstorms and tornados are driven away "by the sight of a naked, menstruating woman" (? *mense nudato*); likewise, storms at sea are turned aside by the sight of a naked woman (?), even without menstruation (*etiam sine menstruis*, 28.77). Menstrual blood has general powers to cure diseases, especially epilepsy (28.44), rabies, fevers (28.82–86)—all illnesses involving loss of bodily control.[13] And it is particularly useful to the farmer. Columella lists a whole series of spells to rid the garden of pests, things like caterpillars (*Rust.* 10.337–68). But the best, he says, is to send a menstruating virgin to walk around the fields (10.357–68):

> But if no medicine [*medicina*] has the power to repel the pests,
> bring on the Dardanian arts, and let a woman with bare feet,
> who, first occupied with the regular laws of a girl,
> drips chastely with her obscene blood,
> with her dress and hair unbound, and serious face,
> be led three times around the fields and garden hedge.
> And when she has purged them by walking, amazing to see! ...
> The caterpillars roll to the ground with twisted bodies.

Columella repeats this advice elsewhere (11.3.64), without specifying that the woman needs to be a virgin, and citing a Greek text, Democritus's *On Antipathies*. Pliny repeats the same advice for getting rid of caterpillars, worms, and beetles, along with other pests (28.78); the woman should be naked. He also there cites a recommendation of Metrodorus of Scepsis, derived from Cappadocia, for getting rid of cantharides in the fields: he says the woman should go through the middle of the fields with her dress pulled up above her buttocks. (Presumably Columella, with his "Dardanian arts," is also thinking of Metrodorus; Scepsis is in the Troad.) Other possibilities are for her to go barefoot, with her hair hanging down and her dress unfastened; but care should be taken lest she do this at sunrise, for this will dry up the crops. Moreover, if she touches them, young vines will be permanently damaged, and rue and ivy, those "most medicinal things" (*res medicatissimos*), will die on the spot. In a discussion of ridding trees of pests (17.266–67), Pliny repeats that many people say caterpillars (*urucae*) can be killed by having a woman just beginning her period walk around each of the trees, barefoot and with her tunic ungirt (*recincta*). Since both writers cite Greek or Asian sources, we cannot tell to what extent such rituals may have been practiced in the Italian countryside, but we gain the added idea that they may have been practiced throughout the Mediterranean. Moreover, we note that even in Columella's discussion of the useful powers of a menstruating woman, the blood itself is referred to as "obscene blood" (*obsceno cruore*, 10.360). The semantic range of *obscenus/a/um* in Latin leaves us in no doubt that Columella associates the blood with things both sexual and repulsive, things that should not be seen or spoken about (Richlin 1992a: 9; cf. von Staden 1991: 284–86). The mixed emotions attested here are echoed by Pliny's warning about the danger to crops.

Thus it is no surprise to find that, in Pliny's *materia medica*, menstrual blood can do harm. Pliny introduces both of his discussions of menstrual blood with warnings: "Nothing may easily be found more monstrous than the flux of women" (7.64); and "Indeed, from the menses themselves, elsewhere monstrous, . . . they rant dire and unspeakable things" (28.77). Intercourse with menstruating women can be "deadly" for men (28.77–78). Speaking of the *violentia* of menstrual blood, Pliny gives a list of its effects (28.79–80): it can put bees to flight, stain linens black, dull barbers' razors, tarnish bronze and give it a bad smell, cause pregnant mares to abort (even when the women are only seen at a distance, if this is the first menstruation), make she-asses sterile if they eat grain contaminated by menstrual blood, and ruin dyes (cf. 28.78, where purple is said to be "polluted" by menstruating women during the times of especially deadly menstruation). Even women themselves, usually "immune among themselves to their own evil" (*malo suo inter se inmunibus*), can be forced to abort by a smear of menstrual blood, especially if a pregnant woman walks over some (28.80). Pliny cites Bithus of Dyrrachium as the authority for one remedy: mirrors that have been dulled by the glance of a menstruating woman can recover their shine by having the woman look at the back of the mirror; and this whole problem can be averted by having the menstruating woman carry a mullet (fish) with her (28.82).

In another list of the harmful properties of menstrual blood (7.64), Pliny says: contact with it sours new wine; crops become barren when touched by it; grafts die; the seeds are burned up in the gardens; fruit falls off the trees; mirrors are dimmed by menstruating women looking into them; the edge of iron tools is dulled; the shine on ivory is dulled; beehives die; bronze and iron corrode, and bronze smells bad; and dogs who taste it contract rabies and their bites are infected with incurable poison (*venenum*). Even ants, people say, can sense it, and will spit out fruit tainted by it, nor will they go back to it afterwards (7.65). Likewise, bees, who appreciate cleanliness, hate both scurf and women's menstrual blood (11.44). All kitchen plants grow yellow at the approach of a menstruating woman (19.176).

Many of these beliefs have an agricultural context, and, indeed, Columella includes a few remarks on menstrual blood among his most humdrum comments on gardening. Like Pliny, he says that plants will dry up if touched by a menstruating woman (*Rust.* 11.3.38); this passage, like most of Columella, is down-to-earth in its tone, and explicitly takes its authority from peasants (*ut rustici dicunt*, 11.3.43, 12.10.1) and from Columella's own experience (11.3.61). Moreover, no women at all should be allowed near cucumbers (hmm . . .) and gourds, for "the growth of green things droops at contact with them." This is even worse if the women are menstruating, at which time they will kill the new growth just by looking at it (11.3.50).

These beliefs are in keeping with attitudes expressed toward menstruation in other kinds of Roman texts. Menstruation and menstrual blood are mentioned only a few times in Roman satirical and moralizing literature, uniformly negatively (discussed in Richlin 1992a: 169, 281–82). Attitudes toward the female genitalia generally in Roman texts are highly negative; descriptions appear only in invective, and invective of a most savage sort.[14] Thus Festus lists the word ANCUNULENTAE, which he says is used to refer to "women . . . at the time of menstruation," and suggests that the Latin word *inquinamentum*, which means "stain," comes from this word (10L). *Inquinamentum* is not a neutral word, and it appears with some frequency in sexual contexts (Richlin 1992a: 27).

It is not just menstrual blood, though, that comes into these medical texts. Another peculiarly female body fluid, breast milk, plays a large part in Pliny's account of the female body. And unlike menstrual blood, breast milk is uniformly helpful. Pliny rates women's milk as one of the most useful remedies (28.123):

Foremost we will expound the common and particular remedies from animals, for example the uses of milk. Mother's milk is the most useful thing
for anybody. . . . Moreover, human milk is the most nourishing for any purpose, next goat's milk; the sweetest after human [milk] is camel's, the most
effective [after human milk] comes from donkeys.

Again, we might be startled to find women listed here among animals,
and take this as similar to the attitudes that link menstruating women
with animals, crops, and the monstrous. Still, Pliny has many good things
to say about women's milk. It is an antidote to poisons, and cures many
illnesses, especially illnesses of the eye. A man anointed with the milk of
a mother and daughter at the same time, Pliny says, is freed from all fear
for his eyes throughout his life (28.73).[15]

Moreover, it is not just these special body fluids that have medical
properties. Other effluvia from women's bodies are also powerful, including urine, hair, and saliva. Pliny says, for example, that the saliva of
a fasting woman is good for bloodshot eyes and fluxes; the corners of the
eye are to be moistened with the saliva occasionally. This works better if
the woman has fasted on the previous day as well (28.76).

With all these recommendations, we find ourselves wondering how
often people actually used cures like this. We have one valuable attestation in a story about the father of the emperor Vitellius. Suetonius is not
sure he approves of him, and describes the senior Vitellius as "a man
harmless and industrious, but thoroughly notorious for his love of a
freedwoman. He used to bathe his windpipe and throat as a remedy with
a mixture of her saliva with honey, and not secretly or occasionally but
daily and right out in the open" (*Vit.* 2.4). Presumably what is disgraceful here is the openness and the breach of class boundaries; Suetonius
does not really seem to question the belief that the woman's saliva would
have curative powers. And as will be seen, there are several accounts of
the use of women's saliva to protect babies from harm.

It seems, overall, that Roman medical uses of the female body tie in
with a set of beliefs about the female body that is characterized by a deep
ambivalence. The body is powerful, but in a frightening way. There is a
familiar division between the lower-body fluids and the upper-body fluids—the fluids from the lower body having the power both to help and
to harm, while the fluids from the upper body are just helpful. Menstrual
blood protects, or harms, a long list of products of culture—crops, metal
tools, domesticated animals, dye. So when Pliny puts on that brassiere, he
is using the female body to think with in more ways than one.[16]

But who gave him the brassiere? Several of the cures from the female
body involve a large degree of cooperation and participation on the part
of women themselves: for example, the caterpillar-removal procedure, in

which a woman has to walk through the fields barefoot. This certainly implies a scenario with a woman and her powers as the center of attention, and this is not the only such case. One female practitioner whom Pliny quotes, the *obstetrix* Sotira, recommends a cure in which the soles of the patient's feet are smeared with menstrual blood; she notes that this works especially well if done by the woman herself (*HN* 28.83). The saliva to be obtained from a fasting woman implies her cooperation not only in providing the saliva but in fasting as well. We might guess that the elder Vitellius got the saliva from his mistress with her knowledge. And likewise for the other cures and harms. We might indeed extrapolate that this body of medical knowledge implies a great deal about women's experience of themselves in the world. We might further expect that women's beliefs about their bodies might vary according to class, or urban/rural divisions; in any case, we might well turn our attention from the man wearing the brassiere to the woman he got it from.

The Woman Behind the Brassiere

> I did not spend the next two weeks worrying about my
> period. If it did not show up, there was no question in my
> mind that I would force it to do so. I knew how to do this.
> Without telling me exactly how I might miss a menstrual
> cycle, my mother had shown me which herbs to pick and boil,
> and what time of day to drink the potion they produced, to
> bring on a reluctant period. She had presented the whole idea
> to me as a way to strengthen the womb, but underneath we
> both knew that a weak womb was not the cause of a missed
> period. She knew that I knew, but we presented to each
> other a face of innocence and politeness and even went so
> far as to curtsy to each other at the end.
> (Jamaica Kincaid, *Lucy*)

Feminist historians of medicine have made us familiar with the idea that women played an important part in "folk" medicine in western Europe.[17] In the Roman period, the divisions among different kinds of medicine were much blurrier than they are today. There evidently were such divisions; Pliny spends a lot of time complaining about the kinds of medicine he disapproves of, especially "magical" cures—that is, the cures of the Magi, practitioners from Asia Minor (cf. Lloyd 1979: 13 n. 20; 1983: 140–41). But for us, it is very hard to tell the difference between the Roman forms of what we would call folk medicine, scientific medicine, and magic. This section looks at how women themselves might have taken an active role in their cures. And these cures definitely sound folksy. But the reader should be aware that they do not sound more folksy than the general run of cures in Pliny's *Natural History*.

Pliny certainly does not cite many female medical authorities as sources. His sources are most often male, when he cites them, and it is always a question how much descriptive validity we can ascribe to his recommendations. Still, what I will try to do is to recover from Pliny's *Natural History* some idea of women's own health practices in first-century c.e. Rome.

How might we imagine women involving themselves in medical practice? The epigraph to this section comes from the Antiguan writer Jamaica Kincaid; her protagonist is living in contemporary New York. This young woman and her mother are both active and knowledgeable, and the sort of medicine they practice is immediately recognizable in the pages of Pliny's *Natural History*.

If we look long enough, we find that some of Pliny's recipes do involve action by the woman herself. For pains in the *muliebria loca*, women are to wear "constantly" a bracelet containing the first tooth of their child to fall out, which should never have fallen on the ground (28.41). So we can imagine women saving, in their medicine boxes, their children's first baby teeth. To stop menstruation, Pliny recommends catching a spider spinning a thread as it ascends again, crushing it, and applying it (30.129). For a variety of ills, Pliny recommends calf's gall sprinkled on the genitals during menstruation, just before intercourse (28.253); so we have to imagine a woman saying, "Excuse me, dear, while I just sprinkle on some of this calf's gall." Taking a purge could apparently be a complex and drawn-out process: women are to take a decoction of linozostis in food on the second day of menstruation (*purgatio*) for three further days; on the fourth day, after a bath, they are to have sex (25.40). In a rare ethnographic description of actual female practice, Pliny says that the *agrestes feminae*, "peasant women," in Transpadane Gaul wear amber necklaces, mostly as ornaments, but also as *medicina*, to ward off throat problems (37.44).

Another branch of ancient *medicina* that demands active involvement of its consumers is love medicine. Despite disclaimers, Pliny describes more than sixty different aphrodisiacs and more than twenty-nine different antaphrodisiacs. He even has several lists of such materials (26.94–99; 32.139), including one from the Magi (30.141–43), and credits a range of sources, all male.[18] These are mostly given without comment, though Pliny chides Theophrastus for his description of a plant that produces the lust to have sex seventy times (26.99). Considering the common Roman idea that women specialize in potions (see below), this all-male cast is surprising; Metrodora does include a number of aphrodisiacs in her book (1.26, 1.38, 1.39, 4.20–23).[19]

The market for these products seems to be mixed. Some are listed specifically as "for men" (a total of twelve) or "for women" (a total of seven); scandix is for those "exhausted by sex or shriveled from old age" (22.80).[20] Rarely are circumstances specified; Pliny does not tell us of limits on use for self as opposed to use on others. Hyena genitals in honey are said to stimulate desire, "even when men hate intercourse with women"; and so (what's a wife to do?) "the harmony of the whole house is preserved by keeping these genitals, along with a vertebra with some of the skin attached" (28.99).[21] For antaphrodisiacs, several motives seem to be in play. Repeatedly these drugs are said to stop wet dreams (*libidinum imaginationes in somno*, literally "imaginings of lusts in sleep") or sex dreams (*somnia veneris*) (20.68, 20.142–43, 20.146, 26.94, 34.166). Some aphrodisiacs are clearly aimed at influencing an object's desires without his/her knowledge—sprinkling seeds on a woman to augment her eagerness (20.227), placing a southernwood sprig under the pillow (21.162). Others would be harder to miss: putting hyena muzzle hairs on a woman's lips (aphrodisiac, 28.101) or rubbing her groin with blood from a tick or giving her he-goat's urine to drink (antaphrodisiac, 28.256). Erynge root (22.20) is said to make a man who gets hold of it *amabilis*; this, Pliny says, is how Phaon of Lesbos made himself beloved by Sappho. The Magi, among many other powers they attribute to the hyena (including a cure for *probrosa mollitia*, "disgraceful effeminacy"), claim that a hyena anus worn on a man's left arm will make any woman follow him the minute he looks at her (28.106). By way of comparison, Metrodora seems equally to be writing for a mixed audience; five of her eight aphrodisiacs are "for erection" (4.20–23), while one is headed "So that she will howl and make all kinds of sounds" (1.39, Parker trans.). A remedy entitled "For a woman, so she will not be promiscuous" (1.36) requires the man to rub medicine on his penis; another charm promises "to make her confess her lovers" (1.37).[22]

Nowadays we expect that abortion would be something with which women would concern themselves. Roman culture, though, set a high value on women's fertility, and Pliny's text reflects that attitude. His expressed attitude toward abortion is negative, and he mostly gives recommendations for ways to increase fertility and to promote successful delivery of a child. However, he does in fact give formulas for abortifacients, as well as for emmenagogues. (These remedies are referred to by Pliny as "calling forth the menses," much like the cures described by Jamaica Kincaid's narrator; the distinction between such a medicine and an abortifacient is obviously a fine one.[23]) In this context, it seems significant that Pliny attributes the invention of abortion to women; he exclaims (10.172), "Males have figured out all the back alleyways of sex, crimes against nature; but women figured out abortions." This despite evident ideological disincentives.

Pliny himself connects abortion not only with "unnatural" sex, as here, but with magical potions leading to insanity and/or love and lust (25.25):

> But what excuse could there be for showing how minds could be unhinged, fetuses squeezed out, and many similar things? I do not discuss abortifacients (*abortiva*), nor even love potions ... nor other magic portents, unless when they are to be warned against or refuted, especially when confidence in them has been undermined.

One such refutation concerns two female practitioners, Lais and Elephantis. In his summary of their accounts of the abortifacient powers of menstrual blood, he faults them for contradicting each other, and concludes (28.81): "When the latter says that fertility is brought about by the same methods by which the former pronounces barrenness [is], it is better not to believe [them]." This tells us a good deal. On the one hand, Pliny's attitude is quite negative: he sums up their accounts as *monstrifica*, in keeping with the general tone of his remarks on menstrual blood. And he is hardly deferential to them as female authorities on abortion. On the other hand, we know through him that these female medical writers talked both about abortion and about fertility. He reproduces their lists of *abortiva*, along with a warning that barley tainted by menstrual blood will block conception in she-asses.

Furthermore, Pliny himself tells us some things about women's practice. A section headed "Wine, too, has its amazing qualities" moves from fertility to poisons, taking in abortion along the way. Wine flavored with hellebore, cucumber, or scammony, he notes (14.110), is called *phthorium* ("destructive") because it produces abortions (*phthorios pessos* is the term for "abortifacient" in the Hippocratic Oath). One wine from Arcadia produces *fecunditas* in women and madness (*rabies*) in men (14.116), but in Achaia, there is a wine reported to expel the fetus (*abigi partum*), "even if pregnant women eat one of the grapes." An Egyptian wine has the nickname *ecbolada* (Gk. "throw-out"), because it brings on an abortion (14.118). Similarly, ground pine has the Latin name *abiga* ("push-out"), "because of abortions" (24.29). These descriptive names may possibly be folk terms; in a discussion of the properties of the willow tree, Pliny notes (16.110) that Homer calls the willow *frugiperda*, "destroys-fruit" (*olesikarpon*, *Od.* 10.510); he comments, "Later ages have interpreted this conceit according to their own wickedness, since it is known that the seed of the willow is a *medicamentum* of barrenness for a woman." The reported accounts in Lais and Elephantis may have been part of a how-to guide; similarly, in a discussion of the gynecological properties of mallow, Pliny notes that another female practitioner, Olympias of Thebes, says that mallows with goose grease bring on abortion (20.226). That a woman might not wish to conceive is recognized by another recipe, directed at a male market: a woman unwilling to conceive is forced to, by means of hairs taken from the tail of a she-mule, pulled out while the animals are mating, and woven together when the man and woman are (30.142).[24]

Pliny's connection between female practitioners, abortifacients, and love potions is common in literary and legal texts. Apart from whatever doctors may have done, Roman writers portray a market of female consumers whose needs are met by women who concoct potions. Thus Juvenal, writing fifty years after Pliny, in his sixth satire, against women (6.594–98):

> Hardly ever do you find a woman giving birth in a gilded bed.
> So great is the power of the arts and medicines of that woman
> who makes women sterile, and contracts to kill human beings
> in the womb. Rejoice, unfortunate man, and yourself give her
> whatever it is she has to drink.

The point is that wealthy women, who can afford the cost, would rather pay for an abortion than bear a child; (cuckolded) husbands are Juvenal's intended audience. Similarly, at least one legal text envisions the makers of potions as female; the jurist Marcian, writing in the early third century C.E. on serious crimes on a level with murder, writes: "But by law that woman is ordered to be relegated who, even if not with malice aforethought, but setting a bad example, has given any medicine to promote conception by which the woman who took it died" (*Dig.* 48.8.3). Here the line between the practice of doctors and of other practitioners grows particularly blurry. Pliny disapproves, but provides a list that seems to reflect folk practice as much as "medicine"; and at least by the early third century C.E., abortion was considered a serious crime, when self-inflicted (*Dig.* 48.8.8) or performed by others by means of "potions" (*Dig.* 48.19.38.5). Yet it is not clear that abortion itself, when brought about by a doctor, was illegal, or that this female market was ever rigorously controlled.[25]

Pliny devotes much more attention to the methods by which women may cure barrenness and promote conception. He recommends a wide variety of substances, from cow's milk to partridge eggs, and he strongly implies an active female market for these medicines.[26] He even cites from one of his sources a text unfortunately lost: a poem by a woman crediting a gemstone with helping her to conceive (37.178): "What paneros is like is not told us by Metrodorus, but he quotes a not-inelegant poem by Queen Timaris on it, dedicated to Venus, in which it is understood that the stone aided her fertility."

A picture begins to emerge of activities undertaken, mostly by women, in order to ensure the fertility that was so essential to them. The waters of Sinuessa are said to cure barrenness in women (31.8); a spring at Thespiae and the river Elatum in Arcadia help women conceive, while the spring Linus in Arcadia prevents miscarriage. We might imagine women making pilgrimages to these rivers in order to attain their goals, much like the well-attested fourth-century B.C.E. pilgrimages to the temple of Asclepius at Epidaurus, where women sought help toward conception, among other cures, via incubation (Lefkowitz and Fant 1992: 285–87). "Some people," says Pliny, "out of superstition, believe that mistletoe works more effectively if it is gathered from an oak at the new moon without iron or touching the ground, and that it cures epilepsy and helps women to conceive if they just keep it with them" (24.12). Women are also advised to keep cucumber seeds fastened to the body, without letting them touch the ground (20.6); thus we imagine the hopeful mother bedecked with seeds and plants. Another recommendation (*tradunt*) is to smell the plant ami during sex (20.164); so we might imagine rituals of the bedroom. (Compare Serenus Sammonicus's recommendation that a woman and her husband pluck the "herb of Mercury" together when they are hurrying to bed at night, *Liber medicinalis* 32.13–14.) Various medicines are said to foster conception, and some of them are not so appealing: the Magi promise that a barren woman will conceive in three days if she takes a hyena eye in her food with licorice and dill (*HN* 28.97); small worms taken in drink promote conception (30.125), as do snails applied with saffron (30.126); likewise hawk's dung in honey wine (30.130).

We might pause here to notice how awful some of the medicines sound. A lot of Pliny's recipes suggest how different the experience of medicine would have been for a Roman than for a modern patient. For the breasts, Pliny recommends crabs applied locally (*inliti*, 32.129); this sounds impossible, but elsewhere he recommends tying frogs backwards onto a baby's head for siriasis (literally "dog-star-itis," a name for infant sunstroke, 32.138); the skull has to be moistened, he notes soberly. Other recommendations for women include the use of beaver testicles, scrapings from the gymnasium, chewed-up anise, earthworms taken in sweet wine, beetles, and a wide variety of kinds of animal dung. There are recommendations for tying on fish, and for fumigation with a dead snake, or with lobsters. The example of the frogs on the baby shows that it is not just women who get stuck with this kind of medicine; however, there does seem to have been an association between disgusting ingredients and women patients. Heinrich von Staden, in a recent study (1992), has pointed out how overwhelmingly such cures are reserved for women, especially the use of dung.

So far we have seen women actively engaged in medical treatments affecting menstruation, abortion, and conception. Once conception was achieved, expectant mothers ran tests to determine the child's sex. For example, Pliny (10.154) says that, as a young woman, Livia, wife of Augustus, was eager to have a boy, and, when she was pregnant with Tiberius, used a special way, "common among girls" (*hoc usa est puellari augurio*), to tell the sex of her baby. Suetonius (*Tib.* 14.2) gives a more detailed description:

> Livia, when pregnant with [Tiberius], wanted to know whether she would give birth to a male [child], and tried to find out by various omens; she took an egg stolen from a setting hen and cherished it continually, sometimes in her own hand, sometimes in her maidservants', taking turns (*nunc sua nunc ministrarum manu per vices ... fovit*), until a chick was hatched, with a marked crest.

Here this procedure is made into a joint effort by mistress and slaves, all participating together, though the practice is focused on the body of the dominant woman.

Pliny also lists recommendations for materials that will affect the sex of the baby, not just tell the mother what it is. And many of these aim at helping to conceive a male child. Some involve activities by father and mother together (for example, taking crataegonos in wine before supper for forty days before conception, 27.63); often the recommendations are for special additions to the mother's diet.[27] Once in a while, the properties of substances to produce either a girl or a boy are listed; so maybe some people were trying for girls (compare the short list of such medicines in Metrodora, "for the birth of a boy or the birth of a girl," 1.33). On the other hand, there are hints here and there that boy babies are better, and a complete absence of recommendations aimed solely at conceiving a girl baby. So though there is nothing here to indicate any widespread gynecide, there does seem to be an assumption that women will be trying to have male children.[28]

By far the bulk of Pliny's material on fertility has to do with pregnancy, and especially with childbirth. It is ironic that one of the very few reported sayings we have from Roman women has to do with a subversion of what seems to be the norm expected by Pliny. A joke attributed to Julia, daughter of Augustus, has her claiming to use her pregnancies to enable her to have sex with men other than her husband (Macrob. *Sat.* 2.5.9): "And when those who knew of her sins used to marvel at how she gave birth to sons resembling Agrippa, when she made such public property of her body, she said, 'Why, I never take on a passenger until the ship is full.'" Julia, in contemporary histories, has the character of a renegade, a woman who goes against what is expected of women (Richlin 1992c).

Certainly, if the list of remedies in Pliny is anything to go by, we would expect that many Roman women were deeply concerned about carrying a baby to term.

Pliny's encyclopedia contains more than 140 remedies concerned with pregnancy and childbirth. A significant category contains substances that help hold off miscarriage or are to be avoided because they will cause miscarriage. Pliny includes miscarriage among the hazards of sexuality, saying that "a yawn indeed is fatal [to a woman] in labor, just as sneezing during sex causes miscarriage" (7.42). Some substances are to be avoided by pregnant women as dangerous, even by proximity; sometimes miscarriage is a risk or side effect. Thus the cases in which activity by the women is demanded include many aimed at staving off miscarriage. Most interesting is a group that involves things women should not step over: these include menstrual blood (28.80); a viper or a dead amphisbaena (30.128); a raven's egg, which will cause a woman to miscarry through the mouth (30.130); and beaver oil, or a beaver (32.133). These are among the most hallucinatory episodes in the *Natural History*: How is it imagined that a woman might accidentally step over a beaver? Did anyone really believe in oral miscarriage? Additional information only raises further questions. Pliny (30.128) offers two remedies for stepping over a dead amphisbaena—a snake with a head at each end of its body. One was to carry a live amphisbaena on your person in a box; the other was to step immediately over a preserved amphisbaena. So we have to imagine the household in an uproar, and somebody yelling, "Marcus! Quick, run down to the drugstore and get a preserved amphisbaena!" The dangers of raven's eggs are clarified by Pliny's notes on the raven (10.32); he says it is a popular belief (*vulgus arbitratur*) that ravens lay eggs or mate through their beaks, and hence a pregnant woman, if she eats a raven's egg, will bear her child through her mouth, and will have a difficult labor if a raven's egg is brought into the house. Though Aristotle is cited for a counteropinion, it seems at least possible that Pliny is preserving a folk belief here—though one that can hardly have had much in women's experience to support it.

Most of the miscarriage insurance is less exotic, and involves amulets, like this one (36.151):

> Eagle stones, wrapped in skins of sacrifical animals, are worn as amulets by women or quadrupeds (*mulieribus vel quadripedibus*) while pregnant to hold back the birth (*continent partus*); these are not to be removed until they give birth, otherwise the vulva will prolapse. But if the amulet is not taken away while they are in labor, they cannot give birth at all.

This kind of recommendation is found for other amulets as well, so when we think of amulets, we also should imagine that each one carries with it its proper procedure.

Indeed, the recommendations here imply women's activities and involvement with the medical care of their own bodies. A woman might experiment with a range of pessaries, ointments, and potions. Pliny recommends tying thirty grains of git to the body with linen to aid in removing the afterbirth (20.183). A woman might also use a hare-rennet ointment, unless she had bathed the day before (28.248); if she takes sow-thistle potion, she must then go for a walk (22.89). Substances or objects she might keep with her or carry include not only the preserved amphisbaena but a stick with which a frog has been shaken from a snake (30.129); a vulture's feather under the feet (30.130); a torpedo fish, brought into the room (32.133); and a "round ball of blackish tufa" taken from the second stomach of a heifer and not allowed to touch the ground (11.203). Amulets to aid labor include those made from plants sprouting inside a sieve thrown away on a cross-path (24.171); a stone eaten by a pregnant doe, found in her excrement or womb (28.246); and chameleon tongue (28.114). Some amulets or substances have to be placed on certain parts of the woman's body: the afterbirth of a bitch (30.123) and the snakeskin (30.129) have to be put on the woman's groin; the stingray-sting amulet is to be worn on the navel (32.133); the stone voided by a bladder victim is to be tied over the groin (28.42). And some procedures are very elaborate indeed, involving the central participation of other people. To hasten birth, the father of the baby is to untie his belt and put it around the woman's waist, and then untie it, saying the *precatio*, "I bound you, and I will set you free"; he then leaves the room (28.42). Another remedy involves someone throwing over the house where the woman is in labor one of two things: a missile that has killed with one stroke each a human being, a boar, and a bear; or a light-cavalry spear pulled from a human body without touching the ground (28.33–34). Or someone might just bring the spear into the house.

Pliny also lists some medicines that counteract the effects of witchcraft against conception, pregnancy, and childbirth. Some of these indicate women's concern to protect themselves against witchcraft, a sense of the vulnerability of a pregnant woman. The stone called aetites, found in eagle's nests, is also said to protect the fetus "against all plots to cause abortion" (*contra omnes abortuum insidias*, 30.130). Eating wolf meat is recommended for women about to give birth, or else having someone who has eaten wolf meat sit next to them as they go into labor; this prevails even against *inlatas noxias*, "harmful things carried in" (28.247–48). The idea that it is harmful specifically to bring certain things into the house where a woman is in labor recurs in several cases, and the implication is that ill-wishers might do this on purpose. The same may be true of the objects not to be stepped over; perhaps these should be thought of as placed in the woman's path—like the beaver, for example. These all seem to be actions it would be hard to do unintentionally, and so are to be understood as malicious; likewise, Pliny notes that hanging the left foot of a hyena above a woman in labor is fatal (28.103). So we should imagine pregnant women as on their guard, having to be vigilant to make sure nobody is surrounding them with beavers and hyena feet.

Similarly, women are vigilant in protecting the babies once they are born. A fascinating set of texts talks about the use of amulets and other medicines by mothers or *nutrices* to protect young babies.[29] Baby amulets cited by Pliny include branches of coral (32.24); amber (37.50); gold (*ut minus noceant quae inferantur veneficia*, 33.84); malachite (37.114); galactitis (37.162); beetles (11.97); a dolphin's tooth, for children's "sudden terrors" (*pavores repentinos*, 32.137); similarly a wolf's tooth or wolf's skin (28.257); a horse's baby teeth (28.258); and bones from dogs' dung, for siriasis (30.135). One cure especially for girl babies is an amulet of goat's dung in cloth (28.259), recalling von Staden's association of dung therapy with women. The use of protective medicine could continue past babyhood; Suetonius says that Nero continued to wear on his right arm the cast-off skin of a snake, enclosed in a gold bracelet, "at his mother's wish" (*ex voluntate matris, Ner.* 6.4). This suggests to us (1) that the amulets do not just appear in some Greek medical sources collected by Pliny, but reflect actual Roman practice, (2) that they were used and controlled by concerned mothers, and (3) that they were worn by children as a sign of their mothers' protection.[30] Moreover, David Soren's excavation of an infant cemetery from the late ancient period in the Italian countryside suggests that animals like those recommended in Pliny were indeed fastened onto ailing children.[31]

The classic baby amulet is the *fascinum*, a phallic amulet of which many exemplars survive today. The paramount example of a *male* body part with beneficial properties, the phallus has powers to counteract witchcraft and the evil eye, as has been widely discussed.[32] But Pliny introduces his account of the *fascinum*—protector, he remarks, of babies and generals alike—in the context of women's pediatric practice. Dismissing some practitioners' claims about the use of saliva, he remarks, scornfully, "If we believe those things are done aright, we must think likewise of these, too: that the wet nurse (*nutrix*), at the approach of a stranger (*extraneus*), or if the infant is looked at while sleeping, spits [*adspui*, on the baby? at the onlooker?] three times" (28.39). Here, as elsewhere, the *nutrix* is the protector of the baby, and her saliva has a protective force against the evil eye.[33]

The satirist Persius, Pliny's contemporary, describes the same practice. He is talking about what is best to pray for, and he uses as a negative illustration a picture of a baby and the women who are taking care of him (*Satire* 2.31–40):

Behold, a grandmother or gods-fearing mother's sister (*matertera*)
has taken the boy from his cradle and averts evil (*expiat*) from
   his forehead and wet lips
with her middle finger (*infami digito*) and her purifying (*lustralibus*) saliva,
skilled at holding back burning (*urentis*) eyes;
then with shaking hands and suppliant prayer she sends her hungry hope,
now toward the fields of Licinius, now toward the house of Crassus:
"May king and queen choose him for son-in-law, may girls
fight over him; whatever he steps on, let it turn into a rose."
But I don't trust my prayers to a wet nurse (*nutrici*). Deny,
Jupiter, these things to her, though she ask you clad in white (*albata*).

Persius, perhaps the most uninterested in women of all Roman satirists, here affords the reader a sidewise glance at women's folk practice. He lists as possible baby-minders not only the *nutrix*, but two important female kin: the grandmother and the mother's sister, the *matertera*—a family member who shows up elsewhere as important in a child's life (Hallett 1984: 151, 183–86; Richlin 1997). He depicts these women as actively concerned to protect the baby, and using their saliva as an important means of protection against the evil eye. These women pray for riches for the baby, for a good marriage, and for love; and they get dressed up to pray. They have health care down to a system.

Beyond Lingerie

And so we leave Pliny, sitting up late at night, laboring away at the *Natural History*, with a bra on his head. This is surely a case where the cup, so to speak, is both half empty and half full. What Pliny tells us certainly gives us information about Roman women's lives that is both new and disturbing. If we want to view Rome as an oppressive patriarchy, we can carry with us the image of Pliny's recommendation that a menstruating woman should carry a mullet with her so as not to dull the shine on mirrors (28.82). Pliny and the other encyclopedic sources provide a rich supply of fears about the female body—but also show beliefs about its powers. We might compare this ambivalence with Judith Hallett's model (1989b) of "woman as same and other" in day-to-day relationships in the Roman elite; or with the perilously permeable boundaries so characteristic of Roman culture, where slave could become freed, Greek could come to Rome, and Pliny could write the *Natural History* and loathe doctors at the same time. The picture of the female body in Pliny also sheds further light on what Roman men feared when they accused each other of effeminacy, as they so frequently did (Richlin 1992a: passim). On the other hand, thanks to Pliny, we are able to fill in a picture of women's lives otherwise only known from material remains and from the somewhat more one-sided view of medical writers. Archaeology can give us votive offerings, dedications, and burials; Pliny and his friends can give us more of a context for them—can help us connect the dots. Pliny and his bra bring us just a little closer to Roman women themselves.

Notes

1. See Boston Women's Health Book Collective 1992: 15, 205. The current edition of this basic women-centered women's health book contains an eighty-page section on sexuality, along with sections on birth control and abortion, pregnancy, childbirth, and menopause, among others. On attacks on *Our Bodies, Ourselves*, see Hunter 1986: 28 (entries for 1977, 1981), apparently using the BWHBC's own "file on backlash."

2. For studies that link medical theories with their cultural context, see Dean-Jones 1992, on the social function of Hippocratic theories of women's sexual pleasure; and, on Rome, French 1986 (on Pliny and Soranus); Gourevitch 1984 (largely a sourcebook); A. E. Hanson 1990: 330–31 (Soranus and Roman culture); Pinault 1992 (Soranus and the rise of asceticism).

3. For discussion of Pliny on doctors, see Nutton 1986, who argues that Pliny overstates his case.

4. On the remarkable life of the elder Pliny, see the younger Pliny, *Ep.* 3.5, 6.16. The extant fragment of Suetonius's *Life* of the elder Pliny may conveniently be found in Rolfe 1914, 2:505. On Pliny's thought generally, see Beagon 1992; French and Greenaway 1986.

5. So also French 1986: 69. The text of Metrodora will someday be available in a new authoritative version (H. N. Parker, n.d.).

6. G.E.R. Lloyd points out (1983: 137) that, when Pliny says *invenio* ("I find"), he often seems to be reporting on what he has read in the course of his research, rather than on his personal experience. My imaginings about Pliny, then, must be taken more for their symbolic value than as an idea of Pliny's actual practice.

7. This question has not been the primary focus of work on Greek and Roman gynecology, due to the nature of the extant sources, which are written from the doctor's point of view. For discussion, see A. E. Hanson 1990: 309–11 (with bibliography); 1992: 47–48; Dean-Jones 1994: 26–40, 247–48; H. King 1993: 105, 109–10; and especially H. King 1995 and Lloyd 1983: 62–79 (on the Hippocratic corpus), 181–82 (on Soranus). Riddle 1992 treats the history of birth control as a slow erosion of women's rights over their bodies; see esp. 165.

8. For women's-culture approaches to antiquity, see Hallett 1989b; Skinner 1993; Zweig 1993. Buckley and Gottlieb (1988a: 12–15, 31–34) argue vigorously for women's agency within menstrual symbolic systems.

9. The major discussion is at 28.70–86, and note the apology at 28.87. Book 28 begins a long section on remedies from animals, which goes on through book 30. Remedies from human beings begin at 28.4, and include a discussion of ver-

bal charms and superstition, the use of human saliva (28.35–39), human hair (28.41), and other body parts (28.41–44), gymnasium scrapings (28.50–52), and urine (28.65–69). The discussion of the female body follows, and from there Pliny proceeds directly to elephants, apologizing for telling the reader so many disgusting things. The discussion in book 7 comes in a book-long general discussion of the properties of human beings, and commences with the statement *solum autem animal menstruale mulier est* (7.63). Then Pliny labels the *profluvium* as *monstrificum*, and gives a concise but full list of its properties.

10. Buckley and Gottlieb 1988a: 7–8, 35–38; they are among the few writers to discuss Pliny in this context, basing their remarks on a 1916 article in the *Johns Hopkins Hospital Bulletin*. They point to Pliny as an example of a positive attitude toward menstrual blood; as will be seen, this is only half the picture. For brief discussion, see Dean-Jones 1994: 248–49.

11. Thus also S.J.D. Cohen 1991: 287. Cole (1992, esp. 109–11) discusses various conditions in which women were considered polluting in Greek sanctuaries, among them post-childbirth and miscarriage, and during menstruation; cf. Dean-Jones 1994: 223–53 on Greek attitudes toward menstruation. On the application of biblical law on menstruation in ancient and medieval Judaism and in ancient Christianity, see S.J.D. Cohen 1991. On menstruation in rabbinic literature, see Wegner 1991: 77–78, 82. On the increase in misogyny in attitudes toward menstruation from the classical rabbinic period through the Middle Ages, see Boyarin 1993: 90–97. On the meaning of menstruation in the medieval church, see Bynum 1987: 122–23 (holy women's bodies as sources of food), 211, 214, 239. On early Islamic attitudes, see Wegner 1991: 91 n. 28. For a women's-culture approach (early modern Jewish women's own prayers, including those concerning menstrual purity), see Weissler 1991, esp. 165–66.

12. It is enticing to speculate that this prohibition, more severe than any attested for Italy, may reflect a pre-Islamic Arab system underlying beliefs like those examined in Delaney 1988.

13. Other powers are listed at *HN* 28.80–86: menses act as a solvent on bitumen (also at 7.65); menses cure gout, and menstruating women can cure by their touch scrofula, parotid tumors, abscesses, erysipelas, boils, and runny eyes. Lais and Salpe, as well as a male source, recommend menstrual blood for relief of the bites of rabid dogs and of fevers. The *obstetrix* Sotira recommends relieving fevers and epilepsy by smearing the soles of the patient's feet with menstrual blood. Icatidas *medicus* says fevers are ended by intercourse when the menses are just beginning. A menstrual cloth can counteract the effects of rabies, due to the fact that rabies is caused by dogs tasting menstrual blood. The blood is also good for ulcers of draught animals, women's headaches, and protecting the house from the arts of the Magi. Cf. Serenus Sammonicus (*Liber medicinalis* 12.163), who recommends the "obscene dews" of a virgin as a cure for pains in the ears.

14. See Richlin 1992a: 67–69, 115–16; Richlin 1984. Cf. von Staden 1991: 277–80 on Celsus's analogies between womb and anus, labia and wound.

15. On the meaning of the eye in Roman culture, see Barton 1993: 91–98.

16. On the female body in symbolic systems, see Buckley and Gottlieb 1988a: 26–30, including discussion of Mary Douglas and the concept of pollution; on the upper body vs. lower body, see Bakhtin 1984.

17. This model, which has gained great popular currency (e.g., students' comments in class), is well exemplified by Ehrenreich and English 1973. The model is somewhat contemptuously dismissed by Green (1989), who produces a set of sophisticated and historically informed questions concerning women practitioners and women patients in the medieval and early modern periods. For a brief but compelling account of the historical vicissitudes of knowledge of herbal contraceptives, see Riddle, Estes, and Russell 1994.

18. Sources are given at 20.19, 20.28, 20.32, 20.34, 20.227, 26.99, 28.256.

19. For some examples of texts featuring women who use aphrodisiacs on their husbands, see Faraone 1992: 98–99; add Juvenal 6.133–35, 610–26.

20. For men: *HN* 8.91, 10.182, 22.20, 26.96, 26.98, 27.65, 28.99, 30.141 (four), 30.143. For women: 20.227, 22.87, 28.101, 28.106, 28.256, 30.143 (two).

21. A cure of the Magi. The text says lust is stimulated *ad sexus suos*, "for their own sex"; this does not make much sense with the following clause, and so Mayhoff conjectured *ab sexu suo*, "away from their own sex," i.e., the wife lures the husband away from his desire for other males.

22. The aphrodisiacs in Pliny and Metrodora would then not support the argument made by Faraone for Greek aphrodisiacs (1992): that they tend to aim at controlling the ardent male but arousing the passive female. For more on the gender politics of Greek love-charms, see Winkler 1990: 90–91, 95–98.

23. On emmenagogues, see Riddle 1992: 27 and passim.

24. On abortion and contraception in antiquity, see Riddle 1992; Riddle, Estes, and Russell 1994. On abortion in Pliny, see Beagon 1992: 216–20. On abortion in the Hippocratic Oath, see Riddle 1992: 7–10.

25. *Dig.* 48.8.8 (Ulp.): "If it is proved that a woman has brought force to bear on her own innards in order to avoid giving birth, the provincial governor should send her into exile"; *Dig.* 48.19.38.5 (Paulus): "Those who make potions, either to cause abortions or love, even if they do not do this fraudulently, still, because it sets a bad example, those of the lower class are sent to the mines, while those of the upper class are relegated to an island and fined part of their property. But if they have caused a woman or man to die, they must undergo the supreme punishment." Gardner (1986: 158–59) is of the opinion that it is the drugs, rather than abortion itself, that are prohibited here. See further, on the availability and legality of abortion, Riddle 1992: 7–10, 109–12; Hopkins 1965, on Roman contraception generally; Gamel 1989, on abortion in Ovid's poetry.

26. For conception aids, see *HN* 20.51, 22.83, 23.53, 27.63, 28.52, 28.249, 28.253, 28.255, 30.131. Serenus Sammonicus devotes section 32 of the *Liber medicinalis* to *Conceptio et partus*; he cites Lucretius as his authority on the mysteries of conception, and goes on to offer several cures for barrenness (32.607–14).

27. See *HN* 20.263, 25.97, 28.248, 28.254, 30.123.

28. Gender-selective infanticide in antiquity has been the subject of extensive scholarly debate. See discussion in Golden 1992: 235–30, with bibliography; also Boswell 1990c: 54 n. 2 (bibliography), 100–103 (primary sources), and in general 53–137; Dixon 1988; Riddle 1992. For reports on the current practice of infanticide in India and on women's statements about the practice, see Dahlburg 1994.

29. On the care of young children by mothers and/or *nutrices*, see Dixon 1988, esp. 120–33.

30. The persistence of some of these amulets is remarkable. Klapisch-Zuber (1985: 149–50, with plate 7.1) publishes a detail of a sixteenth-century Italian painting showing a coral branch and a wolf's-tooth amulet for teething, and discusses the wet nurse's responsibility for the child's health (also at 105 n. 25, on protection from the *maldocchio*). She notes that "dog teeth or wolf teeth" figure in the lists of possessions of four fifteenth-century male babies (149 n. 64). An eighteenth-century American representation of the "coral and bells" may be seen in the Henry Huntington Library and Art Gallery, San Marino, California, in the "Portrait of Mrs. Elijah Boardman and Her Son William Whiting Boardman," by Ralph Earl (c. 1798), displayed alongside a contemporary English specimen.

31. See Soren 1997; Soren, Fenton, Birkby, and Jensen 1997. Soren found puppy bones in with the baby bones; as well as recommending frogs for siriasis (above), Pliny recommends puppies applied to the painful parts of patients for the transfer of the illness, after which the puppies are to be buried (30.42, 30.64).

32. On the phallus and the evil eye, see Barton 1993: 95–98, 171, 189 and fig. 2; Johns 1982: color plate 10 (phallic amulets), 68 fig. 51 (phalluses sawing an eye in half), and in general 62–75.

33. For other examples of apotropaic spitting in Roman belief, see *HN* 28.35–39; the nurse as protector of the baby can be attested in Greek culture at least as early as the seventh century B.C.E. (*Hymn. Hom. Cer.* 228–30). Johnston 1995 provides full treatment and excellent analysis of ancient Greek and Near Eastern beliefs about harm to babies from demons and witchcraft, including discussion of apotropaic spitting. For similar beliefs in Jewish folk culture, see Trachtenberg [1939] 1961: 121 ("threefold expectoration"), 159, 162; my own grandmother, born in Lithuania in the late nineteenth century, practiced the same behavior described by Pliny.

NINE

FEMALE DESIRE AND THE DISCOURSE
OF EMPIRE: TACITUS'S MESSALINA

Sandra R. Joshel

What a pigmy intellect she had, and what giant propensities!
How fearful were the curses those propensities entailed on
me! Bertha Mason, the true daughter of an infamous mother,
dragged me through all the hideous and degrading agonies
which must attend a man bound to a wife at once
intemperate and unchaste. . . .
Disappointment made me reckless. I tried dissipation—never
debauchery: that I hated, and hate. That was my Indian
Messalina's attribute: rooted disgust at it and her restrained
me much, even in pleasure. Any enjoyment that bordered
on riot seemed to approach me to her and her vices,
and I eschewed it.
(Charlotte Brontë, *Jane Eyre*)

OFTEN READ as a feminist text, *Jane Eyre* recounts a woman's attainment of selfhood within a particular imperial moment. The morally healthy empire of the present, associated with the civilizing mission in India, is distinguished from the corrupt empire of the past, associated with the plantation system in the West Indies. Images of women participate in the construction of this distinction. Jane belongs to the moral empire of the present. The creole Bertha Mason, the debauched, mad wife of Edward Rochester, marks the corrupt empire of the past. Historical imagination and the Roman empire provide the means for evoking the "giant propensities" of the creole. Using the name of the third wife of the Roman emperor Claudius, infamous for her sexual depravity and violence, Rochester calls his own wife "an Indian Mes-

This is a slightly revised version of an essay that originally appeared, under the same title, in *Signs: Journal of Women in Culture and Society* 21.1 (1995): 50–82. Copyright 1995 by The University of Chicago. All rights reserved. Reprinted here with the kind permission of the University of Chicago Press.

salina"—a Messalina from the West Indies (Brontë [1847] 1984: 338). Brontë associates the British imperial past with Rome, which in the imagination of the mid-nineteenth century was seen as the corrupt root of Western civilization. In Brontë's collapse of discrete imperial moments, her nineteenth-century female representative of the decadent planter class in Jamaica is conflated with a first-century Roman empress. The name of a particular woman, Valeria Messalina, becomes the proper name for uncontrolled female sexuality that can be specified by an adjective of place or race.[1]

Yet, as Peter Brooks notes, "All tales may lead back not so much to events as to other tales, to man as a fiction he tells about himself" (1985: 277). Indeed, a search for the Roman Messalina turns up little that fits modern notions of historical facts, not even her precise age. When Claudius married her in 39 or 40 c.e., he was forty-eight and she was fourteen by some calculations and eighteen by others. She bore him two children, Octavia and Britannicus. The latter was heir to the throne until, after Messalina's death and Claudius's remarriage to Agrippina, the emperor adopted Agrippina's son Nero. Messalina was killed in 48 c.e. for an involvement with the noble Gaius Silius that Roman authors describe as a sexual liaison and modern historians as a political one. What we can know of the affair and her other deeds must be read through stories in which her chief features are unbridled sexuality, violence, and ferocity.[2] Messalina is not alone: adulterous, cruel, deceitful women populate both the ancient Roman sources and modern images of Rome. Along with gladiators, elaborate banquets, and legions, these women belong to a popular fantasy about the Roman empire, nurtured by Baroque opera, Enlightenment history, French revolutionary literature, Robert Graves's novels ([1934] 1989, [1935] 1989), and their dramatization by the BBC, aired in turn on U.S. public television.[3]

All tales may lead back to other tales, but not always to "man as a fiction." I follow the tale of Bertha Mason's prototype, Valeria Messalina, to woman as a fiction, focusing on Tacitus's account in the *Annals* (11.1–4, 12, 26–38), written sixty to seventy years after her death. Rather than try to uncover the actual woman beneath Tacitus's narrative, I read his Messalina as a fiction for the terms through which the Romans experienced their own present and its history. I am concerned with the writing of history, not with history as a set of events. The issues, it seems to me, are these: How is the imperial past represented, and what role does Messalina play in that representation? What are the implications of that representation for our ability to talk about Roman women and the uses to which images of women are put? What are the politics of a particular intersection of gender and empire? I argue that modern scholars' attempts to define Messalina's agency as a historical figure cannot escape Tacitus's construction of her violence, her excessive desire that produces chaos and emasculates, and her ambiguous voice that moves the narrative but is essentially mute. Like Brontë's Bertha Mason, Tacitus's Messalina is a representation that enables the historian to draw a difficult distinction between present and past, good empire and bad. As such, Messalina functions as a sign in a discourse of imperial power that simultaneously informs, if not determines, her image. I contend that this paradox is the result of a double move made by Roman imperial discourse: woman figures empire, and yet, at the same time, empire becomes the woman.[4]

This study is intended to contribute to feminist work on Tacitus, Roman women, and gender in ancient Rome. Its limits will be obvious: I say little of other imperial women in Tacitus, like Livia, Agrippina the Younger, Agrippina the Elder, Poppaea, or barbarian queens like Boudicca. I do not assume that these women are simple variations of Messalina, nor do I want to make Messalina emblematic of "Woman in Tacitus." Rather, I look at Tacitus's Messalina as a test case for the application of a theoretical model. The point is to suggest that analyses of other female figures might usefully consider the ways in which their representations, too, are shaped by a discourse of empire, albeit differently in certain aspects from Messalina.

Tacitus's Narrative of Messalina

Messalina belongs to a history of empire in the sense of a single state ruling distant states, peoples, and territories, and to a history of imperial power in a particularly Roman sense, concerned with the power of the emperor. Tacitus's political career made him familiar with both. In the early second century, Tacitus looked back over more than a century of the Principate in which the senatorial class had struggled with the emperor to find its political place in the order founded by Augustus. Older Republican families had died or were killed off; increasingly, the emperor drew on new men from Italy and the Romanized elites of the provinces to be senators, magistrates, and commanders. Many were ready to uphold the ancient tradition of service to the state while lacking either the family history or the personal experience of political dominance. Tacitus, a provincial from Gaul or Northern Italy, came from such a background. Without the Principate, he would not have become a senator, a well-known orator at Rome, a consul, or a provincial governor (on Tacitus's life, see Syme 1958: 59–74; Martin 1981: 26–38). When Tacitus recounts the history of the earliest generations of the Principate under Augustus's successors, he does so from the complex point of view of a senator, a member of the ruling class whose action and speech was constrained by the power of the *princeps*, and of a provincial, whose very position as senator depended on the institution of the Principate.

In his account of Claudius, Tacitus worked within a senatorial tradition that depicted the emperor as a fool and a pedant, either ignorant of the machinations of his freedmen and wives or else subservient to their wishes (Suet. *Claud.* 29; Dio Cass. 60.2.4, 2.6, 8.4–6). Yet even hostile accounts implicitly acknowledge the growth of an imperial state under Claudius. Claudius's invasion of Britain in 43 c.e. extended the boundaries of empire. His generous grants of citizenship to Romanized provincials and extension of senatorial status to the upper class of Gallia Comata spread membership in the imperial state and its elite to those who had been conquered under the Republic. Although a subject of scholarly debate, Claudius's administrative changes and absorption of administrative responsibilities enlarged the reach of imperial government and perhaps represented a realignment of state power at the expense of the senate. The freedmen who play an important role in Tacitus's narrative of Messalina and the rest of his account of Claudius's reign should be considered in this context, for they were administrators, not domestic servants. Like other Roman nobles, the emperor relied on his slaves and freedmen to manage his property and business affairs. In the emperor's case, they became the nucleus of a bureaucracy, dealing with matters of public administration and finance. Although the emphasis on freed slaves and wives in the Roman sources presents the emperor as ruled by those he should rule within his household, it also highlights the domestic setting of the emperor's exercise of power within the dominating metropolitan center of empire, a concern that figures importantly in Tacitus's history of the Principate.[5]

We do not have Tacitus's account of the first six years of Claudius's reign and hence of his wife Messalina. Tacitus's story opens in 47 c.e. with the trial of the noble Valerius Asiaticus in the emperor's bedroom with Messalina present (*intra cubiculum auditur, Messalina coram*, 11.2.1). Messalina has pushed the senator Suillius and her son's tutor, Sosibius, to accuse Asiaticus, ostensibly because his power and wealth threaten the throne. Messalina's motives, the real motives in Tacitus's account, are jealousy and greed. She believes that Asiaticus is a former lover of Poppaea Sabina, who had had an affair with one of Messalina's lovers, an actor and ex-slave named Mnester (11.1.1, 11.2.1, 11.4.2). She also wants the gardens of Lucullus that Asiaticus was refurbishing (*hortis inhians, quos ille a Lucullo coeptos insigni magnificentia extollebat*, 11.1.1). Just when Asiaticus's speech in his defense moves Claudius and even causes her to cry, she urges another senator, Vitellius, to act, and he convinces the emperor of Asiaticus's guilt (11.2.3–4). Messalina goes off to drive Poppaea to suicide (*ipsa ad perniciem Poppaeae festinat*, 11.2.5). Asiaticus is allowed to commit suicide. Two equestrians are also killed on the pretext that they had had an inauspicious dream about Claudius (11.4.5). The accuser, Messalina's agent Suillius, and what Tacitus identifies as the real cause of their deaths—they had lent their house to Poppaea and Mnester (*at causa necis ex eo quod domum suam Mnesteris et Poppaeae congressibus praebuissent*, 11.4.2)—suggest Messalina at work behind the scene.

Tacitus's story of Messalina continues in chapter 12 with Messalina's affair with Gaius Silius, consul-elect and the most handsome young noble in Rome (*iuventutis Romanae pulcherrimum*, 11.12.2). This "new and almost mad love" (*novo et furori proximo amore*) diverts her attention from an attack on Claudius's niece Agrippina, great-granddaughter of Augustus and mother of the ten-year-old Nero. Messalina so desires Silius that she forces him to divorce his noble wife. Claudius, preoccupied with his duties as censor, knows nothing of the affair (*Claudius matrimonii sui ignarus et munia censoria usurpans*, 11.13.1). In chapter 26 Tacitus reports that Silius proposes marriage: he would adopt Messalina and Claudius's son, Britannicus, and Messalina would have the same power as before. When Claudius goes to Ostia to perform a sacrifice, Messalina celebrates all the solemn observances of marriage with Silius (*cuncta nuptiarum sollemnia celebrat*, 11.26.7). Implicitly, she divorces the emperor.[6]

According to Tacitus, the emperor's household is frightened by what appears to them as a coup d'état (quite literally, the household shudders: *domus principis inhorruerat*, 11.28.1). Tacitus refers to the emperor's freedmen administrators, although he ignores their official posts, recounting only their activities in the domestic sphere or commenting on the inappropriate power and influence of what for him are merely ex-slaves (11.28–29). They arrange to have Claudius told of Messalina's marriage to Silius by his mistresses during his stay at Ostia (11.30). Claudius is "so overwhelmed by terror that he ask[s] again and again 'Am I still emperor? Is Silius still an ordinary citizen?'" (*satis constat eo pavore offusum Claudium ut identidem interrogaret, an ipse imperii potens, an Silius privatus esset*, 11.31.3). Tacitus follows this image of a frightened, uncertain Claudius with a depiction of Messalina playing maenad to Silius's Bacchus at a wild party celebrating the new vintage (11.31.4–5). When the news arrives of Claudius's return, the guests scatter (11.32). In contrast to the passive Claudius, Tacitus's Messalina takes decisive action (*haud segniter*, 11.32.4). She determines (*intendit*) to face Claudius, sends (*misit*) her children to their father, and begs (*oravit*) the senior Vestal Virgin to intercede with the *pontifex maximus*. With only three companions and on foot (*tribus omnino comitantibus—id repente solitudinis erat—spatium urbis pedibus emensa*), she walks from the gardens of Asiaticus, near the modern Piazza del Popolo, to what is now the Porta S. Paulo, finding only a cart that was used to haul off the rubbish from gardens to carry her out of the city.

In chapters 33 through 38, Tacitus's narrative cuts back and forth between husband and wife. Claudius returns to Rome, avoiding a direct confrontation with Messalina on the road, visits the praetorian camp to reaffirm his position, views Silius's house, and then presides over the summary trial of Messalina's lovers and associates (11.35–36). Finally, he returns to the palace and dinner. Heated with wine (*vino incaluit*, 11.37.2), he orders the "poor woman" (*miserae*) to be told to come the next day to plead her case. Fearing Claudius's attraction to his wife, Narcissus, Claudius's freedman, rushes out and gives the order to have Messalina killed, pretending it came from the emperor (*prorumpit Narcissus denuntiatque centurionibus et tribuno, qui aderat, exequi caedem; ita imperatorem iubere*, 11.37.3). Messalina, for her part, encounters her husband on the road between Rome and Ostia and demands to be heard, but she is shouted down by Narcissus (*Messalina clamitabatque audiret . . . cum ostrepere accusator*, 11.34.3) and outmaneuvered (cf. 11.32.4–5 and 11.34.4–5). She ends up lying on the ground (*fusam humi*, 11.37.4) in the gardens she had taken from Asiaticus—crying, complaining, and helpless. Her mother, with her at the end, urges Messalina to commit suicide and seek "dignity in death" (*neque aliud quam morti decus quaerendum*, 11.37.4), but this advice goes unheeded. Soldiers, sent by Narcissus, break through the gates. Surrounded by them and insulted by a freedman, Messalina can only stab ineffectually at her throat and breast, until the blow of a tribune pierces her through. When Claudius is informed of her death, he finishes his meal without asking how she died. In the following days he shows no signs of any human emotion (*ne secutis quidem diebus . . . ullius denique humani adfectus signa dedit*, 11.38.3).

The Problems of Reading Messalina

In these chapters dealing with Claudius's reign, an adulterous, rapacious wife and anxious, bossy freed slaves determine events. Passive, manipulated, or befuddled, the emperor seems incapable of independent action; senators are objects of female desire or toadies. Although other accounts suggest that Messalina's involvement in Asiaticus's fall and her marriage to Silius were well established in Tacitus's sources (Juv. 10.329–45; Suet. *Claud.* 26.2; Dio Cass. 61.29.4–6a, 61.31.3–5), the historian crafts his own narrative within the senatorial tradition hostile to Claudius (Martin 1981: 144, 150–51). Some scholars have assumed that this narrative contains a core of pure political fact encrusted with sexual disinformation that can be removed by the application of common sense. But the distinction between disinformation and fact is not always clear (Edwards 1993: 4–12). As I shall argue below, the sexual clings to the political.

Attempts to write about Messalina's words, motives, and actions encounter a general problem of interpretation familiar to classicists: the actions assigned to agents in ancient sources depend on the rhetorical strategies of male authors (Baldwin 1972; Rutland 1978; Kaplan 1979; Syme 1981b; Vinson 1989; Santoro L'hoir 1992 and 1994).[7] Especially important for Messalina, the ancient sources are unreliable on sexual misconduct. Adultery is a commonplace of political invective, sexual deviance a trope of satire (Richlin 1981a, 1983, 1984, 1992a; Vinson 1989; Edwards 1993: 35–36, 57). Exposing the incongruities and logical flaws of the Roman sources, scholars have teased out a story that satisfies a modern canon of objectivity from scattered items in the sources. The process depends on rationalizing elements in the sources' rhetorical strategies and determining what seem the more likely events and circumstances. In some cases, sexual activity has been translated literally into political activity: "alleged lovers" have been read as political "allies" (Levick 1975: 33; see also 1976). When not dismissed as pure invective, female lust has been explained as political manipulation, as by Barbara Levick, who rejects the image of Messalina as "an adolescent nymphomaniac" and asserts that "in the main she used sex as means of compromising and controlling politicians" (1990: 56). Yet the process entangles modern historians in problems of agency in their own narratives as they assign actions and motives to historical figures constructed by discourses of sexuality and power. Without attention to such discourses in imperial literature, reconstructions of events continue to work within sexual terms or those that make women passive victims or active villains.[8] Levick, for example, still represents Messalina in terms that tie a woman to her body. Her Messalina remains within a discourse that makes her either controlled (captive of her desires) or controlling (manipulator of others' desires).

Rhetorical strategies that serve Tacitus's discourse of imperial power shape the raw material of modern constructions of agency. Messalina belongs to Tacitus's efforts to create a weak Claudius, the effects of which trouble historical interpretations of Messalina. Tacitus's Claudius perceives neither Messalina's manipulation of the men who persuade him nor her rather public affair with Silius. In every episode involving his wife or freedmen, Messalina's agents or his own freedmen put words in his mouth. His wife's adultery frames Claudius's censorship so that his official acts appear trivial (Ryberg 1942: 404 n. 83). Tacitus's censor-emperor, the arbiter of public morals, harbors immorality at home; he displays his knowledge of Rome's past but is ignorant of affairs in his own home (11.13–15, 24–25). Throughout the confrontation with Messalina on the Ostian road, Claudius is silent (*mirum inter haec silentium Claudi*, 11.35.1), and Narcissus the freedman, not Claudius the patron, determines the events that follow. "Everything obeyed a freedmen" (*omnia liberto oboedie-*

bant, 11.35.1). Appropriately, the narrative bears the stamp of comedy, with Claudius in the stock role of the old man (*senex*), deluded by an adulterous wife and outwitted by his clever servant (Dickison 1977; Vessey 1971). In "an intricate set of reversals," agency belongs to those who should be ruled—wives and ex-slaves (Dickison 1977: 636).

Tacitus's effort to transfer agency from the emperor to his wife and freedmen produces tropes, improbabilities, and nonsensical elements that constitute key aspects of his characterization of Messalina (Colin 1956: 29–30; Mehl 1974: 35–37; Seif 1973: 111; Levick 1990: 61–67). To establish Messalina's motives for accusing Asiaticus, Tacitus must string a convoluted line of who had sexual relations with whom: Asiaticus is the former lover of Poppaea, who had an affair with the actor Mnester, who had an affair with Messalina. To confirm Messalina's responsibility for the deaths resulting from the trial of Asiaticus, Tacitus interrupts his narrative of the trial with the notice of a scene that follows several days later. Ignorant of events, Claudius asks Poppaea's husband why she is not at dinner (*ignaro Caesare*, 11.2.5): that is, the emperor does not know she is dead and he is not responsible—Messalina is. A variation on virtually the same anecdote in Suetonius's biography of Claudius makes it clear that Claudius's question is a trope for the emperor's feeble-mindedness in which the names of dead women are exchangeable (*Claud.* 39). In the biographer's version, Claudius asks about Messalina's rather than Poppaea's absence, forgetting that he himself had put her to death a few days before. Where the biographer's version makes Claudius forgetful, the historian's makes him the dupe of a vicious wife. To exemplify Messalina's greed, Tacitus describes her desire for the elaborate gardens of the man she was trying to have killed. He uses a metaphor, *hortis inhians* (her mouth opens in hunger for [Asiaticus's] gardens, 11.1), that he will repeat verbatim about Claudius's next wife, Agrippina, who reprises Messalina's role in Asiaticus's demise with a different noble (12.59.1, *Statilium Taurum opibus inlustrem hortis eius inhians pervertit accusante Tarquitio Prisco*). *Hortis inhians* is not simply "suitably applied," as Ronald Syme (1981b: 48) contends; it, too, is a trope—for imperial rapacity. The trope informs Tacitus's shaping of the narrative. What remains of book 11 begins with Messalina swallowing up Asiaticus's property and in the process destroying him, and ends with Messalina stretched on the ground of that property, unable to prevent her own destruction. The "poetic justice" D.W.T.C. Vessey (1971: 399) sees in Messalina's death in Asiaticus's gardens is just that—poetic or, more accurately, a piece of theater staged by Tacitus. Obsessive returns to these gardens construct a fantastical itinerary, especially since some of it requires Messalina to travel back and forth across the entire breadth of the city on foot: from the party to the gardens, across Rome to the Ostian road, back to Rome, and across the city again back to the gardens. Messalina's marriage to Silius is so unbeliev-able Tacitus himself calls it *fabulosus* ("storylike, theatrical," 11.27.1) and portrays himself as not unaware (*haud ignarus*, as opposed to the *ignarus* . . . *Claudius*, 11.13.1) that it appears so. He then recounts a sensational tale of her supposed marriage and a wild party, disclaiming the effects of his own narrative devices with an appeal to the sort of evidence that, else-where, he evaluates critically (1.76.6–7, 3.16.1–2, 4.10–11, 4.57, 13.20, 14.2, 14.58.1–2, 15.53.4–5): "Nothing is written for the purpose of amazement, but in fact I have related and shall relate what was heard and written down by older men [men of an earlier generation]" (*sed nihil com-positum miraculi causa, verum audita scriptaque senioribus tradam*, 11.27.2). By anticipating his reader's disbelief, Tacitus's aside solicits faith in his own story and its representation of Messalina's desire.[9]

The sexuality of Tacitus's Messalina haunts modern interpretations of the marriage as a plot, led by Silius or Messalina, to overthrow Claudius and put Silius in his place, in some versions as regent for Britannicus (see Levick 1990: 64–67 with refs.). Although in Tacitus's account Messalina initiates the liaison with Silius, her agency consists in sexual obsession. This structuring of the narrative produces a contradictory Silius, passive and resigned as a lover, yet active and bold as the proposer of marriage (ibid.: 66–67). For a coup d'état, the conspirators—Silius, Messalina, and friends—are strangely unprepared and unconcerned. Instead, Tacitus de-scribes a wild Bacchic fete that furthers his depiction of Messalina's li-cense, and, by implication, of her incompetence. Tacitus's narrative and his Messalina trouble even Levick's interpretation of the marriage as a political ploy with more limited aims (ibid.: 66). She suggests that a struggle within the court led Messalina to ally herself with senators and equestrians who together sought to regain influence with Claudius, not to assassinate him. According to Levick, the marriage ceremony was only a "charade" to prove Messalina's commitment to her senatorial allies rep-resented by Silius. Levick's examples of other such charades, Nero's mar-riages to two male freedmen, strain credulity; the ceremonies, in which Nero took the role of wife with one freedman and husband with the other, were used by ancient authors as examples of the emperor's deprav-ity (Tac. *Ann.* 15.37; Suet. *Ner.* 29; Dio Cass. 62.28.2–3, 63.13.1–3).

Although Levick usefully uncovers the limits and inconsistencies of Tacitus's account, her discussion assumes that there are political facts buried in Tacitus's narrative of sexual relations and that the political can be disentangled from the sexual. Like other political reconstructions of Tacitus's sexual narrative, Levick's cannot interrogate the discourse that shapes the raw material of the political story—the affair, the marriage, and Messalina's agency. Her method implicitly creates Messalina as an agent whose rationality consists in political calculation. Where Tacitus's

Messalina desires but does not calculate, Levick's Messalina calculates but does not desire. This writing of history cannot "accommodate, on the one hand, female power and desire, and, on the other, gender restrictions and sexual subordination" (Sharpe 1993: 11). It omits what feminist scholars have pointed out: that Roman women in the upper classes had wealth and influence but, at the same time, no public political roles and limited legal rights and were, moreover, the objects of a misogynist invective and an ideology that rewarded female subservience. Without attention to agency in representations of women, we reinscribe the villain/victim dichotomy in our attempt to uncover the lived reality of Roman women; we cannot observe how representations of women serve male discourse, sexual, political, and moral. In Messalina's case, woman's vision, action, and voice function as a discursive screen that displaces female agency (see Bal 1984). Ironically, Messalina may be more absent than if she was not in the narrative at all. In her place, a figure of desire becomes woman's desire, whose most powerful representation is sexual.

Tacitus's Construction of a Desiring, Savage Woman

As in other imperial representations, the desire of Tacitus's Messalina is excessive.[10] That excess consists in more than a list of individual lovers. Sated by simple adulterous acts, Tacitus's Messalina wants to expand pleasure beyond illicit sexual relations per se. Bored by the very ease of committing adultery, Messalina "[is] flowing out into untried lusts" (*ad incognitas libidines profluebat*, 11.26.1) when Silius, her lover, proposes marriage. Tacitus attributes her acceptance of his proposal to a desire beyond that for an individual man, for a married life with her lover, or even for the power Silius promises in what amounts to a proposal to overthrow Claudius. She assents, in Tacitus's view, because "she desired the name of wife on account of the magnitude of the *infamia* that is the last source of pleasure for the licentious" (*nomen tamen matrimonii concupivit ob magnitudinem infamiae cuius apud prodigos novissima voluptas est*, 11.26.6).

Tacitus here stretches to depict excess by switching cause and effect. His Messalina does not simply engage in sexual affairs that bring disgrace; she seeks the resulting disgrace of adultery rather than adultery itself, even at the moment when marrying Silius would legitimize their adulterous liaison. His representation turns on the Roman legal concept of *infamia*. Certain crimes or occupations (actor, gladiator, pimp, prostitute) brought *infamia*; it diminished a person's status among his or her fellow citizens and meant real legal disabilities (see Edwards, this volume). A woman condemned for adultery incurred *infamia* as a legal penalty (*Dig.*

22.5.28; Gardner 1986: 129). Yet the quest for *infamia* motivates Messalina's acceptance of Silius's marriage proposal. The very ease of illicit sex acts has sated her. Seemingly, Tacitus's Messalina can only find pleasure in the effects of illicit relations: unlike the female stereotypes of satire, this adulterous wife wants not an actor or a gladiator but their social condition, and that of the prostitute, a role she plays in other authors as well (Pliny *HN* 10.172; Juv. 6.115–32; Dio Cass. 61.31.1). Such excess connotes a collapse of social categories as well as epistemic ones: the top of society becomes the bottom, and the object of illicit desire is conflated with its results. Confusion infects the senses, property and symbols, family and class distinctions, and the constitution of the woman herself in Tacitus's construction.

Drawing on a commonplace of Roman moral rhetoric that associates uncontrolled female sexuality with chaos, Tacitus creates an adulterous wife whose desire creates disorder in the family, household, and social hierarchy (Edwards 1993: 43). Messalina's desire takes her across the boundaries between households and between families. She leaves her own home and comes frequently to Silius's, carrying with her gifts—slaves, freedmen, and the emperor's furniture—objects that are also signs of the rank and dignity of the *princeps* (11.12.3–4, cf. 11.30.3). Later, when Narcissus, Claudius's freedman, opens Silius's house to Claudius's gaze, the objects Narcissus displays are the heirlooms of the Drusi and Nerones, Claudius's family (11.35.2). Messalina has taken Claudius's family signs into another family's home, and the marks distinguishing families are mixed; in Tacitus's words, family signs have been degraded by becoming the price of scandal (*in pretium probri*). By failing to act as a proper limit for her husband's desires, Messalina allows transgression within the family: her crimes and consequent removal open the way for Claudius to "burn" for an incestuous union with his niece Agrippina (*ardesceret in nuptias incestas*, 11.25.8). Nor do her adulteries observe class lines: the lovers named in the *Annals* include senators, equestrians, and a freedman.[11]

Messalina's desire itself is chaotic. Listed among Messalina's lovers is Traulus Montanus, a handsome but modest young man, who was called to the palace and dismissed in a single night by Messalina; he becomes evidence for the equal capriciousness of Messalina's desires and aversions (*paribus lasciviis ad cupidinem et fastidia*, 11.36.4).[12] Tacitus's Messalina lacks anything that could be named a proper order (*honestum*): "There was nothing honorable present in a heart corrupted by lusts," comments Tacitus on her inability to kill herself honorably at her mother's request (11.37.5). In a metonymy that slips from the woman who crosses social and familial boundaries to her means of transportation in the narrative, Tacitus recounts that the only vehicle she can find to ride in after Claudius's freedmen stir him to action is a cart "by which the rubbish of gardens is carried off" (*quo purgamenta hortorum eripiuntur*, 11.32.6); he uses a verb that usually conveys a fraudulent or forceful seizure of property. The woman who carried imperial goods and signs into a private household and who took her husband's family images into another family's home now occupies the place of discarded objects. This detail reverses Messalina's expropriation of Asiaticus's gardens: having taken the gardens, she now becomes their filth that is forcibly carried off. The sexual desire that constitutes the perception and thought, feeling and memory of Tacitus's Messalina creates disorder in the historian's narrative world and "dirties" the female agent herself.

Tacitus also associates Messalina's desire with violence. Indeed, one of those typically unnamed Tacitean speakers later calls her a "savage whore" (*saevienti impudicae*, 13.43.5). In the Asiaticus affair, three men and one woman lose their lives to her lust for bodies and things (generalizations on her savagery: 11.28.2, 11.32.6; cf. Dio Cass. 60.8.5, 14.3, 15.5, 18, 22.4–5). Tacitus represents Messalina's desire for Silius in violating terms: she burns for him, drives out his wife, and takes possession (*exarserat ut Iuniam Silanam . . . matrimonio eius exturbaret vacuoque adultero poteretur*, 11.12.2). Her ex-lover, Mnester, the actor and freed slave, bears the marks of a convertible exchange of desire and violence in the scars of floggings apparently administered by Messalina (11.36.1–2).

With one exception, male agents in Tacitus's narrative do not actively desire Messalina in return. Mnester's scars testify to the necessity of submission to her lust. Tacitus's Silius does not want Messalina, the woman. He thinks of the affair's political rewards and knows that in any case his refusal means his destruction. Neither freed actor nor consul-designate can fend off Messalina's attentions. This inability may be appropriate for an ex-slave whose sexual vulnerability is a commonplace in Latin literature; it is not for a noble. Reducing noble to the position of ex-slave, Messalina's sexuality effects a social castration. Significantly, catalogued with Messalina's adulterers and associates is Suillius Caesoninus, who took a woman's sexual role, presumably at Messalina's wild party (*in illo foedissimo coetu passus muliebria*, 11.36.5). While we do not have to make Messalina the penetrator, Caesoninus's presence among her named lovers like Mnester, the ex-slave who must submit, and Traulus Montanus, the young man who was summoned and dismissed in a single night, signals the implications of Messalina's desire and the male inability to refuse her: men become women. A man's loss of agency is figured by imagining that, like woman, he is penetrable.[13]

Claudius, the one male who is genuinely attracted to Messalina in Tacitus's account, is emasculated too. Claudius's freedmen connect his dull-wittedness and lack of energy to his relations with his wife, and there is a sense that she has tied him up and subjugated him (*hebetem . . . et uxori devinctum*, 11.28.2). Indeed, the paralysis of Tacitus's Claudius results not only from his anxiety about the throne, but also from an oscillation between anger at his wife's crimes and thoughts of married life and children (11.31.3, 11.34.1). Later, once his power is secure, Claudius, heated with wine, grants Messalina a hearing (11.37.2). His freedman Narcissus, seeing the return of Claudius's love for Messalina, fears the emperor's memory of Messalina's bedroom (*uxorii cubiculi memoria*), apparently because the image of her as a sensuous woman will soften Claudius's anger and inhibit punishment of Messalina (11.37.3). According to Tacitus, the freedman must step in and order her death. The only moment of hardness for Claudius comes after Messalina's death, when he neither asks how she died nor shows any emotion, even in response to his tearful children (11.38.2–3).[14]

Claudius's lack is Messalina's gain, but the result is a contradictory agency for Messalina. The freedmen associate Claudius's weakness and attachment to Messalina with the many murders perpetrated at her order (*multasque mortis iussu Messalinae patratas*, 11.28.3). These murders are the result of what Silius calls her *potentia* (11.26.4). As it is acquired by force or improper influence, *potentia* is used by Tacitus as a pejorative synonym for legitimate authority (*auctoritas*) (Syme 1958: 413; Benario 1964: 100–101). Messalina's *potentia* ensures the submission of any object of her sexual desire, yet, as noted above, when her adultery with Silius develops into marriage with its implications of a coup d'état, it is Silius who is the agent of change. He, not she, proposes marriage and outlines the political implications (11.26.2–4). In Tacitus's narrative, Messalina's action is constituted only in a consent figured as insatiable desire. Her collapse into a passive, helpless, tearful woman lying on the ground at the end of Tacitus's narrative suggests the fragility of her power. It depends on a husband with eyes and ears open to her attractions and on other male agents who, acting on her behalf, influence Claudius. The truth of the social intrudes on Tacitus: in reality, only men can exercise *auctoritas*, so to move the narrative, Tacitus's Messalina must move men.

Messalina would seem to influence male agents by speech. Claudius's freedmen fear the power of her voice, coupled with her physical presence, to move him (11.32.4, 11.28.3). Silencing her is the key to their success in bringing her down: the emperor's ears must be closed to her voice (*in eo discrimen verti, si defensio audiretur, utque clausae aures etiam confitenti forent*, 11.28.3). In the confrontation between husband and wife on the road into Rome, therefore, Claudius's freedman Narcissus intervenes and literally shouts Messalina down (*Messalina clamitabatque audiret . . ., cum obstrepere accusator*, 11.34.3–4). Yet Tacitus oscillates between his need for a powerful female voice and his reluctance to describe or quote female speech. Tacitus's story cannot work without the power of Messalina's voice: it is necessary to his depiction of social castration, to his portrait of Claudius, and to his representation of the Principate itself under Claudius. However, his narrative reduces female speech to a minimum and to its effects.

In the fall of Asiaticus, Messalina's voice operates through other men whose speech (on political matters) achieves what she wants (satisfaction of her greed and sexual jealousy). She has Suillius accuse Asiaticus and Sosibius outline his threat to the emperor. And when Asiaticus's words in his own defense soften Claudius, Messalina sets in motion the voice of Vitellius to maneuver Claudius in the direction she wants him to go. The relation between female desire, male speech, and violence is elongated but direct. The emperor has the authority to give orders that make violent action happen. He is moved by the talk of men, and they are moved to speech by Messalina.

Yet Tacitus's representation of Messalina's speech exposes his fiction-making and ideological bias, for her speech is banished to the interior spaces of his narrative world and interiorized in the historian's rhetoric. Except for the confrontation of husband and wife on the Ostian road, all instances of Messalina's speaking take place in private, as with the trial of Asiaticus in Claudius's bedroom. In that confrontation on the Ostian road, Tacitus reduces her words to noise—she clamors (*clamitabat*, 11.34.3).[15] More often, he simply collapses Messalina's words, her cadences, and her tone into verbs of motion. She "sets on" Suillius to accuse Asiaticus and Poppaea (11.1.1, *immittit*); Sosibius "is added" (associated with Suillius in attacking Asiaticus, 11.1.2, *adiungitur*); "persons are introduced/set up" by Messalina to push Poppaea to suicide (11.2.5, *subditis*). Tacitus's representation of other events fails even to substitute such verbs of motion for those of speech, although the events he recounts make no sense without assuming that Messalina spoke. Her supposed seduction and affair with Silius, for example, cannot have taken place without her speech (11.12), yet, in the critical scene where Messalina decides to marry Silius, Tacitus represents what he says (in indirect discourse) but what she thinks (in omniscient narration).

This confined and collapsed description of the speech of a woman who is depicted as obsessively desiring raises a question about the represented relation between the female voice and the female body. In his depiction of two other powerful female agents, Agrippina, the next wife of Claudius and mother of the emperor Nero, and Poppaea, wife of Nero (daughter of the Poppaea destroyed by Messalina), Tacitus represents woman's speech in indirect discourse (13.13.6, 13.14.3–5, 13.46.3–4, 14.2, 14.61). As the mother of Nero, his Agrippina speaks directly (13.21, 14.8.5–6). Neither Poppaea nor Agrippina is chaste, but their difference from Messalina lies in the nature of their sexuality—their use of their bodies. Tacitus's Poppaea, never mastered by either her own or her lovers' desire, transfers her affections to the man from whom she has the most to gain (*neque adfectui suo aut alieno obnoxia, unde utilitas ostenderetur*, 13.45.3). His Agrippina, austere in her public behavior, is unchaste only where it is expedient for power (12.7.5–6). In contrast, desire and lust are said to master Messalina. According to Tacitus, she plays with state affairs not for political ends but to satisfy her wantonness (*per lasciviam, ut Messalina, rebus Romanis inludenti*, 12.7.5). If the female body is deployed for political gain, a goal outside its own pleasure, the utterance of the female voice in Tacitus is allowed a representation similar to that granted male agents. But, where the female body serves only its own pleasure, the female voice, necessary in a narrative that seeks to displace male agency, expresses no specific thoughts: it simply moves men to speak or makes noise.[16]

It is in these terms that we should consider an elision of Messalina's mouth and her vagina in Tacitus's characterization of Vitellius's mouth as dirtied, when he has listened to Messalina and spoken on her behalf. Tacitus's Asiaticus (11.3.2) announces that he was destroyed by female deceit (*fraude muliebri*) and the shameless (or foul) mouth of Vitellius (*impudico Vitellii ore*). Tacitus's words evoke the sense observed by Richlin of a mouth stained by oral sex (1983: 26–29). The equation of political enemies and informers with men who perform oral sex is a commonplace of Roman invective (Skinner 1982: 204; Richlin 1983: 99, 151). Although cunnilingus is not always the mode of sex invoked, the association of a fouled male mouth with female deceit, where the man has listened to a female mouth and done its bidding, suggests that Vitellius's mouth becomes *impudicum* because it has served a woman, and a woman in whom many men have had their penises. The instability of the meaning of a female mouth open in greed for luxurious gardens and ready to toy with state affairs to satisfy lust is furthered by Tacitus's account of an attack on Messalina's agent Suillius during the reign of Nero. When Suillius is blamed for the destruction of prominent men and women under Claudius, he claims that he acted under orders from Messalina (after Nero disallows his claim that he acted on Claudius's orders). Why, asks an unnamed speaker, was no one else selected to put his voice at the service of the "savage whore?" (*cur enim neminem alium delectum qui saevienti impudicae vocem praeberet*, 13.43.5). Seemingly, speaking for or at the order of a "savage whore" stains the male mouth by an association with cunnilingus. Listening to the utterance of a woman characterized by her voracious sexuality becomes attention to her female body: her mouth is equated with her vagina.[17]

The Historian's Project and
the Senator's Agency

The excess of Messalina's desire and Tacitus's tendency to substitute motion for Messalina's speech translates into an elision of body and voice that augments Tacitus's construction of Messalina as a figure of unconstrained desire. His depiction of a former empress who enacts her desire recurs in a political context in which his own actions as senator were constrained by the power of the emperor and by his own recommended code of senatorial self-control. Tacitus projects onto Messalina power and action he lacks as a senator, though he structures a narrative in which she is silenced and hunted down. In doing so, I argue, he figures the relation between his imperial present and its past, achieving in the writing of history an agency he lacks in politics. Tacitus's representation of Messalina's agency, of her body and its uncontrolled desires, allows him to speak as a critical commentator on the forces that have silenced good men.

The change of regimes that marked the beginnings of Tacitus as a writer threw into high relief senators' loss of agency in their dealings with the *princeps*. Tacitus testifies to their encounter with the undisguised despotism of Domitian, the last Flavian and the very emperor who had advanced Tacitus's own political career: they witnessed "the extreme of servitude, when the work of informers deprived us even of the exchange of speaking and hearing. We should have lost memory itself as well as voice, if we had been as able to forget as to be silent" (*nos quid in servitute, adempto per inquisitiones etiam loquendi audiendique commercio. memoriam quoque ipsam cum voce perdidissemus, si tam in nostra potestate esset oblivisci quam tacere, Agr. 2.3*). When Tacitus (*Agr. 3.1*) hails the present under Nerva and Trajan as "the dawning of a most happy age" (*beatissimi saeculi ortu*), he praises the reconciliation of *principatus* (sovereignty of the *princeps*) and *libertas* (freedom of the senator). Now, men can feel what they wish and say what they feel, he claims in his first historical work (*sentire quae velis et quae sentias dicere licet, Hist. 1.1.4*). In terms of narrative agency, Domitian appropriated the senators' action and speech, leaving them only vision (perception and thought, feeling and memory; Bal 1984: 348). Although Tacitus claims the new regime restored speech, aligning it with action, we should (as Ahl points out) "beware of taking Tacitus 'at his word'" (1984: 207).

The realities of power under Trajan limited senators' speech as well as their actions, making the distinction between present and past problematic. The difference between regimes lay in the style in which emperors exercised their absolute power. Tacitus's fellow senator Pliny makes this clear when he celebrates Trajan: "You order us to be free: we shall be; you order us to speak what we feel in public: we shall express ourselves" (*iubes esse liberos: erimus; iubes quae sentimus promere in medium: proferemus*, Pan. 66.4). The ambiguity embedded in the notion of acting freely and speaking openly on demand preserves both the senators' dignity and the imperial appropriation of their agency. Tacitus (*Agr.* 42.5) himself negotiates the potential conflict between the *princeps*'s power and the senatorial tradition of achievement by promising renown to senators who combined deference and restraint (*obsequiumque ac modestiam*) with activity and vigor (*industria ac vigor*). In a system openly acknowledged as autocratic, a senator advanced his own career by serving the emperor and state (Martin 1981: 33–35 with refs.). However, *obsequium*, Tacitus's term for "deference," also referred to the compliance, maintained by threat of force, that freed slaves owed their ex-masters. The compliance of the ex-slave that included speech as well as behavior finds an echo in the limits on the voice of the senator. He could speak ill of the past, but "for the current regime only praise was permissible, in Trajan's time as in Domitian's" (Waters 1969: 399). In this context, figuring the difference between past and present might present difficulties for senators who, as slaveholders, knew this meaning of *obsequium* from the other side.

Tacitus's words about his *immediate* past—"We should have lost memory itself as well as voice, if we had been as able to forget as to be silent"—are significant in terms of the writing of history. Without imputing a systematic program to Tacitus, it may be said that he undertook an extensive project of remembering. His texts map an imaginary construction of empire in time and space. Beginning with his own genealogy, a biography of his father-in-law Agricola, he recounted the story of a good man under a bad emperor as a model of senatorial service and rectitude, commenting along the way on the imperial project at the frontier (*Agricola*). From family, he turned exclusively to the frontier: an ethnography of the Germans describes people outside the empire (*Germania*). Then came a shift from the boundaries of empire to its center and from present to past. An imaginary debate on the decline of oratory in the Principate set in the Rome of Tacitus's youth plays on the questions of speech and liberty and the relations of imperial present and Republican past. From a history overlapping his own lifetime (*Histories*), he moved back toward a place of origins, the earliest generations of the Principate, which include the reign of Claudius (*Annals*).

By writing of the Principate's beginnings, Tacitus is able to represent the genesis of the current imperial order and to differentiate that order from preceding ones. According to Michel de Certeau, history makes the relations of past and present ambiguous because it separates the present from the past and, at the same time, draws a determinative connection between them.

> If, in one respect, the function of history expresses the position of one generation in relation to preceding ones by stating, "I can't be that," it always affects the statement of a no less dangerous complement, forcing society to confess, "I am other than what I would wish to be, and I am determined by what I deny." It attests to an autonomy and a dependence whose proportions vary according to the social settings and political situations in which they are elaborated. In the form of a "labor" immanent to human development, it occupies the place of the myths by means of which a society has represented its ambiguous relations with its origins and, through a violent history of Beginnings, its relations with itself. (1988: 46)

Tacitus's writing displays this tension. The record of imperial despotism and senatorial servility under the first emperors that Tacitus recounts in all its bloody detail offers the senatorial historian and his senatorial readers a field in which to explore the practice of power and the behavior of senators like themselves. On the one hand, Tacitus disassociates his imperial present from this early history of the Principate that included the reign of Claudius. The events' distance from his own day allows the historian's famous contention that he spoke without anger or partisan spirit (*sine ira et studio*, 1.1.6). Yet, on the other hand, his claim that the past provides lessons for the present establishes a continuity between past and present (4.33.2–4). Beyond the traditional Roman view that history establishes a range of behaviors to be followed or avoided, Tacitus offers the very process of history as an object lesson for what the future can inflict on the present—"the dread of posterity and infamy for debased words and deeds" (*pravis dictis factisque ex posteritate et infamia metus sit*, 3.65.1; cf. 4.35.6–7). How senators judge their predecessors in relation to former emperors suggests how succeeding generations may regard them in their relation to their present rulers. This threat makes an observed similarity between present and past especially disturbing: "Though the families themselves may now be extinct, you will find those who, because of a similarity of conduct, will think that another's crimes are cited to condemn them; even fame and virtue have enemies, condemning their opposites by too close a contrast" (*utque familiae ipsae iam extinctae sint, reperies qui ob similitudinem morum aliena malefacta sibi obiectari putent. etiam gloria ac virtus infensos habet, ut nimis ex propinquo diversa arguens*, 4.33.4). The historian could distinguish constitutional forms, state institutions, and the practices of daily life; his problem seems to have been the sameness of past and present.[18] An agent like Messalina in the narrative of the past helps to disrupt the isomorphism of imperial past and imperial present.

History, Empire, and Wives

The figure of excessive desire that circulates in the person of Messalina gives Tacitus an opportunity to express both the present's difference from and its similarity to the past, thus representing his society's "ambiguous relations with its origins and . . . its relations with itself." I argue that the historian's desiring, savage Messalina enables him to distinguish his present from a corrupt imperial past in which a woman is empowered to enact her desire; at the same time, as the desiring woman signals any and every exercise of imperial power, she allows him to recount the growth of the emperor's power, acknowledged as autocratic at his moment of writing. The distinction between present and past is a distinction between good and bad empire, and, as in *Jane Eyre*, the difference between imperial orders is represented by figures of woman, especially as wife. Messalina's desire makes her a bad wife; its effects produce a bad empire. In contrast, images of the virtuous wife inscribed across the map of empire constructed by Tacitus's works suggest what is necessary for good empire: Tacitus's German women depict good wives at the frontiers of empire; the Roman women in his own family represent good wives within the empire.[19]

Tacitus's report on the severe marriage code of the Germans describes female bodies in male control and wives who live for and in terms of men (*Germ.* 18–19). He praises those states in which only virgins marry, and only once (19.3). In a husband who is the sole object of her thoughts and desires, a wife has one body and one life (*sic unum accipiunt maritum quo modo unum corpus unamque vitam*, 19.4). Gifts useful in war cement the marital bond: nothing Tacitus would imagine to please female interest enters the transaction of marriage (*munera non ad delicias muliebres quaesita nec quibus nova nupta comatur*, 18.2). Wedded to considerations of manly virtues and the fortunes of war, a wife shares her husband's labors and dangers (*laborum periculorumque sociam*, 18.4). In Tacitus's view, the marriage transaction firmly guards women's chastity, and, with sexuality controlled, other dangerous pleasures—the allurements of spectacles and the stimuli of banquets—are foreclosed (*saepta pudicitia agunt, nullis spectaculorum inlecebris, nullis conviviorum irritationibus corruptae*, 19.1). Adultery is rare, and apparently only women are guilty of it, for Tacitus reports only the punishment of the wife, offering his readers a graphic representation of a punished, unchaste female body, expelled from home, stripped of clothes, head shaven, and flogged (*abscisis crinibus nudatam coram propinquis expellit domo maritus ac per omnem vicum verbere agit*, 19.2). In effect, Tacitus's discourse in the *Germania* associates desire with women in their role as wives and then displays male control of that desire. Tacitus's German wives can then serve their husbands' preeminent interest—war-making. Wives under male control contribute to the *virtus* (manliness, courage) that makes the Germans formidable in war; they make men toughened warriors.

Tacitus makes a contrast between the decadence of Roman society and the uncorrupted mores of barbarians—between the self and the externalized other, as it were—and he sees in that other the persistence of archaic Roman virtues (Dudley 1968: 221; Dorey 1969: 14; Martin 1981: 49–52). Tacitus's ethnocentrism and misunderstanding of certain practices create an imperialist erasure of difference (Martin 1981: 51–52), inscribing upon an external other what Roman marriage and wives are imagined to have been. The erasure of cultural difference allows for the importation of images from the border to the center of empire to serve as an object lesson in the control of internal others—Roman women. Examples of such control appear in Tacitus's biography of Agricola, his father-in-law and his model of the virtuous imperial senator. These Roman wives are as subservient to the interests of sons and husbands as are the historian's German women. Julia Procilla, a virtuous and affectionate mother, acts only to stem a son's inappropriate ardor for philosophy (*Agr.* 4.2–3). Domitia Decidiana, a wife of illustrious birth advancing a husband's career, appears to live in harmony and mutual affection with Tacitus's hero Agricola and then disappears from the story (6.1). Tacitus's own wife, Agricola's daughter, who gave the historian his link to his model, remains nameless.[20]

Borrowing Tacitus's words to describe the relations between the model emperor and the current imperial wife (Bruère 1954: 163), Pliny, Tacitus's contemporary, presents the vision of the good wife at the center of empire that was publicly disseminated at Tacitus's moment of writing. In his *Panegyricus*, a speech delivered in the senate and then published, Pliny follows a celebration of the emperor's physical prowess and self-control with a picture of a devoted, modest, and unassuming wife (*Pan.* 83–84; see Temporini 1978: 177–80). She is her husband's subject, taking orders rather than giving them. Pliny is careful to remark on the wife's silence (*ipsa cum silentio incedat*, 83.8), and he himself does not name her. Controlled, the wife signals and indeed reproduces the husband-emperor's power over himself and others. Pliny is quite explicit about this: "Many distinguished men have been dishonored by an ill-considered choice of wife or weakness in not getting rid of her; thus their fame abroad was damaged by the loss of reputation at home, and their relative failure as husbands denied them complete success as citizens" (*multis inlustribus dedecori fuit aut inconsultius uxor adsumpta aut retenta patientius; ita foris claros domestica destruebat infamia, et ne maximi cives haberentur, hoc efficiebatur, quod mariti minores erant*, 83.4, LCL).

It could be objected that Tacitus and Pliny simply draw on an ancient tradition of wifely virtues or that, in the case of Agricola, women are not central to the career of a consul, provincial governor, and successful general. But that is precisely the point. Banished to the sidelines, women are subsidiary to or excluded from public and political arenas. The exclusion of women constructs these activities as male ones; women become merely ideological capital in a political discourse of empire. The image of the good wife is central to the depiction of the good empire as one that is militarily strong, served by selfless administrators, and ruled by a *princeps* who has reconciled his own sovereignty with the freedom of senators. Good wives submit to their husbands' control and lack desire—or, at least, any desire of their own. Messalina, the desiring woman out of male control, epitomizes the bad wife. She belongs to Tacitus's hostile portrayal of Claudian Rome, which must be seen in terms of the geography and economy of imperial power generated by Tacitus's Augustus, founder of the Principate. Moving from the outside in, "the State organized under the name of the *princeps*" (*principis nomine constitutam rem publicam*) consists of boundaries, provinces, capital; within, all things (legions, provinces, fleets) are linked (*Ann.* 1.9.6). In the center of Tacitus's map is the city of Rome and the *princeps*, who had drawn to himself the functions of senate, magistrates, and laws (1.2.1). Around the *princeps* is his household (*domus*): hence, in Tacitus's view, the importance of his strength and fitness to maintain himself, his household, and the peace— that is, order within the empire (*seque et domum et pacem*, 1.4.1). Power is pulled in; its administration flows out from the man, the household, and the city to the provinces.[21] In this structure, it may be said that German wives indicate what is necessary to maintain the frontiers of empire, Agricola's women what is required inside, and Trajan's wife what is vital at the center.

Plotted on the Augustan map of *ego, domus, pax* (the emperor's person, his household, the empire), the Claudian economy appears deformed. Like the founder of the Principate, Claudius is said to have drawn to himself all the functions of laws and magistrates. But by doing so he opens up the opportunity for plundering (*cuncta legum et magistratuum munia in se trahens princeps materiam praedandi patefecerat*, 11.5.1).[22] The emperor's submission to his wife's attractions dissolves the boundaries of *ego*; power flows to contingent others within the imperial *domus*—women and freedmen. Men's property is devoured, and they are dragged into the imperial household on female whim. Violence and violation proceed from lust, greed, and the most petulant motives. Where Claudius consumes state power, Messalina expends honors and wealth on a lover. The signs of imperial rank pass carelessly from one house to another. A wife's desire creates a crisis in the very geography of imperial power: Who is citizen and who emperor? Which house is the imperial *domus*? Who holds the city (11.31.3, 12.4, 30.5)?

The implications for *pax* are made clear in Tacitus's depiction of affairs at the borders of the empire. The language in Tacitus's account of the political chaos in Parthia and its chronological misplacement draws an analogy between disorder at the edge of empire and disorder at the center (11.8–10). Similar clusters of words characterize both Parthian princes and Claudian wives (Keitel 1978: 462–66). The uncontrolled extravagance and savagery of the Parthian princes wreak havoc at the edge of empire and portend the destruction of the Roman order by uncontrolled wives. In a convoluted account of affairs at the German frontier, Tacitus uses the successful Roman general Corbulo to show up the timidity of Claudius (11.18–19). Although Corbulo's restoration of ancient military discipline strikes fear in the Germans and inspires the *virtus* (manliness, courage) of his own men, Claudius halts attacks on the Germans and pulls the Roman forces back across the Rhine. Tacitus's Claudius, who fails to exert self-control and lacks *virtus* himself, endangers the German border and dooms imperial expansion.[23]

Woman Becomes Empire

It is within this economy of imperial power that we can fully observe how Tacitus's construction of Messalina's agency functions as a discursive screen. Obsessively desiring and savage, Messalina serves as a device to comment on imperial power and empire. Although Tacitus represents a specific woman, his representation refers to something other than a particular female subject or even a culturally defined femininity. In Tacitus's account of the Claudian Principate, the flow of Messalina's desire signals corruption and disorder across the Augustan geography of empire. In a discourse of imperial power, Tacitus's Messalina functions as a sign of the imperial household, the city, and imperial power itself. Tacitus's representation of Messalina and his construction of her agency serve this signifying process. Woman becomes empire or, more precisely, elements of imperial geography and imperial power itself.[24]

With Messalina, we are dealing very specifically with woman as sign. Tacitus implicitly codes her behavior as feminine in contrast with that of Claudius's next wife. As noted earlier, Tacitus contrasts Messalina, who plays with matters of state to satisfy her lust, with Agrippina, whose liaisons serve political ends and whose unchastity in the service of power he sees as an "almost masculine subjection" (*quasi virile servitium*, 12.7.5–6). The male historian posits a gendered relationship between means and ends; when the ends are political, the agent's behavior is comprehensible and at least malelike, as opposed to Messalina's chaotic and implicitly female fooling around.[25]

In a metonymic slip, woman-wife becomes the inner sanctum of the imperial household, the space at the very center of Tacitus's map of empire. When an actor danced in the emperor's bedroom (clearly a reference to Messalina's sexual relations with Mnester), the freedmen of Claudius's court observe, it brought dishonor, but not the ruin threatened by Messalina's marriage to a noble (11.28.1). The issue turns not only on who is in the imperial bedroom but also on who is in the woman. An unchaste woman, like a room, can be entered, and entrance—penetration—brings shame. Woman's body is equated with male space (here, his bedroom); her unchastity represents an alien invasion of that space (Joshel 1992). The desiring woman invites traffic, so to speak. She turns the household into the street, conflating the imperial household and the imperial city.

Similarly, woman stands in for the city of Rome. Narcissus tells Claudius, "Unless you act at once, the [new] husband holds the city" (*ni propere agis, tenet urbem maritus*, 11.30.5). In this equation of woman and city, female desire again has its signifying uses. Tacitus uses images of flow to describe Messalina's desire and the resulting disorder, echoing his image of Rome under the Julio-Claudians.[26] Messalina's "flowing out into untried lusts" before Silius's marriage proposal is reinforced by Tacitus's vivid description of the wild party that follows the marriage. This celebration of the new vintage invokes the traditional sins of the Roman wife—unchastity and wine-drinking. Everyone and everything is out of control. Messalina is never freer, looser, more fluid in extravagance (*non alias solutior in luxu*, 11.31.4): wine, and Messalina's hair, flows (*fluere lacus, crine fluxo*). Likewise, Tacitus's comments on society in the capital note its extravagance (3.53–54, 14.58.2, 15.42.1), loose morals (13.25.1, 14.15.4–5, 14.20–21), and corrupt sexual standards (2.85, 14.35); money, goods, and bodies flow. At the center of empire, "all that is horrible and shameful flows together and flourishes" (*cuncta undique atrocia aut pudenda confluunt celebranturque*, 15.44.4).[27]

Of course, at another level, Narcissus's statement—and the entire story—works on a simple logic: the man who holds the woman holds the power. In Tacitus's telling, Silius, the imperial freedmen, and Claudius all understand Messalina's marriage as a transfer of power, indeed, as a coup d'état. Here, it is wife as mother who is important. Silius's marriage proposal comes with the plan to adopt Britannicus (11.26.3); in her confrontation with Claudius on the Ostian road, Messalina demands to be heard as the mother of Britannicus and Octavia (11.34.3). Where succession is dynastic, woman's body is the vehicle of transmission of power:

woman's reproductive capacity reproduces power. Home and public life, husband and public man (citizen) are dependent terms, as we have seen in Pliny's depiction of the correct relations of the successful Trajan and his wife. A husband must rule his wife's body at home to rule others outside it. The instability of Messalina's affections, the excess of her desire, and her disinterest in marriage proper make the holding of this woman and power unstable. She may reproduce her husband in producing the heir, but she does not reproduce her husband's control over city or empire. Messalina displays Claudius's failure to hold power in the Augustan formula—*ego, domus, pax* (the emperor's person, his household, the empire).

Yet the desiring woman who gets what she wants, seizes property, deals with men in the inner sanctum of the palace, calls and dismisses them on whim, and levels social distinctions between men is a sign of the nature of imperial autocracy. Although Tacitus's depiction of these actions is pejorative, they are all possible behaviors for any *princeps* in firm control of the legions. Of course, from the point of view of the senator, actually taking such actions is a "bad" exercise of power. It does not allow for the reconciliation of *principatus* (sovereignty of the *princeps*) and *libertas* (freedom of the senator) that allows men to feel what they wish and say what they feel. *Obsequium* as the rational deference to authority that Tacitus recommends for the senator only too easily becomes the required servility of ex-slave for former master. Tacitus is not merely blaming Messalina for the events of her husband's reign. Rather, she functions in his narrative as a sign both of the concentration of state functions in the person of the *princeps* that Tacitus attributes to the founder of the Principate and to Claudius (1.2.1; 11.5.1), which in turn belonged to Trajan, and of the corrupt exercise of that power. Thus, woman and her desire ultimately serve to represent in negative terms an exercise of male power disapproved by Tacitus as senator and historian: the emperor's power appears as a voracious female desire that drags in men and property and flows out to create a mess in the family, the social order, and the empire.[28]

The polyvalence of the sign of the desiring woman, representing both bad empire and imperial power itself, serves both to separate Tacitus's present from the earliest generations of the Principate and to affirm his generation's dependence on and continuity with the past. As a sign of the corruption of power, the desiring woman participates in the disassociation of present and past produced by the writing of history. Trajan's silent, obedient wife marks the present. Messalina, the unchaste, savage woman, belongs to a story of origins; she signals the corruption, decadence, and dangers of that past from which Tacitus would distinguish his present. The work of narrative effects the disassociation by tracking and killing a sign of "bad" empire. In contrast to other authors (Suet. *Claud.* 26.2, 36;

Dio Cass. 61.31.3–5), Tacitus expends considerable detail elaborating not only Messalina's fall but her descent into inanimate matter. His narrative achieves its closure only when it can name her a corpse (11.38.1). In the process, as author of the narrative of empire, the senatorial historian garners a particular agency for himself in terms of the action and speech that were unavailable to senators under Trajan. The work of narrative asserts a senator's efficacy (in the writing of history at least) against an emperor's failure. Tacitus gets rid of Messalina, as his Claudius could not. If Tacitus could not control the present as senator, he could control the narrative of origins as historian.

At the same time, as a sign of imperial power itself, Messalina also participates in the continuity between present and past established by the writing of history. Although he could be accounted a failure as a husband, Claudius participated in the growth of the *princeps*'s power and the development of an imperial state, conditions that determined the historian's moment of writing. Even by the evidence of the hostile senatorial tradition, Claudius extended Roman citizenship to many provincials, brought the Romanized elite of Gallia Comata into the Senate, and strengthened the imperial bureaucracy, augmenting imperial institutions.[29] In important ways, Claudius contributed to the making of Trajan, and Messalina is a sign of that making. She signals not Claudius's acts but the growth of the emperor's power and the development of an imperial state that are the effects of those acts. In other words, Messalina figures in a story of an accumulation of power determining Tacitus's present, in which the emperor orders senators to be free.

Echoes of the past in the present perhaps added urgency to Tacitus's deployment of woman as a sign to distinguish his generation of the Principate from its origins and yet to figure a history of the present. While the image of the martial Trajan forms a stark contrast to the limping, scholarly Claudius of tradition, we can observe similarities in imperial practices, policies, and projects. Both emperors expanded the boundaries of empire with new conquests—Britain under Claudius and Dacia under Trajan. Like Claudius, Trajan enlarged the responsibilities of the imperial bureaucracy. Involvement in the details of imperial administration and paternalistic care for the ruled, depicted as a ridiculous pedantry and interference in Claudius's case, characterized both emperors. Their special concern for Italy extended to work on the harbor at Ostia to insure Rome's grain supply, a project begun by Claudius and renewed by Trajan.[30]

The expansion of external boundaries and the breaking down of internal boundaries mark the material moment of Tacitus's use of the desiring woman as sign. Trajan's conquests pushed the boundaries of empire that separated Roman from non-Roman. Inside the empire, the extension of an imperial bureaucracy and its responsibilities and the intervention of emperors in municipal governments and finances broke down the old hegemonic division between Italy and the provinces. The Romanization of the provinces, the wide extension of citizenship to propertied provincials, and the inclusion of the provincial elites in the Roman senate furthered the process, making distinctions of class more important that those of location. I want to consider Tacitus's politics of representation in terms of these developments, which are generally discussed either as male or without attention to gender (cf. Richmond 1944: 44).

Klaus Theweleit's observations on the social change and ideological developments of European capitalism offer a paradigm for considering the use made of the representations of women in the context of Roman imperial expansion and the breakdown of older political and social distinctions inside the empire:

> As social structures expand and become more mobile, the system of external limitations and constraints begins to lose its force. At this point, the social framework comes to need internal boundaries for streams of desiring production to wash up against: reservoirs, canals, drainage systems. In other words, if people are to perform the new functions required of them—but are to remain at the same time capable of being subjugated—they have to be given new bodily boundaries. (1987: 311)

Theweleit borrows a conceptual vocabulary from Gilles Deleuze and Félix Guattari. "Desiring production" refers to human energy that seeks to act in the world (or the unconscious understood as a productive force). The expansion of human productive capacity brought by industrial capitalism loosened traditional political and social structures, enlarging the possibilities of "desiring production" in a process Deleuze and Guattari call "deterritorialization." At the same time, a process of "reterritorialization" limited the possibilities by inscribing new social controls that rendered people capable of being ruled (Deleuze and Guattari 1983: 33ff.; Theweleit 1987: 264). Theweleit traces the deployment of women, especially upper-class women, in Western culture to establish new boundaries and render people capable of subjugation. Men construct a chaste, undesiring highborn woman who can be celebrated, admired, even worshiped, and a sexual woman who can be persecuted by being turned into a prostitute and then killed (1987: 229ff.). "Meanwhile lack is maintained in relationships with their own (child-bearing and asexual) women through their exclusion (as nameless wives) from social productions and from the confraternities of men" (ibid.: 367). This system requires the accessibility of female bodies from conquered nations or races and from the upper classes, yet "for the great mass of men, images of women sacrificed in this way are all that is needed" (ibid.: 370).

Quite obviously, we cannot talk about Roman industrial capitalism, but in the developments mentioned above, the external boundaries of empire expanded and older internal political and social boundaries were opened up and crossed in a process of deterritorialization. In Tacitus's account of Messalina, empire is mapped on the uncontained, overflowing body of a woman. Its lack of limits echoes the extension of the geographic boundaries of empire as well as the long-held Roman vision of empire as boundless (Nicolet 1991: 29–56; Edwards 1993: 19–20). As the imperial wife at the center of empire, whose desire takes her across family and class boundaries, Messalina figures a process of deterritorialization, not in terms of industrial capitalism, but in terms of the blurring of older distinctions between conqueror and conquered, Italian and provincial. The loss of constraints provided by these older distinctions is patrolled by the work of a narrative that halts the chaos of Messalina, and by the figures of good wives. Tacitus seems to participate in the sort of deployment of woman for reterritorialization described by Theweleit. The Roman historian inscribes the Roman ideals of control on the female bodies of external others and praises but silences the internal others of his class. In a history of origins, he puts on display Messalina's voracious desire and savagery at a moment of decadence and danger for men of his class. He makes available to the gaze of his male readers the all-encompassing wickedness of the castrating woman. Fear evoked by the image is relieved by a narrative that hunts her down. Step by step, Tacitus drains her of sexuality and life until she becomes a corpse.

Empire Becomes Woman

The modern historian's search for the "real" Messalina encounters Tacitus's representation of a sexually voracious, savage woman. As an unified agent, however, this Messalina is a pretense. She functions as a sign in a Roman imperial discourse that fragments woman, distributing her across the tensions between the private and public spheres, between the city and the provinces, and between the sovereignty of the emperor and the freedom of the senator. As such, Messalina figures empire good and bad, present and past. The discourse of empire and the work of history effect a further displacement. The desiring woman signals the exercise of imperial power, but the exercise and always threatening excess of imperial power become the woman. In the process of displacement, her body becomes what she signifies (Douglas [1966] 1984: 115; Butler 1990: 131–34). The process, evident in the narrative idiosyncrasies that result from Tacitus's ideologized construction of Messalina's desire, violence, and voice, is transparent in the roughly contemporary sixth satire of

Juvenal (115–32). As the climax of a catalogue of unchaste wives, Juvenal's Messalina epitomizes woman's desire where that desire is not appropriately wifely. Unnamed, this Messalina becomes the imperial whore (*meretrix Augusta*) who leaves her bed in the palace for a mat in a brothel. Donning a blond wig, she puts on the hair of a barbarian captive from northern Europe. Removing her clothes, she reveals her nipples and the belly that gave birth to the heir to the throne. Under the name of Lyscisa—evoking, through the Greek *lukos*, "wolf," the Roman slang for prostitute, "she-wolf" (*lupa*)—she services all customers without a break. Tired, but so unsatisfied she burns with a "woman's erection," she returns to the palace. Her darkened cheeks are filthy with the smoke of the brothel lantern; she carries the stink of the brothel to her imperial couch.

Juvenal's Messalina belongs to an account of women's flaws, not, as in Tacitus, to a history of the Principate. Yet the satirist's whore is imperial not only because she is identified as an emperor's wife but also because Juvenal projects elements of an imperial discourse onto her. He puts on a pornographic display of the body that in Tacitus stands in for the emperor's household, his city, and his power. The corruption and decadence of the latter become the prostitute's body, or rather her vagina, where penises, not the signs of families, are mixed.[31] Although she takes her body outside the palace, the "traffic" remains inside. Yet the move from the home, where access to the wife should be limited to the husband, to the brothel, where access is open to all men, produces extreme disorder, or disorder of imperial proportions.[32] Juvenal literalizes the heterogeneity that results from crossed boundaries in the images of dirt—the smoke and smell of the brothel that stains her body and the palace couch to which she returns. The imperial dimensions of unsatiable lust are conveyed in the body of a prostitute who outlasts customers, pimp, and other prostitutes. Wig and name associate her with the barbarian and the bestial. The frontier and nature are imported to the center of empire and Roman culture, collapsing the distinction between Roman and barbarian, empire and its frontier.

More than ten centuries of repetition of imperial discourse shapes Bertha Mason, Brontë's Indian Messalina. An imperial Messalina becomes a "majestic" Bertha. As with her Roman predecessor, words of savagery and dirt cluster around Bertha. She is a "wild beast" and a "monster" (Brontë [1847] 1984: 336). The wolfish name becomes in Bertha "wolfish cries" (335). She is a "filthy burden," "gross, impure, depraved" (334, 336). Feeling "covered with grimy dishonor" in the eyes of others, her husband "resolved to be clean in [his] own sight." Unlike Tacitus's Claudius, this husband "repudiated the contamination of [a wife's] crimes" and locked her up in the inner recesses of his home (334). Where the Roman Messalina burned with her own desire, the creole Messalina burns her husband's home, leaving him blind.

The discourse of empire that employs woman as sign leaves its mythic mark. Culturally, it produces woman as a creature whose desires are inordinately large and dangerous: let loose, they overwhelm and violate men. In male imagination, women do to men what men do to women, and the pursuit of desire results in a flow that produces dirt. Removed from its original signifying system, the figure of woman still carries with it the system's dimensions of desire, which, though they came from empire, will be mythically imputed to *women*.

Notes

1. Bertha Mason, daughter of a merchant-planter, is a decadent white. Whereas in Jamaica the term *creole* applied to the native-born population of both African and European origin, in England, it was used as "a derogatory name for the West Indian sugar plantocracy" (Sharpe 1993: 45–46).

2. For Messalina in Roman imperial literature, see Sen. *Apocol.* 11, 13; [Sen.] *Octavia* 10–17, 257–72, 536–37, 947–51; Pliny *HN* 10.172, 29.8; Tac. *Ann.* 11.1–4, 12, 26–38, 12.7.5–7, 13.11.2, 13.19.2, 13.43.1–5; Juv. 6.115–32, 10.329–45; Suet. *Claud.* 26.2, 29, 36, 37.2, 39.1; *Ner.* 6.4; *Vit.* 2.5; Dio Cass. 60.8.4–5, 14, 15.5–16.3, 17.5–18, 22.2–5, 27–28.5, 29.4–6a, 30.6b–31.5. On her age at marriage, see Syme 1958: 437; 1986: 150; Meise 1969: 152 n. 122. For the affair with Silius, see Levick 1990: 65 with refs. Translations from ancient sources are the author's own, unless indicated otherwise. LCL refers to the Loeb Classical Library.

3. For bibliography on women in Tacitus, see Wallace 1991. Roman imperial women in Baroque opera: Monteverdi, *Incoronazione di Poppea* (1642); Pallavicino, *Messalina* (and derived from it, Vivaldi, *Ottone in villa* [1713]; Vivaldi's and printer's errors call Ottone Claudio and Cleonilla Messalina, see Hill 1983: xviii–xxi); Handel, *Agrippina* (1709). On Roman imperial women in Baroque opera, see Heller 1993. On associations of Marie Antoinette with Roman imperial women, see Hunt 1991. In his studies of atavistic physiognomy, the late nineteenth-century scientist Cesare Lombroso identified Messalina's features as exemplary of a criminal type: "Messalina . . . offers many of the features of the criminal and born prostitute—having a low forehead, very thick, wavy hair, and a heavy jaw" (Lombroso and Ferrero 1899: 98).

4. I use "woman" to mean "the historically specific representation of the female that mediates the relationship of women and men to every individual, concrete woman" (Poovey 1990: 29; see also de Lauretis 1984: 5 and 1987: 1–30).

5. Hostile senatorial tradition on Claudius's acts: Sen. *Apocol.* 3; Tac. *Ann.* 11.5.1, 11.23–25.2, 12.60, 13.29.2; Suet. *Claud.* 24.1–2; Dio Cass. 60.10.3–4, 17.5–8, 24.1–2. For the controversy on Claudius's acts, see Scramuzza 1940;

McAlindon 1956; Momigliano 1961; Levick 1978 and 1990, esp. 81–91; De Vivo 1980; M. T. Griffin 1982; Wiseman 1982; Millar [1977] 1992: 74–77. On the importance of Claudius's freedmen administrators, see Levick 1990: 83 and Millar [1977] 1992: 70, 74–77.

6. Although a woman not in paternal power *(sui iuris)* could dissolve her marriage unilaterally, the marriage to Silius and proposed adoption of Britannicus present legal problems: see Levick 1990: 67 with refs.

7. I follow Mieke Bal's definition of narrative agency as *"Who does what?"* to clarify the elements of Tacitus's portrayal of Messalina that are in question: "The activities distinguished are speech, vision and action. Speech includes all utterance by a linguistic subject . . .; vision includes perception and thought, feeling and memory; action includes any activity involving a change in the situation between actions in the diegesis" (1984: 348).

8. On stereotyping and the politics of representation of female sexuality in Roman imperial literature, see Rutland 1978; Richlin 1981a, 1984, 1992c; Vinson 1989; Santoro L'hoir 1992 and 1994; Wyke 1992; Edwards 1993. Cf. the use made of Clodia in the late Republic, Skinner 1983 and Richlin 1992f: 1327–29. For attempts to distinguish practice and discourse, see Hallett 1984 and Hillard 1992.

9. Messalina's liaison with Mnester, ex-slave and actor, is also a trope: see Richlin 1981a: 241; Vinson 1989: 440–45; Edwards 1993: 52–53. Note, too, the incongruity between the public manner with which Tacitus's Messalina conducts her affair with Silius (11.12.4) and his subsequent suggestion that they make it public (11.26.1–2).

10. Other representations of Messalina's desire: Pliny *HN* 10.172; Juv. 6.115ff.; Dio Cass. 60.8.5, 17.8, 18, 22.4–5, 31. Tacitus draws on tropes of Roman moralizing rhetoric: uncontrolled female sexuality and social disorder; unfaithful wives and politically weak husbands; satiated libertines who crave wrongdoing (see Edwards 1993). The issue here is what he does with them in a history of empire and how his formulation works within a discourse of empire (cf. Martin 1981: 11).

11. Dio Cassius also names Sabinus, prefect of the German bodyguard (60.28.2), and Claudius's freedman Polybius, adviser on literary affairs and "Patronage Secretary" (60.31.2).

12. *Fastidia* in the sense of aversions produced by being filled up (cf. 11.26.1) echoes Tacitus's comment on the effects of power: "There comes a satiety, sometimes to the monarch who has no more to give, sometimes to the favorite with no more to crave" *(satias capit aut illos, cum omnia tribuerunt, aut hos, cum iam nihil reliquum est quod cupiant,* 3.30.7, LCL). In Tacitus, the only element named as organizing Messalina's desire is good looks (11.12.1, 11.36.4).

13. The affair catches Tacitus's Silius in a double-bind of sex or death (cf. Juv. 10.329–45); he chooses the former and tries to grab as much as he can. For the sexual vulnerability of freedmen, see Sen. *Controv.* 4, praef. 10. On penetration and masculinity, see Richlin 1993b; Edwards 1993: 70–75. On the seemingly inconsistent charge that effeminate men are adulterers, see Edwards 1993: 64. The party is a Bacchanalia of sorts; in describing the first introduction of the rites and their suppression in 186 B.C.E., Livy associates female sexual misbehavior, homo-

sexual relations, and men who act like women (39.13.10, 15.9). Young men whose bodily integrity has been corrupted cannot serve as soldiers who defend the chastity of women and children (39.15.13–14). Here, too, effeminacy and lust are seen to lead to private crime and an attack on the state (39.16).

14. The representation of Claudius's weakness requires his surrender to his desire for his wife. The figure of the powerful freedman by itself does not demonstrate Claudius's weakness, as Tacitus's account of Agrippina, Messalina's successor in the marital bedroom, makes clear. If in Tacitus's story of Messalina's fall "everything obeyed a freedman" (*omnia liberto oboediebant*, 11.35.1), with Claudius's marriage to Agrippina "everything obeyed a woman" (*cuncta feminae oboediebant*, 12.7.5).

15. Other verbs of speech: at the trial of Asiaticus she warns Vitellius not to let Asiaticus off (*monet*, 11.2.4); preparing to meet her husband, she beseeches the senior Vestal Virgin to ask for a hearing from the *pontifex maximus* to beg for mercy (*oravit*, 11.32.5). On noise, cf. her tears and ineffectual protests before her murder (11.37.5).

16. The question of women's voices in Tacitus requires further analysis of which women speak and when, what they say, and to what effect. Vinson (1989: 440–41) and Santoro L'hoir (1994) suggest the way female speech in Tacitus can condemn the speaker herself and the political order that allows a woman to move male listeners. Female speech should be associated with the deceit (*fraus*) so often attributed to women in Tacitus (Rutland 1978: 17). Messalina's voice belongs to the larger issue of Tacitus's treatment of speech in the reign of Claudius, itself one step in the degeneration of speech from the dissembling Tiberius to Nero, who does not even write his own speeches (*Ann.* 13.3). Working within a tradition that depicts Claudius as afflicted with speech defects (Sen. *Apocol.* 5, 6.2, 7.4; Suet. *Claud.* 30, cf. 4.6), Tacitus undermines the effectiveness of what the emperor says. Two of Claudius's public speeches in Tacitus, one the inclusion of the elite from Gallia Comata in the senate, purportedly in direct quotation (11.24), and another on soothsayers, in indirect discourse (11.15), include antiquarian musings. In the former, the historian, himself an orator, speaks for the emperor and does a better job. Comparisons with Claudius's actual words preserved on the Lyon tablet reveal how Tacitus condensed and streamlined Claudius's words to give them a more dignified quality and universal scope (M. T. Griffin 1982). Tacitus's succinct excurses on learned subjects (the alphabet, 11.14; the history of the quaestorship, 11.22) show up the emperor's vocal pedantry. The senate had no choice but to approve Claudius's antiquarian musings, but the inability of Tacitus's speeched emperor to get things done is illustrated in Tacitus's notice that Claudius's addition of three new letters to the alphabet did not outlast his reign (11.14.5). The functional effectiveness of Messalina's unreported speech only highlights the functional ineffectiveness of her husband's reported speech. Ironically, at the moment of danger, Messalina, ever active, is finally given verbs of speech by Tacitus (see n. 15), but she fails to save her own life. Tacitus's Claudius, passive and silent in the critical scene (*mirum inter haec silentium Claudi*, 11.35.1), is saved by his active and vocal freedman (11.34.3–5). This scene is perhaps the most vicious condemnation of speech under Claudius: the throne is decided by a

shouting match between a woman and an ex-slave, those who should obey and keep quiet.

17. For *os impudicum* as a trope for the effects on a man who does a woman's bidding, see Cicero's descriptions of Sextus Cloelius (*Dom.* 25, 26, 47, 83). On associations of female mouth and vagina in the ancient medical writers, see A. E. Hanson 1990.

18. Histories of constitutions, law, institutions, and luxury: *Ann.* 1.1–3, 3.26–28, 3.55, 4.33, 11.22. Yet Tacitus himself shows how histories can be self-serving (2.22, 14.21). His repeated comments on the emperor's power and the senators' sycophancy, the disguise of freedom and slavery, the safety of the present and acceptance of autocracy, suggest an attempt to figure how his present was different (*Ann.* 1.2, 1.81, 2.32, 2.38, 3.65; cf. *Agr.* 2.3 and *Hist.* 1.1).

19. My discussion here is only suggestive of a more general "reaffirmation of women's domestic and subordinate roles" in the early second century (Boatwright 1991: 539). Boatwright's discussion of the "domestic and submissive roles embodied by the Trajanic and Hadrianic imperial women" (540) is instructive. I stress here the physical and cultural location of good wives in a geography of empire. For the Roman ideal of marriage, see Treggiari 1991.

20. Messala's diatribe on the failures of contemporary mothers, measured by their female ancestors in Tacitus's *Dialogus* (28–29), sets out comparable ideals of female service to children and male political capacity. In the good old days, the highest praise of a wife and mother was accorded for maintaining the household and devoting herself to her children (*praecipua laus erat tueri domum et inservire liberis*, 28.4). Sons raised in a mother's lap and at her breast and supervised by an elderly female relation rather than turned over to slave child-nurses were not corrupted by the character, speech, and beliefs of ignorant slave women. Proper maternal parenting and female devotion to sons laid the ground for male excellence in oratory.

21. On the metaphoric or isomorphic relations of house, household, or family and state, see Lacey 1986 and Edwards 1993: 138–39. Foucault's claim (1986: 94–95, 148–49) that the hegemonic identification of household and state was being modified at this moment by a new reciprocity in conjugal relations is flawed: see Cohen and Saller 1994.

22. The statement comes as an introduction to a new episode, following the fall of Asiaticus, but it perfectly describes an exercise in power, "in the bedroom . . . with Messalina present" (11.2.1), and property left open to imperial plundering.

23. Yet this was the same emperor who ordered the invasion of Britain, extending the boundaries of empire. Tacitus's narrative, in which the emperor gives in to his wife, reverses public portrayals of Claudius's control over the edges of empire—gendered allegorical representations that show Claudius standing above and holding down a prostrate woman, a figure for Britannia (R.R.R. Smith 1987: 115–17, pl. 6).

24. On woman as a sign, see Cowie 1978. Cowie takes up what she considers "the radical implications" of Lévi-Strauss's contention that kinship structures are systems of exchange and communication in which women are exchanged as objects and as signs (55). Cowie contends that, as a sign, woman is not simply ex-

changed, but "produced within a signifying system" (55–56). Most important for the argument here, Cowie suggests that there is a disjunction between the constitutive elements of the sign of woman, signifier and signified. Although the form of the sign (its signifier), here a representation in words, is a female person, the meaning of the sign (its signified) "is *not* the concept woman" (56). As Blassingame (1979) and Carby (1987) suggest with stereotypes, a sign works in relation to other signs. Here, woman-wife should be considered in terms of the ex-slave. Together, they effect the carnivalistic inversion of the Saturnalia (see Dickison 1977).

25. On Agrippina, cf. Tacitus's description of her mother: "But Agrippina was not willing to submit to equality, greedy for domination, and had doffed feminine vices for manly concerns" (*sed Agrippina aequi inpatiens, dominandi avida, virilibus curis feminarum vitia exuerat*, 6.25.2). Suetonius instances Augustus's masculine alienation from the body: Augustus's friends excused his adulteries because they were committed not from lust but from calculation (*excusantes sane non libidine, sed ratione commissa, Aug.* 69.1). See Edwards 1993: 47–48.

26. Desire is also typically expressed in metaphors of madness and burning; see Walker 1952: 63, 65 n. 1.

27. The association of flow and noise (*procaci choro*) at a party thrown by a disordered and disordering woman who crosses boundaries resounds in Juvenal's roughly contemporary image of imperial Rome as a place where different peoples and cultures intermingle with negative effect (3.62–65): the arrival of provincials and their customs is denigrated in the complaint that the Syrian Orontes has flowed into the Roman Tiber, bringing with it a cacophony.

28. Tacitus's narrative also seems to contain an apprehension of a feminized *imperium*: the operative fear is the rule of women, empowered to pursue their desires. If the emperor draws power into the imperial *domus*, and if he is there ruled by wives and freedmen, then, in Suetonius's words (*Claud.* 29.1), the *studia* and *libidines* of women and ex-slaves are determinative. For what the male and upper-class Tacitus imagines about women, see *Ann.* 1.4.4–5, 1.33.5, 2.85, 3.33–34, 4.3.3, 4.39.1, 4.40, 6.25.2–3, 6.49, 12.2, 12.64, 13.13.1, 14.4.2 (cf. Kaplan 1979; Rutland 1978; Baldwin 1972; Richlin 1992c; Santoro L'hoir 1992, 1994); about freedmen, see *Ann.* 15.54–55.

29. See n. 5 above.

30. Even Levick, who diminishes Claudius's accomplishments, sees him as a predecessor of Trajan for his participation in the invasion of Britain (1990: 140). On Claudius's pedantry and interference, see Sen. *Apocol.* 7, 12; Tac. *Ann.* 11.13.3–5; Suet. *Claud.* 14–15, 16.5; Dio Cass. 60.4.3–4, 60.6.7, 60.10.3–4, 60.24.1–3, 60.26.1. On Trajan's conquest of Dacia, policies, and image, see Syme 1958; Garnsey 1968; Waters 1974, 1975; Paribeni 1975. On the harbor at Ostia and Claudius and Trajan's concern for the grain supply, see Meiggs 1973: 149–71, and Rickman 1980: 73–79, 85–91, 213–17. Whether or not Claudius understood the long-term implications of his actions, Tacitus's revision of Claudius's speech on admitting the elite of Gallia Comata to the senate (11.24) suggests that Tacitus did (see M. T. Griffin 1982).

31. As Kate Gyllensvard has pointed out to me, the prostitute participates in

the exchange of both women and money. Juvenal literalizes this double system of exchange by graphically representing the sexual transactions of a woman whose image appeared on coins that passed from one hand to the other (Mattingly 1923: Claudius, no. 242, pl. 34.8; and Mattingly and Sydenham 1923: Claudius, no. 59): "Sweetly she received those entering and asked for money" (6.125).

32. Juvenal's text reproduces access. Although his narrational voice expresses disgust and poses as critic, his text makes Messalina's body available to the gaze of any man who can read.

TEN

FEMALE HOMOEROTICISM AND THE

DENIAL OF ROMAN REALITY

IN LATIN LITERATURE

Judith P. Hallett

Rogavit alter tribadas et molles mares
quae ratio procreasset. exposuit senex:
"idem Prometheus, auctor vulgi fictilis,
qui simul offendit ad fortunam frangitur,
naturae partis veste quas celat pudor
cum separatim toto finxisset die
aptare mox ut posset corporibus suis,
ad cenam est invitatus subito a Libero,
ubi inrigatus multo venas nectare
sero domum est reversus titubanti pede.
tum semisomno corde et errore ebrio
implicuit virginale generi masculo
et masculina membra applicuit feminis.
ita nunc libido pravo fruitur gaudio."
(Phaedrus *Fabulae* 4.16)

The other person asked what phenomenon had produced tribadic females and effeminate males. The old man explained: "It was the same Prometheus, molder of ordinary people from clay, who as soon as he caused trouble was reduced to unfortunate circumstances. When, working through the day, he had formed the genital parts that modesty hides—separately, so that he might soon attach them to their proper bodies—he was suddenly invited to dine by Bacchus. There, having soaked his veins in much nectar, he returned home late with staggering step. Then, owing to drowsy wits and drunken error, he wove the maiden's part into the breed of men, and attached masculine members to women. Therefore lust now enjoys perverted pleasure."

This essay was originally published in the *Yale Journal of Criticism* 3.1 (1989): 209–27; the footnotes and bibliography do not, therefore, draw upon the rich array of relevant scholarly writings published since I revised it for publication early in that year. Earlier versions of this paper were presented at the Fifth Berkshire Conference on the History of Women, the University of Colorado at Boulder, the University of Ottawa, Emory University, Yale

ALONG WITH such tales as the fox and the grapes, the stag at the brook, and the grasshopper and the owl, amid moralistic fables culled from Aesop so as to inspire laughter and caution, in a collection of stories he himself acknowledged as purely make-believe, the early Roman imperial poet Phaedrus retails a narrative that provides an *aition*, an explanation, for two contemporary and actual human phenomena. The first is those women to whom he refers by the plural of the noun *tribas*, a Latin word of Greek provenance that the *Oxford Latin Dictionary* defines as a "female sexual pervert, a masculine Lesbian" (and which we, in modern slang, might translate "bull dyke").[1] The second are men whom he calls *molles mares*, a phrase that I have rendered "effeminate males," though the adjectives "passive" and "pathic" could also convey the sexual connotations inherent in *molles* (as could the modern slang word "pansies").[2] Phaedrus assigns a common *aition* to these two sexual phenomena by attributing the origins of both to a drunken slip-up by the mythic Greek Titan Prometheus.

To be sure, the fragmentary poem that precedes this one also apparently attributes to Prometheus the origin of another contemporary and actual human phenomenon, the female tongue; in this earlier fragment Phaedrus provides an equally implausible source (the male organ) and a similarly censorious assessment of its impact (*Fabulae* 4.15):

> formavit recens
> a fictione veretri linguam mulieris.
> adfinitatem traxit inde obscenitas.

Lately he formed the tongue of woman from the molding of the male organ. From this source obscenity has attracted a bond of kinship by marriage.

Nevertheless, the contexts of the two poems, inasmuch as both are surrounded by avowedly fictitious representations of talking animals, do not foster the impression that either features contemporary and actual human phenomena. Indeed, by crediting the origin of *tribades* to a Greek figure from the remote past, Phaedrus further dissociates females who engage in same-sex love from the actual and contemporary human scene. What is more, the implication that tribads actually possess male organs (presumably on their groins as well as in their mouths) serves to distance them even more from any claim to present-day Roman reality.

University, and George Washington University. The Berkshire conference version, "Autonomy as Anomaly: Roman, and Postclassical Greek, Reactions to Female Homoerotic Expression," and much of the material that it included, has been cited by Brooten (1985: 66ff.). All translations are my own. I would like to thank David Halperin, Ralph Hexter, Barry Baldwin, Amy Richlin, and Marilyn Skinner for their comments and suggestions.

The following discussion will begin by surveying several portrayals of what the Romans would have called tribadism in Latin authors from the second century B.C.E. through the second century C.E. The aim of this survey is to establish that Phaedrus was far from alone in representing such conduct as he does: namely, as both a Greek practice, geographically and chronologically distanced from present-day Roman behavior, and as abnormal and unreal, involving the use and possession of male sexual apparatus. In the course of this survey I shall maintain that the sole Latin literary representation of tribadism that neither masculinizes nor Hellenizes nor anachronizes (that is, retrojects into the past) this phenomenon does so for deliberate effect, to break with established tradition and thus make an unconventional point more forcefully. Of course, it is not only tribadism that Phaedrus associates with the Greek world and with times past: passive male homoerotic behavior receives the same treatment. But this Hellenizing and anachronizing of tribadism by Phaedrus and other Latin authors is particularly striking, since such a characterization does not seem justified by evidence from earlier Greek sources. Nor, for that matter, does the Roman literary preoccupation with masculinizing, and problematizing, this phenomenon.

For this reason, I would also like to reflect upon two particularly curious aspects of this masculinizing, Hellenizing, and anachronizing tendency in these similar portrayals of tribadism by several Roman authors, and of the refusal to accept tribadism as both Roman and real that such a tendency implies. I shall do so in the larger context of considering some literary and attitudinal factors that seem to underlie these similarities in representation: first, that this refusal contrasts in significant respects with the only acknowledgment of female homoeroticism as a contemporary and actual phenomenon that has been bequeathed by a classical Greek author, a nonjudgmental if mythic and fictive account of how sexual preference began in Plato's *Symposium*; and second, that this refusal contrasts no less with the gradual acceptance and Romanization of male same-sex love by Latin authors and Roman culture. By comparing Roman reactions to female and male same-sex love, I am assuming that Roman thought, perhaps under the influence of the categoric constructions presented in this same passage of Plato's *Symposium*, regarded each as a distinct phenomenon and the two as relatively comparable and parallel phenomena. I do so on the basis of several Latin texts. Some, since they focus on the phenomenon of female homoeroticism, are to be discussed below, such as Ovid's rendition of the Iphis and Ianthe story, and the speech of Laronia in Juvenal's second satire; others, which focus on male same-sex love, have been accorded special attention in studies of the Roman attitude toward male homoeroticism published during the past decade.[3] I recognize that both classicists and modern historians have lately argued that the conceptualization of homosexual desire as a discrete phenomenon—

that is, the categorization of sexual passion according to the gender of both the subject and object choice—ranks as a recent development in medical thought. Inasmuch as the medical authorities (such as Havelock Ellis) who promulgate this view of homosexual desire write extensively about classical texts and topics, I would regard ancient authors such as those we will survey as a major source of this late-nineteenth- and early-twentieth-century scientific conceptualization.[4] But let us now turn to these Roman literary texts themselves, and to the tribadic tradition they represent.

In her magisterial study of homosexuality in Republican and Augustan Rome, Saara Lilja examines a wide range of allusions to homoeroticism in Plautine comedy, including one that she interprets as an unmistakable reference to female homosexuality at *Truculentus* 262. It occurs in an address by the title character, an Athenian slave, to Astaphium, maid of the courtesan Phronesium. When this maid asks Truculentus to calm his rage, *comprime sis eiram*, he responds with a double pun on *comprime*, which can mean "have forced sexual intercourse with" as well as "control"; then on *eira*, an archaic spelling of *ira*, "anger," which sounds like *era*, "mistress."[5] In response to his punning retort—"Why don't you, who've gotten into the habit, get it off with her instead, you who shamelessly pressure a country fellow into sexual disgrace" (*eam quidem hercule tu, quae solita es, comprime / impudens, quae per ridiculum rustico suades stuprum*)—the maid replies, "I said anger, not mistress"; a change of subject ensues.

Here, then, the possibility of sexual relations between women is raised but briefly, in a dramatic context involving fictional characters, as part of an insult engendered by a comic misunderstanding, albeit one that represents such behavior as customary between a sexually experienced woman and her female slave. Yet in this, our earliest extant reference to female homoeroticism in Latin literature, we see the features characteristic of later representations as well. Plautus's Astaphium and Phronesium are Athenian women; the Greek model for the *Truculentus* was composed and set in the first decade of the third century B.C.E., whereas the *Truculentus* is dated to the second decade of the second.[6] In addition to the geographical and chronological distancing of this phenomenon, the attribution of it to the Greek world and to an earlier point in time, we find female homoeroticism associated with masculine conduct. For the verb *comprimere*, here used to accuse a slave woman of sexual relations with her mistress, as a rule describes sexual assault by males; both women are, moreover, portrayed on the comic stage by male actors and were in all probability perceived by the audiences as males no less than females.[7]

The possibility of sexual relations between women receives more extended treatment two centuries later, by the elder Seneca at *Controversiae*

1.2.23. This treatment also associates such conduct with both the Greek world and masculine erotic activity; so, too, Seneca here dissociates tribadism from contemporary Roman reality. The discussion occurs in the context of his reflections about how to declaim publicly, and with proper refinement, on publicly unmentionable sexual practices. Seneca first compares the belabored and unnecessarily explicit attempt at alluding to heterosexual anal intercourse by a nameless ex-praetor with a succinct, erudite, and witty allusion to the same topic by Mamercus Scaurus.[8] He then comments that Scaurus himself attributed the fault of uttering labored, unnecessarily explicit oratorical remarks on publicly unmentionable practices to Greek declaimers. Quoting Scaurus again in illustration, Seneca relates remarks made by two such individuals, Hybreas and Grandaus, when delivering the same *controversia*: that about a man who caught and killed two tribads, one his own wife, *in flagrante*, and was subsequently forced to speak in his own defense. The remarks that Scaurus recalled and Seneca recalls are in Greek, even though Grandaus is quoted as having begun in Latin, switching languages only for a sexually charged punch line. This fact contrasts these remarks with previous mentions of heterosexual anal intercourse, since such conduct was alluded to, both tastelessly and tastefully, in Latin.

Furthermore, what both Scaurus and Seneca judge the quoteworthy treatments of this tribadic *controversia* joke about the masculinity of the woman taken in adultery with the man's wife. Hybreas speaks of her as an *andra*, "man," to be established as natural or fake. Grandaus compares her to a male adulterer. It merits emphasis as well that Seneca mentions the two tribads as a topic for *controversiae*, situations at some remove from routine Roman events. Topics of other *controversiae* that Seneca treats, for example, include "the father who was dragged from the graves of his three sons by a debauched youth, given a haircut, and forced to change his clothes and attend a wild party."[9]

Inasmuch as we have now discussed the earliest extant appearance in Latin literature of the word *tribas* itself, and as *tribas* is the only noun employed by Roman authors to designate women who engage in same-sex love, we might note that the word and its usage have several things in common with literary representations of tribadism. For one, *tribas* is a purely Greek formation, from *tribein*, "to rub," "to wear down." Unlike other Latin nouns derived from this Greek verb—*flagritriba*, "wearer-out of whips," and *ulmitriba*, "wearer-out of elm rods," *tribas* retains its Greek nominative ending. It is also associated with women who appropriate masculine behavior by seeking physical gratification not merely by rubbing, but by penetrating, as one would with a male organ, the orifices of other females; in such instances—such as the passage by the elder Seneca we have just discussed, and Martial's portrayal in 7.67 of a woman he

accuses of male, penetrating, genital acts—it is thus somewhat of a mis-
nomer.[10] Curiously, too, we shall see that *tribas* is not used by two of the
three authors who depict female homoeroticism as a present-day Roman
phenomenon.

But to return to our literary survey. In deference to diachronicity, I
have deferred discussion of Ovid's writings: even though they predate the
elder Seneca's *Controversiae* and Scaurus's reminiscences, they postdate
the heyday of the declaimer Hybreas, who is described by Plutarch as a
contemporary of Mark Antony.[11] Ovid has left us several representations
of female homoeroticism, all involving Greeks from the past (and largely
the remote, mythic past), all linking such behavior with masculine sexual
activity. The most extensive occurs at *Metamorphoses* 9.666ff., which relates the Cretan tale of the male impostor Iphis and her passion for the
maiden Ianthe. Central to Ovid's rendition of the story is a lengthy
lament he has the thwarted Iphis voice. In the course of her agonizing,
she refers to her homoerotic desire as unprecedented and monstrous
(*prodigiosa*, 727), as a strange kind of desire from which the gods should
have spared her. She proceeds to state that if the gods wanted to destroy
her, they should at least have given her an evil that is natural and customary (*naturale malum saltem et de more dedissent*, 730). When establishing that this evil is neither natural nor customary, Iphis even cites various
zoological examples, concluding from sociobiological analysis that among
all of the animals, no female is smitten with love for a female. Fortunately
for the pious Iphis, on the day she is to wed Ianthe, she is transformed
by the goddess Isis into a male. Ovid personalizes and dramatizes this
transformation by addressing Iphis himself (*nam quae / femina nuper eras,
puer es*, 790–91).

Ovid also appears to comment upon female same-sex love in two
poems about the archaic Greek poet Sappho: the first, a letter in the
Heroides, implicitly associates her with the heroines of the mythic past assigned the other letters in the collection; the second, *Tristia* 2, discusses
her among Ovid's earlier Greek male poetic predecessors. At *Heroides*
15.19, his Sappho states to her male beloved Phaon that she loved many
women "not without reproach" (*non sine crimine*); later in that same poem,
she refers to the women of Lesbos as "you who, having been loved, made
me disgraced" (*Lesbides, infamem quae me fecistis amatae*, 201).[12] Significantly, moreover, in line 86 she extols the young man's physical appeal to
her by terming his age "what a man is able to love" (*quos vir amare potest*).
At *Tristia* 2.365, when contemplating his own punishment for writing
about love, Ovid recalls Sappho among his literary antecedents, who celebrated love unscathed. While his words—*quid Lesbia docuit Sappho, nisi
amare puellas*—may be construed as, "What did Sappho of Lesbos teach
if not girls to love?" they also allow the interpretation, "What did she
teach if not to love girls?"

Like his father the elder Seneca, Seneca the Younger has left a contribution to our surviving array of Latin texts dealing with female homoeroticism at *Epistulae morales* 95.20–21. It differs, however, in several key regards from his father's contribution, from those of Phaedrus, Plautus, and Ovid we have already considered, and from those of Martial and Juvenal we shall look at shortly. For one thing, it occurs in a prose letter to an actual friend about contemporary Roman reality—not in verse about the Greek, or Greek mythic, past; not in an oratorical exercise attributed to Greek rhetoricians. For another, it only alludes to female same-sex love obliquely, with the assertion that certain women of the present day "even rival men in their lusts . . . although born to be passive" (*virorum licentiam aequaverint . . . pati natae*), and in its climactic claim that such women, "having devised so deviant a type of shamelessness, enter men" (*adeo perversum commentae genus impudicitiae viros ineunt*). And Seneca does not represent this form of female eroticism as in any way connected with the Greeks or with times past. Still, Seneca's passage appears to have had a powerful impact on (or at least to have derived from other statements that exerted tremendous influence on) the representation of tribadism in Martial that we shall soon examine. And Seneca's text does place great emphasis on the masculinity of the women he describes; in Seneca's eyes, sexual conduct other than passive yielding to men, behavior that would seem to include same-sex love, is clearly and primarily associated with activity viewed as masculine, and indeed, is said to transform women physically into men.

For Seneca's claim that females in his day appropriate male sexual conduct, even the sort for which an erect penis is *de rigueur*, occurs in a passage during which Seneca twice observes that women now disprove a statement by the esteemed Hippocrates: namely, that their sex never loses hair or suffers from foot pain by becoming bald and gouty. At the start of this passage Seneca accuses women of conquering rather than changing their nature; at its conclusion, he remarks that "women have lost the privileges of their sex as a result of their vices, and because they have shed womanliness, they have been condemned to men's diseases" (*beneficium sexus sui vitiis perdiderunt et, quia feminam exuerant, damnatae sunt morbis virilibus*). Between these two statements, Seneca details the "license of men," which women have equaled through equaling the "unsuitable activities of men" (*virilium incommoda aequarunt*). He enumerates various instances of such behavior, among them emulating men in keeping late hours and drinking, challenging men in wrestling and carousing (*et oleo et mero viros provocant*), and rivaling men in vomiting and other efforts to relieve overindulgent eating (*aeque invitis ingesta visceribus per os reddunt et vinum omne vomitu remetiuntur*).

Three of Martial's epigrams—1.90, 7.67, and 7.70—depict women whom the poet explicitly attacks as tribads. The second and third of these epigrams are about a woman whom he calls not only a *tribas* but "tribad of the very tribads," and whom he calls by the Greek name of Philaenis. He describes her involvement in the Greek athletic activities of wrestling and jumping with weights; he also peppers the longer of these two poems with a series of Greek words (*harpasto*, "handball," 4; *haphe*, "yellow sand," 5; *halteras*, "jumping weights," 6; *palaestra*, "wrestling ring," 7; *colyphia*, meat dishes, 12).[13] What is more, he masculinizes Philaenis in both poems by representing her as capable of physical activities requiring a male organ. At 7.67.1 he introduces Philaenis as a tribad who anally penetrates boys with a penis; he next maintains that she, "rather fierce with the erection of a husband, pounds with her axe" at eleven girls daily (*Pedicat pueros tribas Philaenis / et tentigine saevior mariti / undenas dolat in die puellas*, 1–3). The comic point of this poem is that Philaenis may forego fellatio because she deems it unmanly, but nonetheless has failed to achieve the level of manliness to which she aspires: after all, she performs cunnilingus, which only the demented would judge manly (and the wish that she be granted a *mentem* puns on and implies her lack of a *mentula*, male organ).[14] Still, while Martial ridicules Philaenis for her false impression of what true virility in sexual etiquette entails, he also ridicules her as truly virile in body and behavior by attributing to her such male athletic activities as wrestling and jumping. In 7.70 he similarly mocks Philaenis for her inappropriate virility: there he tells her that "you rightly call a girlfriend the woman whom you penetrate vaginally with a penis" (*recte, quam futuis, vocas amicam*).

To be sure, Martial does not distance Philaenis and her homoerotic conduct from contemporary Rome by portraying her as a figure from, or even by linking her conduct with, an earlier point in time. Yet he does link the addressee of 1.90, one Bassa, with the remote past while Hellenizing and masculinizing her as well. He begins this poem by claiming to this woman that he had earlier and mistakenly interpreted her lack of male and crowd of female intimates as proof of her similarity to the legendary Roman female moral paradigm Lucretia. But the truth, he adds, is a different matter: "You, o evil deed, Bassa, were a *fututor* [male who fucks: a female fucker is a *fututrix*].[15] You dare to join two cunts (*cunni*) together, and your monstrous (*prodigiosa*) lust imitates a male." Consequently, Martial rejects this early Roman model for Bassa, and asseverates that she has devised (*commenta es*, 9) a monstrous phenomenon worthy of that great, mythic Greek, sexually portentous riddle, the Theban enigma.

Still, Martial represents both Philaenis and Bassa as individuals with whom he is personally acquainted, and as alive and functioning in the urban scene of his day. His description of Philaenis in 7.67 shares several similarities with the younger Seneca's passage about the conspicuous masculinization of some women in Seneca's own time, that is, the generation prior to his own. These similarities, again, seem to reflect Martial's familiarity with Seneca's text, or at least with a tradition on which Seneca also draws. For, just as Seneca asserts that such women *et oleo et mero viros provocant*, Martial details Philaenis's being whipped by the oiled coach in the wrestling ring and imbibing seven *meros deunces*. As Seneca speaks of these women's vomiting wine and food with *aequo vomitu remetiuntur*, Martial notes that Philaenis *vomuit*. As Seneca remarks upon their rivaling men in *libido* (*libidine vero ne maribus quidem cedunt*), Martial observes that Philaenis *libidinatur* by refusing *fellatio* as *parum virile*. Seneca's claim that such women *perversum commentae* [*sunt*] *genus* is also recalled by Martial's statement in 1.90.9 that Bassa *commenta es dignum monstrum*. And if Seneca's language and motifs in a prose epistle are being echoed and evoked by Martial in hendecasyllabic and elegiac epigrams, it may well be because Seneca—like Martial and unlike the other authors we have discussed so far—treats female homoeroticism as a present-day phenomenon, and thus provides a more suitable literary model than other such authors on this score.

I say this because Martial would appear to be drawing on Ovid as well, with whom he also shares a view of female homoeroticism as Greek behavior, identified with if not restricted to mythic times. After all, he uses the same unusual word for Bassa—*prodigiosa*—in 1.90 that Ovid has Iphis apply to her passion at *Metamorphoses* 9.727.[16] Similarly, he adopts a tone toward Bassa (with such words as *monstrum* and *facinus*) reminiscent of that in Iphis's speech. Admittedly, Iphis's revulsion at female homoerotic passion must not be confused with the view of Ovid himself. Indeed, Ovid's narrative displays immense sympathy toward Iphis's plight, a sympathy contrasting with Iphis's own self-condemnation and negative view of female homoeroticism. As a matter of fact, the transformation of Iphis from human female to human male stands out conspicuously among the changes undergone by characters in the *Metamorphoses*. Here Ovid does not resolve a painful human dilemma in his typical fashion, by turning this particular human into a vegetable, mineral, or subspecies of animal. Rather, Ovid accords Iphis's story an unusually happy ending—inasmuch as Iphis, unlike many others in the *Metamorphoses*, need not relinquish her living human identity and even improves upon the one the gods have created for her. Nevertheless, Martial's evocation of Iphis's condemnatory attitude toward female homoeroticism, rather than Ovid's more sympathetic viewpoint, is best explained by the fact that Martial, like Iphis, is dealing with female homoeroticism as a present and real phenomenon.

Martial is, moreover, himself evoked by a subsequent literary representation of tribads as a present and real phenomenon, lines 36 through 55 of Juvenal's second satire. Juvenal assigns these lines, a sarcastic and contemptuous attack on male pathics, to a Roman woman named Laronia.

She is portrayed as bristling at one particular male pathic for his hypocritical invocation of earlier Roman marriage and adultery laws, and as initially responding to this hypocrite in kind—with a string of allusions to things Roman and respectable. In lines 38–39 she puns on Cicero's *o tempora, o mores* (*felicia tempora, quae te moribus opponunt*); she then speaks of Rome as at last acquiring decency (*babeat iam Roma pudorem*, 39); she subsequently calls this fraudulent pathic a third Cato (*tertius e caelo cecidit Cato*, 40); finally, she urges that he invoke the *lex Scantinia* instead (43–44). Juvenal next has this Laronia compare the entire female sex favorably to the entire male sex on two grounds. First, she alleges that male pathics—*molles*, the same term as that used by Phaedrus—have no female counterparts save in one major and abominable respect. Unlike such men as Hispo, who physically suffers from reciprocal fellatio with young males, Roman women do not perform oral sex on one another (*non erit ullum / exemplum in nostro tam detestabile sexu. / Tedia non lambit Cluviam nec Flora Catullam: / Hispo subit iuvenes et morbo pallet utroque*, 47–50). Laronia then claims that women do not enter the prestigious Roman male field of law, but limit their masculine endeavors to wrestling and meat-eating, and that in small numbers (*numquid nos agimus causas, civilia iura / novimus aut ullo strepitu fora vestra movemus? / luctantur paucae, comedunt colyphia paucae*, 51–53). Men, she contends by way of contrast, outdo even the celebrated Greek female wool workers in undertaking that feminine occupation (54–56).

Like the younger Seneca, Juvenal does not employ the word *tribas* or even explicitly mention female same-sex love in this discussion of what he regards as sexual deviance. That he is dealing with such female behavior must be inferred: from his emphasis on passive male homoerotic behavior in comparing the two sexes, and from his references to female wrestlers and meat-eaters in a clear evocation of Martial's tribadic poem 7.67. Yet Laronia's remarks by no means disavow female homoerotic activity altogether—merely mutual oral gratification of the sort she judges revolting in males. In this regard, then, Juvenal evidently has Laronia challenge Martial's assertion in 7.67 that a woman like Philaenis would "eat girls' middles" and "think cunnilingus manly." Furthermore, Juvenal's challenge to Martial involves having Laronia respond to Martial not only in kind, but in Martial's own words: by denying that women as a sex—even, apparently, those of homoerotic inclination—act as men do save in two endeavors; by defining those endeavors as precisely those linked by Martial with Philaenis while stressing—through the repetition of *paucae* in 53—that only a few women behave in this way; and by employing Martial's own and unusual term *colyphia* to describe, and implicitly defend, such atypical female behavior.[17] We should note as well that with the exception of *colyphia*, Juvenal differs from Martial in avoiding

Greek words in this defense of all females, even the homoerotically inclined, as superior to all males, and as superior because of disgraceful conduct by some men who engage in same-sex love. Juvenal even stresses how thoroughly Roman Laronia's frame of reference is in the language and context of her remarks, which defend all female, and denounce certain aspects of male, sexuality. Indeed, whatever Greek terms and allusions appear in Laronia's speech occur in descriptions of male behavior.

Similarly, in this passage Juvenal does not ascribe any sexual masculinity to females, even to those who take up manly pursuits. Rather, he pointedly dissociates women from what Laronia deems disgraceful in men. Although he, like Phaedrus, "feminizes" male pathics, through Laronia's remark that they reek of perfume and surpass women at woolworking, his dissociation of all women from pathic males sharply distinguishes this passage from Phaedrus's earlier portrayal of *tribades* and *molles mares* as equivalent: indeed, Juvenal seems to contrast male and female same-sex love generally, as well as to the detriment of the former.

Juvenal's treatment of tribadism, then, only resembles Martial's explicit representation (and the younger Seneca's implicit representation) in its contemporary Roman setting and concern with everyday reality. It additionally differs from all of the earlier Roman depictions of female homoeroticism that we have surveyed save that of the younger Seneca in its failure to Hellenize such conduct. No less anomalous is Juvenal's defense of and tolerance for such behavior, behavior condemned outright by Martial, the younger Seneca, and Phaedrus, portrayed as tragic by Ovid and comic by Plautus. For it represents not only a major break with the other extant Latin literary representations of tribadism but also a complete departure from the way in which Juvenal and Martial usually handle similar subjects. We should recall Anderson's important essay (1970) contrasting Martial's distinctive approach with that of Juvenal, an essay that embarks from two texts comparable to Martial 7.67 and Juvenal 2.47–53 in that the Juvenal passage wittily reworks material from an earlier witty epigram by Martial. Anderson concludes that Martial's professed air of *lascivia*, naughty playfulness of a basically tolerant sort, operates in full agreement with his wit: both seek above all to inspire laughter, laughter shared with the poet in relaxed amorality. By way of contrast, Juvenal customarily blends what wit he evinces with anger, *indignatio*: his wit and anger operate together, in their harsh, often extreme, moralizing about Rome's Hellenized degradation, to demand from the reader a complex response that accords some credence to the moralistic criticism voiced.

Nevertheless, it is not Juvenal but Martial who condemns female homoeroticism in savage if witty tones. It is Martial, too, who intolerantly and unplayfully characterizes Philaenis and Bassa as Greek and extremely degenerate in their behavior. It is Juvenal who, albeit through the ironic characterization of Laronia, defends and displays witty tolerance toward all female sexual activity, tribadism included; such an attitude is absent not only in Martial, but in other earlier Latin literary tribadic representation as well. Despite his penchant for wit, Juvenal notes for laughs only the inappropriate masculine and nonerotic conduct of a few women. Why have Juvenal and Martial reversed their usual literary and attitudinal stances? Why, for that matter, has Juvenal broken so completely with the earlier literary tradition of tribadic representation?

It warrants emphasis, of course, that Juvenal only addresses the topic of tribads obliquely, through implicit contrast with male conduct and intertextual allusion. It merits note as well that Laronia's speech does voice sarcastic, if not *saeva*, *indignatio* at male pathics: the acerbic tone and moralizing position Anderson regards as quintessentially Juvenalian permeate this poem, but with male pathics rather than female homosexuals as their target. I would, therefore, consider Juvenal's anomalous treatment of female homoeroticism as a form of what J. P. Sullivan has labeled "literary opportunism," the inconsistent and unexpected abandonment of a traditional literary stance in the service of a more immediate literary aim.[18] Such literarily opportunistic writing reminds us that Juvenal's indignation can vary with the individual speaker and that the moralism voiced by the speaker is itself relative and rhetorical: a moralism so bent on discrediting the phenomenon under attack as to sanction other discreditable practices—if such a strategy strengthens the attack in question.

Furthermore, I would maintain that Juvenal's literary opportunism here is made possible by, and itself confirms, the strength and influence of a literary tradition that as a rule masculinizes, usually Hellenizes, and more often than not anachronizes, the phenomenon of tribadism. In other words, I would argue that this literary tradition is strong enough, and recognized enough, to permit Juvenal to make an effective point by dispensing with it. In fact, Juvenal pays further homage to, and further establishes the power of, this tradition, this topos, by evoking Martial, who in turn evokes the younger Seneca and Ovid. I would go so far as to contend that this tradition itself conditions its participants and perpetuators to represent tribadism as they do, that over time it has created its own momentum and power.

Yet the three latest contributors to this tradition all break with their predecessors in acknowledging tribadism as a present and actual contemporary phenomenon rather than a literary notion out of earlier Greek culture. Two of these, moreover—the younger Seneca and Martial—nonetheless resemble the Hellenizing and anachronizing Phaedrus by portraying such behavior in a completely *unrealistic* fashion: as involving physical acts not only culturally associated with men but actually necessitating the possession of a male organ. How do we account for this denial of biological reality, of anatomical plausibility? And can this denial of biological reality illuminate the parallel denial of tribadism as a contemporary Roman phenomenon?

The younger Seneca's assertion that women, though "born to be passive," even rival men in their lust would seem to have special relevance here. So would two learned Roman explanations, by the elder Pliny (*HN* 7.36) and by Aulus Gellius, who quotes him (*NA* 9.4.12ff.), of a mythic Greek story: this tale, alluded to by Vergil and related at length by Ovid, resembles the story of Iphis in that its protagonist—the maiden Caenis— was also transformed physically into a male.[19] Both Pliny and Gellius regard such a transformation as altogether plausible; Pliny even retails, and Gellius quotes him as retailing, four actual episodes that render this female-to-male metamorphosis "no fiction." And what about these episodes? The first supposedly took place in an Italian town, but did so on the authority of annalistic records rather than eyewitness accounts, far earlier (in 171 B.C.E.) than the other incidents, and at some distance from Rome. Two of the other changes—by individuals Lucius Mucianus claimed to have seen—are located in the Greek world, at Argos and Smyrna respectively. The fourth—whom Pliny himself inspected—is called a citizen of a Greekly named town, Thysdrus, in North Africa. In other words, these descriptions of what purport to be actual occurrences represent "masculinization" as having taken place either long ago or in a Hellenic far away, and thus resemble our representations of fictive and even real tribadism. The woman who became a man in Argos is, moreover, said to have been wed to a man before her sex change and subsequent marriage to a woman; the individual Pliny actually met—like the legendary Iphis—is said to have become a man on her wedding day. Noteworthy, too, is that both Pliny and Gellius describe these changes in the context of discussing hermaphrodites, women who are also men and vice versa, and their present-day employment as sources of sexual pleasure.

It would appear, then, that these female-to-male sex changes interest these two authorities in part because they illuminate, justify, and render more comprehensible the sexual involvements of women with other ostensible women. Several aspects of Pliny's and Gellius's accounts would suggest as much: the similarities between these Hellenizing and anachronizing representations of biologically masculinized females and our Latin literary descriptions of tribads; the resemblances between one of the scenarios related by Pliny and Gellius and the plot of Ovid's lengthy reflection on same-sex love; and the context in which these four cases are reported—a discussion of the erotic pleasures offered by partners of the same sex. It would appear that Roman authorities were similarly eager to deny the essential femininity of those women who themselves denied what the younger Seneca would have called their "natural" passivity by engaging in male-free sexual acts. As Seneca accuses such women of rivaling the lust of males, so our Roman sources attribute male activities and apparatus to such women. This widely held Roman notion that female homoeroticism could not be expressed without masculine sexual parts and practices is, of course, itself a denial of biological and social reality. After all, the Roman use of *tribas*, a term from a Greek word meaning "to rub," itself acknowledges that women were capable of providing mutual pleasure by friction alone. Such purveyors of the tribadic tradition as Martial themselves acknowledge—through references to the clitoris and to cunnilingus—that female sexual pleasure did not demand penile penetration.[20] The "true stories" of sex changes reported by Pliny and Gellius may not have been true and certainly were not common occurrences. But for Roman males who wrote about tribadism, it was evidently easier to deny the actual and avow the unlikely than to abandon assumptions about how, according to biological nature and Roman culture, women ought to behave.

I am disconcerted by two further aspects, mentioned earlier, of this Roman denial of cultural reality—namely, that tribadism did go on in the Rome and among the Romans of the classical period—and of this Roman denial of biological realism—namely, that tribads can give one another pleasure without male organs, and that women do not possess male organs. The first is that the Roman effort to associate tribadism with masculine, and earlier Greek, conduct finds little support in our surviving classical Greek texts. Only one reference to same-sex love as a contemporary and actual phenomenon survives, in Aristophanes' speech at 189c–193d of Plato's *Symposium*. There the diversity of human sexual attraction is explained by a fantastic tale, that all human beings have descended from primitive bisectees belonging to three original sexes: the androgynous, the all-female, and the all-male wholes. A drive to seek one's missing half, says Aristophanes, initially sparked erotic desire in those bisectees and continues to do so in their descendants. Plato's description of these descendants starts with those from the androgynous wholes: men who love women, including adulterers, and women who love men, including adulteresses. He then identifies women descended from all-female wholes as those who do not pay attention to men, but are attracted to other women, terming the *hetairistriai* of this type. Last, he claims that halves of an all-male whole pursue males and include the best and most manly young men, who enter public life, become lovers of boys, and only marry and sire children under compulsion of custom. While Plato's Aristophanes may not regard the *hetairistriai*—women who love other women—as highly as he does men who love other men, he says nothing negative about this group; by way of contrast, he emphasizes the presence of adulterers among descendants of androgynous wholes. More significantly, he does not liken these women to men.[21]

Second, it warrants emphasis that this Roman literary representation of female same-sex love as alien and earlier Greek behavior can claim a patent parallel in Republican Roman references to male same-sex love as a Greek import. Such references include Polybius 31.25, which lists love affairs between Roman young men and youths among manifestations of "Greek licentiousness," and Cicero *Tusculanae Disputationes* 4.70, in which pederasty is said to have originated in Greek gymnasia, and 5.58, which describes a young man surrounded by lovers "in the fashion of Greece."[22] Two negatively charged words used by Roman authors to describe male pathics—*pathicus* and *cinaedus*—are, like *tribas*, adopted from the Greek as well.[23] But as time went by, Latin authors increasingly portrayed male same-sex love as common in the contemporary Roman elite milieu of their audience, and as familiar to and tolerated by these readers. Most of these authors—Catullus, Tibullus, Ovid—furnish literary and imaginative treatments rather than documentary reportage about actual incidents.[24]

Still, elite Roman culture had so completely absorbed and accepted pederasty by the time of Juvenal that the contemporary Greek author Plutarch, in a Greek narrative, uses a Latin word, *deliciae*, presumably for want of a good Greek equivalent, in describing a homoerotically desirable boy favored by the moralistic Roman emperor Augustus.[25] Martial not only waxes rhapsodic about a host of beloved boys, but even seems to flatter the emperor Domitian by extolling the charms of his particular boy favorite.[26] Some Roman authors, of course—such as Phaedrus and Juvenal—provide negative and feminizing representations of mature men who inappropriately assumed the passive role in homoerotic liaisons. There is, however, a clear distinction drawn by Latin authors between active, penetrating and passive, penetrated participants in male same-sex love. It is accompanied by the recognition that individuals who adopted the active role did not customarily adopt the passive and acquire the opprobrium attached to its improper assumption.[27] Curiously, and by way of contrast, our Roman sources on female same-sex love both attach opprobrium to active, masculine behavior and fail to make clear distinctions between active and passive tribadic partners: indeed, the elder Seneca seems to use the word *tribades* for both. Clearly these Latin literary sources, and the culture they come from, did not sort out, systematize, and rank their thoughts and feelings about the phenomenon of tribadism in the way that they did their reactions to male same-sex love, much less integrate tribadism into their cultural milieu. To them, female homoeroticism was an undifferentiated, unassimilated conglomeration of alien and unnatural Greek behaviors, which did not really take place in their own milieu, or—if it did occur—did so in a completely unrealistic way.

Further investigation into why these Roman sources fail to accept and tolerate female homoeroticism as they did male same-sex love is needed. So is investigation into why so many Roman authors deny tribadism as a cultural and physical reality.[28] We should recognize, though, that such denial was by no means limited to the phenomenon of tribadism. The emperor Augustus succeeded in convincing a great many Romans to deny that he had instituted a monarchy.[29] Such denials seem to involve other activities in which Roman women participated: research on the Latin literary representation of male and female friendship has led me to conclude that, contrary to all kinds of evidence, several major Roman writers denied that men and women were friends.[30] That Roman authors were perfectly capable of deluding themselves and their audiences is significant in itself: this capacity for self-deception also warrants study, and theorizing about, as a general cultural phenomenon. This capacity makes it all the more understandable that we moderns have such difficulty in distinguishing the prescriptive and ideal from the descriptive and actual in our Roman sources. In particular, it compounds the difficulty that feminist scholars such as myself have in recovering Roman women—since practically nothing written by women themselves survives, and since the evidence we have from men blurs the prescriptive and the descriptive. But it reminds us that we must look within as well as beyond our literary evidence to understand both Roman literature and Roman reality better: by surveying representations of a given notion or practice in several literary genres, fictional and nonfictional; and by focusing on anomalous as well as typical representations.

Notes

1. *Oxford Latin Dictionary* s.v. *tribas*. Ker 1968 translates *tribas* in Mart. 7.67.1 as "Lesbian." I have not, however, used the latter term as the English equivalent of *tribas* in this chapter, since—as I hope my discussion will establish—the connotations of Latin *tribas* are both far more limited and far more negative than those of English "Lesbian."

2. For *mollis* in the sense of "effeminate," the diminutive *molliculus* (used to characterize "unmanly" poetry in Catull. 16), and the noun *mollitia* (used for pathic behavior by, e.g., Tac. *Ann.* 15.49), see the *Oxford Latin Dictionary* 1127–28.

3. E.g., Cic. *Cat.* 2.8 and *Tusc.* 4.70ff.; Livy 39.13.10–11; all of which are discussed by Lilja 1983. Other recent studies focusing on Roman representations of male homoeroticism include Boswell 1980 and MacMullen 1982.

4. See, e.g., Halperin (1986) and Chauncey (1982–83: 114ff), who notes (134

n. 56) the use of Greek evidence not only by Ellis, but also by I. H. Coriat, James Kiernan, and Douglas McMurtrie, the last two in discussions of female homosexuality.

5. Lilja 1983: 28, 32. In the latter discussion she notes that Plautus reverses the customary homosexual insult to males—which charges them with passive behavior—by charging the maid with active "masculine" behavior. Lilja additionally observes that both *Epidicus* 400 and *Persa* 227 may be interpreted as allusions to female homoerotic conduct, but neither unambiguously so.

6. For the date of the *Truculentus*, see Cic. *Sen.* 14, which attributes both the *Truculentus* and the *Pseudolus* to Plautus's old age. As the latter is known to have been written in 191 B.C.E., and Plautus is known to have died in the late 180s, a date in the early 180s seems likely. The date of the Greek model is inferred from lines 91–92 and 530–32, which refer to historical events in the early 290s B.C.E.

7. For *comprimere*, see Adams 1982: 182–83.

8. I follow the interpretation of Winterbottom 1974: 86–87; the allusion, labeled "that Ovidian phrase" (*Ovidianum illud*), consists of two words—*inepta loci*—from a pedicatory poem traditionally known as *Priapea 3*.

9. *Controv.* 4.1, *pater a sepulchris a luxurioso raptus*; for the tendency of the themes of declamation, even those in Seneca's collection, "to stray far from reality," see Winterbottom (1974: xii–xiii), who, while conceding that "genuine parallels in Roman law exist for many of the laws on which the themes are based," notes that "the fact remains that declamation *could* have been far nearer to reality than it was."

10. Although Adams (1982) discusses a wide variety of Greek words used to describe sexual activities and apparatuses in Latin, he does not consider the etymology and connotations of *tribas*. For *flagritriba*, see Plaut. *Pseudolus* 137; for *ulmitriba*, Plaut. *Persa* 279. Both are masculine nouns of the Latin first declension for frequent victims of flogging.

11. Plut. *Ant.* 24.5; cf. also Strab. 660 on Hybreas's defense of his city in 36 B.C.E.

12. Scholars have long debated over whether or not *Heroides* 15 is genuinely Ovidian and whether or not it in fact belongs among the *Heroides*. For the debate generally, see, e.g., the bibliography provided by Kenney 1982: 208; for the view that the poem is by Ovid, but does not belong among the *Heroides*, see Baca 1971: 29ff. Additional discussion in Gordon, this volume. It merits note that some texts of this poem—e.g., the second edition (1977) of the Loeb Classical Library volume—would substitute *hic* for *non* in line 19 and thus read this line as stating "whom I loved here to my reproach."

13. In connection with Martial's portrayal of Philaenis here, it perhaps warrants mention that in a paper delivered on February 15, 1989, at the University of Maryland, College Park, entitled "The Meaning of Jewish Hellenism," Tessa Rajak observed that the gymnasium and athletic activities are represented in *2 Maccabees* as institutions not only central to, but also symbolic of, Greek culture.

14. It is possible that the name Philaenis itself is also a (bilingual) pun—on the Greek *phil-*, "love," and the Latin *anus*; although Martial does not use *anus* for the "fundamental opening" elsewhere, it is so employed by, e.g., Phaedrus 4.19.19 (in a poem following shortly after his verses on the genesis of tribads).

15. Indeed, Martial himself uses *fututrix* at 11.22.4 and 11.61.10.

16. For the rare word *prodigiosa*, see the *Oxford Latin Dictionary*, which lists no attestation earlier than the Ovidian passage.

17. For the problematic nature of *colyphia*, which the scholiast on this passage interprets as a word for the male organ, see Adams 1982: 49–50.

18. Sullivan 1968: 267ff. As Zeitlin (1971: 645) has observed, Sullivan primarily employs this phrase for Petronius's capricious moves "from style to style as a display of technical virtuosity and wit"; nevertheless, attitudinal as well as stylistic changes may be included in this form of literary display.

19. For the story of Caenis/Caeneus, see Verg. *Aen.* 6.448 and Ov. *Met.* 12.171ff. On Vergil's use of the legend, see West 1980.

20. For Martial's ridicule of the clitoris, see, e.g., 3.72.6; for his condemnation of cunnilingus, see, e.g., 1.77, 1.84, 3.81, 3.96, 4.43, 7.95, 11.47, 11.61, 12.59, and 12.85. As Chauncey (1982–83: 131ff.) points out, turn-of-the-century medical authorities also assumed that "female inverts" "simply could not be women" and therefore possessed "structural cellular elements of the opposite sex" (e.g., excessive hair growth, unusually large clitorises, and menstrual irregularities).

21. As Brooten (1985: 65–66) notes, Plato later (*Leg.* 636b–c) outlaws, as "contrary to nature," sexual relations between members of the same sex, be they male or female, in his blueprint for an ideal city; this proscription, however, is not only brief and prescriptive, but also at variance with other evidence for the widespread acceptance of pederasty in the Greece of Plato's day. Brooten additionally mentions a Hellenistic epigram, *Anth. Pal.* 5.207, that alludes to the defiance of Aphrodite's laws, and the embrace of "not-beautiful practices," by two Samian women; while this poem may be construed as referring, in a negative fashion, to tribadism, its date and opacity disqualify it as solid evidence for classical Greek disapproval of such conduct.

22. On these passages, see also MacMullen 1992, and Lilja 1983: 123ff.

23. For these terms, see MacMullen 1982: 486; Adams 1982: 190 and 194; Lilja 1983: 22, 26, 56–57.

24. On these portrayals, which include Catull. 15, 16, 21, 23, 24, 40, 48, 81, and 99, and Tib. 1.4.8 and 1.4.9, as well as Ov. *Am.* 1.1.20 and 1.8, 1.34, and 1.68, see, for example, the discussions of Lilja 1983: 51–85, and Richlin 1983: 114–16, 119, 121, and 141–42.

25. Plut. *Ant.* 59.4.

26. Mart. 9.11–13, 13, 36, discussed by Boswell (1980: 67).

27. See the discussions of Lilja 1983: 130 and 135; and Richlin 1983: 220–26.

28. In the original version of this paper, quoted by Brooten (1985: 68), I suggested that "this male preoccupation with physical masculinity and particularly penis possession, as a necessary component of female sexual autonomy and homoeroticism, and this characterization [of such female sexual conduct] as distanced and non-Roman, seems to reflect an effort to describe such female behavior in symbolic language, as an imaginary super-deviation from the limits of prescribed female sexuality explicable to Roman males only in male terms." I argued that "whereas Roman men passed beyond the passive sexual stage during which they could be penetrated by another male when they reached their early twenties,

Roman women were to remain in the passive role throughout their adult lives. The easiest way to understand women's rejection of the passive sexual role was to imagine that they, like the men, had passed on to the next stage," which involved "penetrating behavior."

29. See, for example, Yavetz 1984, and Millar 1984.

30. "Male-Female Friendship Among the Classical Roman Elite: The Strengths and Limitations of Literary and Philological Approaches," Meeting of the Friends of Ancient History, annual meeting of the American Philological Association, Baltimore, Maryland, January 7, 1989.

ELEVEN

THE LOVER'S VOICE IN *HEROIDES* 15:

OR, WHY IS SAPPHO A MAN?

Pamela Gordon

TO THE CLASSICAL GREEKS, Sappho was "the tenth Muse," a title that recognized not only the mythic proportions of her lyric genius, but also her unique status as a highly revered woman poet.[1] Imperial Rome, however, seems to have had less confidence in Sappho's womanliness.[2] This essay examines one text in which Roman uncertainty about Sappho's gender verges on a travesty of her erotic desire.

My text is *Heroides* 15 (also called the *Epistula Sapphus*), an elegiac poem that appears in our printed editions as the last installment of Ovid's unanswered letters from abandoned heroines. This fictional work presents the legendary Sappho writing to her lost lover Phaon. Ovid's Phaon is a young man who has left the Greek poet for the girls of Sicily; his Sappho is an unattractive older woman who has lost her Muse along with her lover (lines 13–14 and 195–98). Like Penelope, Dido, and the dozen other mythological authoresses of the *Heroides*, Sappho claims she cannot endure life without her man. In the course of her letter she reveals her intention to try the cure for unrequited love: a leap from the cliffs of Leucas (157–92).

Sappho's letter is absent from the earliest manuscripts of the *Heroides*, and seems to have joined (or, as I think, rejoined) the corpus only in the twelfth or thirteenth century. Several Renaissance manuscripts assert, however, that the Sapphic epistle is doubly authentic: they present it as

My title pays tribute to Marilyn Skinner's "Woman and Language in Archaic Greece, or, Why Is Sappho a Woman?" in Rabinowitz and Richlin 1993. Skinner's title is a rejoinder to David Halperin's essay "Why Is Diotima a Woman?" (in Halperin 1990a: 113–51).

I presented earlier versions of this chapter at meetings of the Classical Association of the Middle West and South (Hamilton, Ontario, 1991) and the American Philological Association (Washington, D.C., 1993), and at Texas Tech University (April 1993) for the symposium, "Foucault's History of Sexuality: Revisions and Responses." Acknowledgment of my work was inadvertently omitted from early printings of Margaret Williamson, *Sappho's Immortal Daughters* (Cambridge, Mass., and London: Harvard University Press, 1995), 177. For their encouragement, I am grateful to the audiences at those meetings, and to Betty Banks, Amy Richlin, Harold Washington, and Kathleen Whalen. This investigation was supported by the University of Kansas Graduate Research Fund.

Ovid's own translation into Latin of a genuine Greek text by the Lesbian poet.[3] Although today's readers do not take that claim literally, scholarship has focused upon the questions it suggests: Is the poem by Ovid? Does it belong with the rest of the *Heroides*? Does the poem translate or allude to genuine Sapphic lyrics that are now lost?[4] This essay shifts the focus to another sort of authenticity: Does this Sappho write "like a woman"? Is the configuration of desire in this poem evocative of Sappho's own lyrics? Or can the poem's slant on Sappho's erotic persona be described as Roman rather than Hellenic?

Several recent studies have drawn attention to opposing aspects of Sappho's gender as it is constructed in *Heroides* 15. Kauffman argues (1986: 55–61 and passim) that the letter rejects stereotypically masculine conceptions of sexuality, and presents instead alternative, nonaggressive, feminine models for erotic desire. According to Kauffman, Ovid found his source for the language of female desire in Sappho's authentic lyrics (61). In contrast, Lipking suggests that Ovid simply feminizes Sappho (Lipking 1988: 67–70). That is, rather than recalling Sappho's true voice, Ovid forces the eccentric poetess to fit the mold of the archetypal forsaken woman. Thus, Ovid's Sappho plays the role played by all other women in the *Heroides* (and in the literatures of many cultures), for "to be a heroine, for Ovid and his legion of followers, means being abandoned" (ibid.: xv). DeJean (1989: 64–67 and passim), like Kauffman, suggests that Ovid joins his voice with Sappho's in order to subvert traditional male paradigms. For DeJean, the resulting persona upsets the male poetic order, but is not entirely female: behind Sappho lurks Ovid the male ventriloquist.

These three studies (Kauffman 1986, Lipking 1988, and DeJean 1989) deal with Ovid and his influence upon later (mostly nonclassical) literatures. The work of Cantarella (1988) and Hallett (1989a, reprinted in this volume) on the portrayal of female homoeroticism in a wider spectrum of Latin authors introduces another consideration: Ovid's treatment of Sappho fits a pattern that emerges when we view the treatment of female homoeroticism in Roman literature in general. Almost all *tribades*[5] (women who desire other women) who appear in ancient Latin texts are explicitly masculinized, sometimes so radically that their very bodies become male. In this chapter I, like Hallett, suggest that Ovid's Sappho is no exception. Focusing upon the construction of Sappho's erotic desire in *Heroides* 15, I suggest that the Ovidian Sappho writes so much "like a man" that the poem would work well as a parody of what French psychoanalytic critic Luce Irigaray has called "hom/m/osexuality" (a play on *l'homme*), or what Esther Newton has dubbed the "Mythic Mannish Lesbian."

The word "lesbian" denotes, of course, a twentieth-century category (or rather, many twentieth-century categories), and I wish to call atten-

tion to some striking similarities between Ovid's fictional Sappho and Esther Newton's formulation without claiming that the Mythic Mannish
Lesbian is necessarily a transhistorical or cross-cultural phenomenon.[6] In
fact, one point I wish to stress is that the mannish Sappho seems to be a
Roman construction with few roots in the early Greek tradition. Since I
do not assume that Ovidian personas are made up of universal "masculine" and "feminine" components, and since I wish to concentrate on
constructions of desire in Rome, I measure Ovid's Sappho by the rules for
gendered writing provided by the other *Heroides*.[7] That is, I attempt to
compare Ovid's Sappho not to my own conception of Woman, but to
other male and female Ovidian voices. Although full discussion of the
gendered writing of "the real Sappho" lies outside the realm of this chapter, I shall begin with a look at the way Sappho brings Phaon into her
own lyrics.

Why Phaon (and Not Anactoria)?

At first glance it may appear that the main strategy of *Heroides* 15 is, as
Lipking suggests, to transform Sappho into an ordinary forsaken woman:
like the fourteen preceding heroines, she is just another woman who has
lost her particular man. Some readers may take this as a "heterosexualiz-
ing" of Sappho; others may take it as confirmation that there was no notion of fixed sexual identity in classical antiquity. In my reading, however,
the elements of this Sappho's gender are more contradictory than either
of these first impressions allows.

Unlike the warriors, gods, princes, and kings lamented by Ovid's other
heroines, Phaon is hardly a hero in his own right. An elusive mythological figure who appears, like Ganymede, in Attic red figure paintings with
attractive long hair,[8] Phaon is remembered as the boatman who ferried
Aphrodite (disguised as an old woman) across the sea for no fare, a deed
for which he was rewarded with youth and beauty. A dim picture of this
Phaon is provided by an extant fragment of Sappho's poetry, and Sappho's
nonextant lyrics may well have been Ovid's source of inspiration for the
descriptions of Phaon's loveliness. *Heroides* 15 is rich in Sapphic allusions,
and Roman readers certainly had access to Sapphic lyrics that are lost to
us now (Jacobson 1974). As Nagy (1973) and Stehle (1990) have demonstrated, our evidence suggests that some of Sappho's lyrics treated the
theme of Aphrodite's love for Phaon, as well as the passions of other goddesses for other beautiful young mortals.

We need not assume, however, that Sappho's allusions to lovely young
men replicated the paradigms for erotic desire found in the lyrics of her
male predecessors and contemporaries. Several recent interpretations of

Sappho have claimed (appropriately, in my view) that her lyrics about women stress reciprocity and mutuality, rather than the lover's desire for possession,[9] and a recent essay by Stehle (1990) suggests that Sappho approaches love between women and men in an equally unconventional spirit. Rejecting the narrow confines of the traditional roles of both the dominant lover and his passive object of desire, Sappho dissolves the customary hierarchy and uses the mythic pattern of the goddesses' liaisons with young mortals to create, as Stehle puts it, "an open space for imagining unscripted sexual relations" (ibid: 108). Thus Sappho portrays what the dominant culture suppresses: "Images of the desiring woman, the sexual mother with her son, the submissive but responsive man" (106). In my reading of *Heroides* 15, I imagine Ovid recalling these Sapphic texts, in which he, too, reads the unconventional erotic images that Stehle's reading brings out. Ovid sides, however, not with Sappho but with the dominant culture.[10] As I shall show below, the Ovidian Sappho usurps one of the very roles—that of the dominant *erastēs*—that the lyric Sappho declines.

Although Phaon seems to have appeared in Sappho's lyrics as the legendary favorite of Aphrodite, later generations remembered him as one of Sappho's real-life consorts. In the late fourth century B.C.E., Menander cast Phaon as Sappho's runaway lover in a (nonextant) comedy. Lacking other evidence, we may view Menander (perhaps along with other comic poets) as the main source for the outlines of the Sappho/Phaon liaison as it is presented in *Heroides* 15 (cf. Nagy 1973; Stehle 1990; Knox 1995). Thus the tradition of Sappho's love for Phaon, a tradition that implies that neither Atthis nor Anactoria (nor any of the "hundred other girls," 19) could break Sappho's heart, predates imperial Rome and is at least as old as New Comedy. What seems to be new in *Heroides* 15, however, is the idea that Sappho's love for Phaon represents a shift tantamount to conversion. Instead of ignoring Sappho's reputation as a *gunaikerastria* (a lover, or *erastēs*, of women),[11] the Ovidian poem plays up Sappho's conquest of girls as the most noteworthy aspect of her past. This leads to an interesting juxtaposition. If *Heroides* 15 is the work of the young Ovid, not only is it our oldest unobscured commentary on Sappho's homoeroticism (as the 1924 Pauly-Wissowa article on "Lesbische Liebe" claims);[12] it is also the earliest source in which she renounces her love for girls (15–20):

> nec me Pyrrhiades Methymniadesve puellae,
> > nec me Lesbiadum cetera turba iuvant;
> vilis Anactorie, vilis mihi candida Cydro,
> > non oculis grata est Atthis, ut ante, meis,
> atque aliae centum quas non sine crimine amavi:
> > improbe, multarum quod fuit, unus habes.

> The girls of Pyrrha, the girls of Methymna?
> No, thank you.
> None of that Lesbian crowd for me.
> Anactoria? Cheap.
> Ditto pale Cydro.
> And Atthis, my ex?
> I want her out of my sight,
> along with the hundred others I loved
> despite public censure.
> You (one worthless male) now possess
> what once belonged to a bevy of girls.[13]

Whether we accept the majority reading for line 19, *non sine crimine* ("not without censure"; or possibly, "not without fault") or the variant *hic sine crimine* ("here without censure"; "here without fault")—whether Sappho is alluding to being censured for loving girls, or whether she is asserting that in Lesbos loving girls is not disgraceful—the point is: she loved girls. As Palmer writes in his commentary on this line, "Little is gained by reading *hic* for *non*" (1898: 427). At any rate, "Sappho" later reveals that her reputation was indeed damaged by her love affairs (*Lesbides, infamem quae me fecistis amatae*, "Lesbians loved to my disgrace," 201). Thus in the Ovidian version of Sappho's biography, the mature Sappho has become convinced that one man is preferable to the community of women celebrated in Sappho's lyrics, and that community has been degraded to a horde of discarded girlfriends. As DeJean writes, Ovid makes Sappho repudiate desire for women as a "youthful transgression." When Ovid is finished with her, "deviant female sexuality has been tamed, and the female bond often presented as the inspiration for Sapphic poetic creation has been erased" (DeJean 1989: 68).

Sappho has been transported far from her original archaic Greek context, which not only valorized homoerotic passion in general (see Cantarella 1992: 81) but also nourished a tradition of women's writing (Skinner 1993). The notion that Sappho's love for women is shameful may be traceable to postclassical Greek origins,[14] but the idea becomes full-fledged in first-century B.C.E. Rome, where female homoeroticism is, as Cantarella puts it, almost univocally considered the "worst form of female depravity" (1992: 166; for the monstrous traits assigned to *tribades* in Rome, see Hallett 1989a). The Roman slant on Sappho's erotic history is also discernible in the triumphalist notion of conversion implied in her repudiation of female lovers. For contrast, consider a dictum of Foucault, which serves as a valid generalization on the classical Greek material: "The Greeks did not see love for one's own sex and love for the other sex as opposites, as two exclusive choices, two radically different types of behavior" (1985: 187). In classical Greek texts, a person may have free choice between male and female lovers, "but for them this option was not referred to a dual, ambivalent, and 'bisexual' structure of desire" (187). The Ovidian Sappho, however, seems to view her life with Phaon and her life with the girls of Lesbos as two separate modes of existence. As in the other Roman texts cited by Hallett (1989a) and Richlin (1993b), homoerotic behavior is construed as something unnatural or peculiar at best.

Once this unnatural and "radically different" realm has been established, one can imagine the notion of escape. Thus a repudiation of female homoeroticism is implied in our ersatz Sappho's expression of eagerness to leave Lesbos—*quid mihi cum Lesbo?* ("What's Lesbos to me?" Ov. *Her.* 15.52)—and her repeated naming of her homeland toward the end of the poem (199–202):

> Lesbides aequoreae, nupturaque nuptaque proles,
>   Lesbides, Aeolia nomina dicta lyra,
> Lesbides, infamem quae me fecistis amatae,
>   desinite ad citharas turba venire mea!

> Lesbian islanders,
>   married, engaged,
> Lesbians catalogued on my Aeolian lyre,
> Lesbians loved to my disgrace:
>   Crowd around to hear my zither no more.

In archaic and classical Greek texts, the island of Lesbos is associated with good wine, beautiful women, and certain sexual acts, but not necessarily with female homoeroticism: verbs formed from the Greek root *lesb-*, for example, refer to oral sex, often in the context of women servicing men.[15] As long as Greek culture did not recognize sharp divisions between people based on the gender of their sexual partners, homoeroticism—male or female—was unlikely to be associated exclusively with any particular region. In imperial Rome, as in earlier Greece, the usual vocabulary of female homoeroticism alludes neither to Lesbos nor to Sappho: the use of adjectives and verbs with the root *lesb-* to connote tribadism can be traced in Greek only as far back as the tenth century c.e., and in Latin only back to the fifteenth century.[16] In my view, however, the general association of the island of Lesbos with female homoeroticism is another matter. Though the connection is not obvious in archaic or classical Greek texts (unless we take this to be the sense of Anacreon 358),[17] Lesbos is explicitly called the home of female homoeroticism in Lucian's *Dialogi meretricii* (5), a Greek text from the Roman empire (second century c.e.). It is clear that Lucian has the central *tribas* in his dialogue hail from Lesbos precisely because Lesbos was indeed associated with female homoeroticism, at least in some contexts, in some circles. The Ovidian Sappho, I assert, belongs to this same tradition.

A character named Clonarium makes explicit the connection between Lesbos and woman-to-woman sex at the beginning of Lucian's dialogue. Clonarium's friend Leaena has just confessed that she has a new girlfriend named Megilla who is "terribly mannish" (*deinōs andrikē*), and Clonarium responds (289):

> I don't get what you mean, unless she's some sort of *hetairistria* (a woman who consorts with women).[18] They say there are women like that in Lesbos, with masculine faces, who don't want to have sex with men, but only with women, as though they themselves were men.

Leaena concedes that Clonarium has grasped the situation, and proceeds to answer more questions about her experience with her mannish lover. When Clonarium asks how sex between two women could possibly work, Leaena's answer fits in well with the portrayal of phallic tribads in the sources that Hallett (1989a) surveys: as her name implies, Megilla/us ("Big Girl"/"Big Boy") has a substitute phallus.[19]

Readers who are not convinced that Lucian's invention of a lesbian from Lesbos has anything to do with a broader connection between Lesbos and female homoeroticism have pointed to the fact that Megilla herself has a long-term female lover named Demonassa who is "similarly skilled" (*homotekhnos*, 290), and Demonassa comes from Corinth, not Lesbos. This is an issue to which I shall return below; for now I turn to Ovid's portrayal of the masculine side of his fallen Lesbian.

The Mannish Muse

Ovid's stance is best illumined by the contrast he draws between Sappho and his other *Heroides*. The laments of each of Ovid's other heroines stress not passion for the absent lover, but the predicament in which he has left her. The women claim to have had limited experience of sex before the arrival (and sudden departure) of their hero; most of them describe themselves as (formerly) chaste virgins or faithful matrons. Emblematic of their sexual passivity is their habit of dwelling on their own physical appearance while ignoring the man's. They rarely mention the man's attractiveness, but frequently allude to their own physical humiliation and repeatedly draw the reader's gaze to their inert, trembling, or grief-stricken bodies (cf. *Her.* 3.14–15, 3.59–60, 11.3–5, 14.3). As Fredrick has argued (1991), it is as though the heroines were inviting the reader to join the mythological addressee in a voyeuristic act; in the *Heroides* as elsewhere in Ovid, a woman's fear is beautiful (Richlin 1992e: 162). Sappho reverses the pattern: while celebrating Phaon's godlike appearance (*Her.* 15.21–23, 93–95, 123–24), she rejects his gaze and insists that she has skills (artistic and sexual) that compensate for her own ugliness (31–34):

> si mihi difficilis formam natura negavit,
> ingenio formae fama repende meo.
> sim brevis, at nomen, quod terras inpleat omnes,
> est mihi; mensuram nominis ipsa fero.

> If spiteful nature has denied beauty to me,
> balance my genius
> against my looks.
> I may be short, but my reputation extends
> to every land:
> this is my stature.

In *Heroides* 15 it is the male who plays the passive role; the other letters allude to the men's heroic exploits or bold actions, and most of them quote at least a phrase or two of the men's erotic or affectionate remarks. Unlike the other addressees—Odysseus, Jason, Hercules, *et alii*—Phaon provides no heroic exploits for his lover to praise or criticize. Phaon seems not to do or say anything at all; Sappho has nothing to quote except something he failed to say.[20] As Verducci says: "[Phaon] has no history, no clearly delineated or (as in other poems) misunderstood character, no motives, no ambitions. Phaon is merely, and consummately, beautiful" (1985: 154).

Whereas the other heroines never describe sexual contact directly, Sappho boasts of her own sexual expertise and indulges in the most graphic descriptions of sex in the *Heroides*. Her memories of Phaon lead her into vaunting descriptions of love play (44–50), "deep tongue kisses" (129–30), and fantasies during which she "can't stay dry" (134). *Heroides* 15 presents, moreover, a Sappho who has done to Anactoria, Atthis, Cydro, and "one hundred other girls" (*atque aliae centum*, 19) precisely what the mythical male heroes have done to the preceding fourteen heroines. Like Aeneas, Jason, and Hercules, Sappho has discarded her old girlfriends for someone new. Ovid's other heroines lament this sort of behavior as something peculiarly masculine. Penelope, for example, derides herself for fearing for Odysseus's life, while he, as is usual for men (*quae vestra libido est*, 1.75), is probably in some stranger's arms. Dido recognizes her fate as a repetition of what happened to Aeneas's first wife, and she knows he has left her not just for another country, but for "yet another Dido" (*et altera Dido*, 7.17). Medea and Hypsipyle need not dwell on male infidelity (although they do); they have been abandoned by the same hero. It is feminine credulity that makes women the ideal victims—as Phyllis writes, she was fooled by Demophoon's words simply because she was a woman in love (2.65).

Phaedra, the mature stepmother in love with her young stepson, and a mythical exemplum of lechery and illicit passion, provides the closest parallel among the heroines for Sappho's lust. Whereas our other heroines barely mention their lover's looks, in *Heroides* 4 Phaedra dwells upon Hippolytus's pleasing appearance almost as much as Sappho does upon Phaon's. The link between Sappho and Phaedra is also brought out by Sappho's description of herself running "like a woman possessed" (15.139) through the woods and caves, an image that recalls Phaedra's longing (in both Ovid and Euripides) for the wild realm of the hunter Hippolytus (cf. 4.37–50 and 15.135–45). Phaedra, however, is in love for the first time (*venit amor gravius, quo serius*, "The later love comes, the deeper it strikes," 4.19), and she shrinks from describing sexual acts or fantasies. Phaedra sees her passion for Hippolytus as an egregious female vice that runs in the family—something comparable to the passion for bulls experienced by her mother Pasiphae and her ancestor Europa (4.53–66).

True parallels to Sappho's explicit language and lecherous gaze are to be found not in the women's letters of the *Heroides*, but in the male voices of Ovid's other works and the male letter-writers in the three pairs of male/female exchange that follow the letter from Sappho in some manuscripts and in most modern editions of the *Heroides*. Also paralleled in the stories of male lust in other Ovidian works (where only the beautiful are raped) is Sappho's suggestion that Phaon is so lovely that some promiscuous goddess—Aurora, Phoebe, or perhaps even Venus—might swoop down and steal him (15.87–91). Mortal Ovidian women seldom pursue men, and forceful abduction is attempted only by the occasional witch, maenad, or goddess. For men in Ovid, however, rape is a compliment paid to an attractive woman (Richlin 1992e). The only Ovidian female to trespass into this male preserve is the naiad Salmacis, who rapes the beautiful boy Hermaphroditus. As Nugent (1990) and Richlin (1992e) point out, however, Ovid treats Salmacis's behavior as a threatening usurpation of male privilege for which punishment is swiftly exacted. Male rapists in Ovid usually enjoy their prey and move on to a new victim, but Salmacis the female ceases to exist. Her body is joined to the boy's, and the female mind and voice disappear.

Like Martial's Philaenis (see Hallett 1989a: 215), Ovid's Sappho may even have a masculine body. When she writes to Phaon of her dreams about him, she breaks off her description with *ulteriora pudet narrare, sed omnia fiunt, / et iuvat, et siccae non licet esse mihi* ("I'm embarrassed to say more, but it all happens, and it feels so good, and I can't stay dry," 15.133–34). Various copyists and editors have been unsure what to make of *sicca* ("dry"), but I follow Palmer (1898), who writes in his apparatus criticus *spurca sed certa lectio*, "Dirty but the right reading." Elsewhere *sicca* clearly describes a woman who is unresponsive or unaroused (cf. Mart. 11.16.8, 81.2), and the sexual sense is at least implicit in Ovid's *odi quae praebet quia sit praebere necesse, / siccaque de lana cogitat ipsa sua*, "I hate a woman who submits out of duty, while frigidly (*sicca*) thinking about her knitting" (*Ars Am.* 2.685–86).[21] Thus, according to the language of erotic elegy, Sappho describes herself in vocabulary technically appropriate for a woman. The context crosses over into male territory, however: because she "can't stay dry" precisely at the climax of her fantasy (just before she wakes up), it is clear, as Verducci says, that Sappho has had a "wet dream."[22] Thus it seems that in Rome Sappho, like other *tribades*, has acquired a phallus.

All this masculinity is of course incompatible (in Ovid's scenario) with the surest emblem of womanhood: mother love. Sappho's daughter Kleis holds a firm place in the biographical tradition; Sappho mentions her three times in the extant fragments alone.[23] One reference is especially lovely "despite obscurity and corruption" (Page 1955: 131).

> I have a beautiful child, her form
> like golden flowers, beloved Kleis,
> whom I would not trade for all of Lydia
> or lovely. . . . [24]

To Ovid's Sappho, however, Kleis is a burden: *et tamquam desint, quae me sine fine fatigent, / accumulat curas filia parva meas*, ("And as if all this weren't enough to wear me out, I have a little daughter to top off my worries," 15.69–70). One suspects that Ovid's Sappho would gladly give up Kleis to get Phaon back. She grieves for Phaon as though she has lost a son (115–16); when her brother Charaxas witnesses her lamentations, he (indulging in an intertexual rejoinder)[25] reproaches her for forgetting her real maternal obligations: *quid dolet haec? certe filia vivit!* ("What's wrong with her? Surely her daughter still lives!" 120).

The Mythic Mannish Lesbian

From her lecherous gaze and her faithless treatment of women, to her apparent *membrum virile*, the Ovidian Sappho fits Ovid's mold for men. Thus Ovid's portrayal of Sappho anticipates a familiar modern description of lesbianism, according to which the lesbian has no sexuality of her own, but simply acts out a charade of male sexuality. The early work of

Luce Irigaray exposes this masculinizing of the lesbian in twentieth-century thought as one aspect of Freud's inability to describe women as anything but deficient men. According to Freudian theory, "The instincts that lead the homosexual woman to choose an object for her satisfaction are, necessarily, 'male' instincts" (Irigaray 1985a: 99). Thus, punning on *l'homme*, Irigaray asserts that because Freudian analysis maps no separate realm for the lesbian, it allows only for female hom/m/osexuality, not female homosexuality.

Wittig (1980: 108) puts it another way: "When thought by the straight mind, homosexuality is nothing but heterosexuality." As in the ideology Wittig describes, so in *Heroides* 15: the Lesbian apes the Man. Wittig's literary works suggest a world of other options, and when Wittig concludes her essay "The Straight Mind" with the statement, "Lesbians are not women" (ibid.: 110), she writes of "Man" and "Woman" as political (rather than biological) concepts. Thus she envisions the lesbian as a woman freed from obligatory social relationships to Man. Wittig's lesbian has a woman's body, but conforms to the role of neither Woman nor Man (cf. Wittig 1981).

Ovid's scheme is not so flexible. His lesbian resembles instead Stephen Gordon, the trousered hero(ine) of Radclyffe Hall's *The Well of Loneliness*. As Newton (1984) points out, Hall could have developed her character along the lines of the feminine lesbians in (for example) the novels of Colette, but Hall and her contemporaries had other beliefs: "The 'womanly' lesbian contradicted the convictions that sexual desire must be male and that a feminine woman's object of desire must be a man." Thus Mary, the object of Stephen Gordon's affections, is a shadowy and inconsistent figure. Her lesbian liaison makes her less than a woman, but her passivity, youth, and prettiness prevent her from being a "lesbian." Hallett (1989a) points to a similar phenomenon in the depiction of female homoeroticism in Roman literature: while the model for female homoerotic behavior seems to require a passive recipient, Roman writers could not imagine her.

Why Is Phaon a Boy?

Sappho's repeated references to Phaon's good looks, her allusions to her long history of sexual exploits, her bold descriptions of lovemaking, and her acceptance of the notion that to rape is to flatter are among the subtler aspects of Sappho's machismo. Ovid's Sappho is so masculine that when she chooses a man, she chooses a boy. Or rather, as she puts it, she selects a pretty youth (of all the heroes in the *Heroides*, only Phaon is *formosus*) who is at that delectable stage of pubescence: *o nec adhuc iuvenis, nec iam puer, utilis aetas,* / *o decus atque aevi gloria magna tui,* "Not yet a man but no longer a boy, a useful age, / glory of your generation, paradigm of your time" (93–94). Here the Roman vantage point for this view of Sappho emerges more fully. In pursuing a pretty boy, Sappho conforms to the Greek stylistics of male sexual behavior as formulated by Dover (1978) and Foucault (1985): men pursue not other men, but boys (or women, or slaves).[26] A man's partner, whether male or female, submits. Thus Sappho entreats Phaon to resume his passive role: *huc ades inque sinus, formose, relabere nostros!* / *non ut ames oro, verum ut amere sinas,* "Glide back to my arms, O beautiful, / not to love but to let yourself be loved" (95–96).

As though forgetting her own gender, Sappho explicitly equates her passion with a masculine drive: *quid mirum, si me primae lanuginis aetas* / *abstulit, atque anni quos vir amare potest?* "But it's no wonder his peach fuzz blew me away: / a guy can really fall for a boy that age" (85–86). Sappho suspects one "real man" in particular of having a weakness for Phaon's type: Mars (god of war) would go for him if he ever saw him (92). Or he would have, if he had seen him soon enough. Apparently Sappho has failed to notice that Phaon the *erōmenos* has begun to grow up the way Greek boys must.[27] Hence his shift from Sappho (the older, more experienced *erastēs*) to pretty girls. Here Phaedra provides a telling contrast to Sappho's erotic desire: even when Phaedra calls herself (wishfully) a girl, she refers to Hippolytus as an adult (*puella* and *vir,* 4.2). She admires not prettiness, but masculinity: his strength, his disheveled hair, the dust on his face (4.77–83). Phaedra is explicit about her preference: *sint procul a nobis iuvenes ut femina compti!* / *fine coli modico forma virilis amat,* "Keep youths primped like women out of my sight! / Male beauty should be nurtured in moderation" (4.75–76).

The implied requirement—that a couple can have only one active, virile partner, and that the other must be passive (and preferably young and pretty)—is also met by Lucian's female pairs in *Dialogi meretricii* (5). Returning to that text, we find that our "informant" Leaena has reluctantly consented to let Megilla make love to her. Significantly, Leaena herself seems to be neither mannish nor particularly interested in women. The main reason she gives for her compliance is that Megilla begs her, and follows up with some ladylike gifts: a necklace and a fine linen dress (292). As for Demonassa, Megilla's regular partner: although the dialogue at first suggests that Demonassa is just like Megilla (having "the same accomplishments," 290), once the three are in bed it turns out that Demonassa is Megilla's "wife" (*gunē,* 291). Demonassa has none of the masculine attributes of Megilla, who gives herself the masculine name "Megillus," has a shaved head, and has "the mind, the desire, and everything else of a man" (291–92). Demonassa's status as the "wife" explains why Demonassa is not from Lesbos. It is not a case of tribadism being attributed to both Lesbos and Corinth,[28] a coupling that would indeed undermine any claim that imperial Rome regarded Lesbos as the home of female homoeroticism. Rather, as the passive, more feminine partner in a female couple, Demonassa is not herself completely a *tribas*, but an inhabitant of that unmapped territory of the tribad's lover (see Hallett 1989a: 223, on this phenomenon in the Latin sources).

As Hallett (1989a) demonstrates, there are few Latin texts that do not attempt to masculinize, anachronize, and Hellenize women who engage in homoerotic activity. Thus, the attribution of boy-love to the Greek Sappho fits the pattern (in some Roman circles) of disowning homoeroticism by naming it "Greek" (MacMullen 1982). The conception of homoerotic desire in *Heroides* 15 is Hellenic only on the surface, however. As Foucault put it (1985: 192), "The Greeks could not imagine that a man might need a different nature—an 'other' nature—in order to love a man."[29] It seems that the Roman imagination suspected that a different nature was in fact required, especially if a woman were to love a woman (a possibility the Greek sources cited by Foucault usually avoid). In the Roman conception, this different nature runs so deep that the Roman tribad cannot convert or go straight simply by choosing a partner of the opposite sex. In fact, the tribad's object choice seems to be viewed as a symptom of her masculine makeup, rather than the essential core of her tribadism. Martial's Philaenis does not become normal when she turns from girls and has sex with a boy (7.67.1). Instead, contrary to the Foucauldian notion that the ancients had no concept of fixed sexual types,[30] Philaenis, like Sappho, is out of bounds wherever she goes.

Snyder mentions the difficulties some modern readers have in reconciling Sappho's wedding songs with the love poetry Sappho addressed to other women and judiciously concludes:

> In the absence of any independent concrete evidence about the social structures of sixth-century Lesbos, all that can be said with certainty is that for whatever reasons, Sappho herself evidently did not regard marriage and lesbianism as mutually exclusive. In Sappho's world, there is room for coexistence. (1989: 32–33)

For the imperial Roman audience, as for a legion of modern readers, the Greek tradition that counted men and women among Sappho's lovers is problematic, and peaceful coexistence is impossible. According to Roman (il)logic, Sappho's problematic sexuality was in need of comic resolution. The Ovidian Sappho, as a notorious lover of women, must have a masculine nature. This "other" nature is so integral to her character that, although she may turn her gaze to a male, Sappho must remain, absurdly, a hom/m/osexual.

Epilogue: A Glimpse of the Roman Lesbian

In her recent essay about *cinaedi*—Roman men who desired to be penetrated by men—Amy Richlin writes that "a historian might doubt their very existence, attested as it is only by hostile sources." She puts forth the possibility, however, that the history of the *cinaedus* may one day be retrieved from the silence, and "the hostility of the sources be considered as a fact of these men's lives" (Richlin 1993b: 524). Can the same be said of the *tribas*? Despite the implicit denials in the Roman sources that these women even existed in Rome, and despite the "Roman denial of biological realism" inherent in the phallic behavior attributed to the *tribas* (Hallett 1989a: 222), can these texts accord us a glimpse of Roman women who loved women? Can we someday retrieve these women from the shadows?

Because of the disavowal of reality that Hallett's article spells out, and because of the comparative scarcity of the sources, in the case of the Roman lesbian we are even worse off than we are with the *cinaedi*. I would hazard to suggest, however, that one way to find a material lesbian beneath the surface of our hostile sources would be to approach the tribad's allegedly masculine form with new sets of assumptions. In this essay, I have adduced Irigaray's hom/m/osexual and Newton's Mythic Mannish Lesbian in order to expose the ludicrous side of a phallic conception of sex that imagined that "sex could only occur in the presence of an imperial and imperious penis" (Newton 1984: 561). Newton begins her essay by asking whether the mannish lesbian could be a male pornographic fantasy, but ends it by asserting that the notion needs to be challenged "not because it doesn't exist, but because it is not the only possibility." She asks: "Why should we as feminists deplore or deny the existence of masculine women or effeminate men? Are we not against assigning specific psychological or social traits to a particular biology?" (ibid.: 575). Newton's questions point toward one way I might temper my approach, but Wittig's claim that the lesbian is neither woman nor man suggests an even more productive angle (Wittig 1981).

As Newton observes, historical portrayals of mannish lesbians may sometimes be inspired by actual women who adopt traditionally "masculine" garb or behavior. But what if one were to describe these women as "gender-rebellious" rather than masculine?[31] Ann Ferguson, who is optimistic that lesbian theorists can develop a notion of lesbian culture that is not "so narrow as to exclude us from any authentic lesbian history before the nineteenth century," suggests in a recent essay the potential gains such a change in vocabulary may offer (1991: 138). Objecting to what she sees as an ahistorical bent in Wittig's theorizing, Ferguson outlines an "approach to thinking of lesbian cultures as potential cultures of resistance within historically specific patriarchal cultures" (1990: 84). Thus we might conjecture that the Mythic Mannish Lesbian is likely to appear (in historically specific forms) when a dominant culture perceives female homoerotic behavior as an unseemly usurpation of the privileged role of the male.[32] With this formulation in mind, we can imagine the masculinized lesbians of the Roman texts not as monsters or fools (as their creators intended), but as dauntless rebels. Despite its efforts to assert that such creatures cannot exist, the dominant culture has left us a promising glimpse of the women who challenged the very notion of Roman womanhood.

Turning back to *Heroides* 15, we might find something redemptive after all in the Roman stereotyping of Sappho. The association of Sappho with Rome's negative view of female homoeroticism may debase "the tenth Muse," but when turned on its head, the Sappho/*tribas* connection brings to the Roman lesbian the notions of intellect, creativity, and the capacity for full erotic expression. Because the authenticity of the poem is not assured, we cannot be completely secure in assigning this development to the age of Augustus. My own view is that the similarities between the portrayals of homoeroticism in this text and in the texts discussed by Hallett make the Ovidian Sappho look quite at home in first-century Rome. Lucian's second-century reference to lesbianism in Lesbos may convince others, however, that our text belongs instead to an era slightly later in the Roman empire.

Scholars who regard *Heroides* 15 as inauthentic point to various apparently anomalous turns of phrase and metrical patterns, but stress in particular the fact that Sappho's epistle is missing from the earliest (ninth- or tenth-century) manuscripts of Ovid's *Heroides* (Tarrant 1981). There is evidence, however, that these manuscripts belong to a separate tradition that had excised "Sappho to Phaon," jumping from the fourteenth epistle to what is now known as *Heroides* 16. Some thirteenth-century anthologies, whose archetype may be as old as the manuscripts that omit Sappho, preserve excerpts of the *Heroides*; and when they quote "Sappho to Phaon," the poem appears right between excerpts of *Heroides* 14 and 16 (Palmer 1898: 422). With Palmer, I take this as "striking confirmation" that the Sapphic epistle belongs with the rest of the *Heroides*, and that the fifteenth slot is indeed Sappho's rightful place, poised as she is between the penultimate lonely heroine and Ovid's three pairs of male/female correspondents.

To my mind this excision bears comparison to the fate of Sappho's own lyrics. W. R. Johnson has written recently:

> The legends about the burnings of Sappho's poems are, doubtless, mostly legends merely. But where, in matters such as these, there is smoke, there is usually some fire, even if it is essentially symbolic. If Gregory VII did in fact

burn her poems publicly in 1073, his act—it was more than a gesture—was hardly intended to get rid of her for good and all, since he was doubtless not silly enough to think that he was destroying the only remaining copies of the Poetess from Hell; rather, lacking an Index, he was sending a message, to his contemporaries and to the future, about this evil and the other poetic evils of whom she herself was symbolic.[33]

My suspicion is that despite her repudiation of the Lesbian girls, "Sappho's" frank acknowledgment of her love for women ultimately led to the judgment that Sappho had no place in the authoritative catalogue of womankind that forms the *Heroides*. Like Ovid, she was exiled. Like the original Sappho, she was suppressed. A few centuries later, when readers had begun to long anew for the voice of the tenth Muse, Ovid's poem was given a second life, and its eager readers were promised that this was the real thing.

Notes

1. See Hallett 1979.

2. Cf., e.g., Horace's reference to *mascula Sappho* ("virile Sappho," *Epist.* 1.19.28), a passage that certainly alludes to the issue of gendered writing, even if it does not comment upon Sappho's sexuality per se. The Greece/Rome dichotomy is, of course, not always clear-cut; there is much variation between regions and periods, and Sappho's lyrics about women had already become problematic in Hellenistic society. Cf. Dover 1978: 182.

3. The following are two of the many manuscript headings listed by Dörrie (1971: 313) with my own translations: *epistula Saphos vatis ad phaonem amatorem suum quae ab Ovidio translata fuit de graeco in latinum*, "A letter from Sappho the poet to Phaon her lover, which was translated by Ovid from Greek to Latin"; and *Saphos Lesbiae poete opusculum sequitur*, "The following is a minor work of the Lesbian poet Sappho."

4. Although I do not consider the attribution to Ovid a settled issue, in this essay for convenience I will refer to our author as "Ovid." For some arguments against authenticity (with bibliography), see Tarrant 1981, and Knox 1995: 12–14; see also Reynolds 1983: 272–73. On Sapphic allusions and parodies, see the chapters on Sappho in Jacobson 1974 and Verducci 1985.

5. See Hallett 1989a on the term *tribas* (plural: *tribades*), which is a Roman borrowing from the Greek.

6. See Dover 1978: 182–83. See also Stimpson 1990, and Richlin's remarks (1993b) on the word "homosexual." For a recent general discussion of essentialism (by a classicist), see Kennedy 1993.

7. This method can be justified even if the epistle is not Ovid's, as it was clearly composed as a companion piece to the other *Heroides*.

8. Cf. Dover (1978: 78), who cautions that, although long hair is often associated with youthful *erōmenoi*, it does not necessarily have this connotation.

9. See Cantarella 1992: 83; Dover 1978: 177; Stigers 1979; Snyder 1994; and Greene 1994, 1996. DuBois (1995: e.g., 155) challenges this approach.

10. DeJean writes of the Ovidian Sappho's "acceptance of the superiority of an *ars amatoria* much like Ovid's over that which she had formerly preached" (1989: 68).

11. See *POxy.* 1800 fr. 1 col. i.16f., which says that some people call Sappho a *gunaikerastria*, a "(female) *erastēs* of women"; cited by Dover (1978: 174). Dover speculates that the writer may have been following a Hellenistic source.

12. Kroll 1924. Other authorities agree that our earliest extant references to Sappho's homoeroticism date to the Augustan age, even if they do not consider *Her.* 15 as the first example. Dover cites Hor. *Carm.* 2.13.5 and Ov. *Tr.* 2.365 as our earliest commentaries on "Sappho's eros for her own sex" (1978: 174), and Jocelyn cites Hor. *Epist.* 1.19.28 and *Epod.* 5.41, along with *Her.* 15 and later works such as Mart. 7.69.9–10 and 10.35.15–16 (1980: 48 n. 66).

13. This and all other translations of the *Heroides* in this essay are by Stanley Lombardo and Pamela Gordon (Lombardo and Gordon, n.d.). Pyrrha and Methymna (15) are towns on Lesbos.

14. Welcker ([1816] 1845) "freed Sappho from a prevailing prejudice" (as his title asserts) by identifying Attic comedy as the source of stories about her liaisons with women. More recent scholarship, however, has stressed that the comic Sappho seems to have engaged in excessive sexual activity with men. Cf. Lardinois 1989.

15. Cf. Hallett 1979; Jocelyn 1980: 48 n. 66; Cassio 1983; Dover 1978; and Kroll 1924.

16. Cf. Cassio 1983 and Hallett 1989a. Even in English and other modern languages, the use of the word "lesbian" to denote female homoeroticism has a shadowy history that begins in the late nineteenth century (cf. Hallett 1979, Cassio 1983).

17. Dover cites Anac. fr. 358 as an archaic text in which there appears prima facie to be an association between the island Lesbos and female homosexuality, but cautions that the text may suggest simply that the women of Lesbos were associated with erotic license (Dover 1978: 183–84).

18. On *hetairistriae*, see Hallett 1989a: 222. The translations of Lucian are my own.

19. Clonarium is eager to know all about the mechanics, but Leaena's punch line leaves us wondering whether to imagine an *olisbos* (a dildo) or an enlarged clitoris: "Don't press for details; it's an ugly story. So, by Aphrodite, I won't tell you!" (Lucian *Dial. Meret.* 292).

20. In a flippant allusion to Catull. 8, Ovid's Sappho says that she wishes Phaon had at least bid her farewell: *si modo dixisses "Lesbi puella, vale!"*, "If only you had said, 'Girl of Lesbos, goodbye'" (100).

21. Tarrant (1981: 146) argues that *sicca* in the *Ars* means "sober" or "temperate," and that the explicitly sexual connotation of the word does not appear before Martial.

22. Verducci (1985: 166), who earlier translates lines 133–34 as "I hesitate to say what happens next, but it all happens, / there's no choice, just joy, and I'm inundated with it" (130). Verducci does not discuss Sappho's masculinity explicitly,

and she may understand the text to refer to female ejaculation, which is possible if we consider the mechanics of reproduction as presented in ancient Hippocratic texts. See A. E. Hanson 1990: 314.

23. DuBois (1995: 148) questions the modern tendency to assume that Kleis is Sappho's daughter and suggests that the relationship may be more erotic than modern readers have assumed. See Hallett 1982 for earlier attempts to dislodge Kleis from the biographical tradition.

24. Translation by Diane Rayor. Copyright 1991, Diane Rayor. Originally published in Rayor (1991: 72), and reprinted here through the kind permission of the author and the University of California Press, publisher of that volume.

25. In several of Sappho's poems, Charaxas is upbraided or lamented for his involvement in an unseemly love affair.

26. As many critics of Foucault have pointed out, Foucault's scheme is based on philosophical texts, and does not take into account the very different picture presented by, e.g., the comedies of Aristophanes. For my purposes here, this is not a problem; the scheme Ovid parodies is the stereotypical model of the Greek elite.

27. Or does she have a taste for overripe boys? On the ideal age for a boy to leave his lover, see Foucault 1985, esp. 199–201. One example Foucault cites is Pl. *Prt.* 309a, where the razor that shaves the boy's first beard must also cut his ties to his lover.

28. *Pace* Dover (1978: 183). Instead, Corinth's reputation as a center for female prostitution highlights Demonassa's role as the receptive feminine partner.

29. See Foucault (1985: 190): "A man who preferred *paidika* did not think of himself as being 'different' from those who pursued women." Cf. "The Greeks did not see love for one's own sex and love for the other sex as opposites, as two exclusive choices, two radically different types of behavior. The dividing lines did not follow that kind of boundary" (187).

30. See Richlin 1993b: 526–28.

31. Against the idea that "butch" women are imitation men, see Butler's remarks on butch/femme identities (1990: esp. 123 and 137).

32. Cf. Cantarella (1992: 170): "In the Roman imagination, female homosexuality could only mean an attempt by a woman to replace a man, and an attempt by another woman to derive from homosexual intercourse, quite unnaturally, the pleasure which only men were able to confer."

33. From the foreword to Rayor 1991: xvii.

PART FIVE

FEMALE CONSTRUCTION OF

THE DESIRING SUBJECT

TWELVE

TANDEM VENIT AMOR: A ROMAN
WOMAN SPEAKS OF LOVE

Alison Keith

D ISCUSSION OF sexuality and gender in Augustan Rome commonly appeals to a standard opposition: scholars have interpreted
the literature of the period as "for" or "against" an "Augustan"
sexual ideology that they reconstruct from Augustus's legislative inter-
ventions into the morality of the Roman elite.[1] The *leges Iuliae de adulteriis et de maritandis ordinibus*, promulgated in the name of Augustus in
18 B.C.E., addressed marriage and adultery among the upper classes with
particular attention to the regulation of female sexuality in the interests
of the state.[2] Under these laws, sexual union outside of marriage or con-
cubinage became a criminal offense against the state, and penalties for
conviction were severe.[3] Livy, Vergil, and Horace are commonly cited as
supporters of this ideology, while the elegists Propertius, Tibullus, and
Ovid are usually identified as its critics.[4] Scholars who have challenged
this *communis opinio* (e.g., Kennedy 1992: 40–47) continue to rely on the
frame of reference provided by the terms "Augustan" and "anti-Augustan," even as they demonstrate the complicity of one with the other. The
female-oriented discourse of Sulpician elegy has rarely been drawn into
the debate about Augustan sexual ideology, perhaps because women's perspective is routinely subsumed under men's in histories of ideology. Yet
Sulpicia's poems constitute our only extant female-authored treatment of
sexuality from ancient Rome, and therefore offer valuable evidence whose
congruence with either Augustan ideology or the "oppositional" stance of
male-authored elegy cannot be simply assumed. To explore the small corpus of Sulpicia's elegiac poetry is to open up further alternative perspectives about sexuality in Augustan Rome.

I shall argue that the Dido episode in Vergil's *Aeneid* establishes an important context for Sulpician elegy. Such a view depends on assumptions
about Sulpicia's identity and the literary culture of early Augustan Rome.
While her dates are a matter of speculation, scholarly consensus accepts

My thanks to Judith Hallett, Marilyn Skinner, and Stephen Rupp for comments and suggestions on earlier versions of this article.

the identification, first proposed by Haupt (1871), that Sulpicia is the daughter of Servius Sulpicius Rufus, the son of Cicero's friend, the jurist of the same name (*cos.* 51 B.C.E.), and Valeria, the sister of Augustus's general Messalla Corvinus.[5] Syme (1955; cf. 1981a) has argued for a date of birth anywhere from the mid-40s to the mid-30s B.C.E., and the composition of Sulpicia's *elegidia* is usually dated to the antepenultimate decade of the century (Lowe 1988; Snyder 1989; Hallett 1992a). These years span the period in which Vergil wrote, with the composition of the *Aeneid* securely dated from 29 to 19 B.C.E.

It is clear that the *Aeneid* provoked a great deal of interest in elite Roman circles long before its official "publication" in 17 B.C.E. Propertius refers to the *Aeneid* as *nescio quid maius Iliade* ("something greater than the *Iliad*," 2.34.66) and summarizes the plot in phraseology indebted to the opening lines of the epic in the mid-twenties B.C.E. (2.34.61–64), while Tibullus seems to have been inspired by Vergil's project to offer his own account of Aeneas's arrival in Rome (Tib. 2.5). Vergil presented portions of the *Aeneid* (certainly books 2, 4 and 6) at both private and public recitations in Rome, and Suetonius attests to the poem's impact on at least one female member of the Augustan elite, Octavia (Suet. *Vita Vergili* 32–33). It is scarcely credible that Sulpicia was unfamiliar with Vergil's undertaking, especially in view of her relationship to Messalla.[6] This is implicitly acknowledged in recent critical discussion of the close relations between Sulpicia's poetry and contemporary male-authored elegiac poetry.[7] But contemporary elegy offers Sulpicia little precedent for exploring female erotic desire, since the genre is almost exclusively concerned with the male poet-lover's rejection of the standard careers available to wellborn men at Rome in favor of a life given over to the pursuits of poetry and love.

Dido's passion for Aeneas offers a much closer literary parallel for the amatory situation in Sulpicia's elegies. Surprisingly little attention has been paid to the points of contact between Sulpicia's elegies and the *Aeneid*, despite the prominence of Vergilian themes and vocabulary in the small Sulpician corpus.[8] Yet a sympathetic interest in Dido's character can be paralleled in other ancient writers (Ov. *Her.* 7; Macrob. *Sat.* 5.17.5; August. *Confessiones* 1.13), and in Sulpicia's case would furnish early evidence of Roman women's interest in the Dido episode, an interest attested by Ovid (for his own reasons) at *Tristia* 2.533–36. I shall argue that Vergil's portrayal of the love of Dido and Aeneas provides Sulpicia with a framework in which to articulate a woman's love for a man, and that Sulpicia's imaginative engagement with the Dido episode in the *Aeneid* exposes the inadequacy of our standard either/or model of "pro-" or "anti-" Augustanism for investigating the relations among female subjectivity, agency, and sexuality in Augustan Rome.

Infelix Dido

The sexual ideology implicit in the Dido episode of the *Aeneid* shows significant points of contact with the social and moral concerns addressed in the *leges Iuliae* of 18 B.C.E., the year after Vergil's death. While it would be naive to suppose that the *Aeneid* is no more than an Augustan policy statement circulated as literature, there is compelling evidence that the poem was in broad accord with the politics of the new regime. Suetonius tells us that the *Aeneid* was preserved and published on Augustus's orders, despite Vergil's deathbed wish that the poem be burned (Suet. *Vita Vergili* 37, 40–41). The close temporal conjunction between the promulgation of the moral legislation of 18 B.C.E. in the name of Augustus and the publication of the *Aeneid* on the authority of Augustus in the following year suggests that Dido's sexual transgression may be related to Augustan efforts at appearing to regulate female sexuality.[9]

Vergil represents Dido against a background of specifically Roman cultural norms in her political, religious, legislative, and architectural practice.[10] But a narrative concerning the origins of the political, religious, and military institutions of a state that places a woman at its head (*dux femina facti*, *Aen.* 1.364) poses a serious threat to Roman cultural conventions, since these institutions were reserved almost exclusively for upperclass male citizens at Rome.[11] As a woman operating in the public sphere, Dido necessarily constitutes and is constituted as a disruptive force in the *Aeneid*. In accordance with Roman discursive codes about the female, therefore, the focus of the narrative "naturally" narrows to Dido's sexuality, so that her political and military ambitions come to be subsumed by her inappropriate erotic desires.

The banquet to which Dido hospitably invites Aeneas (*Aen.* 1.627) after welcoming the shipwrecked Trojans to her city is the site of her transformation in the narrative from an effective political leader (*dux*) into a politically disabled, lovesick woman (*femina*). Vergil's descriptions of Dido's richly appointed banquet (*Aen.* 1.701–6, 723–24, 736–47) and the sumptuous luxury of her palace (*Aen.* 1.697–700, 707–8, 725–30) implicate her character in Roman moralizing discourses linking excessive wealth with excessive lust.[12] In this overly luxurious setting, Dido is necessarily, (ideo)logically, represented as succumbing to excessive erotic desires: *nec non et vario noctem sermone trahebat / infelix Dido longumque bibebat amorem*, "Unhappy Dido drew out the night in varied conversation and drank deeply of love" (*Aen.* 1.748–49; cf. *Aen.* 1.715–22). By the outset of book 4, excessive desire constitutes the whole of her identity: *at regina gravi iamdudum saucia cura / vulnus alit venis et caeco carpitur igni*, "But the queen, long since stricken with a grievous passion, nourishes the wound in her veins and is consumed by an invisible flame" (*Aen.* 4.1–2). Driven by *amor*, Dido is no longer an effective political leader. Building projects stand unfinished throughout Carthage (*Aen.* 4.86–89), as Dido abandons her political and military projects in favor of dalliance (*Aen.* 4.74–79). Her political decline is complemented by her abuse of religious ritual throughout book 4 to further erotic rather than political goals (*Aen.* 4.56–67, 300–303, 452–65, 483–98, 504–21, 634–65, 676).

The transgressive sexuality of the Carthaginian queen is delineated within the peculiarly Roman framework of *pudor*, a "sense of what is seemly" (especially in sexual matters), and *fama*, "reputation." At the outset of *Aeneid* 4 Dido swears an oath to *Pudor* (4.27) in which she undertakes to respect the sexual proprieties dictated by modesty and regard for her good name by remaining faithful to the memory of her dead husband rather than succumbing to passion (*Aen.* 4.18–29). Her oath accords with the Roman ideal of the "one-man woman," *univira*, the widow who refuses to remarry out of steadfast loyalty to the memory of a dead spouse.[13] Dido breaks her oath, however, first in her sexual communion with Aeneas, and then, without regard for her good name (*fama, Aen.* 4.170), in her open assertion of their union as *coniugium*, "marriage" (*Aen.* 4.172). The related noun *coniunx*, "marriage partner," is used by both Venus and Dido of Dido's first husband Sychaeus (*Aen.* 1.343, 1.354, 4.21), but Dido alone uses *coniunx* of Aeneas (*Aen.* 4.324); for his part, the Trojan leader pointedly denies ever having assumed the responsibilities of a husband (*nec coniugis umquam / praetendi taedas, Aen.* 4.338–39).[14] Moreover, Vergil undermines the validity of their union by labeling it *culpa*, "crime" (*Aen.* 4.172), in a decisive echo of Dido's initial definition of any sexual relationship after Sychaeus's death as *culpa* (*Aen.* 4.19).

The scandalous relationship of the lovers excites malicious gossip, *fama*, throughout Africa (*Aen.* 4.173–74, 189–95),[15] and Dido herself is represented as lamenting her loss of *pudor*, "chastity," and *fama*, "reputation," when she reproaches Aeneas for abandoning her (4.320–23):

> te propter Libycae gentes Nomadumque tyranni
> odere, infensi Tyrii; te propter eundem
> exstinctus pudor et, qua sola sidera adibam,
> fama prior.

Because of you the peoples of Libya and the Numidian leaders hate me, the Tyrians are hostile; because of you, too, my chastity has been obliterated along with my earlier good name, my sole claim to immortality.

Sexual union with Aeneas not only disables Dido politically but leads, apparently inevitably, to her death: *ille dies primus leti primusque malorum / causa fuit*, "That day first was the cause of her death and the cause of her troubles" (*Aen.* 4.169–70). In the depiction of Dido's excessive passion and her resulting political downfall and death, a pattern of protocols promoting female sexual "purity" can be discerned that overlaps with Augustan elite ideology concerning the state regulation of female sexuality. Viewed through this androcentric elite Roman perspective, Dido's nationality and gender (ideo)logically render her socially disruptive and therefore sexually deviant.

Servi filia Sulpicia

But of course Augustus's control over discursive practices, let alone interpretive practices, was by no means hegemonic or uncontested at Rome (and especially in the *Aeneid* itself).[16] The genre of elegy in particular "represents itself, and is often represented as, 'oppositional'" in Augustan Rome.[17] Attention has accordingly been drawn (Sullivan 1972; Hallett 1973) to the predilection of the elegists Propertius, Tibullus, and Ovid for critiquing the culturally validated standards of conduct espoused most forcefully in epic.[18] The recent scholarly exploration of the literary and sexual politics of the Roman elegists, however, has for the most part failed to consider the poetry of the single extant female elegist, Sulpicia ([Tib.] 3.13–18 = [Tib.] 4.7–12), and has thereby elided valuable evidence of alternate strategies for articulating female sexuality in Augustan Rome.

Sulpicia's opening poem ([Tib.] 3.13) ponders the impropriety necessarily involved in a Roman woman's avowal of love:

> Tandem venit amor, qualem texisse pudori
> quam nudasse alicui sit mihi fama magis.
> exorata meis illum Cytherea Camenis
> adtulit in nostrum deposuitque sinum.
> exsoluit promissa Venus: mea gaudia narret,
> dicetur siquis non habuisse sua.
> non ego signatis quicquam mandare tabellis,
> ne legat id nemo quam meus ante, velim,
> sed peccasse iuvat, voltus conponere famae
> taedet: cum digno digna fuisse ferar.

At last love has come; and such a love it is that the rumor of having concealed it would shame me more than having bared all. Entreated by my Muses' prayers, Cythera's mistress has brought and placed him in my lap. Venus has fulfilled her promises. Let my joys be told by all of whom it can be said that they have missed their own. I would not choose to entrust anything to sealed tablets, so that no one might read it before my lover. Instead my sin delights me, and I am tired of composing a mask for rumor. Let me be said to have been worthy of my worthy beloved.[19]

Sulpicia's daring freedom of speech finds expression in the offer of her tale of love to others, as she invites those who lack their own joys (5–6) to narrate as their own her private compact with the goddess of love (3–5). This oral dissemination constitutes the initial informal publication of her love poetry, and a figure for its formal literary publication (7–8) follows in the image of the unsealed tablets that make our poet's *amores* available to any reader. Her unsealed tablets contrast strikingly with the conventionally sealed tablets surreptitiously conveyed by a go-between from elegiac poet-lover to beloved (e.g., Ov. *Am.* 1.11, 1.12). This love affair is a story for others to tell (*mihi fama*, 2; *mea gaudia narret*, 5; *ne legat id nemo*, 8; *digna fuisse ferar*, 10).[20]

It is difficult to know how quickly the voice of our elegiac poet-lover would have been recognized as female by a Roman reader. The rest of the extant corpus of Latin elegy is male-authored, but in the Tibullan collection (as we have it), the alternation of the voice of a male observer with the voice of "Sulpicia" in the five poems immediately preceding the univocal sequence of six elegies perhaps invites the assumption that the speaker of *tandem venit amor* will be "Sulpicia."[21] The gender of the poet-lover in the initial poem can be securely identified as female only in the last line of the poem, where the nominative adjective *digna*, "a worthy woman," withheld to the second half of the line, is placed beside the masculine form of the ablative *digno*, "a worthy man." Yet the audacious new gender politics of the speaking voice may be signaled as early as the first line through the prominence of the noun *pudor*.

As we have seen in connection with Dido, *pudor* is a quality much praised in Roman women, and contemporary Latin elegy offers little precedent for its association with the male poet-lover. The Roman elegists conventionally characterize the elegiac poet-lover's lifestyle as *nequitia*, "depravity," and embrace it in defiance of social norms, but they do not make *pudor* programmatic to their rejection of the standards of conduct endorsed at Rome.[22] A much closer literary parallel for Sulpicia's attention to the proprieties dictated by *pudor* occurs in Vergil's depiction of Dido's passion for Aeneas. Vergil represents Dido striving to conduct herself in accordance with the dictates of *pudor* despite her growing love for Aeneas (*Aen.* 4.27, 55, 322); moreover, her downfall originates in the ill repute (*fama*, *Aen.* 4.170, 323) arising from her neighbors' gossip (*fama*, *Aen.* 4.170–97, 219–21, 296–99, 665–66) about their sexual relations. In Sulpicia's poem, likewise, the constraints of *pudor* ([Tib.] 3.13.1) are closely associated with the maintenance of her reputation (*fama*, [Tib.] 3.13.2), as is particularly clear in the reference to composing a mask for rumor (*fama*, [Tib.] 3.13.9).[23] But Sulpicia, as the author of "Sulpicia's" literary destiny, can both contest Roman suspicion of female sexuality and redefine the terms of moral judgment. She tacitly suggests that deception (*texisse*, [Tib.] 3.13.1) is a frequent companion to *pudor*, and deftly reorients the sphere of *pudor* from dissimulation to openness. The regulation of female sexuality by innuendo and rumor ([Tib.] 3.13.2, 9), so injurious to Dido in the *Aeneid* (4.170–97), is rejected outright. Instead, our poet emphasizes her extraordinary distance from Roman norms of female propriety through the pervasive sexualization of the process of poetic composition in the use of sexually charged verbs denoting covering and uncovering (*texisse, nudasse*), in the imagery of "pelvic" reception (*adtulit in nostrum deposuitque sinum*), and in the claim of misbehavior (*peccasse*) to describe her writing as well as her physical conduct.[24]

Vergil's portrait of the lovesick Dido resonates throughout the opening *mise-en-scène* of Sulpicia's elegiac sequence. In the *Aeneid*, Venus receives the epithet *Cytherea*, "of Cythera" (*Aen.* 1.657), when she instructs her son Cupid to disguise himself as Ascanius and, by sitting in Dido's lap, to inspire her with love for Aeneas (*Aen.* 1.657–60, 683–88). The success of Venus's stratagem is confirmed at the outset of *Aeneid* 4, in Vergil's portrait of the Carthaginian queen's longing for the absent Aeneas (83–85):

> illum absens absentem auditque videtque,
> aut gremio Ascanium genitoris imagine capta
> detinet, infandum si fallere possit amorem.

> In Aeneas's absence she hears and sees him, or she holds Ascanius in her lap, captivated by his likeness to his father, as if he could deceive her unspeakable love.

The divine machinery of Vergilian epic is strikingly echoed in Sulpicia's formulation of the success of her love affair in the second couplet, where Cythera's queen is said to have answered her prayers by dropping love into her embrace: *Amor*, "love," is another name for Cupid, while Sulpicia's "embrace," *sinum*, varies the Vergilian Dido's "lap," *gremium*. Although *gremium* and *sinus* are not, strictly speaking, interchangeable, their usage overlaps to a very great extent, especially in contexts where someone is being hugged or cuddled.[25] Recent scholarship has rightly emphasized that Sulpicia uses *sinus*, "pocket," because her beloved bears a name, Cerinthus, that functions as a metonymy for her tablets (Roessel 1990: 245–48), and the Romans carried their writing materials in the folds of their garments. Nonetheless, the surface sense of *sinus* here, "embrace," is synonymous with standard contemporary usage of *gremium*, and coheres with Vergil's usage of the term in the *Aeneid*.[26] Sulpicia has thus sympathetically reimagined Dido's ignorance of the divine machinery of the *Aeneid* in her own informed personal relation with the Muses and Venus, and has recast Dido's pursuit of a love undertaken against the will of Rome's gods as a love fully in accordance with divine will. Like the

Vergilian Dido, who does not conceal her "fault" (*culpa*) but calls it marriage (*Aen.* 4.170–72), "Sulpicia" delights in her fault (*peccasse*, [Tib.]
3.13.9) and revels in its publication. Where Dido is the object of rumors
purveyed by *Fama*, however, "Sulpicia" publishes her transgressive passion to gain a literary reputation.

The poem closes with the affirmation that the poet-lover and her
beloved are "each worthy of the other," *digno digna* ([Tib.] 3.13.10), and
the Latin underscores their mutual worth through the rhetorical device
of polyptoton. The phrase *digno digna* echoes an earlier elegist's claims for
his achievement in the field of elegy: *tandem fecerunt carmina Musae / quae
possem domina deicere digna mea*, "At last the Muses have made poems that
I could utter, worthy of my mistress," (Gallus *P. Qasr Ibrîm* 6–7).[27] The
Latin elegists emulate Gallus in expressing the desire to produce poems
worthy of their mistresses' beauty and taste, but there is no elegiac parallel for Sulpicia's evocation of the mutual worthiness of poet-lover and
beloved.[28] Once again, however, the *Aeneid* furnishes a precedent. Dido
draws Aeneas's attention to the parallels in their experiences and their social standing (1.628–30):

> me quoque per multos similis fortuna labores
> iactatam hac demum voluit consistere terra;
> non ignara mali miseris succurrere disco.

A similar Fortune buffeted me, too, through many labors until she wished
to set me to rest at last in this land; I have learned through suffering to come
to the assistance of those in need.

Sulpicia refracts the echo of Gallus through the apparent equality between Aeneas and Dido in the opening book of the *Aeneid*. More
poignantly, she combines Gallus's diction with the very words with which
Rumor maliciously indicts Dido's passion for Aeneas: *venisse Aenean ... /
cui se pulchra viro dignetur iungere Dido*, "To Libya had come Aeneas, a
man whom beautiful Dido deemed worthy of union" (*Aen.* 4.191–92).[29]
Vergil's innovative depiction of a woman who deems her lover worthy of
herself furnishes Sulpicia with a model for representing the reciprocity of
her erotic relations with Cerinthus.

Since a paucity of references to mythology has been noted in Sulpicia's
elegies, it is surprising that her evocations of the Vergilian Dido in [Tib.]
3.13 have gone unnoticed.[30] The most obvious effect of Sulpicia's adap-
tation of the Vergilian third-person epic narrative for a first-person female elegiac persona lies in the loss of political resonances. Paradoxically,
however, this reorientation of the Dido episode from public to private allows Sulpicia to disrupt the logic of subsuming the transgressive political
ambitions of a woman in her deviant sexuality. Sulpicia thereby challenges,

however slightly, the protocols regulating the sexual conduct of Roman women. The pervasive reminiscences of the Dido episode in this opening poem invite us to consider such evocations in the poems that follow.

In two birthday poems ([Tib.] 3.14 and 15), Sulpicia explores the elegiac topos of the separation of lovers from the perspective of a female lover abandoning her male beloved. Contemporary elegy often depicts the separation, real or threatened, of lover from beloved, and another elegiac commonplace is the poet-lover's polite refusal to leave Rome (and the beloved) to accompany a Roman magistrate or general on official business in the provinces. But the separation of poet-lover from beloved at the behest of a figure such as Messalla, who is in a position to compel obedience, is far less frequent in elegy ([Tib.] 3.14):

> Invisus natalis adest, qui rure molesto
>   et sine Cerintho tristis agendus erit.
> dulcius urbe quid est? an villa sit apta puellae
>   atque Arretino frigidus amnis agro?
> iam, nimium Messalla mei studiose, quiescas;
>   non tempestivae saepe, propinque, viae.
> hic animum sensusque meos abducta relinquo,
>   arbitrio quamvis non sinis esse meo.

My hateful birthday has arrived, and I have to spend the dismal day without Cerinthus in the tiresome countryside. What is more delightful than the city? Do you really think a villa or a cold stream in the farm country of Arezzo suits a girl? Now relax your excessive concern for my welfare, Messalla. Journeys, uncle, are often ill-timed. Carried off, I leave here my soul and my senses, though you do not allow me to live according to my wish.

When "blocking" figures appear in male-authored elegy, they are cast in the role of the *puella's* man or bawd, and characteristically effect the separation of the lovers by removing the *puella* from the poet-lover just as Messalla is here portrayed as inadvertently proposing to separate "Sulpicia" from Cerinthus. But the beloved's emotional response to these separations is never explored in male-authored elegy; we must turn rather to the *Aeneid* to find a literary model for the articulation of a woman's distress at impending separation.

As the guardian of "Sulpicia," Messalla is represented as the ultimate arbiter for determining her plans, in a role not dissimilar to that of Jupiter, whose envoy Mercury commands Aeneas to leave Carthage (and desert Dido) in order to resume his divinely appointed mission to Rome (*Aen.* 4.265–76). In the face of Mercury's command, Aeneas is silent and burns only to be gone (*Aen.* 4.279–82). By contrast, although our poet-lover represents herself as the recipient of an authoritative command to leave her beloved, in a position analogous to that of Aeneas, "Sulpicia" disputes her guardian's dictum and voices her discontent. Neatly reversing the example of Aeneas, "Sulpicia" defends her desire to remain with her beloved in the city, and her excuse (*non tempestivae saepe, propinque, viae,* [Tib.] 3.14.6) is phrased in such a way as to recall Dido's arguments to Aeneas about the untimeliness of the season chosen for her lover's departure from Carthage (*Aen.* 4.309–11; cf. 4.51–53, 430).

Unlike Vergil's *infelix Dido,* whose pleas fail to dissuade Aeneas from leaving Carthage, however, "Sulpicia" receives a reprieve. The following poem celebrates the unexpected pleasure of enjoying her birthday in the city ([Tib.] 3.15):

> Scis iter ex animo sublatum triste puellae?
> natali Romae iam licet esse suo.
> omnibus ille dies nobis natalis agatur,
> qui nec opinanti nunc tibi forte venit.

Do you know that the hateful journey has been put off, relieving your girl's spirit? Now her birthday can be spent at Rome. Let us all celebrate that birthday which comes to you now by an unexpected chance.

Many readers have recognized an "implied cause and effect relationship between the two poems; the attempt to persuade Messalla in the first of the pair may be what led to the happy occasion proclaimed in the second" (Snyder 1989: 132; cf. Santirocco 1979: 232). In her own small canvas, Sulpicia is able to imagine a very different resolution of competing claims than that available to Dido and Aeneas in the *Aeneid.*

"Sulpicia's" success in frustrating her uncle's plans for her birthday, however, cannot ensure harmonious relations with her beloved. The fourth poem in the sequence ([Tib.] 3.16) introduces conflict between the lovers, as "Sulpicia" rebukes Cerinthus for inconstancy, evoking Dido's reproaches against Aeneas for his faithlessness (*Aen.* 4.305–30, 365–87).

> Gratum est, securus multum quod iam tibi de me
> permittis, subito ne male inepta cadam.
> sit tibi cura togae potior pressumque quasillo
> scortum quam Servi filia Sulpicia:
> solliciti sunt pro nobis, quibus illa dolori est,
> ne cedam ignoto, maxima causa, toro.

I'm glad that, secure in your position, you allow yourself so much regarding me that I may suddenly stumble in some unhappy folly. Let concern for the toga and a prostitute burdened with a wool-basket be more to you than Sulpicia, Servius's daughter. They are anxious on my behalf, for whom the greatest cause of grief is that I may yield to an ignoble lover.[31]

Hinds (1987: 45) observes that the phrasing of Cerinthus's preference for a prostitute (*cura togae* gestures by metonymy to *scortum*, [Tib.] 3.16.3–4) punningly suggests that Cerinthus should prefer matters of state, exemplified by the male citizen's toga, to an erotic liaison. Sulpicia thereby may obliquely present Cerinthus's infidelity to "Sulpicia" as a contrast between public duty and private pleasure. The punning oscillation between concern for the state and interest in another woman in [Tib.] 3.16.3–4 finds a suggestive parallel in Aeneas's justification to Dido for his departure: *sed nunc Italiam magnam Gryneus Apollo, / Italiam Lyciae iussere capessere sortes; / hic amor, haec patria est,* "But now Grynean Apollo and the Lycian oracles bade me seek Italy, great Italy; this is my love, this is my country" (*Aen.* 4.345–47). Like Aeneas, whom Dido accuses of personal betrayal and political treachery in leaving her for Italy, Cerinthus is reproached by Sulpicia for infidelities potentially both personal and political. Her disillusionment provokes Cerinthus to fall in her estimation. Just as Dido was initially impressed by the nobility of Aeneas's lineage (*Aen.* 4.10–14), so Sulpicia celebrated Cerinthus's dignity at the outset of her sequence (*digno*, [Tib.] 3.13.10). Now, however, Cerinthus is no longer a worthy beloved, but has become instead an ignoble bedmate (*ignoto . . . toro*, [Tib.] 3.16.6). A similar trajectory is rehearsed by Aeneas in the course of *Aeneid* 4 as Dido comes to repudiate her earlier estimate of his character (*Aen.* 4.365–67). Moreover, just as there are hints that Dido is besieged by rival suitors (*Aen.* 4.35–38, 211–18), so here our poet implies that the sexual destiny of "Sulpicia" may be a matter of interest to other admirers as well as to her kinsmen ([Tib.] 3.16.5–6).[32]

In the final poems of her sequence ([Tib.] 3.17 and 18), Sulpicia elaborates the metaphor of erotic passion as a fever. Thus 3.17:

> Estne tibi, Cerinthe, tuae pia cura puellae,
> quod mea nunc vexat corpora fessa calor?
> a ego non aliter tristes evincere morbos
> optarim, quam te si quoque velle putem.
> at mihi quid prosit morbos evincere, si tu
> nostra potes lento pectore ferre mala?

Cerinthus, do you have any thoughtful concern for your girlfriend, because the heat of fever now afflicts her exhausted flesh? Ah, I would not otherwise wish to overcome my grievous illness than if I thought you too wished it. But how would it benefit me to overcome my sickness, if you can endure my pains with an unresponsive heart?

As Snyder notes (1989: 134), "The speaker refers to a literal fever that wracks her body but in such a way that she also manages to suggest the fever of passion and the desire on her part for an equally fervent response from the addressee." The metaphor of love as illness is an elegiac commonplace, but the vocabulary with which Sulpicia describes this flame of love finds its closest parallel in Vergil's depiction of the lovesick Dido (*Aen.* 4.1–5):

> At regina gravi iamdudum saucia cura
> vulnus alit venis et caeco carpitur igni.
> multa viri virtus animo multusque recursat
> gentis honos; haerent infixi pectore vultus
> verbaque nec placidam membris dat cura quietem.

But the queen, long since stricken with grievous passion, nourishes the wound in her veins and is consumed by an invisible flame. Many times his manliness returns to her mind, many times the dignity of his lineage; his looks and words stick in her mind and love gives no peaceful rest to her limbs.

Sulpicia conflates the Vergilian imagery of Dido's love as at once flame and wound in the metaphor of love as a feverish illness. Like Dido at the outset of *Aeneid* 4, "Sulpicia" is wracked by the fever of passion. But in the framework of Sulpician elegy, the lovers' mutual devotion fulfills the plans of the gods (Venus and the Muses), rather than contravening the dictates of destiny. Cerinthus's devotion (*cura*) to "Sulpicia" can therefore be characterized as ideally dutiful (*pia*) in an implicit contrast to Dido's painful and excessive love (*gravi . . . cura*) for Aeneas. Yet Sulpicia's deployment of the adjective *pius* in the characterization of Cerinthus's proper concern for his sick girlfriend cannot fail to evoke the very different nature of Aeneas's *pietas* in the *Aeneid*, where the use of *pius* as a personal epithet is reserved almost exclusively for Aeneas and is closely correlated with his performance of public duty.[33] Vergil withholds the epithet during Aeneas's sojourn in Carthage, and the hero regains the epithet only after he has decisively rejected Dido's personal claims on him (*Aen.* 4.393). In returning *pietas* to the private realm of elegy from the public sphere of epic, Sulpicia restores the concept to its pre-Vergilian usage in the *sermo amatorius*.[34] Her reapplication of the adjective *pia* to erotic love, *cura*, reaffirms the elegiac association of *pietas* in the realm of personal relations and constitutes a rejection of Vergil's unprecedented rupture of the two.

"Sulpicia's" fever for Cerinthus proves infectious in the succeeding poem, where his *pia cura* ([Tib.] 3.17.1) has become a love as fevered (*fervida cura*, [Tib.] 3.18.1) as her own:

> Ne tibi sim, mea lux, aeque iam fervida cura
> ac videor paucos ante fuisse dies,
> si quicquam tota conmisi stulta iuventa,
> cuius me fatear paenituisse magis,
> hesterna quam te solum quod nocte reliqui,
> ardorem cupiens dissimulare meum.

My light, let me be no more such a blazing passion as I seem to have been a few days ago, if in the whole of my youth I foolishly did anything which I would confess I regretted more than leaving you alone yesterday night, because I desired to conceal my passion.

This poem brings the collection full circle with its reminiscence of the opening avowal of love in [Tib.] 3.13. There Sulpicia had asserted that the claims of *pudor* required the publication of her passion rather than its concealment, while here at the close of the sequence she professes to regret (*fatear paenituisse*, [Tib.] 3.18.4) not her sexual passion for Cerinthus but her attempt to conceal it. For readers familiar with the Roman narrative conventions that transform female sexual conduct into female sexual misconduct, Sulpicia's celebration of erotic passion is astounding. She takes witty delight in disrupting her reader's expectations concerning the foolish misdeed for which she chastizes herself ([Tib.] 3.18.3), for far from regretting the consummation of her union with Cerinthus, it is her flight from his bed in accordance with the proprieties of *pudor* that she decries. Like Dido after her union with Aeneas in the cave (*Aen.* 4.171), "Sulpicia" no longer thinks of keeping her love a secret. The conclusion of the sequence allows the love narrative to remain open-ended, since the poem reaffirms the poet-lover's passion for her beloved. At the same time, Sulpicia rejects Vergil's endorsement of Aeneas's mastery over emotion implied in the restoration of the epithet *pius* to the epic hero at this point in the narrative (*Aen.* 4.393). Sulpicia's final affirmation of her love leaves open the possibility of its continuation, a possibility that cannot be entertained in the *Aeneid*. Nonetheless, the conclusion of [Tib.] 3.18 subtly evokes the close of the Dido episode, for like Aeneas, whose nighttime departure from Carthage (*Aen.* 4.522, 4.554–83, 5.1–5) precipitates Dido's suicide at the end of *Aeneid* 4, "Sulpicia" abandons her lover by night and therewith brings the sequence to a close.

Throughout these six short elegies, Sulpicia repeatedly evokes the amatory relations of Dido and Aeneas by redeploying Vergilian diction and recombining Vergilian themes and imagery. Alternately adopting the perspectives of both Dido and Aeneas, Sulpicia constructs a multifaceted though distinctively female persona through which to invoke a complex of erotic desires, sensations, fears, and satisfactions. The evocation of the Dido episode in Sulpicia's elegiac poetry insistently contests the devaluation of women's unregulated sexuality so characteristic of Roman culture. Writing from within the framework of Augustan discourses about female sexuality, Sulpicia delicately yet continually presses at the limits of that framework. Her elegiac sequence reveals an acute sensitivity to the transgressive role of female sexuality in Roman society and literature, while it deftly articulates a far less restrictive vision of female passion. Sulpicia's poetry compels our recognition of tensions among competing ideological positions in the construction of sexuality and gender in Augustan Rome all too rarely glimpsed in the male-authored literature of her contemporaries.[35]

Notes

1. See, e.g., Galinsky 1981; Wallace-Hadrill 1982, 1985; Wiseman 1984; Stahl 1985; Purcell 1986; Zanker 1988; and Edwards 1993.

2. On *lex Iulia de adulteriis*, see Galinsky 1981; Wallace-Hadrill 1982, 1985; Gardner 1986; Treggiari 1991; and Edwards 1993: 34–62. On *lex Iulia de maritandis ordinibus* and *lex Papia Poppaea* (of 9 C.E.), see Gardner 1986 and Treggiari 1991.

3. See Gardner 1986: 121–32; Treggiari 1991.

4. On Livy, Vergil, and Horace, see, e.g., Galinsky 1981; Wiseman 1984; Joshel 1992: 119–21; Kennedy 1992: 42–46; Wyke 1992; and Edwards 1993: 42–47. On the elegists, see, e.g., Sullivan 1972; Hallett 1973; and Stahl 1985. For bibliography on all aspects of politics in Augustan poetry, see Little 1982.

5. The identification is accepted by K. F. Smith 1913; Bréguet 1946; Syme 1955; Davies 1973; Santirocco 1979; Currie 1983; Dettmer 1983; Fisher 1983; Hinds 1987; Lowe 1988; Snyder 1989; Lee 1990; Merriam 1990; Tränkle 1990; Butrica 1993; Hallett 1992a; and Parker 1994.

6. Messalla was deeply involved in the literary debates of Augustan Rome: see Sen. *Suas.* 2.20; Serv. ad *Aen.* 8.310; and cf. Davies 1973; Tränkle 1990: 299; and White 1993.

7. See Bréguet 1946: 40–43; Santirocco 1979: 237–38; Currie 1983: 1756–58; Hinds 1987; Roessel 1990; Yardley 1990; Butrica 1993; Wyke 1994: 114–15; and Parker 1994.

8. Noted in Santirocco 1979 and Yardley 1990. For methodological issues in intertextual interpretation, see Conte 1986: 23–95; and Thomas 1986.

9. As Judith Hallett points out to me, in correspondence, Augustus seems to have made no effort to regulate his own daughter Julia until her liaisons became politically dangerous, but he clearly wanted to give the impression of taking action on this front. On Augustus's attitude to Julia's sexual liaisons, see Hallett 1984, and Richlin 1992c.

10. On the Roman sociopolitical background of the Dido episode, see Monti 1981. All translations of Vergil's *Aeneid* are my own.

11. See Finley 1977; Richlin 1992f. The *locus classicus* is Livy 34.7.8–9. On women in Roman political life, see Bauman 1992; Hallett 1984, 1986, 1989b, 1990a, and 1992a; Purcell 1986; Richlin 1992c; Snyder 1989; and Wyke 1992.

12. On this association, see Edwards 1993: 169, 176–83.

13. On the valorization of the *univira* in Roman society, cf. the *Laudatio Turiae* (*ILS* 8393, pag. 1 [27–29]) and Prop. 4.11, with Hallett 1973 and 1986; on its relevance to Dido, see Pease 1935: 110–12, ad *Aen.* 4.27–29; and Austin 1955: 33, ad *Aen.* 4.29.

14. *Oxford Latin Dictionary* s.v. "coniunx" 1a. Austin concludes (1955: 30, ad

Aen. 4.21) that "Sychaeus *is* her lawful husband still" (his emphasis). In this context, Mercury's taunt that Aeneas "belongs to a wife," *uxorius* (*Aen.* 4.266), is richly ironic.

15. Vergil's readers have shown themselves very ready to accept the formulation of *fama* as it is applied to Dido here: see, e.g., Pease 1935: 38–39; Moles 1984 and 1987.

16. Cf. Kennedy 1992, Powell 1992a.

17. See Kennedy 1992: 40–47, quote at 47.

18. Kennedy (ibid.: 47), however, has drawn attention to the complicity of "Augustan" and "anti-Augustan" discourses in contributing to an "Augustan age" through their deployment of the same terms of reference; cf. Stahl 1985.

19. I cite the *elegidia Sulpiciae* from Lenz 1964, except [Tib.] 3.14.6, on which see Lenz 1964: 154. All translations of Sulpicia's elegies are my own.

20. Cf. Wyke 1994: 114. Hinds (1987: 42) has related this tendency to the project undertaken by the so-called *auctor de Sulpicia,* "who really does take it upon himself to tell the story of Sulpicia's love."

21. Throughout my discussion, I distinguish between the author of these six elegies, the historical Sulpicia, and the persona of the speaker in the poems, "Sulpicia."

22. For *nequitia,* see, e.g., Prop. 1.6.26 and Ov. *Am.* 2.1.2. For *pudor* in reference to women (not necessarily the poet's mistresses) in elegiac poetry, see, e.g., Tib. 1.3.83, 1.4.14; Prop. 2.9.18, 3.13.20, 3.13.50, 3.19.3; and Ov. *Am.* 1.5.8, 2.4.12. Propertius and Ovid infrequently invoke the claims of *pudor* in their elegiac poetry (Prop. 1.13.18, 2.24.4; Ov. *Am.* 1.2.32, 1.3.14), but not in programmatic contexts. On the difficulties of interpreting Propertius's claims regarding *pudor* at 2.24.4, Camps (1985: 162) is instructive. By contrast, K. B. Miller (1994: 24–33) has recently argued that Prop. 2.24.3–4 is not just a meaningful parallel to its programmatic occurrence in Sulpicia (because in both cases the publication of erotic verse conceivably threatens to shame the speaker), but is in fact the model to which *tandem venit amor* responds.

23. K. F. Smith (1913: 506) draws attention to the "intrusion of *fama* in the first distich [of Sulpicia's poem], which constitutes the real difficulty of the sentence, and which a man would probably not have used."

24. Cf. Hinds 1987: 43–44.

25. *Gremium* is properly "a person's lap or bosom" (*Oxford Latin Dictionary* s.v. "gremium" 1; cf. *Thesaurus linguae Latinae* 6.2.2319.12–13), but is closely associated with *sinus,* originally "the fold produced by the looping of a garment" (*Oxford Latin Dictionary* s.v. "sinus" 1), already in the late Republic and early Empire: see, e.g., *Rhet. Her.* 4.51; Cic. *Cael.* 59, *Pis.* 91; Ov. *Fast.* 4.436; *Epicedion Drusi* 115; Tac. *Dial.* 28.4.

26. On *gremium* as a synonym for *sinus,* see *Thesaurus linguae Latinae* 6.2.2319.12–76. Vergil deploys *gremium* and *sinus* interchangeably in the *Aeneid:* thus, Venus carries Ascanius off to the Idalian temple precinct in the embrace of her *gremium* (*Aen.* 1.692–93), but Anna comforts the dying Dido in the embrace of her *sinus* (*Aen.* 4.686).

27. See Hinds 1983 on the intertextual diffusion of the Gallan passage in Augustan poetry.

28. Propertius often comments on the mutual worth of other pairs of lovers: see Prop. 1.13.29, 1.13.34, 2.9.4, 3.12.16. Tibullus once expresses a desire for mutual love (1.2.63–64), but eschews Gallan diction. Both Propertius and Tibullus frequently portray the poet-lover's relations with his beloved within the framework of *servitium amoris*, as, e.g., in Prop. 1.4.4, 1.5.19, 1.12.18; Tib. 1.4.40, 2.3.30, 4.1. On *servitium amoris*, see Lyne 1979.

29. For similarities between Dido and Aeneas, see Pöschl 1962: 69–71; Hallett 1989b: 68–69.

30. Judith Hallett points out to me, in correspondence, that there may also be an Iliadic resonance in both the Vergilian and the Sulpician scenes. Although Aphrodite does not drop Paris into Helen's lap in *Iliad* 3, she removes him from the battlefield, drops him into his bedchamber, and brings Helen to him for a rendezvous, even setting up a chair for her.

31. On the difficulties of interpretation in the final couplet, see Lowe 1988: 200–201.

32. Cf. K. F. Smith 1913: 513; Santirocco 1979: 232–33; Hinds 1987: 42; and Snyder 1989: 133.

33. Cf. Santirocco 1979: 233. On *pietas* in the Aeneid, see Pöschl 1962.

34. *Pium*, Catull. 76.2; *pro pietate mea*, Catull. 76.26.

35. Cf. Hallett 1990b and 1992a.

BIBLIOGRAPHY

Abbreviations of ancient works are those used in N.G.L. Hammond and H. H. Scullard, eds., *Oxford Classical Dictionary*, 2d ed. (Oxford, 1970).

Adams, J. N. 1982. *The Latin Sexual Vocabulary*. Baltimore.

Adler, E. 1981. *Catullan Self-Revelation*. New York.

Ahl, F. 1984. "The Art of Safe Criticism in Greece and Rome." *American Journal of Philology* 102: 174–208.

Alfonsi, L. 1945. "L'amore-amicizia negli elegiaci latini." *Aevum* 19: 372–78.

Anderson, W. S. 1970. "*Lascivia* vs. *ira*: Martial and Juvenal." *California Studies in Classical Antiquity* 5: 1–34.

Arkins, B. 1982. *Sexuality in Catullus*. Altertumswissenschaftliche Texte und Studien 8. Hildesheim.

Armstrong, D. 1989. *Horace*. New Haven, Conn.

Arthur, M. B. 1982. "Cultural Strategies in Hesiod's *Theogony*: Law, Family, Society." *Arethusa* 15: 63–82.

Astin, A. 1978. *Cato the Censor*. Oxford.

Austin, R. G., ed. 1955. *P. Vergili Maronis Aeneidos, liber quartus*. Oxford.

Babcock, B. 1978. *The Reversible World: Symbolic Inversion in Art and Society*. Ithaca, N.Y.

Baca, A. R. 1971. "Ovid's Epistle from Sappho to Phaon (Heroides 15)." *Transactions and Proceedings of the American Philological Association* 102: 29–38.

Baehrens, A., ed. 1885. *Catulli Veronensis liber*. 2 vols. Leipzig.

Bagg, R. 1965. "Some Versions of Lyric Impasse in Shakespeare and Catullus." *Arion* 4: 64–95.

Bailey, C., ed. 1947. *Titi Lucreti Cari, De rerum natura, libri sex*. 3 vols. Oxford.

Bakhtin, M. 1984. *Rabelais and His World*. Trans. H. Iswolsky. Bloomington, Ind.

Bal, M. 1984. "The Rhetoric of Subjectivity." *Poetics Today* 5.2: 337–76.

Baldwin, B. 1972. "Women in Tacitus." *Prudentia* 4: 83–101.

Barton, C. A. 1993. *The Sorrows of the Ancient Romans: The Gladiator and the Monster*. Princeton.

———. 1994. "All Things Beseem the Victor: Paradoxes of Masculinity in Early Imperial Rome." In R. C. Trexler, ed., *Gender Rhetorics*, 83–92. Binghamton, N.Y.

Bartsch, S. 1994. *Actors in the Audience: Theatricality and Doublespeak from Nero to Hadrian*. Cambridge, Mass.

Baskin, J. R., ed. 1991. *Jewish Women in Historical Perspective*. Detroit.

Bauman, R. A. 1992. *Women and Politics in Ancient Rome*. London.

Beagon, M. 1992. *Roman Nature: The Thought of Pliny the Elder*. Oxford.

Benario, H. W. 1964. "Tacitus and the Principate." *Classical Journal* 60.1: 97–106.

Berger, A. 1953. *An Encyclopedic Dictionary of Roman Law*. Philadelphia.

Bing, P. 1988. *The Well-Read Muse: Present and Past in Callimachus and the Hellenistic Poets*. Göttingen.

Blassingame, J. W. 1979. *The Slave Community: Plantation Life in the Ante-Bellum South*. Oxford.

Blayney, J. 1986. "Theories of Conception in the Ancient World." In B. Rawson, ed., *The Family in Ancient Rome: New Perspectives*, 230–39. Ithaca, N.Y.

Bloom, A. 1994. "The Body Lies." *New Yorker*, 18 July: 38–49.

Boatwright, M. T. 1991. "The Imperial Women of the Early Second Century A.C." *American Journal of Philology* 112.4: 513–40.

Boedeker, D. D. 1974. *Aphrodite's Entry into Greek Epic*. Leiden.

Bollinger, T. 1969. *Theatralis licentia*. Winterthur, Switz.

Booth, A. 1991. "The Age for Reclining and Its Attendant Perils." In Slater 1991: 105–20.

Boston Women's Health Book Collective. 1992. *The New Our Bodies, Ourselves*. New York.

Boswell, J. 1980. *Christianity, Social Tolerance, and Homosexuality: Gay People in Western Europe from the Beginning of the Christian Era to the Fourteenth Century*. Chicago and London.

———. 1990a. "Concepts, Experience, and Sexuality." In E. Stein, ed., *Forms of Desire: Sexual Orientation and the Social Constructionist Controversy*, 133–73. New York and London.

———. 1990b. "Concepts, Experience, and Sexuality." In Konstan and Nussbaum 1990: 67–87. [A somewhat different and shorter version of Boswell 1990a.]

———. 1990c. *The Kindness of Strangers*. New York.

Boyarin, D. 1993. *Carnal Israel: Reading Sex in Talmudic Culture*. Berkeley.

Bradley, K. R. 1991. *Discovering the Roman Family: Studies in Roman Social History*. New York and Oxford.

Bramble, J. C. 1974. *Persius and the Programmatic Satire*. Cambridge.

Bréguet, E. 1946. *Le roman de Sulpicia*. Geneva.

Bremmer, J. 1992. "Walking, Standing, and Sitting in Ancient Greek Culture." In J. Bremmer and H. Roodenburg, eds., *A Cultural History of Gesture*, 15–35. Ithaca, N.Y.

Brontë, C. [1847] 1984. *Jane Eyre*. New York.

Brooks, P. 1985. *Reading for the Plot*. New York.

Brooten, B. J. 1985. "Paul's Views on the Nature of Women and Female Homo-eroticism." In C. W. Atkinson, C. H. Buchman, and M. Miles, eds., *Immaculate and Powerful: The Female in Sacred Image and Social Reality*, 61–87. Boston.

Brown, P. 1988. *The Body and Society: Men, Women, and Sexual Renunciation in Early Christianity*. New York.

Brown, R. D. 1987. *Lucretius on Love and Sex*. Leiden.

Bruère, R. T. 1954. "Tacitus and Pliny's *Panegyricus*." *Classical Philology* 49: 161–79.

Buckley, T., and A. Gottlieb. 1988a. "A Critical Appraisal of Theories of Menstrual Symbolism." In Buckley and Gottleib 1988b: 3–50.

———, eds. 1988b. *Blood Magic*. Berkeley.

Burkert, W. 1979. *Structure and History in Greek Mythology and Ritual*. Berkeley and Los Angeles.

———. 1983. *Homo Necans*. Trans. P. Bing. Berkeley and Los Angeles. (Originally published as *Homo Necans* [Berlin, 1972]).

———. 1991. "Oriental Symposia: Contrasts and Parallels." In Slater 1991: 7–24.

Butler, J. 1990. *Gender Trouble: Feminism and the Subversion of Identity*. New York and London.

Butrica, J. 1993. "Lygdamus, Nephew of Messalla?" *Liverpool Classical Monthly* 18: 51–53.

Bynum, C. W. 1987. *Holy Feast and Holy Fast*. Berkeley.

Cahoon, L. 1988. "The Bed as Battlefield: Erotic Conquest and Military Metaphor in Ovid's *Amores*." *Transactions of the American Philological Association* 118: 293–307.

Cairns, F. 1972. *Generic Composition in Greek and Roman Poetry*. Edinburgh.

———. 1983. "Propertius 1.4 and 1.5 and the 'Gallus' of the Monobiblos." *Papers of the Liverpool Latin Seminar* 4: 61–103.

Cameron, A. 1976. *Circus Factions: Blues and Greens at Rome and Byzantium*. Oxford.

———. 1995. *Callimachus and His Critics*. Princeton.

Camps, W. A., ed. 1985. *Propertius, Elegies Book II*. Rpt. Bristol.

Cantarella, E. 1988. *Secondo natura: La bisessulatità nel mondo antico*. Rome.

———. 1992. *Bisexuality in the Ancient World*. Trans. C. Ó. Cuilleanáin. New Haven, Conn., and London.

Caplan, P., ed. 1987. *The Cultural Construction of Sexuality*. London.

Carby, H. V. 1987. *Reconstructing Womanhood*. New York.

Carrier, J. M. 1980. "Homosexual Behavior in Cross-Cultural Perspective." In J. Marmor, ed., *Homosexual Behavior: A Modern Reappraisal*, 100–122. New York.

———. 1995. "Mexican Male Bisexuality." In F. Klein and T. J. Wolf, eds., *Bisexualities: Theory and Practice*, 75–85. New York and London.

Carson, A. 1990. "Putting Her in Her Place: Woman, Dirt, and Desire." In Halperin, Winkler, and Zeitlin 1990a: 135–69.

Cassio, A. C. 1983. "Post-Classical Lesbiai." *Classical Quarterly* 33: 296.

Cèbe, J.-P., ed. 1977. *Varron, Satires Ménippées*. Vol. 4. Collection de L'École française de Rome 9. Rome.

Chauncey, G., Jr. 1982–83. "From Sexual Inversion to Homosexuality: Medicine and the Changing Conceptualization of Female Deviance." *Salmagundi* 58–59: 114–46.

Chibnall, M. 1975. "Pliny's Natural History and the Middle Ages." In T. A. Dorey, ed., *Empire and Aftermath: Silver Latin II*, 57–78. London.

Clarke, J. R. 1991. *The Houses of Roman Italy, 100 B.C.–A.D. 250: Ritual, Space, and Decoration*. Berkeley.

Clavel-Lévêque, M. 1984. *L'Empire en jeux: Espace symbolique et pratique social dans le monde romain*. Paris.

Clay, J. S. 1995. "Catullus' *Attis* and the Black Hunter." *Quaderni Urbinati di cultura classica* 50.2: 143–55.

Cohen, D. 1991a. *Law, Sexuality, and Society*. Cambridge.

———. 1991b. "Sexuality, Violence, and the Athenian Law of Hubris." *Greece and Rome* 38.2: 171–88.

Cohen, D., and R. Saller. 1994. "Foucault on Sexuality in Greco-Roman Antiquity." In J. Goldstein, ed., *Foucault and the Writing of History*, 35–59. Cambridge, Mass., and Oxford.

Cohen, S.J.D. 1991. "Menstruants and the Sacred in Judaism and Christianity."

In S. B. Pomeroy, ed., *Women's History and Ancient History*, 273–99. Chapel Hill, N.C.

Cole, S. G. 1992. *"Gunaiki ou Themis*: Gender Difference in the Greek *Leges Sacrae*." *Helios* 19.1–2: 104–22.

Coleman, K. M. 1990. "Fatal Charades: Roman Executions Staged as Mythological Enactments." *Journal of Roman Studies* 80: 44–73.

Colin, J. 1952–53. "Juvénal, les baladins et les rétiaires d'après le MS. d'Oxford." *Atti della Accademia delle Scienze di Torino* 87–88: 315–86.

———. 1955. "Luxe oriental et parfums masculins dans la Rome alexandrine." *Revue belge de philologie et d'histoire* 33: 5–19.

———. 1956. "Les vendanges Dionysiaques et la légende de Messaline." *Les Études classiques* 24: 25–39.

Conte, G. B. 1986. *The Rhetoric of Imitation*. Trans., ed., and with a foreword by C. Segal. Ithaca N.Y. (Originally published in Italian as *Memoria dei poeti e sistema letterario: Catullo, Virgilio, Ovidio, Lucano* [Turin, 1974] and *Il genere e i suoi confini: Cinque studi sulla poesia di Virgilio* [Turin, 1980; enlarged edition 1984].)

Copley, F. O. 1956. *Exclusus Amator*. Madison, Wis.

Courtney, E. 1980. *A Commentary on the Satires of Juvenal*. London.

———, ed. 1993. *The Fragmentary Latin Poets*. Oxford.

Cowie, E. 1978. "Woman as Sign." *m/f* 1: 49–63.

Crawford, M., ed. 1996. *Roman Statutes*. 2 vols. London.

Crook, J. 1967. "A Study in Decoction." *Latomus* 26: 363–76.

Currie, H. M. 1983. "The Poems of Sulpicia." *Aufstieg und Niedergang der römischen Welt* 2.30.3: 1751–64.

Dahlburg, J.-T. 1994. "The Fight to Save India's Baby Girls." *Los Angeles Times*, 22 Feb.: A1, A14.

Dalla, D. 1987. Ubi venus mutatur: *Omosessualità e diritto nel mondo Romano*. Milan.

D'Arms, J. 1981. *Commerce and Social Standing in Ancient Rome*. Cambridge, Mass.

———. 1990. "The Roman *Convivium* and the Idea of Equality." In O. Murray, ed., *Sympotica: A Symposium on the* Symposium, 308–20. Oxford.

Darnton, R. 1984. *The Great Cat Massacre*. New York.

Davies, C. 1973. "Poetry in the 'Circle' of Messalla." *Greece and Rome* 20: 25–35.

Davis, G. 1975. "The Persona of Licymnia: A Revaluation of Horace, Carm. 2.12." *Philologus* 119: 70–83.

Davis, T. C. 1991. *Actresses as Working Women*. London.

Dean-Jones, L. 1992. "The Politics of Pleasure: Female Sexual Appetite in the Hippocratic Corpus." *Helios* 19.1–2: 72–91.

———. 1994. *Women's Bodies in Classical Greek Science*. Oxford.

de Certeau, M. 1988. *The Writing of History*. Trans. T. Conley. New York.

Degrassi, A., ed. 1963. *Inscriptiones Italiae*. Vol. 13.2. Rome.

DeJean, J. 1989. *Fictions of Sappho, 1546–1937*. Chicago.

Delaney, C. 1988. "Mortal Flow: Menstruation in Turkish Village Society." In Buckley and Gottlieb 1988b: 75–93.

de Lauretis, T. 1984. *Alice Doesn't*. Bloomington, Ind.

———. 1987. *Technologies of Gender*. Bloomington, Ind.

Deleuze, G., and F. Guattari. 1983. *Anti-Oedipus*. Trans. R. Hurley, M. Seem, and H. R. Lane. Minneapolis.

Detienne, M. 1977. *The Gardens of Adonis.* Trans. J. Lloyd. Atlantic Highlands, N.J.

Detienne, M., and J.-P. Vernant. 1978. *Cunning Intelligence in Greek Culture and Society.* Trans. J. Lloyd. Atlantic Highlands, N.J.

Dettmer, H. 1983. "The 'Corpus Tibullianum' (1974–1980)." *Aufstieg und Niedergang der römischen Welt* 2.30.3: 1962–75.

De Vivo, A. 1980. *Tacito e Claudio: Storia e codificazione letteraria.* Naples.

Dickison, S. 1977. "Claudius: Saturnalicius Princeps." *Latomus* 36: 634–47.

Dixon, S. 1983. "A Family Business: Women's Role in Patronage and Politics at Rome, 80–44 B.C." *Classica et mediaevalia* 34: 91–112.

———. 1988. *The Roman Mother.* Norman, Okla.

———. 1992. *The Roman Family.* Baltimore.

Dorey, T. A. 1969. "'Agricola' and 'Germania.'" In T. A. Dorey, ed., *Tacitus,* 1–18. London.

Dörrie, H., ed. 1971. *P. Ovidii Nasonis: Epistulae Heroidum.* Berlin and New York.

Douglas, M. [1966] 1984. *Purity and Danger.* London.

Dover, K. J. 1978. *Greek Homosexuality.* London. (Rev. ed., with a new afterword, Cambridge, Mass., 1989).

———. 1984. "Classical Greek Attitudes to Sexual Behaviour." In J. Peradotto and J. P. Sullivan, eds., *Women in the Ancient World: The* Arethusa *Papers,* 143–57. Albany, N.Y.

Drabkin, I. E., ed. and trans. 1950. *Caelius Aurelianus: On Acute Diseases and On Chronic Diseases.* Chicago.

duBois, P. 1982. *Centaurs and Amazons.* Ann Arbor.

———. 1988. *Sowing the Body.* Chicago.

———. 1995. *Sappho Is Burning.* Chicago and London.

Duclos, G. S. 1976. "Catullus 11: Atque in perpetuum, Lesbia, ave atque vale." *Arethusa* 9: 77–89.

Dudley, D. R. 1968. *The World of Tacitus.* London.

Dunbabin, K.M.D., and M. W. Dickie. 1983. "*Invida Rumpantur Pectora*: The Iconography of Phthonos/Invidia in Graeco-Roman Art." *Jahrbuch für Antike und Christentum* 26: 7–37.

Dupont, F. 1977. "La Scène juridique." *Communications* 26: 62–77.

———. 1985. *L'Acteur-roi.* Paris.

Dynes, W. R., and S. Donaldson, eds. 1992. *Homosexuality in the Ancient World.* New York.

Dyson, M. 1973. "Catullus 8 and 76." *Classical Quarterly* 23: 127–43.

Earl, D. 1967. *The Moral and Political Tradition of Rome.* Ithaca, N.Y.

Edwards, C. 1993. *The Politics of Immorality in Ancient Rome.* Cambridge.

———. 1994. "Beware of Imitations: Theatre and the Subversion of Imperial Identity." In J. Elsner and J. Masters, eds., *Reflections of Nero: Culture, History and Representation,* 83–97. London.

Ehrenreich, B., and D. English. 1973. *Witches, Midwives, and Nurses: A History of Women Healers.* New York.

Elder, J. P. 1947. "Catullus' *Attis.*" *American Journal of Philology* 68: 394–403.

Esser, D. 1976. *Untersuchungen zu den Odenschlussen bei Horaz.* Beiträge zur klassischen Philologie 77. Meisenheim an Glan.

Fantham, E. 1991. "*Stuprum*: Public Attitudes and Penalities for Sexual Offenses in Republican Rome." *Échos du monde classique* 35: 267–91.

Faraone, C. A. 1992. "Sex and Power: Male-Targetting Aphrodisiacs in the Greek Magical Tradition." *Helios* 19.1–2: 92–103.

Ferguson, A. 1990. "Is There a Lesbian Culture?" In J. Allen, ed., *Lesbian Philosophies and Cultures*, 63–88. Albany, N.Y.

———. 1991. *Sexual Democracy: Woman, Oppression, and Revolution*. Boulder, Colo., San Francisco, and Oxford.

Finley, M. I. 1977. "The Silent Women of Rome." In *Aspects of Antiquity: Discoveries and Controversies*, 2d ed., 129–42. Harmondsworth, England.

———. 1985. *The Ancient Economy*. London.

Fisher, J. M. 1983. "The Life and Work of Tibullus." *Aufstieg und Niedergang der römischen Welt* 2.30.3: 1924–61.

Fitzgerald, W. 1988. "Power and Impotence in Horace's Epodes." *Ramus* 17: 176–91.

———. 1992. "Catullus and the Reader: The Erotics of Poetry." *Arethusa* 25: 419–43.

———. 1995. *Catullan Provocations: Lyric Poetry and the Drama of Position*. Berkeley, Los Angeles, and London.

Foerster, R., ed. 1893. *Scriptores physiognomonici*. 2 vols. Leipzig.

Fordyce, C. P., ed. 1961. *Catullus*. Oxford.

Forsyth, P. Y. 1976. "Catullus: The Mythic Persona." *Latomus* 35: 555–66.

———. 1991. "The Thematic Unity of Catullus 11." *Classical World* 84.6: 457–64.

Foucault, M. 1976. *La Volenté de savoir*. Vol. 1, *Histoire de la sexualité*. Paris.

———. 1980. *The History of Sexuality*. Vol. 1, *An Introduction*. Trans. R. Hurley. New York. (1st American ed., New York, 1978.)

———. 1985. *The Use of Pleasure*. Vol. 2, *The History of Sexuality*. Trans. R. Hurley. New York.

———. 1986. *The Care of the Self*. Vol. 3, *The History of Sexuality*. Trans. R. Hurley. New York.

Frank, T. 1925. "On Augustus' References to Horace." *Classical Philology* 20: 26–30.

Fredrick, D. 1991. "*Haec scribentis imago*: Ovid's Epistolary Tableaux." Paper presented at the annual meeting of the Classical Association of the Middle West and South, April 10–13, 1991, Ontario, Canada.

———. 1995. "Beyond the Atrium to Ariadne: Erotic Painting and Visual Pleasure in the Roman House." *Classical Antiquity* 14.2: 266–87.

French, R., and F. Greenaway, eds. 1986. *Science in the Early Roman Empire: Pliny the Elder, His Sources and Influence*. London and Sydney.

French, V. 1986. "Midwives and Maternity Care in the Greco-Roman World." *Helios* 13.2: 69–84.

Fry, P. 1985. "Male Homosexuality and Spirit Possession in Brazil." *Journal of Homosexuality* 11.3–4: 137–53.

Galinsky, G. K. 1981. "Augustus' Legislation on Morals and Marriage." *Philologus* 125: 126–44.

Gamel, M.-K. 1989. "*Non sine caede*: Abortion Politics and Poetics in Ovid's *Amores*." *Helios* 16.2: 183–206.

Garber, M. 1991. *Vested Interests: Cross-Dressing and Cultural Anxiety*. New York.

Gardner, J. F. 1986. *Women in Roman Law and Society*. Bloomington and Indianapolis, Ind.

———. 1993. *Being a Roman Citizen*. London.

Garlick, B., S. Dixon, and P. Allen, eds. 1992. *Stereotypes of Women in Power*. New York.

Garnsey, P. 1968. "Trajan's *Alimenta*: Some Problems." *Historia* 17: 367–81.

———. 1970. *Social Status and Legal Privilege in the Roman Empire*. Oxford.

Garnsey, P., and R. Saller. 1987. *The Roman Empire: Economy, Society and Culture*. Berkeley and Los Angeles.

Geffcken, K. 1973. *Comedy in the* pro Caelio. *Mnemosyne* suppl. 30. Lyons.

Genovese, E. N. 1970. "Attis and Lesbia: Catullus' Attis Poem as a Symbolic Reflection of the Lesbia Cycle." Diss., Ohio State University.

Giacomelli, A. 1980. "Aphrodite and After." *Phoenix* 34: 1–19.

Gilmore, D. D. 1990. *Manhood in the Making*. New Haven, Conn.

Giovannini, A. 1993. "Greek Cities and Greek Commonwealth." In A. Bulloch, E. S. Gruen, A. A. Long, and A. Stewart, eds., *Images and Ideologies: Self-Definition in the Hellenistic World*, 265–86. Berkeley and Los Angeles.

Gleason, M. 1990. "The Semiotics of Gender: Physiognomy and Self-Fashioning in the Second Century C.E." In Halperin, Winkler, and Zeitlin 1990a: 389–415. Now incorporated into Gleason 1995: ch. 3.

———. 1995. *Making Men: Sophists and Self-Presentation in Ancient Rome*. Princeton.

Gold, B. K. 1993a. "'But Ariadne Was Never There in the First Place': Finding the Female in Roman Poetry." In Rabinowitz and Richlin 1993: 75–101.

———. 1993b. "The 'Master Mistress' of My Passion: The Lady as Patron in Ancient and Renaissance Literature." In M. DeForest, ed., *Woman's Power, Man's Game: Essays on Classical Antiquity in Honor of Joy K. King*, 279–304. Wauconda, Ill.

Golden, M. 1984. "Slavery and Homosexuality at Athens." *Phoenix* 38: 308–24.

———. 1985. "*Pais*, 'Child' and 'Slave'." *L'Antiquité classique* 54: 91–104.

———. 1991. "Thirteen Years of Homosexuality and Other Recent Works on Sex, Gender and the Body in Ancient Greece." *Échos du monde classique* 35: 327–40.

———. 1992. "The Uses of Cross-Cultural Comparison in Ancient Social History." *Échos du monde classique* 36: 309–31.

Goldhill, S. 1995. *Foucault's Virginity*. Cambridge.

Gonfroy, F. 1978. "Homosexualité et idéologie esclavagiste chez Cicéron." *Dialogues d'histoire ancienne* 4: 219–62.

Gordon, L. 1986. "What's New in Women's History?" In T. de Lauretis, ed., *Feminist Studies/Critical Studies*, 20–30. Bloomington, Ind.

Gourevitch, D. 1984. *Le Mal d'être femme: La Femme et la médecine dans la Rome antique*. Paris.

Gowers, E. 1993. *The Loaded Table: Representations of Food in Roman Literature*. Oxford.

Grant, M., and R. Kitzinger, eds. 1988. *Civilization of the Ancient Mediterranean: Greece and Rome*. 2 vols. New York.

Graves, R. [1934] 1989. *I, Claudius*. New York.

———. [1935] 1989. *Claudius the God*. New York.

Green, M. 1989. "Women's Medical Practice and Health Care in Medieval Europe." *Signs* 14.2: 434–73.

———. 1992. "Conception, Gestation, and the Origin of Female Nature in the *Corpus Hippocraticum*." *Helios* 19.1–2: 31–71.

Greenberg, D. F. 1988. *The Construction of Homosexuality*. Chicago.

Greenblatt, S. 1987. "Capitalist Culture and the Circulatory System." In M. Krieger, ed., *The Aims of Representation*, 257–73. New York.

Greene, E. 1994. "Apostrophe and Women's Erotics in the Poetry of Sappho." *Transactions of the American Philological Association* 124: 41–56.

———. 1996. "Sappho, Foucault, and Women's Erotics." *Arethusa* 29: 1–14.

Greenidge, A.J.H. 1894. *Infamia: Its Place in Roman Public and Private Law*. Oxford. (Rpt., Darmstadt, 1977.)

Griffin, J. 1976. "Augustan Poetry and the Life of Luxury." *Journal of Roman Studies* 66: 87–105. (Rpt. in Griffin 1986: 1–31.)

———. 1984. "Augustus and the Poets: 'Caesar qui cogere posset'." In F. Millar and E. Segal, eds., *Caesar Augustus: Seven Aspects*, 189–218. Oxford.

———. 1986. *Latin Poets and Roman Life*. Chapel Hill, N.C.

Griffin, M. T. 1982. "The Lyons Tablet and Tacitean Hindsight." *Classical Quarterly* 32.2: 404–18.

Griffith, G. T. 1935. *Mercenaries in the Hellenistic World*. Cambridge.

Gutzwiller, K. J. 1992. "Callimachus' *Lock of Berenice*: Fantasy, Romance, and Propaganda." *American Journal of Philology* 113: 359–85.

Gutzwiller, K. J., and A. N. Michelini. 1991. "Women and Other Strangers: Feminist Perspectives in Classical Literature." In J. E. Hartman and E. Messer-Dow, eds., *(En)Gendering Knowledge*, 66–84. Knoxville, Tenn.

Habinek, T. N. 1992. "An Aristocracy of Virtue: Seneca on the Beginnings of Wisdom." In F. M. Dunn and T. Cole, eds., *Beginnings in Classical Literature*, 187–203. *Yale Classical Studies* 29. Cambridge.

Hallett, J. P. 1973. "The Role of Women in Roman Elegy: Counter-Cultural Feminism." *Arethusa* 6: 103–24.

———. 1977. "*Perusinae Glandes* and the Changing Image of Augustus." *American Journal of Ancient History* 2: 151–71.

———. 1979. "Sappho in Her Social Context: Sense and Sensuality." *Signs* 4: 447–64.

———. 1982. "Beloved Cleis." *Quaderni Urbinati di cultura classica*, n.s. 10: 22–31.

———. 1983. Review of Adams 1982. *Liverpool Classical Monthly* 8.7 (July): 102–8.

———. 1984. *Fathers and Daughters in Roman Society*. Princeton.

———. 1986. "Queens, Princeps and Women of the Augustan Elite: Propertius' Cornelia-Elegy and the Res Gestae Divi Augusti." In R. Winkes, ed., *The Age of Augustus*, 73–88. Providence, R.I. and Louvaine-la-Neuve.

———. 1988. "Roman Attitudes Toward Sex." In Grant and Kitzinger 1988: 1265–78.

———. 1989a. "Female Homoeroticism and the Denial of Roman Reality in Latin Literature." *Yale Journal of Criticism* 3: 209–27. (Rpt. in Dynes and Donaldson 1992: 179–97.)

———. 1989b. "Woman as *Same* and *Other* in Classical Roman Elite." *Helios* 16: 59–78.

———. 1990a. "Perspectives on Roman Women." In R. Mellor, ed., *From Augustus to Nero: The First Dynasty of Imperial Rome*, 132–44. East Lansing, Mich.

———. 1990b. "Contextualizing the Text: The Journey to Ovid." *Helios* 17: 187–95.

———. 1992a. "Heeding Our Native Informants: The Uses of Latin Literary Texts in Recovering Elite Roman Attitudes Toward Age, Gender and Social Status." *Échos du monde classique* 11.3: 333–55.

———. 1992b. "Martial's Sulpicia and Propertius' Cynthia." *Classical World* 86.2: 99–123.

———. 1993. "Feminist Theory, Historical Periods, Literary Canons, and the Study of Greco-Roman Antiquity." In Rabinowitz and Richlin 1993: 44–72.

Halperin, D. M. 1986. "One Hundred Years of Homosexuality." *Diacritics* 16.2: 34–45.

———. 1990a. *One Hundred Years of Homosexuality*. New York and London.

———. 1990b. "One Hundred Years of Homosexuality." In Halperin 1990a: 15–40.

Halperin, D. M., J. J. Winkler, and F. I. Zeitlin, eds. 1990a. *Before Sexuality: The Construction of Erotic Experience in the Ancient Greek World*. Princeton.

———. 1990b. "Introduction." In Halperin, Winkler, and Zeitlin 1990a: 3–20.

Hanson, A. E. 1990. "The Medical Writers' Woman." In Halperin, Winkler, and Zeitlin 1990a: 309–38.

———. 1992. "Conception, Gestation, and the Origin of Female Nature in the *corpus Hippocraticum*." *Helios* 19.1–2: 31–71.

Hanson, V. D. 1991a. "The Future of Greek Military History." In Hanson 1991b: 253–56.

———, ed. 1991b. *Hoplites: The Classical Greek Battle Experience*. London.

Harkins, P. W. 1959. "Autoallegory in Catullus 63 and 64." *Transactions and Proceedings of the American Philological Association* 90: 102–16.

Haupt, M. 1871. "Varia." *Hermes* 5: 32–34.

Havelock, E. A. 1939. *The Lyric Genius of Catullus*. Oxford.

Hawley, R., and B. Levick, eds. 1995. *Women in Antiquity: New Assessments*. London and New York.

Heller, W. 1993. "The Queen as King: Refashioning Semiramide for Seicento Venice." *Cambridge Opera Journal* 5.2: 1–22.

Henderson, J. 1975. *The Maculate Muse*. New Haven, Conn. and London.

Henderson, J.G.W. 1989. "Not 'Women in Roman Satire' but 'When Satire writes "Woman".'" In S. H. Braund, ed., *Satire and Society in Ancient Rome*, 89–125. Exeter.

Herdt, G. [1981] 1994. *Guardians of the Flutes: Idioms of Masculinity*. Chicago.

———, ed. 1982. *Rituals of Manhood: Male Initiation in Papua, New Guinea*. Berkeley and Los Angeles.

———, ed. 1984. *Ritualized Homosexuality in Melanesia*. Berkeley and Los Angeles.

Herter, H. 1960. "Die Soziologie der antike Prostitution im Lichte des heidnischen und christlichen Schriftums." *Jahrbuch für Antike und Christentum* 3: 70–111.

Hill, J. W. 1983. "Vivaldi's 'Ottone in villa': A Study in Musical Drama." In J. W. Hill, ed., Domenico Lalli and Antonio Vivaldi, *Ottone in villa*, ix–xlvi. Drammaturgia Musicale Veneta, vol. 12. Milan.

Hillard, T. 1989. "Republican Politics, Women, and the Evidence." *Helios* 16: 165–82.

———. 1992. "On the Stage, Behind the Curtain: Images of Politically Active Women in the Late Roman Republic." In Garlick, Dixon, and Allen 1992: 37–64.

Hinds, S. 1983. "*Carmina digna*: Gallus, P. Qasr Ibrim 6–7 Metamorphosed." *Papers of the Liverpool Latin Seminar* 4: 43–54.

———. 1987. "The Poetess and the Reader: Further Steps toward Sulpicia." *Hermathena* 143: 29–46.

Holland, D., and N. Quinn, eds. 1987. *Cultural Models in Language and Thought*. Cambridge.

Hopkins, M. K. 1965. "Contraception in the Roman Empire." *Comparative Studies in Society and History* 8: 124–51.

———. 1983. *Death and Renewal*. Cambridge.

Hopkinson, N. 1988. *A Hellenistic Anthology*. Cambridge.

Horowitz, M. C. 1976. "Aristotle and Woman." *Journal of the History of Biology* 9: 183–213.

Housman, A. E. 1904. "*Tunica retiarii*." *Classical Review* 18: 395–98.

———. 1931. "Praefanda." *Hermes* 66: 402–12. (=Housman 1972: 1175–84.)

———. 1972. *The Classical Papers of A. E. Housman*. Ed. J. Diggle and F.R.D. Goodyear. Vol. 3. Cambridge.

Hunt, L. 1991. "The Many Bodies of Marie Antoinette: Political Pornography and the Problem of the Feminine in the French Revolution." In L. Hunt, ed., *Eroticism and the Body Politic*, 108–30. Baltimore.

Hunter, N. D. 1986. "The Pornography Debate in Context: A Chronology." In F.A.C.T. Book Committee, ed., *Caught Looking*, 26–29. New York.

Hutchinson, G. O. 1988. *Hellenistic Poetry*. Oxford.

Irigaray, L. 1985a. *Speculum of the Other Woman*. Trans. G. G. Gill. Ithaca, N.Y. (Originally published as *Speculum de l'autre femme* [Paris, 1974].)

———. 1985b. *This Sex Which Is Not One*. Trans. C. Porter. Ithaca, N.Y. (Originally published as *Ce Sexe qui n'en est pas un* [Paris, 1977].)

Jacobson, H. 1974. *Ovid's Heroides*. Princeton.

Janan, M. 1991. Review of Halperin 1990a. *Women's Classical Caucus Newsletter* 17.2: 40–43.

———. 1994. "*When the Lamp Is Shattered*": Desire and Narrative in Catullus. Carbondale and Edwardsville, Ill.

Jocelyn, H. D. 1980. "A Greek Indecency and Its Students." *Proceedings of the Cambridge Philological Society* 206: 12–66.

Johns, C. 1982. *Sex or Symbol? Erotic Images of Greece and Rome*. Austin, Tex.

Johnston, S. I. 1995. "Defining the Dreadful: Remarks on the Child-Killing Demon." In M. Meyer and P. Mirecki, eds., *Ancient Magic and Ritual Power*, 361–89. Leyden.

Joshel, S. 1986. "Nurturing the Master's Child: Slavery and the Roman Child-Nurse." *Signs* 12: 3–22.

———. 1992. "The Body Female and the Body Politic: Livy's Lucretia and Verginia." In Richlin 1992d: 112–30.

Kampen, N. B. 1991. "Between Public and Private: Women as Historical Subjects in Roman Art." In S. B. Pomeroy, ed., *Women's History and Ancient History*, 218–48. Chapel Hill, N.C. and London.

Kaplan, M. 1979. "*Agrippina semper atrox*: A Study in Tacitus' Characterization of Women." In C. Deroux, ed., *Studies in Latin Literature and Roman History*, 1: 410–17. Collection *Latomus* 164. Bruxelles.

Kaser, M. 1956. "*Infamia* und *ignominia* in den römischen Rechtsquellen." *Zeitschrift der Savigny-Stiftung für Rechtsgeschichte*, romanistische Abteilung 73: 220–78.

Katz, J. 1995. *The Invention of Heterosexuality*. New York.

Katz, M. A. 1989. "Sexuality and the Body in Ancient Greece." *Métis* 4.1: 155–79.

Kauffman, L. 1986. *Discourses of Desire*. Ithaca, N.Y.

Keitel, E. 1978. "The Role of Parthia and Armenia in Tacitus *Annals* 11 and 12." *American Journal of Philology* 99: 462–73.

Keith, A. M. 1994. "*Corpus eroticum*: Elegiac Poetics and Elegiac *puellae* in Ovid's *Amores*." *Classical World* 88.1: 27–40.

Kennedy, D. F. 1992. "'Augustan' and 'Anti-Augustan': Reflections on Terms of Reference." In Powell 1992b: 26–58.

———. 1993. *The Arts of Love: Five Studies in the Discourse of Roman Love Elegy*. Cambridge.

Kenney, E. J. 1982. "Appendix of Authors and Works: Publius Ovidius Naso." In E. J. Kenney and W. V. Clausen, eds., *The Cambridge History of Classical Literature*. Vol. 2.3, *The Age of Augustus*, 207–9. Cambridge.

Ker, W. 1968. *Martial: Epigrams*. 2 vols. Loeb Classical Library. Cambridge, Mass.

Kincaid, J. 1990. *Lucy*. Harmondsworth.

King, H. 1993. "Producing Woman: Hippocratic Gynaecology." In L. Archer, S. Fischler, and M. Wyke, eds., *Women in Ancient Societies*, 102–14. London.

———. 1995. "Self-Help, Self-Knowledge: In Search of the Patient in Hippocratic Gynaecology." In Hawley and Levick 1995: 135–48.

King, J. 1980. "The Two Galluses of Propertius' Monobiblos." *Philologus* 124: 212–30.

Kinsey, A. C., W. B. Pomeroy, and C. E. Martin. 1948. *Sexual Behavior in the Human Male*. Philadelphia.

Klapisch-Zuber, C. 1985. *Women, Family, and Ritual in Renaissance Italy*. Trans. L. G. Cochrane. Chicago.

Knox, P. E., ed. 1995. *Ovid, Heroides: Select Epistles*. Cambridge.

Konstan, D. 1977. *Catullus' Indictment of Rome: The Meaning of Catullus 64*. Amsterdam.

———. 1991. "The Death of Argus, or What Stories Do: Audience Response in Ancient Fiction and Theory." *Helios* 18: 15–30.

———. 1993. "Sexuality and Power in Juvenal's Second Satire." *Liverpool Classical Monthly* 18.1: 12–14.

———. 1994. *Sexual Symmetry: Love in the Ancient Novel and Related Genres*. Princeton.

Konstan, D., and M. Nussbaum, eds. 1990. *Sexuality in Greek and Roman Society.* Special issue, *differences* 2.1.

Krenkel, W. 1980. *"Fellatio* and *irrumatio." Wissenschaftliche Zeitschrift der Wilhelm-Pieck-Universität, Rostock* 29: 77–88.

———. 1988. "Prostitution." In Grant and Kitzinger 1988: 1291–97.

Kroll, W. 1924. "Lesbische Liebe." In A. Pauly and G. Wissowa, eds., *Real-Encyclopaedie der klassichen Altertumswissenschaft,* 12.2, cols. 2100–2102.

———. 1933. *Die Kultur der ciceronische Zeit.* Leipzig.

———, ed. 1968. *C. Valerius Catullus.* 5th ed. Stuttgart.

Labate, M. 1984. *L'arte di farsi amare.* Pisa.

Lacey, W. K. 1986. *"Patria potestas."* In B. Rawson, ed., *The Family in Ancient Rome,* 121–44. Ithaca, N.Y.

Lancaster, R. 1988. "Subject Honor and Object Shame: The Construction of Male Homosexuality and Stigma in Nicaragua." *Ethnology: An International Journal of Cultural and Social Anthropology* 28: 111–25.

Laqueur, T. 1990. *Making Sex: Body and Gender from the Greeks to Freud.* Cambridge, Mass.

Lardinois, A. 1989. "Lesbian Sappho and Sappho of Lesbos." In J. Bremmer, ed., *From Sappho to de Sade,* 15–35. London.

Lazenby, J. 1991. "The Killing Zone." In Hanson 1991b: 87–109.

Lebek, W. D. 1990. "Standeswürde und Berufsverbot unter Tiberius: das SC der Tabula Larinas." *Zeitschrift für Papyrologie und Epigraphik* 81: 37–96.

Lee, G. 1990. *Tibullus: Elegies.* 3d ed., revised in collaboration with R. Maltby. Leeds.

Lefkowitz, M., and M. B. Fant. 1992. *Women's Lives in Greece and Rome.* 2d ed. Baltimore.

Lenz, F. W., ed. 1964. *Albii Tibulli aliorumque carminum libri tres.* Leiden.

Levick, B. 1975. " 'Julians and Claudians.' " *Greece and Rome* 22: 29–38.

———. 1976. "The Fall of Julia the Younger." *Latomus* 35: 301–39.

———. 1978. "Antiquarian or Revolutionary? Claudius Caesar's Conception of His Principate." *American Journal of Philology* 99: 79–105.

———. 1983. "The Senatus Consultum from Larinum." *Journal of Roman Studies* 73: 97–115.

———. 1990. *Claudius.* New Haven, Conn.

Lilja, S. 1983. *Homosexuality in Republican and Augustan Rome.* Commentationes Humanarum Litterarum 74. Helsinki.

Lipking, L. 1988. *Abandoned Women and Poetic Tradition.* Chicago and London.

Little, D. A. 1982. "Politics in Augustan Poetry." *Aufstieg und Niedergang der römischen Welt* 2.30.1: 254–370.

Lloyd, G.E.R. 1966. *Polarity and Analogy.* Cambridge.

———. 1979. *Magic, Reason and Experience.* Cambridge.

———. 1983. *Science, Folklore and Ideology.* Cambridge.

Lombardo, S. 1989. *"Technopaegnia:* Hellenistic Pattern Poetry." *Temblor* 10: 200–204.

Lombardo, S., and P. Gordon. N.d. "Ovid's *Heroides:* A Translation." Unpublished manuscript.

Lombardo, S., and D. Rayor, trans. 1988. *Callimachus: Hymns, Epigrams, Select Fragments*. Baltimore.

Lombroso, C., and G. Ferrero. 1899. *The Female Offender*. New York.

Lowe, N. J. 1988. "Sulpicia's Syntax." *Classical Quarterly* 38: 193–205.

Lyne, R.O.A.M. 1979. "*Servitium amoris.*" *Classical Quarterly* 29: 117–30.

———. 1980. *The Latin Love Poets from Catullus to Horace*. Oxford.

McAlindon, D. 1956. "Senatorial Opposition to Claudius and Nero." *American Journal of Philology* 77.2: 113–32.

MacAlister, S. 1992. "Gender as Sign and Symbolism in Artemidoros' *Oneirokritika*: Social Aspirations and Anxieties." *Helios* 19: 140–60.

McDermott, E. A. 1982. "Horace, Maecenas, and Odes 2,17." *Hermes* 110: 211–28.

McDonald, A. H. 1944. "Rome and the Italian Confederation, 200–186 B.C." *Journal of Roman Studies* 33: 11–33.

McGinn, T.A.J. 1989. "The Taxation of Roman Prostitutes." *Helios* 16: 79–111.

———. Forthcoming. *Prostitution and Roman Society*. Ann Arbor: University of Michigan Press.

Macleod, C. W. 1974. "A Use of Myth in Ancient Poetry." *Classical Quarterly* 24: 82–93.

MacMullen, R. 1982. "Roman Attitudes Towards Greek Love." *Historia* 31: 484–502. Rpt. in Dynes and Donaldson 1992: 340–58.

McWhirter, D. P., S. A. Sanders, and J. M. Reinisch, eds. 1990. *Homosexuality/Heterosexuality: Concepts of Sexual Orientation*. New York.

Malamud, M. 1993. "Vandalising Epic." *Ramus* 22.2: 155–73.

Manfredini, A. 1985. "Qui commutant cum feminis vestem." *Revue internationale des droits de l'Antiquité* 32: 257–71.

Martin, K., and B. Voorhies. 1975. *The Female of the Species*. New York.

Martin, R. 1981. *Tacitus*. Berkeley and Los Angeles.

Mattingly, H. 1923. *Coins of the Roman Empire in the British Museum*. London.

Mattingly, H., and E. Sydenham. 1923. *Roman Imperial Coinage*. London.

Mehl, A. 1974. *Tacitus über Kaiser Claudius: Die Ereignisse am Hof*. Studia et Testimonia Antiqua 16. Munich.

Meiggs, R. 1973. *Roman Ostia*. 2d ed. Oxford.

Meise, E. 1969. *Untersuchungen zur Geschichte der Julisch-Claudischen Dynastie*. Vestigia, Bd. 10. Munich.

Merriam, C. U. 1990. "Some Notes on the Sulpicia Elegies." *Latomus* 49: 95–98.

Millar, F. 1984. "State and Subject: The Impact of Monarchy." In Millar and Segal 1984: 37–68.

———. [1977] 1992. *The Emperor in the Roman World*. Ithaca, N.Y.

Millar, F., and E. Segal, eds. 1984. *Caesar Augustus: Seven Aspects*. Oxford.

Miller, K. B. 1994. "Sulpicia's Love Elegies." M.A. thesis, University of Arizona.

Miller, P. A. 1988. "Catullus, *C.* 70: A Poem and Its Hypothesis." *Helios* 15: 127–32.

Moles, J. 1984. "Aristotle and Dido's *Hamartia.*" *Greece and Rome* 31: 48–54.

———. 1987. "The Tragedy and Guilt of Dido." In M. Whitby, P. Hardie, and M. Whitby, eds., *Homo Viator, Classical Essays for John Bramble*, 153–61. Bristol.

Momigliano, A. 1961. *Claudius: The Emperor and His Achievements*. Trans. W. D. Hogarth. New York.

Monaco, G. 1968. *Cicerone: L'excursus de ridiculis*. Palumbo.

Monti, R. C. 1981. *The Dido Episode and the Aeneid*. Leiden.

Moritz, L. A. 1967. "Well-Matched Lovers (Propertius 1.5)." *Classical Philology* 62: 106–8.

Mulroy, D. 1977–78. "An Interpretation of Catullus 11." *Classical World* 71: 237–47.

Mulvey, L. [1975] 1989. "Visual Pleasure and Narrative Cinema." In L. Mulvey, ed., *Visual and Other Pleasures*, 14–26. Bloomington, Ind. (Originally published in *Screen* 16.3: 6–18).

Murray, S. O. 1983. "Fuzzy Sets and Abominations." *Man*, n.s. 18: 396–99.

Myerowitz, M. 1992. "The Domestication of Desire: Ovid's *parva tabella* and the Theater of Love." In Richlin 1992d: 131–57.

Nagy, G. 1973. "Phaethon, Sappho's Phaon, and the White Rock of Leukas." *Harvard Studies in Classical Philology* 27: 137–77.

Näsström, B.-M. 1989. *The Abhorrence of Love: Studies in Rituals and Mystic Aspects in Catullus' Poem of Attis*. Uppsala.

Newman, J. K. 1990. *Roman Catullus and the Modification of the Alexandrian Sensibility*. Hildesheim.

Newton, E. 1984. "The Mythic Mannish Lesbian: Radclyffe Hall and the New Woman." *Signs* 9.4: 557–75.

Nicolet, C. 1980. *The World of the Citizen in Republican Rome*. London. (Trans. of *Le Metier de citoyen dans la Rome republicaine*.)

———. 1991. *Space, Geography, and Politics in the Early Roman Empire*. Ann Arbor, Mich.

Nisbet, R.G.M., ed. 1961. *Cicero: In Pisonem*. Oxford.

Nisbet, R.G.M., and M. Hubbard, eds. 1978. *A Commentary on Horace: Odes, Book 2*. Oxford.

Nugent, G. 1990. "This Sex Which Is Not One: De-Constructing Ovid's Hermaphrodite." In Konstan and Nussbaum 1990: 160–85.

———. 1992. "Vergil's 'Voice of the Women' in *Aeneid* V." *Arethusa* 25: 255–92.

Nutton, V. 1986. "The Perils of Patriotism: Pliny and Roman Medicine." In French and Greenaway 1986: 30–58.

Ober, J. 1991. "Hoplites and Obstacles." In Hanson 1991b: 173–96.

Oliensis, E. 1991. "Canidia, Canicula, and the Decorum of Horace's *Epodes*." *Arethusa* 24: 107–38.

Onians, R. 1951. *The Origins of European Thought*. Cambridge.

Ortner, S. B., and H. Whitehead. 1981. "Introduction: Accounting for Sexual Meanings." In S. B. Ortner and H. Whitehead, eds., *Sexual Meanings*, 1–27. Cambridge.

Otto, A. 1890. *Die Sprichwörter und sprichwörtlichen Redensarten der Römer*. Leipzig.

Page, D. 1955. *Sappho and Alcaeus: An Introduction to the Study of Ancient Lesbian Poetry*. Oxford.

Paglia, C. 1990. *Sexual Personae*. New Haven, Conn. and London.

Palmer, A., ed. 1898. *P. Ovidi Nasonis, Heroides*. Oxford.

Paribeni, R. 1975. *Optimus princeps*. New York.

Parker, H. N. 1992a. "Love's Body Anatomized: The Ancient Erotic Handbooks and the Rhetoric of Sexuality." In Richlin 1992d: 90–107.

———. 1992b. "Other Remarks on the Other Sulpicia." *Classical World* 86: 89–95.

———. 1993. "Sappho Schoolmistress." *Transactions of the American Philological Association* 123: 309–51.

———. 1994. "Sulpicia, the *Auctor de Sulpicia* and the Authorship of 3.9 and 3.11 of the *Corpus Tibullianum*." *Helios* 21: 39–62.

———. N.d. "Metrodora: The Earliest Surviving Work by a Woman Doctor." Unpublished manuscript.

Parker, R. 1985. "Masculinity, Femininity and Homosexuality: On the Anthropological Interpretation of Sexual Meanings in Brazil." *Journal of Homosexuality* 11.3–4: 155–64.

Patzer, H. 1982. *Die griechische Knabenliebe*. Wiesbaden.

Pease, A. S., ed. 1935. *Publi Vergili Maronis Aeneidos Liber Quartus*. Cambridge, Mass.

Pedrick, V. 1986. "Qui potis est, inquis? Audience Roles in Catullus." *Arethusa* 19: 187–207.

Pike, K. L. 1967. *Language in Relation to a Unified Theory of the Structure of Human Behavior*. 2d ed. The Hague and Paris.

Pinault, J. R. 1992. "The Medical Case for Virginity in the Early Second Century C.E.: Soranus of Ephesus, *Gynecology* 1.32." *Helios* 19.1–2: 123–39.

Pollock, G. 1988. *Vision and Difference: Femininity, Feminism and the Histories of Art*. London.

Pomeroy, S. B. 1995. "Women's Identity and the Family in the Classical *Polis*." In Hawley and Levick 1995: 111–21.

Poovey, M. 1990. "Speaking of the Body: Mid-Victorian Constructions of Female Desire." In M. Jacobus, E. F. Keller, and S. Shuttleworth, eds., *Body/Politics: Women and the Discourses of Science*, 29–46. New York.

Pöschl, V. 1962. *The Art of Vergil*. Trans. G. Seligson. Ann Arbor.

———. 1989. *Der Begriff der Würde im antiken Rom und Später*. Heidelberg.

Poulsen, F. 1936. "Les Portraits de Pompeius Magnus." *Revue archéologique* 7, 6th ser.: 16–52.

Powell, A. 1992a. "The *Aeneid* and the Embarrassments of Augustus." In Powell 1992b: 141–74.

———, ed. 1992b. *Roman Poetry and Propaganda in the Age of Augustus*. London.

Price, S.R.F. 1986. "The Future of Dreams: From Freud to Artemidoros." *Past and Present* 113: 3–37. Rpt. in Halperin, Winkler, and Zeitlin 1990a: 365–87.

Puelma, M. 1982. "Die Aitien des Kallimachos als Vorbild der römischen Amores-Elegie." *Museum Helveticum* 39.1: 221–46; 39.2: 285–304.

Purcell, N. 1986. "Livia and the Womanhood of Rome." *Proceedings of the Cambridge Philological Society* 212: 78–105.

Putnam, M.C.J. 1974. "Catullus 11: The Ironies of Integrity." *Ramus* 3: 70–86.

Quinn, K. 1972. *Catullus: An Interpretation*. London.

———. 1973. *Catullus: The Poems*. 2d ed. London and Basingstoke.

———. 1980. *Horace: The Odes*. London.

Rabinowitz, N. S., and A. Richlin, eds. 1993. *Feminist Theory and the Classics*. New York and London.

Rackham, H., W.H.S. Jones, and D. E. Eichholz, eds. and trans. 1938–63. *Pliny: Natural History*. 10 vols. Loeb Classical Library. Cambridge, Mass.

Rankin, A. V. 1962. "Odi et amo: Gaius Valerius Catullus and Freud's Essay on 'A Special Type of Choice of Object Made by Men.'" *American Imago* 19: 437–47.

Rawson, B., ed. 1991. *Marriage, Divorce and Children in Ancient Rome*. Oxford.

Rawson, E. 1987. "*Discrimina ordinum*: The *lex Iulia theatralis*." *Papers of the British School at Rome* 53: 97–113.

Rayor, D., trans. 1991. *Sappho's Lyre: Archaic Lyric and Women Poets of Ancient Greece*. Berkeley and Los Angeles.

Reitzenstein, R. 1912. "Zur Sprache der lateinischen Erotik." *Sitzungsberichte der Heidelberger Akademie der Wissenschaften* 12: 9–36.

Reynolds, L. D. 1983. *Texts and Transmissions: A Survey of the Latin Classics*. Oxford.

Richlin, A. 1981a. "Approaches to the Sources on Adultery at Rome." *Woman's Studies* 8: 225–50.

———. 1981b. "The Meaning of *irrumare* in Catullus and Martial." *Classical Philology* 76: 40–46.

———. 1983. *The Garden of Priapus: Sexuality and Aggression in Roman Humor*. New Haven, Conn. and London.

———. 1984. "Invective Against Women in Roman Satire." *Arethusa* 17.1: 67–80.

———. 1988. "Systems of Food Imagery in Catullus." *Classical World* 81: 355–63.

———. 1991. "Zeus and Metis: Foucault, Feminism, Classics." *Helios* 18: 160–80.

———. 1992a. *The Garden of Priapus*. Rev. ed. New York.

———. 1992b. "Introduction." In Richlin 1992a: xiii–xxxiii.

———. 1992c. "Julia's Jokes, Galla Placidia, and the Roman Use of Women as Political Icons." In Garlick, Dixon, and Allen 1992: 63–91.

———, ed. 1992d. *Pornography and Representation in Greece and Rome*. New York.

———. 1992e. "Reading Ovid's Rapes." In Richlin 1992d: 158–79.

———. 1992f. "Roman Oratory, Pornography, and the Silencing of Anita Hill." *Southern California Law Review* 65.3: 1321–32.

———. 1992g. "Sulpicia the Satirist." *Classical World* 86: 125–40.

———. 1993a. "The Ethnographer's Dilemma and the Dream of a Lost Golden Age." In Rabinowitz and Richlin 1993: 272–303.

———. 1993b. "Not Before Homosexuality: The Materiality of the *Cinaedus* and the Roman Law Against Love Between Men." *Journal of the History of Sexuality* 3.4: 523–73.

———. 1997. "Carrying Water in a Sieve: Class and the Body in Roman Women's Religion." In K. King, ed., *Women and Goddesses*. Philadelphia.

Richmond, I. A. 1944. "Gnaeus Iulius Agricola." *Journal of Roman Studies* 34: 34–45.

Rickman, G. 1980. *The Corn Supply of Ancient Rome*. Oxford.

Riddle, J. M. 1992. *Contraception and Abortion from the Ancient World to the Renaissance*. Cambridge.

Riddle, J. M., J. W. Estes, and J. C. Russell. 1994. "Birth Control in the Ancient World." *Archaeology* (Mar./Apr.): 29–35.

Riley, D. 1988. *"Am I That Name?": Feminism and the Category of "Women" in History.* Minneapolis.

Roessel, D. 1990. "The Significance of the Name *Cerinthus* in the Poems of Sulpicia." *Transactions of the American Philological Association* 120: 243–50.

Rogin, M. 1987. *"Ronald Reagan," the Movie: And Other Episodes in Political Demonology.* Berkeley.

Rolfe, J. C. 1914. *Suetonius.* 2 vols. Loeb Classical Library. Cambridge, Mass.

Ross, D. O., Jr. 1969. *Style and Tradition in Catullus.* Cambridge, Mass.

———. 1975. *Backgrounds to Augustan Poetry: Gallus, Elegy and Rome.* Cambridge.

Rousselle, A. 1988. *Porneia: On Desire and the Body in Antiquity.* Trans. F. Pheasant. Oxford and New York.

———. 1989. "Personal Status and Sexual Practice in the Roman Empire." In M. Feher, ed., *Fragments for a History of the Human Body,* Zone 5.3: 301–33. New York.

Rubino, C. A. 1974. "Myth and Mediation in the Attis Poem of Catullus." *Ramus* 3: 152–75.

———. 1975. "The Erotic World of Catullus." *Classical World* 68: 289–98.

Rudd, N. 1966. *The Satires of Horace.* London.

Rutland, L. W. 1978. "Women as Makers of Kings in Tacitus' *Annals.*" *Classical World* 72: 15–29.

Ryberg, I. S. 1942. "Tacitus' Art of Innuendo." *Transactions and Proceedings of the American Philological Association* 73: 383–404.

Saller, R. 1991. "Corporal Punishment, Authority, and Obedience in the Roman Household." In Rawson 1991: 144–65.

Santirocco, M. S. 1979. "Sulpicia Reconsidered." *Classical Journal* 74: 229–39.

———. 1980. "Strategy and Structure in Horace *C.* 2.12." In C. Deroux, ed., *Studies in Latin Literature and Roman History,* 2:223–36.

Santoro L'hoir, F. 1992. *The Rhetoric of Gender Terms: "Man," "Woman," and the Portrayal of Character in Latin Prose.* Mnemosyne suppl. 118. Leiden.

———. 1994. "Tacitus and Women's Usurpation of Power." *Classical World* 88.1: 5–25.

Scarborough, J. 1969. *Roman Medicine.* Ithaca, N.Y.

Schaps, D. 1977. "The Woman Least Mentioned: Etiquette and Women's Names." *Classical Quarterly* 27: 323–30.

Scramuzza, V. M. 1940. *The Emperor Claudius.* Cambridge.

Sedgwick, E. K. 1985. *Between Men.* New York.

Segal, C. 1982. *Dionysiac Poetics and Euripides' Bacchae.* Princeton.

Seif, K. P. 1973. "Die Claudiusbücher in den Annalen des Tacitus." Inaug. diss., Mainz.

Selden, D. L. 1992. "*Ceveat lector:* Catullus and the Rhetoric of Performance." In R. Hexter and D. Selden, eds., *Innovations of Antiquity,* 461–512. New York and London.

Shackleton Bailey, D. R. 1982. "Notes on Cicero's *Philippics.*" *Philologus* 126: 217–26.

Shackleton Bailey, D. R. 1993. *Martial.* 3 vols. Loeb Classical Library. Cambridge, Mass.

Sharpe, J. 1993. *Allegories of Empire: The Figure of Woman in the Colonial Text.* Minneapolis.

Sienkewicz, T. J. 1981. "Catullus–Another Attis?" *Classical Bulletin* 7: 37–43.

Skinner, M. B. 1979. "Parasites and Strange Bedfellows: A Study in Catullus' Political Imagery." *Ramus* 8: 137–52.

———. 1982. "Pretty Lesbius." *Transactions of the American Philological Association* 112: 197–208.

———. 1983. "Clodia Metelli." *Transactions of the American Philological Association* 113: 273–87.

———. 1986. Review of Richlin 1983. *Classical Philology* 81: 252–57.

———. 1989. "*Ut decuit cinaediorem*: Power, Gender, and Urbanity in Catullus 10." *Helios* 16.1: 7–23.

———. 1991. "The Dynamics of Catullan Obscenity: cc. 37, 58 and 11." *Syllecta classica* 3: 1–11.

———. 1993. "Woman and Language in Archaic Greece, or, Why Is Sappho a Woman?" In Rabinowitz and Richlin 1993: 125–44.

———. 1996. "Zeus and Leda: The Sexuality Wars in Contemporary Classical Scholarship." *Thamyris* 3.1: 103–23.

Slater, W., ed. 1991. *Dining in a Classical Context.* Ann Arbor.

Smith, K. F., ed. 1913. *The Elegies of Albius Tibullus.* New York.

Smith, R.R.R. 1987. "The Imperial Reliefs from the Sebasteion at Aphrodisias." *Journal of Roman Studies* 77: 88–138.

Snyder, J. M. 1989. *The Woman and the Lyre: Women Writers in Classical Greece and Rome.* Carbondale and Edwardsville, Ill.

———. 1994. "The Configuration of Desire in Sappho Fr. 22 L.-P." *Helios* 21: 3–8.

Soren, D. 1997. "Hecate and the Infant Cemetery at Poggio Gramignano." In Soren and Soren 1997.

Soren, D., T. Fenton, W. Birkby, and R. Jensen. 1997. "The Infant Cemetery at Poggio Gramignano: Description and Analysis." In Soren and Soren 1997.

Soren, D., and N. Soren, eds. 1997. *Excavation of a Roman Villa and Late Roman Infant Cemetery near Lugnano in Teverina, Italy.* Rome.

Stahl, H.-P. 1985. *Propertius: "Love and War":* Individual and State Under Augustus. Berkeley and Los Angeles.

Stehle, E. 1989. "Venus, Cybele, and the Sabine Women: The Roman Construction of Female Sexuality." *Helios* 16.2: 143–64.

———. 1990. "Sappho's Gaze: Fantasies of a Goddess and Young Man." In Konstan and Nussbaum 1990: 88–125.

Stigers, E. [Stehle.] 1979. "Romantic Sensuality, Poetic Sense: A Response to Hallett on Sappho." *Signs* 3: 465–71.

Stimpson, C. R. 1990. "Afterword: Lesbian Studies in the 1990s." In K. Jay and J. Glasgow, eds., *Lesbian Texts and Contexts: Radical Revisions,* 377–82. New York and London.

Sullivan, J. P. 1968. *The Satyricon of Petronius: A Literary Study.* Bloomington, Ind. and London.

———. 1972. "The Politics of Elegy." *Arethusa* 5: 17–34.

Sussman, L. S. 1978. "The Birth of the Gods: Sexuality, Conflict and Cosmic Structure in Hesiod's *Theogony*." *Ramus* 7: 61–77.

Sweet, D. R. 1987. "Catullus 11: A Study in Perspective." *Latomus* 46: 510–26.

Syme, R. [1939] 1956. *The Roman Revolution*. Oxford.

———. 1955. "Missing Senators." *Historia* 4: 52–71. Rpt. in E. Badian, ed., *Roman Papers I*, 271–91 (Oxford, 1979).

———. 1958. *Tacitus*. Oxford.

———. 1981a. "A Great Orator Mislaid." *Classical Quarterly* 31: 421–27. Rpt. in A. R. Birley, ed., *Roman Papers III*, 1415–22. (Oxford, 1984).

———. 1981b. "Princesses and Others in Tacitus." *Greece and Rome* 28: 40–52.

———. 1986. *The Augustan Aristocracy*. Oxford.

Syndikus, H. P. 1972. *Die Lyrik des Horaz. Eine Interpretation der Oden*. Vol. 1. Darmstadt.

———. 1973. *Die Lyrik des Horaz. Eine Interpretation der Oden*. Vol. 2. Darmstadt.

———. 1990. *Catull: Eine Interpretation*. Vol. 2, *Die großen Gedichte (61–68)*. Darmstadt.

Tapinc, H. 1992. "Masculinity, Femininity, and Turkish Male Homosexuality." In K. Plummer, ed., *Modern Homosexualities*, 39–49. London and New York.

Tarrant, R. J. 1981. "The Authenticity of the Letter of Sappho to Phaon." *Harvard Studies in Classical Philology* 85: 133–53.

Temkin, O., trans. [1956] 1991. *Soranus' Gynecology*. Baltimore and London.

Temporini, H. 1978. *Die Frauen am Hofe Trajans*. Berlin.

Theweleit, K. 1987. *Male Fantasies*. Vol. 1. Trans. S. Conway. Minneapolis.

Thomas, R. F. 1986. "Vergil's *Georgics* and the Art of Reference." *Harvard Studies in Classical Philology* 90: 171–98.

Thornton, B. 1991. "Constructionism and Ancient Greek Sex." *Helios* 18.2: 181–93.

Thorp, J. 1992. "The Social Construction of Homosexuality." *Phoenix* 46: 54–61.

Tompkins, J. P. 1980. "The Reader in History: The Changing Shape of Literary Response." In J. P. Tompkins, ed., *Reader-Response Criticism*, 201–32. Baltimore.

Trachtenberg, J. [1939] 1961. *Jewish Magic and Superstition*. Cleveland.

Tracy, V. 1976. "Roman Dandies and Transvestites." *Échos du monde classique* 20: 60–63.

Tränkle, H., ed. 1990. *Appendix Tibulliana*. Berlin and New York.

Treggiari, S. 1991. *Roman Marriage: Iusti Coniuges from the Time of Cicero to the Time of Ulpian*. Oxford.

Van Nortwick, T. 1990. "*Huc veniet Messalla meus*: Commentary on Johnson." *Arethusa* 23: 115–23.

Verducci, F. 1985. *Ovid's Toyshop of the Heart: Epistulae Heroidum*. Princeton.

Vermaseren, M. J. 1977. *Cybele and Attis: The Myth and the Cult*. London.

Versnel, H. S. 1970. *Triumphus: An Inquiry into the Origin, Development and Meaning of the Roman Triumph*. Leiden.

Verstraete, B. C. 1980. "Slavery and the Social Dynamics of Male Homosexual Relations in Ancient Rome." *Journal of Homosexuality* 5: 227–36.

Vessey, D.W.T.C. 1971. "Thoughts on Tacitus' Portrayal of Claudius." *American Journal of Philology* 92.3: 385–409.

Veyne, P. 1978. "La Famille et l'amour sous le Haut-Empire romain." *Annales (Économie, Sociétés, Civilisations)* 33: 35–63.

———. 1985. "Homosexuality in Ancient Rome." Trans. A. Forster. In P. Ariès and A. Béjin, eds., *Western Sexuality: Practice and Precept in Past and Present Time*, 26–35. Oxford. (Originally published as "L'Homosexualité à Rome," *Communications* 35 [1982]: 26–33.)

———. 1988. *Roman Erotic Elegy: Love, Poetry, and the West*. Trans. D. Pellauer. Chicago.

Vidal-Naquet, P. 1986. "The Black Hunter and the Origin of the Athenian *Ephebia*." In *The Black Hunter: Forms of Thought and Forms of Society in the Greek World*, trans. A. Szegedy-Maszak, 85–156. Baltimore.

Ville, G. 1981. *La Gladiature en occident des origines à la mort de Domitien*. Rome.

Vinson, M. 1989. "Domitia Longina, Julia Titi, and the Literary Tradition." *Historia* 38.4: 431–50.

———. 1992. "Party Politics and the Language of Love in the Lesbia Poems of Catullus." In C. Deroux, ed., *Studies in Latin Literature and Roman History*, 6: 163–80. Brussels.

von Staden, H. 1991. "*Apud nos foediora verba*: Celsus' Reluctant Construction of the Female Body." In G. Sabbah, ed., *Le Latin médical: La Constitution d'un langage scientifique*, Mémoires du Centre Jean Palerne, 10, 271–96. Saint-Étienne.

———. 1992. "Women and Dirt." *Helios* 19.1–2: 7–30.

Walker, B. 1952. *The Annals of Tacitus: A Study in the Writing of History*. Manchester.

Wallace, K. G. 1991. "Women in Tacitus, 1903–1986." *Aufstieg und Niedergang der römischen Welt* 33.5: 3556–74.

Wallace-Hadrill, A. 1981. "*Civilis princeps*: Between Citizen and King." *Journal of Roman Studies* 71: 32–48.

———. 1982. "The Golden Age and Sin in Augustan Ideology." *Past and Present* 95: 19–36.

———. 1985. "Propaganda and Dissent? Augustan Moral Legislation and the Love Poets." *Klio* 67: 180–84.

———. 1988. "The Social Structure of the Roman House." *Papers of the British School at Rome* 56: 43–97.

———. 1989a. "Introduction." In Wallace-Hadrill 1989c: 1–13.

———. 1989b. "Patronage in Roman Society: From Republic to Empire." In Wallace-Hadrill 1989c: 63–87.

———, ed. 1989c. *Patronage in Ancient Society*. London and New York.

———. 1994. *Houses and Society in Pompeii and Herculaneum*. Princeton.

Waters, K. H. 1969. "Traianus Domitiani Continuator." *American Journal of Philology* 90.4: 385–405.

———. 1974. "Trajan's Character in the Literary Tradition." In J.A.S. Evans, ed., *Polis and Imperium: Studies in Honour of Edward Togo Salmon*, 233–52. Toronto.

———. 1975. "The Reign of Trajan and Its Place in Contemporary Scholarship (1960–72)." *Aufstieg und Niedergang der römischen Welt* 2.2: 381–431.

Watson, A., ed. and trans. 1985. *The Digest of Justinian*. 4 vols. Philadelphia.

Weeks, J. 1981. "Discourse, Desire and Sexual Deviance." In R. Plummer, ed., *The Making of the Modern Homosexual*, 76–111. London.

Wegner, J. R. 1991. "The Image and Status of Women in Classical Rabbinic Judaism." In Baskin 1991: 94–114.

Weissler, C. 1991. "Prayers in Yiddish and the Religious World of Ashkenazic Women." In Baskin 1991: 159–81.

Welcker, Fr. [1816] 1845. *Sappho von einem herrschenden Vorurtheil befryt*. In *Kleine Schriften*, 2: 80–144. Bonn.

West, G. S. 1980. "Caeneus and Dido." *Transactions of the American Philological Association* 110: 315–24.

White, P. 1993. *Promised Verse: Poets in the Society of Augustan Rome*. Cambridge, Mass., and London.

Whitehead, H. 1985. Review of Herdt 1984. *Journal of Homosexuality* 11.3–4: 201–5.

Wiedemann, T. 1992. *Emperors and Gladiators*. London.

Williams, C. A. 1995. "Greek Love at Rome." *Classical Quarterly* 45: 517–39.

Williams, F. 1978. *Callimachus: Hymn to Apollo: A Commentary*. Oxford.

Williams, G. 1962. "Poetry in the Moral Climate of Augustan Rome." *Journal of Roman Studies* 52: 28–46.

———. 1968. *Tradition and Originality in Roman Poetry*. Oxford.

Williams, W. 1986. *The Spirit and the Flesh: Sexual Diversity in American Indian Culture*. Boston.

Winkler, J. J. 1990. *The Constraints of Desire*. New York.

Winterbottom, M., trans. 1974. *The Elder Seneca I: Controversiae I–VI*. Loeb Classical Library. Cambridge, Mass.

Wiseman, T. P. 1982. "Calpurnius Siculus and the Claudian Civil War." *Journal of Roman Studies* 72: 57–67.

———. 1984. "Cybele, Virgil and Augustus." In A. J. Woodman and D. A. West, eds., *Poetry and Politics in the Age of Augustus*, 117–28. Cambridge.

———. 1985. *Catullus and His World: A Reappraisal*. Cambridge.

Wistrand, M. 1992. *Entertainment and Violence in Ancient Rome: The Attitudes of Writers in the First Century A.D.* Göteborg.

Wittig, M. 1980. "The Straight Mind." *Feminist Issues* 1.1: 103–10.

———. 1981. "One Is Not Born a Woman." *Feminist Issues* 1.3: 47–54.

Woodman, A. J. 1993. "Amateur Dramatics at the Court of Nero." In A. J. Woodman and T. J. Luce, eds., *Tacitus and the Tacitean Tradition*, 104–28. Princeton.

Woolf, V. [1929] 1957. *A Room of One's Own*. New York.

Wyke, M. 1987. "Written Woman: Propertius' *scripta puella*." *Journal of Roman Studies* 77: 47–61.

———. 1989a. "In Pursuit of Love, the Poetic Self and a Process of Reading: Augustan Elegy in the 1980s." *Journal of Roman Studies* 79: 165–73.

———. 1989b. "Mistress and Metaphor in Augustan Elegy." *Helios* 16: 25–47.

———. 1989c. "Reading Female Flesh: *Amores* 3.1." In A. Cameron, ed., *History as Text: The Writing of Ancient History*, 113–43. London.

———. 1992. "Augustan Cleopatras: Female Power and Poetic Authority." In Powell 1992b: 98–140.

———. 1994. "Taking the Woman's Part: Engendering Roman Love Elegy." *Ramus* 23.1–2: 110–28.

Yardley, J. C. 1990. "Cerinthus' *pia cura* ([Tibullus] 3.17.1–2)." *Classical Quarterly* 40: 568–70.

Yavetz, Z. 1969. *Plebs and Princeps*. Oxford.

———. 1984. "The *Res Gestae* and Augustus' Public Image." In Millar and Segal 1984: 1–36.

Zanker, P. 1988. *The Power of Images in the Age of Augustus*. Trans. A. Shapiro. Ann Arbor.

Zeitlin, F. I. 1971. "Petronius as Paradox: Anarchy and Literary Integrity." *Transactions and Proceedings of the American Philological Association* 102: 631–84.

———. 1985. "Playing the Other: Theater, Theatricality, and the Feminine in Greek Drama." *Representations* 11: 63–94.

———. 1990. "The Poetics of *Erōs*: Nature, Art, and Imitation in Longus' *Daphnis and Chloe*." In Halperin, Winkler, and Zeitlin 1990a: 417–64.

———. 1995. "Signifying Difference: The Myth of Pandora." In Hawley and Levick 1995: 58–74.

Zweig, B. 1993. "The Primal Mind: Using Native American Models for the Study of Women in Ancient Greece." In Rabinowitz and Richlin 1993: 145–80.

CONTRIBUTORS

ANTHONY CORBEILL, Associate Professor of Classics at the University of Kansas, is the author of *Controlling Laughter: Political Humor in the Late Roman Republic* (Princeton 1996). His current research treats the social and political connotations of gesture in the Roman world.

CATHARINE EDWARDS is Senior Lecturer in the Department of Classics and Ancient History at the University of Bristol. Her publications include *The Politics of Immorality in Ancient Rome* (Cambridge 1993) and *Writing Rome: Textual Approaches to the City* (Cambridge 1996). She is presently working on an edition of selected letters of Seneca for the Cambridge Greek and Latin Classics series.

DAVID FREDRICK, Assistant Professor at the University of Arkansas, is currently editing *The Roman Gaze*, a collection of essays on vision, gender, and representation in Roman culture, forthcoming from The Johns Hopkins University Press in conjunction with the journal *Arethusa*.

PAMELA GORDON, Associate Professor of Classics at the University of Kansas, is the author of *Epicurus in Lycia: The Second-Century World of Diogenes of Oenoanda* (Ann Arbor 1996). Her current project, whose working title is "Women, Eunuchs, and Epicureans," concerns the cultural history of the Garden.

JUDITH PELLER HALLETT, Professor and Chair of Classics at the University of Maryland at College Park, has published widely on Latin literature and on women, sexuality, and the family in Roman antiquity. She is the author of *Fathers and Daughters: Women and the Elite Family* (Princeton 1984) and co-editor of *Compromising Traditions: The Personal Voice in Classical Antiquity* (London and New York 1997).

SANDRA R. JOSHEL teaches in the Department of Liberal Arts at the New England Conservatory of Music. Her research interests focus on women, gender, and slavery in ancient Rome. Her publications include: *Work, Identity, and Legal Status at Rome* (Norman, Oklahoma 1992); "The Body Female and the Body Politic: Livy's Lucretia and Verginia," in Amy Richlin, ed., *Pornography and Representation in Greece and Rome* (Oxford 1992); and "Nurturing the Master's Child: Slavery and the Roman Child-Nurse," *Signs* 12.1 (Autumn 1986). She is the co-editor (with Sheila Murnaghan) of a forthcoming volume of essays on gender and slavery in ancient Greece and Rome, *Differential Equations: Women and Slaves in Greco-Roman Culture* (Routledge) and is now working on a book-length study of the construction of gendered subjects in imperial narratives.

ALISON KEITH is Associate Professor of Classics at Victoria College, University of Toronto. She is the author of *The Play of Fictions: Studies in Ovid's* Metamorphoses *Book 2* (Ann Arbor 1992), and *Engendering Rome: Women in Latin Epic* (forthcoming from Cambridge University Press). She is now working on a commentary on Ovid's *Metamorphoses*, Book 4.

ELLEN OLIENSIS is Assistant Professor of Classics at Yale University. Her work focuses on the social and sexual dynamics of Augustan poetry. In addition to articles on Horace, Vergil, and Ovid, she is the author of a book forthcoming from Cambridge University Press, entitled *Horace and the Rhetoric of Authority*.

HOLT N. PARKER is Associate Professor of Classics at the University of Cincinnati and a Fellow of the American Academy in Rome. He has published articles on various aspects of gender and literature in the ancient world. He is currently preparing an edition, translation, and commentary on Metrodora, the earliest surviving work by a woman doctor.

AMY RICHLIN is Professor of Classics and Gender Studies at the University of Southern California. She is the author of *The Garden of Priapus* (rev. ed. New York and Oxford 1992), editor of *Pornography and Representation in Greece and Rome* (New York and Oxford 1992), and co-editor, with Nancy Sorkin Rabinowitz, of *Feminist Theory and the Classics* (New York and London 1993). Her present research projects include a book on gender production in the Roman rhetorical schools and a study of Roman witches, from which "Pliny's Brassiere" is drawn.

MARILYN B. SKINNER is Professor of Classics at the University of Arizona and editor of *Transactions of the American Philological Association*. She is the author of *Catullus' Passer: The Arrangement of the Book of Polymetric Poems* (New York 1981) and numerous articles on both Latin poetry and the Greek female poetic tradition. Her current critical project, tentatively entitled *Catullus in Verona*, will offer a new reading of the poet's elegiacs and elegiac epigrams.

JONATHAN WALTERS spent seventeen years in nonacademic employment after gaining a B.A. in Islamic History at Oxford University, including several years working in the gay community in London. He returned to academic life to take a Ph.D. at Cambridge University. In 1996–97 he was Latin Lecturer at Trinity College, Dublin, and holds the Mellon Fellowship at the University of Southern California for 1997–98. Walters' main scholarly interests are twofold: first, in the area of Roman gender and sexuality; second, in education and rhetoric in the Roman world.

INDEX

abortion, 184–85, 197, 208–10
actors, 66–95; and *infamia*, 69–76; and prostitution, 81; political role of, 79; sexual deviance of, 79–80; social status of, 78–79
Adams, J. N., 12, 43n28, 50, 56, 64n14, n15, 125n39, 170n27, 271n10, 272n17
Adler, E., 131, 144, 147n2, n3
adultery, 25, 36, 58, 59, 112, 119, 126n42, 143, 227, 230–31, 233; in Augustan Rome, 295; punishment of, 39, 50–51, 75, 81, 88, 239–40. *See also* betrayal; fidelity; infidelity
agency: of Messalina, 236–38, 242–47, 250n7; of Roman senators, 236–38, 245
Ahl, F., 236
alterity. *See* otherness
amicitia, 4, 18, 150n30; and *amor*, 154–55, 171n39; in Horace, 153–54, 162–68; in love elegy, 143–44, 151–71; in Propertius, 157–62; in Tibullus, 155–57. *See also* friendship; patronage
Anderson, W. S., 151, 265
androgyny, 110–12. *See also* effeminacy
anthropology, 131–33
aphrodisiacs, 208
architecture: and gender, 12–13. *See also* space
Armstrong, D., 170–71n32
Arthur, M. B., 134. *See also* M. A. Katz
Attis (in Catullus), 133–42, 146
Augustus: as patron, 166; sexual ideology of, 295–310
Aulus Gellius: on transsexuality, 267
Austin, R. G., 308–9n14

Baca, A. R., 271n12
Baehrens, A., 148n14
Bailey, C., 149n22
Bakhtin, M., 191n20, 218n16
Bal, M., 230, 236, 250n7
Baldwin, B., 227, 256
Banks, B., 274
banquets: and dancing, 104–7; and masculinity, 16–17, 99–128; and gluttony, 101–4; and sexuality, 297

Barton, C. A., 12, 65n31, 68, 92n41, n45, 93n70, 94n75, n78, n80, 149n24, 172
Batstone, W., 129
beating: of adulterers, 239–40; and *infamia*, 73–74; in love elegy, 172, 175, 186–87; by Messalina, 232; and sexual passivity, 38–39; of slaves, 37–38, 76; and social status, 14, 37–41, 66, 73–75. *See also* violence
Benario, H. W., 233
Berger, A., 34–35
betrayal, 160. *See also* adultery; fidelity
Blassingame, J. W., 253n24
Blayney, J., 125n30
Bloom, A., 125n37
Boatwright, M. T., 252n19
Bodel, J., 151
bodies, female: ambivalence toward, 205, 216; equated with texts in love elegy, 173–90; and female speech, 234–35; and imperial power, 244; in medical writers, 201–20; social construction of, 172–93
Boedeker, D., 147n7
Booth, A., 127n53
Boswell, J., 60, 64n5, n10, 123n9, 126n47, 127n50, 131, 219n28, 270n3
boundaries: defense of, 30; of empire, 241–42; of gender, 30, 32, 59; of masculinity, 41–42; physical, 38, 41; social, 37, 88–90, 109, 231; transgression of, 12, 49–50, 231, 245–47
Boyarin, D., 218n11
Bradley, K. R., 9, 133
Bramble, J. C., 169n2
Bremmer, J., 127n57
Brontë, Charlotte, 221
Brooks, P., 222
Brooten, B. J., 256, 272n21, n28
Brown, P., 125n31, n36, 149n21
Bruère, R. T., 240
Buckley, T., 201, 218n10, n16
Burkert, W., 134
Butler, J., 247, 291n31
Bynum, C. W., 218n11

Printed in Great Britain
by Amazon.co.uk, Ltd.,
Marston Gate.